**DISCARDED**

# THE NEW MIDDLE AGES

BONNIE WHEELER, *Series Editor*

*The New Middle Ages* is a series dedicated to transdisciplinary studies of medieval cultures, with particular emphasis on recuperating women's history and on feminist and gender analyses. This peer-reviewed series includes both scholarly monographs and essay collections.

PUBLISHED BY PALGRAVE:

*Women in the Medieval Islamic World: Power, Patronage, and Piety*
edited by Gavin R. G. Hambly

*The Ethics of Nature in the Middle Ages: On Boccaccio's Poetaphysics*
by Gregory B. Stone

*Presence and Presentation: Women in the Chinese Literati Tradition*
by Sherry J. Mou

*The Lost Love Letters of Heloise and Abelard: Perceptions of Dialogue in Twelfth-Century France*
by Constant J. Mews

*Understanding Scholastic Thought with Foucault*
by Philipp W. Rosemann

*For Her Good Estate: The Life of Elizabeth de Burgh*
by Frances A. Underhill

*Constructions of Widowhood and Virginity in the Middle Ages*
edited by Cindy L. Carlson and Angela Jane Weisl

*Motherhood and Mothering in Anglo-Saxon England*
by Mary Dockray-Miller

*Listening to Heloise: The Voice of a Twelfth-Century Woman*
edited by Bonnie Wheeler

*The Postcolonial Middle Ages*
edited by Jeffrey Jerome Cohen

*Chaucer's Pardoner and Gender Theory: Bodies of Discourse*
by Robert S. Sturges

*Crossing the Bridge: Comparative Essays on Medieval European and Heian Japanese Women Writers*
edited by Barbara Stevenson and Cynthia Ho

*Engaging Words: The Culture of Reading in the Later Middle Ages*
by Laurel Amtower

*Robes and Honor: The Medieval World of Investiture*
edited by Stewart Gordon

*Representing Rape in Medieval and Early Modern Literature*
edited by Elizabeth Robertson and Christine M. Rose

*Same Sex Love and Desire Among Women in the Middle Ages*
edited by Francesca Canadé Sautman and Pamela Sheingorn

*Sight and Embodiment in the Middle Ages: Ocular Desires*
by Suzannah Biernoff

*Listen, Daughter: The Speculum Virginum and the Formation of Religious Women in the Middle Ages*
edited by Constant J. Mews

*Science, the Singular, and the Question of Theology*
by Richard A. Lee, Jr.

*Gender in Debate from the Early Middle Ages to the Renaissance*
   edited by Thelma S. Fenster and Clare A. Lees

*Malory's* Morte Darthur: *Remaking Arthurian Tradition*
   by Catherine Batt

*The Vernacular Spirit: Essays on Medieval Religious Literature*
   edited by Renate Blumenfeld-Kosinski, Duncan Robertson, and Nancy Warren

*Popular Piety and Art in the Late Middle Ages: Image Worship and Idolatry in England 1350–1500*
   by Kathleen Kamerick

*Absent Narratives, Manuscript Textuality, and Literary Structure in Late Medieval England*
   by Elizabeth Scala

*Creating Community with Food and Drink in Merovingian Gaul*
   by Bonnie Effros

*Representations of Early Byzantine Empresses: Image and Empire*
   by Anne McClanan

*Encountering Medieval Textiles and Dress: Objects, Texts, Images*
   edited by Désirée G. Koslin and Janet Snyder

*Eleanor of Aquitaine: Lord and Lady*
   edited by Bonnie Wheeler and John Carmi Parsons

*Isabel La Católica, Queen of Castile: Critical Essays*
   edited by David A. Boruchoff

*Homoeroticism and Chivalry: Discourses of Male Same-Sex Desire in the Fourteenth Century*
   by Richard Zeikowitz

*Portraits of Medieval Women: Family, Marriage, and Politics in England 1225–1350*
   by Linda E. Mitchell

*Eloquent Virgins: From Thecla to Joan of Arc*
   by Maud Burnett McInerney

*The Persistence of Medievalism: Narrative Adventures in Contemporary Culture*
   by Angela Jane Weisl

*Capetian Women*
   edited by Kathleen Nolan

*Joan of Arc and Spirituality*
   edited by Ann W. Astell and Bonnie Wheeler

*The Texture of Society: Medieval Women in the Southern Low Countries*
   edited by Ellen E. Kittell and Mary A. Suydam

*Charlemagne's Mustache: And Other Cultural Clusters of a Dark Age*
   by Paul Edward Dutton

*Troubled Vision: Gender, Sexuality, and Sight in Medieval Text and Image*
   edited by Emma Campbell and Robert Mills

*Queering Medieval Genres*
   by Tison Pugh

*Sacred Place in Early Medieval Neoplatonism*
   by L. Michael Harrington

*The Middle Ages at Work*
   edited by Kellie Robertson and Michael Uebel

*Chaucer's Jobs*
   by David R. Carlson

# THE MIDDLE AGES AT WORK: PRACTICING LABOR IN LATE MEDIEVAL ENGLAND

*Edited by*

*Kellie Robertson and Michael Uebel*

THE MIDDLE AGES AT WORK
© Kellie Robertson and Michael Uebel, 2004.

All rights reserved. No part of this book may be used or reproduced in any manner whatsoever without written permission except in the case of brief quotations embodied in critical articles or reviews.

First published 2004 by
PALGRAVE MACMILLAN™
175 Fifth Avenue, New York, N.Y. 10010 and
Houndmills, Basingstoke, Hampshire, England RG21 6XS
Companies and representatives throughout the world

PALGRAVE MACMILLAN is the global academic imprint of the Palgrave Macmillan division of St. Martin's Press, LLC and of Palgrave Macmillan Ltd. Macmillan® is a registered trademark in the United States, United Kingdom and other countries. Palgrave is a registered trademark in the European Union and other countries.

ISBN 1–4039–6007–0 hardback

Library of Congress Cataloging-in-Publication Data
    The Middle Ages at work : practicing labor in late medieval England / edited by Kellie Roberston and Michael Uebel.
      p. cm. — (New Middle Ages)
    Includes bibliographical references and index.
    ISBN 1–4039–6007–0
    1. Labor—England—History. 2. Working class—England—History.
3. Middle Ages. I. Robertson, Kellie, 1968– II. Uebel, Michael. III. Series.
HD8389.M53 2004
331'.0942'09024—dc22
                                           2003063971

A catalogue record for this book is available from the British Library.

Design by Newgen Imaging Systems (P) Ltd., Chennai, India.

First edition: October 2004
10  9  8  7  6  5  4  3  2  1

Printed in the United States of America.

# CONTENTS

| | | |
|---|---|---|
| Introduction | Conceptualizing Labor in the Middle Ages<br>*Michael Uebel and Kellie Robertson* | 1 |
| **Part 1** | **Gender Trouble** | **17** |
| 1. | The Idioms of Women's Work and Thomas Hoccleve's Travails<br>*Catherine Batt* | 19 |
| 2. | "As If She Were Single": Working Wives and the Late Medieval English *Femme Sole*<br>*Brian W. Gastle* | 41 |
| **Part 2** | **Spiritual Employment** | **65** |
| 3. | "The Workman is Worth his Mede": Poverty, Labor, and Charity in the Sermon of William Taylor<br>*Kate Crassons* | 67 |
| 4. | The Naked and the Dead: The Carpenters' Company and Lay Spirituality in Late Medieval England<br>*Mark Addison Amos* | 91 |
| **Part 3** | **Labor and the Law** | **111** |
| 5. | Reconstructing English Labor Laws: A Medieval Perspective<br>*Anthony Musson* | 113 |
| 6. | Branding and the Technologies of Labor Regulation<br>*Kellie Robertson* | 133 |
| **Part 4** | **Producing Poetics** | **155** |
| 7. | The Displacement of Labor in *Winner and Waster*<br>*Britton J. Harwood* | 157 |

8. Scribal Hermeneutics and the Genres of
   Social Organization in *Piers Plowman*  179
   *Andrew Cole*

## Part 5  Book Work  207

9. Poetic Work and Scribal Labor in Hoccleve and Langland  209
   *Ethan Knapp*

10. The Erasure of Labor: Hoccleve, Caxton, and
    the Information Age  229
    *William Kuskin*

*List of Contributors*  261
*Index*  263

# INTRODUCTION

# CONCEPTUALIZING LABOR IN THE MIDDLE AGES

*Michael Uebel and Kellie Robertson*

## I

From the mid-fourteenth to the end of the fifteenth century, work arguably shaped social identity to a much greater extent than in either earlier or later times. We know that labor ordinances issued in the wake of the 1348 Black Plague not only restricted wages but also demanded the textual encoding of identity in the form of letters patent issued for migrating laborers among villages. Sumptuary laws determined how a person could dress and what could be eaten depending on what the person did. Estates satire criticized all classes of society for failing to fulfill their professional duties, and hence their obligations to the rest of society. The equation of what you did with who you were was an almost inviolate one (unless, of course, you were a woman; in which case, who you were was likely to be dependent on what your husband did).

Assuming labor was one of the determinant factors of social identity in late medieval Europe, this volume thinks about the multiple historical forms such identities take when they are framed in terms of the processes and materialities of labor. The essays collected here are predicated upon not only an antiphonal movement between literary and historical documents but a similar metahistorical movement between nineteenth- and twentieth-century social theory and the Middle Ages. In part, this volume proposes a reexamination of the commitments of historicism in the wake of New Historicism. It seeks to contribute to the construction of a materialist historicism while, at the same time, proposing that discussions of work need not be exclusively framed in terms of the clash between labor and capital.

Aaron Gurevich eloquently defines the historian's task as the "persistent and relentless questioning of the past by the present...an approach characterized by interrogating the legacies of the past with those questions which past cultures could not put to themselves."[1] In attempting to formulate such questions, medieval scholars are more and more frequently turning to postindustrial theoretical models to explain the social value of labor as represented in medieval texts. While this line of approach has recently resulted in suggestive studies on individual authors (like Langland) as well as the medieval intellectual marketplace more generally,[2] the questions raised by these economic models for medieval historiography are equally in need of historicization. For ultimately, labor theory cannot be "applied" to the Middle Ages the way that, say, lipstick is applied; or, if it is, similar results obtain: despite all claims to permanence, it eventually rubs off.

Several of the essays in this collection propose to turn Gurevich's insight around, to think about how medieval labor practice (and its representations) can relentlessly question our present understanding of Marxist or postmarxist theory in ways neither positivist nor weighted with a teleological imperative. It is no longer sufficient simply to ask that these models not be reductively applied to the Middle Ages; the challenge facing medievalists now is to explore how such theories stand up to the problems posed by medieval texts, and how medieval texts can, in turn, not only modify existing models but also generate new ones. To this end, all of the essays in this collection encourage discussion of several related questions: for example, how have representations of the Middle Ages been used to structure postindustrial models of production and consumption? To what extent does the assumption of a univocal Middle Ages (along with the perennial and related question of the periodization of the Middle Ages) hinder the use of such theories? Finally, in the broadest sense, how can medieval practice transform modern theories of social and intellectual labor?

Such questions are pressing now because social critics have begun to chronicle the "end of work." Economists and cultural critics alike are debating the materiality of contemporary labor and its relation to a postmodern, global economy. Jeremy Rifkin, for example, has asserted that we live in a post-market era where information technology will soon produce a near "workerless" society. Instead of an economic disaster, Rifkin believes this mass redundancy will result in new opportunities for the growth of a non-profit sector geared toward transformative social change. In a similar vein, writers like Antonio Negri and Michael Hardt have heralded the appearance of so-called "immaterial" labor, labor that "produces an immaterial good, such as a service, a cultural product, knowledge or communication."[3] "Immaterial labor" is not just synonymous with a clique of cyber information workers but is a new form of labor-power that has the potential to become the basis for a newly cohesive class consciousness. Interestingly, both these analyses (despite their radically different political persuasions) envision labor history as a teleological progression from feudalism to Fordism to a near-workerless wonderland, wherein the end of work ushers in a (surprisingly) utopian vision of the future.

What is most striking in these pronouncements to a medievalist, however, is the insistence that this emerging bio-political order is marked by a "new" interest in the materiality (or immateriality) of labor. Those familiar with European medieval history know that similar questions could be found at the center of the most fraught and prolonged controversies of the high- and late–Middle Ages. The polemical atmosphere at the University of Paris that emerged in the 1250s, for instance, grew out of heated exchanges between secular masters and mendicant friars over the extent to which preaching, praying, and the hearing of confessions could be considered "work." The activities of seculars and mendicants overlapped in many areas, but an important question remained: how to weigh the mendicant's fasting and silent meditation against the secular's pastoral care and administration of the sacraments? Ultimately, mendicant defenders (like Aquinas and Albertus Magnus) had to validate the benefits of immaterial spiritual labor, while regular defenders sought to validate the secular, material work of their members in the community. Similarly, the question of the extent to which manual and artisanal labor was material, and therefore regulatable, was a pivotal concern in the framing of the much hated, post-plague labor laws in England, laws that would later be blamed (in part) for both the 1381 rising and Cade's Rebellion of 1450. The question of how labor gets embodied is one that links the medieval, modern, and postmodern periods. The challenge for critics then is to find a vocabulary that allows us to discuss the relationships among these periods in a truly comparativist (rather than a merely compartmentalizing) way.

This volume of essays thus offers more than a strictly historical view of the complex terms (social and literary) within which labor was treated in the medieval period. It attempts to rethink the critical language framing the categories of labor and work through a continually doubled engagement with modern theories of labor and medieval theories and practices of labor. In this context, one of the larger questions the volume addresses is the "troubled" history of the category of labor itself: in what ways can this historically mercurial concept ground an understanding of "mass work(er)" as agent of historical change? What value does labor have *outside* of capital(ism)? Marx claims that it has none, of course, but this volume—by examining forms and practices of labor at a time before capitalist hegemony—begins to think about precisely what an *outside* or, better, a *beyond* capital might look like. Thomas Aquinas's articulation of the fourfold aim of labor is one such *beyond*:

> First and principally to obtain food; wherefore it was said to the first man (Gen. 3:19): "In the sweat of thy face shalt thou eat bread," and it is written (Ps. 127:2): "For thou shalt eat the labors of thy hands." Secondly, it is directed to the removal of idleness whence arise many evils; hence it is written (Sirach 33:28–9): "Send" thy slave "to work, that he be not idle, for idleness hath taught much evil." Thirdly, it is directed to the curbing of concupiscence, inasmuch as it is a means of afflicting the body; hence it is written (2 Cor. 6:5–6): "In labors, in watchings, in fastings, in chastity." Fourthly, it is directed to almsgiving.[4]

The Thomist definition makes it clear that the aim of labor is neither individual nor collective economic accumulation and progress but rather simply providing what is necessary, subsistence. The corporeal act of labor, legitimized by *necessitas*, also points to the beyond in the spiritual and moral sense, where the body becomes the site of mortification and the defeat of temptation as well as the production of charity.

Continuing to imagine this *beyond* requires that we consider, for example, the relation of the value of work to the value of labor in the Middle Ages. *Work* in the Middle Ages was never precisely equivalent to medieval *labor*. Although we use these two terms synonymously in this Introduction, as do the volume's contributors, we will be now making the argument that to confuse their ethical and social meanings is to obscure an important dimension of the cultural value of human production in the Middle Ages. It is a rather curious fact that every European language, ancient and modern, preserves a distinction between two words we have come to regard as referring to the same practice.[5] The persistent synonymous usage of *work* and *labor* masks the fact that these are two etymologically, as well as phenomenologically, unrelated practices. Latin *laborare/facere (fabricari)*, French *travailler/ouvrer*, German *arbeiten/werken*, Greek *ponein/ergazesthai*: in each case, only the equivalents for laboring have an unambivalent connotation of pain, suffering, and fatigue. Indeed, this sense of pain and trouble is especially clear in French: *travailler* replaced the older *labourer*, and derives from *tripalium*, an instrument of torture consisting of three stakes designed to rack the body. In addition, something must be made of the Latin homographs *labor* (work) and *labor* (to slip, a verb often joined to *cadere*, to fall).

This association between work, exhaustion, and death was traced out linguistically by the psychoanalyst Georg Groddeck, who is perhaps best known for being credited as having suggested to Freud the term *das Es* (the It or Id),[6] which of course became a key concept in Freud's psychical topography. For Groddeck, the etymological affinities marking the nexus of work and death operate, like those linking death and eros, to dramatize the ways in which humans are constantly striving to unite the disparate and antagonistic elements of their very beings. Labor always already involves death, as Groddeck's etymologies appear to indicate:

> The German verb *sterben*, to die (dc. English starve), originally meant to take pains, to work; Old Norwegian *starf*, work, *starfa*, to take pains, *stjarfe*, rigid spasms. The same association is seen in Greek, where *kamno* means to take pains, and *kamontas*, the dead. The base is *kam-*, *cema-*, *cme–*, to take pains, to grow tired.[7]

Among the ancients, there is a marked distrust of labor and laborers, primarily because bodily labor is associated with the humiliating and painful activity of slaves and animals.[8] Hesiod, in his *Works and Days*, distinguished labor (*ponos*) from work (*ergon*), with the former, like all evils, issuing from Pandora's box, a punishment from Zeus for Prometheus's famous deception.

Contempt for laboring, Hannah Arendt reminds us, arose originally out of

> a passionate striving for freedom from necessity and a no less passionate impatience with every effort that left no trace, no monument, no great work worthy of remembrance.[9]

Laboring is not only purely physical—slavish because necessitated by bodily needs—but it is also antiphysical; it leaves nothing lasting behind, the result of its effort consumed nearly as quickly as the effort is expended. Labor is thus antimemorial and antimaterial: the intangible (what is remembered) and the utopic (what is hoped for) are prevented from materializing. Several of the essays collected here (Robertson, Cole, Knapp, Kuskin) open up an inquiry of this tension, inherent in labor, between the creative or physical and the unrealizable or immaterial. While Marx of course never lost sight of labor as a physiological condition ("the metabolic interaction [*Stoffwechsel*] between man and nature"[10]), one that can only be ended with death, we might say that loss inhabits labor from its inception in capitalism since it entails the total independence of the laborer from his own products. Capitalism is thus not only characterized by its transformation of all objects into commodities but, as Marx saw more deeply, the loss of the objects themselves: the laborer "is related to the product of his labor as to an alien object."[11] The forfeiture of the laborer's object-world means that man, defined now as *animal laborans*, is forever forced to repeat the effort of labor. The metabolisms of nature and the body immediately incorporate, consume, and annihilate the product of labor.

It would seem, and this is a point the volume addresses implicitly, that the contempt for laboring in ancient theory (Aristotle) and in late antique thought (the Eastern monastic tradition and, in the west, Carthaginian monasticism),[12] its increasing, though far from total, valorization in medieval thought (as Paul Freedman has recently shown[13]), and of course its glorification in modern theory (Marx) all issue from what has always been theorized from the outside—that is, the subjective attitude and affectivity of the laborer himself, either not trusting his painful exertion or extolling his productivity.[14] The material and spiritual condition of medieval serfs, slaves, vagabonds, and prostitutes turned ideologically on questions not only of church doctrine but also of philosophy, such as Aristotle's concept of "natural slavery", and of legal definition. The categories of peasant, slave, vagabond, and whore were far from fixed in the Middle Ages.[15] Neither the church nor secular authorities (literary and legal) promoted anything resembling a univocal understanding of these different labor groups. Medieval labor, its agents and practices, resists, however incompletely, the forms of objectivity and discipline we associate with historical institutions of dominion like the Church or the King's Bench. This challenge to objectivity carries with it ethical implications, how strategies of resistance are formulated around labor, in Ricardian England for instance; but it also indicates something of the moral and political commitments of the modern historian. Ruth Karras has emphasized, in her treatment of medieval prostitutes, that there is a danger in considering a form of labor independent from its nature, which in the case of prostitution is obviously sexual and thereby confers upon it social and moral stigmata.[16] The history of women's sexual objectification and social subordination can hardly be approached neutrally, likewise any history of labor that attends to issues of social inequality and the human costs and pains of laboring.

This volume, then, strives to rethink the terms in which a subjective approach to labor is even possible. The subjectivity of approaching laboring may be obvious in the medieval distinction between intellectual labor and *labor corporalis*, or craftsmanship, the *artes mechanicae* (a false distinction argued St. Bonaventure, who viewed, at least at one point in his writings, the different modalities of laboring as a single *artifex*[17]). Or the subjective approach may be apparent in the distinction, so crucial to theologians, between laboring and not laboring. This latter distinction was of course the frequent subject of popular sermons. Jacques de Vitry's sermon 61, *Ad agricolas et alios operarios*, for example, warns against the paralyzing effects of *otium* and *accidia*, recommending to its listeners the careful performance of their labor on earth so that it cannot be said of them that they are like mice, born only to consume.[18] Humbert of Romans (sermon 78) sees in the labor of the peasants the most laudable existence precisely because, though they produce no lasting monuments, they alone lead a life in accordance with the penance and punishment called for by original sin.[19] In fact, the very misery of their existence ensures the peasants' reward in the world to come. Laboring was viewed as a cheerless necessity, a constant, if not masochistic, reminder of the Fall and the degraded state of mankind. For this reason, the *Distinctiones* of Alan of Lille equates laboring (*laborare*) with repenting (*poenitere*) and the condition of suffering (*patientem esse...id est fui patiens*).[20]

In the scientific and philosophical traditions, laboring is repudiated as that which is antagonistic to the *vita contemplativa* and as that which actually debilitates the subject.[21] Robert Kilwardby's *De ortu scientiarum* (1246–50) is typical in this regard:

> Physical activity is more suited to insignificant and common people, the peace of meditation and study to the noble elite; in this way, everyone has an occupation fitting his station of life.[22]

In the concordance of Jean de St.-Amand, who was canon at Tournai and provost of Mons at the end of the thirteenth century, we find a crucial bit of information concerning the evolution of the term *laboring*. Citing Hippocrates, Jean defines laboring as a condition of anguish or malady (*morbus*).[23] Laboring in the sense of suffering a malady is well attested in the classical sources (e.g., Plautus, Cicero, Virgil, and Tacitus), but Jean's concordance reminds us of the extent to which this negative connotation of laboring was carried into the Middle Ages. In Middle English, the *laborante* is one who suffers from disease or pain.

This volume aims to offer a fuller history of labor, at the same time that it eschews any teleology of labor as historical agency for change or revolution. Marx's insight, updated by Karl Polyani, that the "great transformation"[24] bringing the industrial order into being was the separation of laboring from the rest of life—more specifically, the treatment of labor as a commodity rather than as an integral function of an indivisible way of life—may be reformulated with respect to the pre-industrial meanings of laboring. That is, well before the industrial period the cleavage of productive activities from everyday pursuits allowed bodily and mental exertion to condense into a phenomenon in its own right—an undesirable, even morbid, 'thing'. It would become, then, the work of medieval preachers to strengthen the connection between laboring and the totality to which it naturally belongs. In the pre-industrial vision, this totality was of course land, complete with those who tilled and harvested it and the promise of spiritual rewards in the afterlife.

In postmarxist discussions, the history of the medieval *laborante* has become inextricably linked with debates over the proper writing of history itself. Much of the medieval and early modern work associated with the influential *Annales* school and the development of the so-called "new historiography" takes the problem of labor as its point of departure, from its early founders (Febvre and Bloch) through Braudel and its later practitioners. Jacques Le Goff, for instance, expands on the methodology of *mentalité* criticism—the taking of 'successive soundings' from different types of sources (legal, literary, hagiographic, iconographic) in order to trace collective cultural beliefs—in his meditation on changing attitudes toward manual and artisanal labor across the early Middle Ages. Similarly, Georges Duby's discussion of a tripartite society composed of *oratores, bellatores,* and *laboratores* not only set the tone for most postwar discussions of medieval work, but provided a model of interdisciplinary scholarship that asked the historian to occupy simultaneously the positions of ethnographer, psychologist, economist, art historian, and literary critic. Both Le Goff and Duby lamented the silent presence of workers unable to speak for themselves, and, consequently, both saw medieval discourses on work as acts of communal ventriloquism. The elite classes promulgated idealized visions of labor that served their own unified, seigniorial interests, producing images of manual work and its heavenly reward that served, first and foremost, to legitimate aristocratic and ecclesiastical privilege.[25]

While critics of the *mentalité* school rejected the implicit partitioning of the material from mental conceptions of work in this view, recent scholarship has sought to create a more nuanced estates model. Instead of an ideological fantasy of order imposed on the inarticulate, oppressed lower orders (with a concomitant masking of the "realities" of medieval working life), historians now recognize the potentially transformative nature of the estates' rhetoric of mutuality. Paul Freedman, for example, has argued that the divisions of labor that informed the estates model was more than mere 'mystification'; rather, the inherent reciprocity of the model made it a vehicle that was available not only "for justifying but also for criticizing exploitation, for one could protest the failure of social reality to live up to this model."[26] This understanding of the medieval world view has produced a series of more localized demographic studies such as those by Barbara Hanawalt and Bruce Campbell, whose contributions to medieval social and economic history have sought to uncover the lived experience of the third estate rather than merely to extrapolate their situation from hegemonic sources. These historians are less concerned with collective cultural attitudes than with the specific material parameters of work in a given manor or village (based on sources like field and village plans, household architecture, wills, coroners' inquests, and other legal and manorial documents).[27] By finding alternative means of documenting the lives and experiences of the laboring classes, these scholars have shifted the emphasis in medieval studies away from the search for a disembodied 'voice' of labor, toward an inquiry into the surviving traces of individual workers, communities, and activities.

Just as the body of the medieval laborer became the site of the contested legacy of postwar 'new historiography', it serves a similar function in scholarship that defines itself (positively or negatively) in relation to the literary movement of New Historicism. Prior to the advent of New Historicism, considerations of literary work tended to take the form of genre studies, arguably the most influential being Jill Mann's magisterial *Chaucer and Medieval Estates Satire*, a book that explores the historical and literary contexts of the General Prologue's occupational satire.[28] Mann showed that in critiquing the various orders of society, Chaucer wrote within a literary tradition that stretched back several centuries while providing social stereotypes about labor readily recognizable to his contemporaries. Mann's methodology encourages us to focus on the form of the *Canterbury Tales* as a vehicle for its wider commentary on fourteenth-century mores. The advent of New Historicism in literary studies—an approach which has tended to privilege questions of social interest and production, sequestering them from considerations of genre and formal innovation—has meant that critics thinking about literary images of labor were less likely to comment on relatively open-ended aesthetic modes of affiliation and more likely to map the social 'pressures' that can be detected in a single moment of textual production.

In thinking about Langland's representations of literary labor, for example, Anne Middleton reads the narrator's "autobiography" (found in *Piers Plowman* C 5) as an intervention in late fourteenth-century debates about vagrancy, themselves part of a broader ethical inquiry into the nature of true labor (rather than reading the passage solely in relation to literary traditions of *apologia*). While Middleton's self-conscious negotiation of the dividing line between text and context as well as her antiphonal use of legal and literary sources is certainly inflected by New Historicism, she sees a need for "different models of the relations between literary history and [the] history of institutions or events than either Old or New History has proposed."[29] This need is felt particularly strongly, we would argue, when critics attempt to piece together the labors of the past—where, that is, they must make sense of its transient, physical aspects as well as the concrete record of its epiphenomenal presence. The essays collected here may be seen as a response to Middleton's call to rethink the relation between the material and the textual, meditating on how the two are mutually constitutive rather than uniquely separate realms. Recognizing the Foucauldian maxim that no event has a single cause, these essays are less likely to suggest a unique literary or historical context and rather more likely to sketch the plural social ambits in which a given representation of labor might circulate, whatever its provenance.

## II

Collectively, the contributors to this volume seek then to redefine labor, broadening the category beyond strictly agricultural work to include forms of feminine labor, literary and scribal production, guild work, and legal regulation. The essays collected here all highlight the tensions between the making visible and the making invisible of labor, the ways in which labor is at once recovered and elided, named and silenced. Labor leaves traces in the written records of the Middle Ages in a curious way: its immateriality as lived event places it beyond the reach of language at the same time that there is always detectable a linguistic pressure to domesticate labor. In other words, it seems language, especially poetic language, is adept at controlling labor even if it cannot articulate it fully or even name it at all.

The first section of this volume examines the implications of gender for understanding medieval labor and the social divisions structuring it. Examining the rhetoric and iconography of medieval women's work, Batt demonstrates the ideological ambiguities, what she calls 'the self-unraveling', inherent in such verbal and visual imagery. The image of the woman-with-distaff operates as a 'regulatory fiction', masking simultaneously the diversity and narrowness of medieval women's work. Images of the materiality of work, such as the distaff and spindle, assign women a place in the social order (e.g., the domestic as opposed to the intellectual) at the same time that such images metonymically prescribe the shape of the medieval social order, idiomatically defining both feminine and masculine types of labor. In the work of Hoccleve, Batt finds images of women's labor working as projections of masculinist concerns, occluding feminine work at the same time, and more dramatically, such images betray his own insecurity concerning his position as religious authority. The image of having 'tow on one's distaff', one that Hoccleve uses to refer to his domestic situation in *The Regiment of Princes*, is likewise read by Batt as revealing the failures and anxieties of masculine intellectual labor.

Gastle's essay also treats the precise language used to define feminine labor, in this case, the late medieval English legal discourses concerning the *femme sole*, the woman who, for instance, takes up merchant activities independent of her husband's concerns. Like Batt, Gastle detects a set of anxieties below the surface of such language. Designed at their inception to legitimate and, to a certain extent, police feminine mercantile activities, the laws concerning the *femme sole*, as they developed, were most significant, according to Gastle, for the ways they transformed medieval notions of obligation and equity traditionally associated with the marriage debt. As the laws change, particularly in the fourteenth century, feminine power becomes institutionalized to the extent that now the wife is legally dissociated from her husband, and is able to act as a genuine *sole* merchant.

The second section of the collection examines the interanimated meanings of secular work and spiritual labor. William Taylor's 1406 sermon is the focus of Crasson's analysis of the conflicting logics of the antifraternal tradition and the Wycliffite contention that poverty is an essential social and spiritual value. At the same time the sermon opposes the emergent antipoverty ethos of the late medieval period, it also celebrates almsgiving as a moral necessity, a necessity, according to Taylor, that extends institutionally to the disendowment of the church. Taylor's critique of spiritual culture stops short, however, of making poverty the ultimate Christian virtue; instead, the sermon promotes a socioeconomic condition in which labor emerges as the crucial virtue. Labor is not only and obviously the virtuous antidote to poverty; it is, in Taylor's vision, a fundamental Christian responsibility, upon which support of church and society depend.

Amos's assessment of guild life in the late Middle Ages examines how the economic, social, and political interests of craft guilds were colored by religious purposes. Amos's essay is a useful reminder of just how intricately the institutionalization of medieval labor is bound up with the cultivation of worldly and spiritual success. Taking as his example the Carpenters' Company, Amos shows how guild life operates as a buffer against future privations, measured culturally and spiritually. A 'theology of work' emerges where secular activities dovetail with religious missions. Such a theology of labor justifies the inevitable exploitative dimensions of an emergent capitalism in terms of salvific benefits, for example, prayers performed for the dead. Remarkably, labor is symbolically contiguous to death.

The third section turns to problems of labor and medieval law, specifically how the latter conditions the former. The contiguity of labor and death is reflected in the legislation known as the Ordinance of Laborers (1349) and the Statute of Laborers (1351), as the British royal government responds to perceived difficulties in labor relations brought about by the plague. Musson demonstrates how, with working practices coming increasingly under the purview of the royal government, the actual adjudication of labor disputes continued to be as much a matter of local judicial practices as so-called national ones, represented by the rulings of royal justices. Musson, for example, finds continuities in the personnel charged with enforcing the new labor laws at the local and at the national levels. More generally, such continuities point to an ideology of labor refigured by, yet certainly preexisting, the labor legislation of the mid-fourteenth and its refinements into the fifteenth century. This is an ideology of self-conscious participation in and dispute over, often by ordinary people, the very terms of everyday life structuring power and powerlessness in late medieval England.

The terms by which power is exercised and powerlessness is experienced bodily, and hence rendered visible to those in power, is the concern of

Robertson's essay on the material effects of the 1351 statute and its successive legal developments. The punitive dimensions of this legislation installed, Robertson shows, new protocols of reading (reading the body, interpreting the law) and writing (e.g., branding the renegade laborer), protocols aimed at making abstract labor itself legible and thus manageable. The worker's body becomes a text upon which the value of his or her labor can be inscribed, a text nonetheless, like any contract, inherently subject to negotiation and thus revaluation. Marked now by labor laws and ecclesiastical penances as public, the laborer's tremulous private body is transformed into an instrument of status, a model of what "bad" or transgressive labor looks like from both a political and a spiritual perspective. These two perspectives—the natural juridical and the ideal theological one—created an ideologically twinned, if split, laborer, a worker subjected to dialectical fantasies of control: "the idle recalcitrant worker who was always already suspected of labor violations and therefore always already regulated, and the good laborer incapable of such violations."

The next section looks at the literary terms and forms into which labor is cast in the Middle Ages. In an essay exploring the generic instabilities of the Middle English *Winner and Waster* that issue from the poet's sympathetic, if conflicted, relation to the aristocracy and its value system, Harwood demonstrates how the poem neutralizes the prospect of interclass violence. The poem repeatedly displaces threats of class-motivated hostility (the historical referent of which is the violence in Cheshire put down by the Black Prince in 1353), turning aggression into a kind of symptom haunting the text's surface. The demands of labor are elided in this poem, erased under the pressure of what Harwood terms the poet's "ideological imperative" to suppress acknowledgment of this basic struggle at the core of feudalism. Harwood's nuanced essay evokes the terms of psychoanalysis (viz., as in dreams, substitution, and displacement), sensitive to the real stakes of the allegorical battle between Winner and Waster, namely, the modes of expenditure and consumption governing feudal economy.

Like Harwood, Cole detects in the poetic tendency toward allegorical abstraction an elision of the realities of labor that can never be fully successful. The allegorical mode of *Piers Plowman* is, Cole suggests, finally less revealing of the complex organization of human labor than Langland's own multiple habits of composition all working to memorialize work in different ways. Cole's essay opens up new ways to appreciate the operations of allegory, without losing sight of the material conditions these very operations tend to generalize or suppress. Theological, literary, legal, and allegorical modes combine in Langland's hybrid vision of labor to generate novel private and communal affectivities around the material center of work.

The last section of the volume focuses on the significance of literary culture and the labors such as writing and book production that support it. Scribal work, in the business of preserving, through replication, literary culture itself, is a pointed example of immaterial labor, that is, the kind of labor that produces affectivities, values, and imagination rather than (or along with) mechanical or agricultural products. Knapp looks at the imaginary contours of scribal production in the *apologias* of Hoccleve and Langland, suggesting that the figure of manual agricultural labor, to which medieval scribes often metaphorically compared and contrasted their own work, transforming, sometimes negatively, the ideological meaning and role of writing within late medieval culture. In the Middle English tradition, Knapp suggests, scribal labor becomes that form of work always in the process of emerging from under the shadows of mercantile, agricultural, or ecclesiastical systems of labor.

The historical transition from manuscript to print culture in fifteenth-century England is usually discussed in terms of changing modes of production, especially the ways these allegorize the emergence of the modern. Similar claims about the emergence of "immaterial" culture are made for the more recent change from print to electronic culture. For Kuskin, these periodizations must be rethought, reframed in terms of the precise ways in which technologies articulate social relations through which subjectivity is produced by the labor and capital implicated in such changes. Like Knapp, Kuskin reads Hoccleve's "writerly body" as a sign of impaired or troubled subjectivity, and hence one that is subject to contradictory forces. Hoccleve, as laborer, is made and unmade in relation to the social and economic systems in which he is immersed—Lancastrian usurpation of the throne, the continuous French war, a radically changed Chancery, capitalist book production, and, perhaps above all, the emergent development of an English poetic canon. The English printer Caxton, Kuskin shows, is an example of how labor is erased in order to generate a myth of technological effortlessness, where the book becomes an object, autonomous and idealized.

## Notes

1. Aaron Gurevich, "Historical Anthropology and the Science of History," in *The Historical Anthropology of the Middle Ages*, ed. Jana Howlett (Cambridge, UK: Polity Press, 1992), p. 6 [3–20].
2. On Langland, see *Written Work: Langland, Labor, and Authorship*, ed. Steven Justice and Kathryn Kerby-Fulton (Philadelphia: University of Pennsylvania Press, 1997). On fourteenth-century labor, both intellectual and physical, see the essays collected in *The Problem of Labour in Fourteenth-Century England*, ed. James Bothwell, P.J.P. Goldberg and W.M. Ormrod (York: York Medieval Press, 2000).

3. Michael Hardt and Antonio Negri, *Empire* (Cambridge, MA: Harvard University Press, 2000), p. 290. For the economic arguments about post-work culture, see Jeremy Rifkin, *The End of Work: The Decline of the Global Labour Force and the Dawn of the Post-Market Era* (New York: Putnam, 1994). For further discussion of the term 'immaterial labor', see also Maurizio Lazzarato, "Immaterial Labor," in *Radical Thought in Italy: A Potential Politics*, ed. Michael Hardt and Paolo Virno (Minneapolis: University of Minnesota Press, 1996), pp. 133–47; and Michael Hardt, Antonio Negri, and Ronald A. T. Judy, "Dossier: Scattered Speculations on Value," *Boundary 2* 26 (1999): 75–100, esp. pp. 93–98.
4. St. Thomas Aquinas, *Summa theologica secunda secundae partis*, q. 187, art. 3.
5. A useful discussion of the development of the word 'labor' is Lucien Febvre, "Travail: Evolution d'un mot et d'une idée," *Journal de psychologie normale et pathologique* 41.1 (1948): 19–28. On the distinction between work and labor, see G. Keel, *Laborare und Operari: Verneudungs und Bedentrengs geschichte zweier Verben fur "arbeiten" im Lateinischen und Galloromanischen*, Inaugural-Dissertation der Philosoph. Fak. der Universitat Bern, St. Gall, 1952.
6. Sigmund Freud, "The Ego and the Id," in *The Standard Edition of the Complete Psychological Works of Sigmund Freud*, 24 vols., ed. and trans. James Strachey et al. (London: Hogarth Press, 1953–74), 19:23.
7. Georg Groddeck, *The World of Man*, trans. V.M.E. Collins (New York: Funk and Wagnells, 1951), pp. 221–22.
8. The connections between labor, slavery, and need or service is explored in the volume *The Work of Work: Servitude, Slavery, and Labor in Medieval England*, ed. Allen J. Frantzen and Douglas Moffat (Glasgow: Cruithne Press, 1994).
9. Hannah Arendt, *The Human Condition* (Chicago: University of Chicago Press, 1958), p. 81.
10. Karl Marx, *Capital: A Critique of Political Economy*, 3 vols., trans. Ben Fowkes (New York: Penguin, 1976), 1:290.
11. Karl Marx, *Economic and Philosophic Manuscripts of 1844*, ed. Dirk J. Struik, trans. Martin Milligan (New York: International Publishers, 1964), p. 108.
12. The ancient attitudes toward labor are well covered in Arthur T. Geoghegan, *The Attitude Towards Labor in Early Christianity and Ancient Culture*, The Catholic University of America Studies in Christian Antiquity 6 (Washington, D.C.: Catholic University of America Press, 1945).
13. See Paul Freedman, *Images of the Medieval Peasant* (Stanford: Stanford University Press, 1999).
14. Cf. Arendt, *Human Condition*, p. 93.
15. See, for example, Freedman, *Images*; Charles Verlinden, *L'Esclavage dans l'Europe médiévale*, vol. 1, *Péninsule Ibérique, France* (Brugge: De Tempel, 1955), vol. 2, *Italie, Colonies italiennes du Levant, Levant latin, Empire byzantin*, Rijkuniversiteit te Gent, Werken uitgegeven door de Faculteit van de Letteren en Wijsbegeerte 162 (Ghent: Rijkuniversiteit te Gent, 1977); Ruth Mazo Karras, *Slavery and Society in Medieval Scandinavia*, Yale Historical Publications 135 (New Haven: Yale University Press, 1988); Karras, *Common Women: Prostitution and Sexuality in Medieval England* (Oxford: Oxford University Press, 1996);

Steven A. Epstein, *Speaking of Slavery: Color, Ethnicity, and Human Bondage in Italy* (Ithaca: Cornell University Press, 2001); Bronislaw Geremak, "The Marginal Man," in *Medieval Callings*, ed. Jacques Le Goff, trans. Lydia G. Cochrane (Chicago: University of Chicago Press, 1990), pp. 347–73; and Jacques Le Goff, *Time, Work, and Culture in the Middle Ages*, trans. Arthur Goldhammer (Chicago: University of Chicago Press, 1980), pp. 58–121.
16. See Karras, *Common Women*, p. 9.
17. See Birgit van den Hoven, *Work in Ancient and Medieval Thought: Ancient Philosophers, Medieval Monks and Theologians and Their Concept of Work, Occupations and Technology*, Dutch Monographs on Ancient History and Archaeology 14 (Amsterdam: J.C. Gieben, 1996), p. 141.
18. Jacques de Vitry, sermo LXI (Ad agricolas et alios operarios), in *Analecta novissima Spicilegii Solesmensis altera continuatio*, ed. J.B. Pitra (Farnborough, Hants., UK: Gregg, 1967).
19. Humbert of Romans, sermo LXVIII (Ad laicos in villis), ed. Marguerin de La Bigne (1677).
20. Alan of Lille, *Liber in distinctionibus dictionum theologicalium*, in PL 210:825.
21. A useful study here is William Ovitt, *The Restoration of Perfection: Labor and Technology in Medieval Culture* (New Brunswick: Rutgers University Press, 1987).
22. Robert Kilwardby, *De ortu scientiarum*, ed. Albert G. Judy (London: British Academy, 1976), pp. 128–29.
23. Julius Leopold Pagel, *Die Concordanciae des Johannes de Sancto Amando nach eine Berliner und zwei Erfurter Handschriften zum ersten Male herausgegeben* (Berlin: Reimer, 1894).
24. See Karl Polyani, *The Great Transformation* (Boston: Beacon Press, 1957).
25. For the work of the *Annales* school on medieval labor and society, see Febvre, "Travail"; Marc Bloch, *La société féodale* (Paris: Albin Michel, 1940); Ferdinand Braudel, *Civilisation matérielle, économie et capitalisme: XVe-XVIIIe siècle*, 3 vols. (Paris: A. Colin, 1979); Jacques Le Goff, *Time, Work, and Culture*; and Georges Duby, *Les trois ordres: ou l'imaginaire du féodalisme* (Paris: Gallimard, 1978).
26. Freedman, *Images*, p. 23.
27. Barbara Hanawalt, *The Ties that Bound: Peasant Families in Medieval England* (Oxford: Oxford University Press, 1986); and Bruce M.S. Campbell, *English Seigniorial Agriculture, 1250–1450* (Cambridge, UK: Cambridge University Press, 2000).
28. Jill Mann, *Chaucer and Medieval Estates Satire: The Literature of Social Classes and the General Prologue to the* Canterbury Tales (Cambridge, UK: Cambridge University Press, 1973).
29. Anne Middleton, "Acts of Vagrancy: The C Version 'Autobiography' and the Statute of 1388," in *Written Work*, ed. Stephen Justice and Kathryn Kerby-Fulton, p. 213.

# PART 1

# GENDER TROUBLE

# CHAPTER 1

# THE IDIOMS OF WOMEN'S WORK AND THOMAS HOCCLEVE'S TRAVAILS

*Catherine Batt*

> *This essay considers the imagery of women spinners and spinning as an ideological trope, its relation to historical women's experience, and its deployment in Hoccleve's poetry.*

## Idiom, Ideology, and Historical Practice

*Whan Adam dalf and Eve span, Who was thanne a gentelman?*

The so-called democratic proverb, associated with the rising of 1381 (by which time it was already a familiar saying), demands equality for men on the grounds of common descent from our first parents.[1] There have been claims for the proverb as a tool of social change (i.e., for the male laboring classes).[2] Most recently, however, Paul Freedman, surveying the literature on the subject, suggests that medieval culture could, more readily than one might imagine, accommodate these words' evident radicalism by viewing them primarily as a recommendation of mutual service on the part of the different ranks of society.[3] If academic investigation judges that the revolutionary potential of the proverb's program of reform is open to interpretation, it seems hardly to notice, much less to interrogate, the way the proverb essentializes its already postlapsarian division of gendered labor roles at the same time as it proclaims an apparently utopian social equality. It is perhaps in part because the interpretive stress is primarily on the social placing of both women and men rather than on the work of women per se, that this proverb apparently forestalls debate about either gender role or gender equality. The blindness inherent in the critical reception and historical deployment of this proverb to what it might encode or convey beyond a desire for male equality is also, however, arguably a function of the saying's form. The binary of gender in which the question couches its 'radical' address inherently assumes the inequality of the very terms it uses, and so supports the subordination of female to male even as it specifies and crystallizes woman's role as that of spinner.[4] The proverb then bypasses questions of *women's* working identities, and of how Eve's spinning might relate to female social enfranchisement and rights; Eve and her distaff exist primarily to supplement and consolidate Adam's definition as a tiller of the soil.

In taking this position, the proverb (and its reception) reveals something of western culture's ideology. It partakes of the same strategy as medieval iconography, which in general naturalizes and universalizes the ready association of woman with the labor of spinning, and so deflects inquiry from what may lie behind this essentialist placing of her function. According to Frances M. Biscoglio, "pictorial images of the woman with distaff and spindle are a more authentic representation of popular culture than is the written word," while there is no single equivalent emblem in traditional visual representations of men.[5] At the same time, the woman as spinner is indeed historically specific; medieval men appear not to spin for a living.[6] While, then, women's working role as spinners appears fixed and unquestionable, in iconography and in common proverb, we need to appreciate the extent to which this positioning of women entraps them ideologically, in ways that write large, and form part of, the *pro* and *contra* arguments of antifeminism and feminism, and may indeed serve more to delineate the interests and self-definitions of men than of women. At the same time, the potential complexity endemic to how ideological placings and lived lives inter-relate further complicates the picture.

Laura Hodges reminds us that one must gauge the meaning of each iconographic representation of spinning contextually, for the image of the spinning woman is open to a dynamic range of interpretation, from that of obedient humility, in the picture of the domestic working woman, to that of riotous disobedience in (e.g.) the presentation of Noah's Wife-with-distaff as a type of Eve.[7] The iconography of the Virgin Mary as spinner, meanwhile, shows her reworking, as a benign influence, the spinning of the indifferent classical Fates who determine human destinies.[8] Rhetorically also, the image of spinning may belong to a language of praise or blame; Marbod of Rennes, for example, eulogizes spinning as women's work that is necessary to the community.[9] Spinning can also feature in derogatory contexts; Chaucer has his most prominent apologist for women, the Wife of Bath, subscribe to the traditional essentialization of women's work in the same breath as her revelations of sexual intrigue:

> Deceite, wepyng, spynnyng God hath yive
> To wommen kyndely, whil that they may lyve.[10]

The Wife's provocative assertion of the 'naturalness' of spinning to women, as of her inherent ability to dominate and trick a hapless husband, is a vernacular echo of a Latin proverb beloved of misogynist writing (and Chaucer slyly leaves us to measure from it for ourselves the extent to which dominant ideologies control the Wife's sense of identity). Christine de Pizan's Reason, meanwhile, in *The Book of the City of Ladies*, robustly counters the assertion that women (in her version) only "weep, talk, and spin," and assigns a positive Christian and moral value to all these activities. Spinning she declares (somewhat briefly, in comparison with the space she allocates the good that comes of women's speech), is "an activity which is essential for serving (God) and for the good of all rational beings. Without it, the world would be in a vile state."[11]

These uses of the proverbial idiom, positive and negative, expose its untenably essentialist view of women, and act out the tensions inherent in such essentialism. Christine's and Marbod's defenses, vigorous as they are, nevertheless hold them in the trap that Slavoj Žižek identifies for the "ideological dream"; it is ultimately useless to counter a position by declaring that the historical reality proves the situation to be otherwise. What the position masks is, as Žižek observes of anti-Semitism, "the inconsistency of our own ideological system."[12] Ideology, as Žižek describes it, assumes a certain lack of awareness on the part of those who exist within the social reality that it constitutes. We should be asking why we formulate social and gender relations in the way we do, not what is 'unfair' or inaccurate in the formulation's specificities. To interrogate the treatment of, and responses to, the idioms of women's labor with this awareness is to see how misogynist rhetoric in general operates, and also to uncover some of the power of that rhetoric as a cultural phenomenon, for how is one to step outside of one's social reality? Žižek's discussion of inconsistencies and internal contradictions that are implicitly both recognized and ignored in the adoption of any ideological position (e.g., that one's notion of 'freedom' may entail servitude for others), is also germane to an investigation of the rhetoric around women and their work. In the formulation the 'democratic' proverb offers, Eve's presence is integral, but she also threatens to throw its proclaimed vision of ideal social and working conditions off-balance, for she both guarantees and undermines it. Examination of the rhetoric and iconography of women's work exposes the self-constitutive ambiguity surrounding an essentialist vision of woman, what I term the 'self-unraveling' of misogynist techniques of representation.

If the rhetoric of misogyny effectively structures reality, the difficulty lies in teasing apart the historical actuality of women's work and the language that claims to define it (and one has also to acknowledge the degree to which these might be inseparable). J.K. Gibson-Graham writes of the need to break down essentialist categories of class, labor, and economic structure if one is to determine the particular nature of interacting economic frameworks and individuals' dynamic and fluctuating participation in them. For Gibson-Graham, to attempt to define an individual's "true and singular" class identity may be simply (to borrow a term from Judith Butler's investigation of gender coherence) to engage with a "regulatory fiction," one that, in terms of working lives, misrepresents the diversity of labor processes in which people might take part.[13] For medieval working women (as still for many modern women), the question of 'identity' may be even more complex because of the cultural imbrication of sexuality and marital status with their status as workers. The recording of their identities is in the service of others' interests. The "regulatory fiction" of the stereotypical icon of woman-with-distaff ignores the variety and actuality of women's work. It also draws in its wake a set of associations and assumptions. And yet, when Chaucer combines spinning and (sexual) fraud in the Wife of Bath's dealings with men, which we saw above, he cannily, if obliquely, reflects a world, historical details of which one may attempt to reconstruct, in which women's working, sexual, and marital-status identities, and assumptions about those identities, elide, but may also interrelate culturally with some sophistication.

The Wife of Bath is of course a literary construction, and one that transparently holds up to us, for our examination, its own rhetorical procedures. Historically, women were certainly heavily involved in the spinning and cloth industries, but culturally normative representations of women at work may not necessarily reflect the historical reality and complexity of their work patterns and practices.[14] The reality of women's labor is largely absent from literary texts, although this is also part of medieval literature's general tendency to ignore manual labor (while it might accord it some respect).[15] As Karma Lochrie points out, the nature and variety of women's labor, and other factors, such as their marital status, may lead to their occlusion in the records.[16] At the same time, several pragmatically arrived-at concerns may inform how record-keepers and document-providers represent female identities. Cordelia Beattie notes from her researches into women's work identities in the England of the later fourteenth century that "(t)exts classify people according to their own interests."[17] Beattie identifies, from poll tax returns and related documentation, and from accounts of consistory court and King's Bench cases, representations of women that diversely accord greater or lesser importance to their marital, social, sexual, economic, and occupational status, and observes that these modes of identification may conflict, compete, or elide with one another. The King's Bench case she discusses relating to Joan Garton, an ale-seller, is particularly interesting for its overlap of the professional and the sexual. Accused of immoral behavior by John atte More (who turns out to be a brewer and tavern-owning competitor), who says he broke into her home to prevent illicit sexual activity, Garton successfully counters the charge with a narrative that exposes John's motive as one of economic rivalry; it would be to his profit to have her leave the area. In this context, she responds to the charge of immorality not by asserting her sexual continence, but by declaring her honesty and competence as a good worker, and the court appears to interpret this as tender of her moral rectitude.[18]

In historical practice, the elements of women's identity formation may prove adaptable and flexible, and their configuration may even work in women's favor, as when Garton's dedication to her job serves as a serious index of her probity. Garton overcomes an all-too-familiar aggressive strategem (one undermines a woman by questioning her sexual mores) by nimbly exploiting social values and ideological positions. The rhetoric about women's work, meanwhile, especially the invocation of the tools and materials of her trade—distaff, spindle, and wool—would appear to be more prescriptive in application, invoked in a variety of cultural, literary, and social contexts, to control women, but also to confirm 'natural' roles for men. Mention of a distaff may reinforce the appropriateness of gendered labor and, by implication, disenfranchise women from intellectual 'work', as when, in the twelfth century, Abelard reports that Eloise presents the artifacts of a feminized domesticity as inimical to her lover's higher philosophical occupation: "What harmony can there be between pupils and nursemaids, desks and cradles, books or tablets and distaffs, pen or stylus and spindles?"[19] Correlatively, distaffs may twit men with a lack of masculinity; the spinning man is, iconographically, a satirical figure of fun.[20] Recent work on the Third Crusade (1187–92) draws attention to a story in the *Itinerarium Peregrinorum et Gesta Regis Ricardi* that describes how, in reaction to homiletic exhortation to join the crusade: "A great many men sent each other wool and distaff, hinting that if anyone failed to join this military undertaking they were only fit for women's work."[21]

The distaff as metonym of women's work reflects on men's definition of their masculinity in later as well as earlier medieval culture and on occasion, as we shall see, literature and law appropriate the distaff as shorthand for male sexual humiliation and for male social shame. This further satirical deployment of distaff imagery ratifies and expands its ideological importance (rather than its usefulness as a historical descriptor). The troping of women's work as male burlesque writes large the tensions of the original spinner image, with its play on order and disorder, control and disobedience, and self-evidently belongs to the 'unraveling' propensities of a particular misogynist discourse; but it also opens up an uneasy arena in which to position men in relation to dominant ideologies.

## Thomas Hoccleve

In the context of appropriations of the distaff/spindle image, whereby the instruments of labor may speak to men's rather than to women's concerns, I want to consider two instances where Hoccleve invokes women's traditional work of spinning. While Hoccleve hardly pays full attention to the nature and importance of women's work, his apparently casual mentions of women's industry and the instruments of their labor reward examination precisely for the way in which they trouble, or even seek to occlude, women's presence, or serve as projections of masculine concerns. Hoccleve often links the representation of women in general with the problematics of interpretation.[22] Mentions of women's work link with those points at which Hoccleve appears highly anxious about the legitimacy and authority of his own intellectual labors.

In Hoccleve's "Address to Sir John Oldcastle" (1415), the tone of which is so difficult to gauge, women's communities, activities and words, feature (if only briefly) as the poet's displacement of anxieties about order and authority. Through the contradictory images of female activity and verbal (in)continence we glimpse something of a projection of the tensions in Hoccleve's own non-clerical position as promulgator of religious orthodoxy—though this is not to suggest, for reasons I examine in my analysis, that Hoccleve thereby 'feminizes' his own situation. In the slightly earlier book of advice to the future King Henry V, *The Regiment of Princes* (1411–12), an apparently fleeting reference to the technique of spinning serves as an awkward supplement to the rather fuller (and critically more closely examined) images of writing and labor Hoccleve employs elsewhere in the poem. Extra-textual legal and literary contexts for interpolated idiom suggest that Hoccleve feels the isolation and ambiguity of his position, and that through the image of having "tow on his distaff" he conveys something of the problematic nature of his intellectual labor, its vexed status and articulation. In the "Address," then, the view of working women uncovers (perhaps unwittingly) rhetorical and ideological tensions, while the distaff idiom in the *Regiment* marks out an ambiguous space of self-identification.

## "The Address to Sir John Oldcastle"

The "Address," as an anti-Lollard poem, denounces the heretical and treasonous rebellion of one identified as the most prominent of the movement, John Oldcastle, and is written while Oldcastle is still evading capture after the failure of a plot against the crown in which he has been implicated.[23] Recent work emphasizes the extent to which the "Address" genders the heterodox as female in its anxieties over the policing of what constitutes appropriate devotional and interpretive behavior. Ruth Nissé, for example, offers a powerful analysis of the poem as Hoccleve's attempt to outline a masculinized program of reading and chivalric action as a counter to a Lollard interpretive practice perceived as perfidiously 'feminine'.[24] Hoccleve classically combines sexual and verbal 'looseness' when he enjoins "lewde calates" [ignorant sluts] to keep out of theological debate they are too feeble-minded to understand:[25]

> Some wommen eke, thogh hir wit be thynne,
> Wole argumentes make in holy writ.
> Lewde calates, sittith down and spynne
> And kakele of sumwhat elles, for your wit
> Is al to feeble to despute of it.[26]

Hoccleve appears here to be impeccably orthodox in his deployment of an accepted and familiar trope.[27] His linking of woman-as-preacher with misinterpretation through a reminder of woman's proper business is a cultural commonplace. Throughout and beyond the medieval period, the orthodox tell recalcitrant women, defined as dissenting religious (and vice versa) to take up the distaff rather than scripture. John Swetstock, for example, whose writings are contemporaneous with Hoccleve, advises the female audience for his sermons: "tak þe to þi distaff, coveyt not to be prest ne prechour, schal never cloc henne be wel crowing cok."[28] As we saw above, the woman and her distaff are susceptible to diverse interpretations, depending on her location, and mention of the obedient spinner also raises the specter of her opposite.

The distaff-wielding woman out of doors, rather than safely cooped inside, may in practice, however, connote a range of meanings. She may figure female unruliness, and even female riot, but she can also represent the indignant call to arms of a wronged community. Chaucer's *Nun's Priest's Tale*, for example, gives us just such an image, in the pursuit of the fox at the end of the story, when "Malkyn, with a dystaf in hir hand" (3383–84) features among the local people who give chase.[29] *The Book of Margery Kempe* also finely exploits the resonances of the distaff-wielding woman in and out of doors, and their contrasts, in the episode that forms part of the account of Margery's travels through Yorkshire, in which angry women, in the service of orthodoxy, run out of their houses, distaffs in hand, to demand that Margery be burned as a heretic, while individuals concerned for her welfare advise that she would be better off taking up women's work and so removing herself from the public gaze:

> Then thei browt hir ayen into Hesyl, and ther men callyd hir "Loller," and women cam rennyng owt of her howsys wyth her rokkys, crying to the pepil:
> "Brennyth this fals heretyk!"
> So, as sche went forth to-Beverle-ward wyth [. . .] yemen and frerys [. . .] thei mettyn many tymes wyth men of the cuntre, whech seyd unto hir:
> "Damsel, forsake this lyfe that thu hast, and go spynne and carde as other women don, and suffyr not so meche schame and so meche wo" [. . .].[30]

The "Address" and *The Book of Margery Kempe* are alike here in imagining a topographical 'placing' of women that returns them to a domestic female community of 'safe' (and largely invisible) labor.[31] But just as the image of a crowd of women out of doors may carry different nuances of meaning, so Hoccleve's poem problematizes domestic space and its significance. He cursorily inscribes the home not only as a means to contain nuisance women, but also (nostalgically) as a place for the communication of orthodox piety:

> Oure fadres olde and modres lyued wel
> And taghte hir children as hemself taght were
> Of holy chirche, and axid nat a del
> "Why stant this word heere? and why this word there [. . .]?" (153–56)

How have the good-living mothers who taught their children transformed into—or produced—"lewde calates"? As Patricia Meyer Spacks notes, "(g)ossip as a phenomenon raises questions about boundaries, authority, distance, the nature of knowledge."[32] The treatment and 'placing' of women's speech here declares an authorial control over a group of individuals, but it also crystallizes the difficulty of determining, let alone maintaining, the meaning of spaces and boundaries. The juxtaposition of outspoken women, gossips seemingly rendered harmless through domestic enclosure, and maternal instructors in the faith, raises historical questions about the status of women's talk and learning and the form of women's teaching of others.[33] The poem does not stop to consider its contradictory presentation of women here. Ethan Knapp generously reads Hoccleve's married state (and his concomitant lack of automatic rights to clerkly authority) as providing him with the opportunity to negotiate a new relation to writing and gender, which manifests itself, in his reworking of Christine de Pizan's *Epistre au dieu d'Amours*, at least, in an 'authorial voice' that tries to maintain a 'skeptical distance' from conventional auctorial categories of gender and textual tradition alike.[34] The unresolved tensions of the "Address," however, look more like an ideological blind spot on Hoccleve's part. His own (uncertain) authority has to be gained, in the poem, at the expense of the women he condemns, while he is himself involved in the very strategies he projects onto them; he claims obedience to the Church ("Auctoritee of Preest excedith alle / Eerthely powers" [291–92]), yet he also 'speaks out'.

While the tantalizing glimpse of historical women, irreducible to their traditional tropes of representation, to some extent troubles Hoccleve's gendered political language in this poem, it is the implicit invitation to narrativize those tropes that raises greater difficulties (and Spacks notes in general that the impulse to narrativize is itself an attribute of gossip). The problems inherent in the representation of woman as religious instructor and commentator—her 'transgression' denounced, and her role then redefined, but not analyzed—tacitly reflects on Hoccleve's own situation as lay promulgator of religious truth and political obedience. It has been noted that as a vernacular author claiming orthodox conformity, the scriptural knowledge he both demonstrates and recommends "impinges on clerical prerogatives."[35] Hoccleve advises Oldcastle on how he may reinvent himself as a "manly" knight, with a reading program that will (ostensibly) keep him safe from heresy but, as I have discussed elsewhere, Hoccleve's complicated literary taxonomy of "legitimate," religiously orthodox, writings here generates its own interpretive difficulties and possible heterodoxies, so that the poem undoes itself, and, rather than leading us to concentrate on Oldcastle's crimes against religion, implicitly leads us to recognize the ineluctably political nature of both writing and its interpretation.[36]

The presentation of another 'active' woman, Judith, contributes further to this simultaneous poetic 'making' and 'undoing,' on the level of gender. The "Address" presents as unproblematic secular narratives that have clearly political and moral implications, such as the siege of Troy and the story of Lancelot, and recommends militaristic books of the Old Testament as "safe" for chivalric consumption. Yet, in the context of a strategy that ranges the chivalric, the manly and the orthodox against the heretical feminine, it seems extraordinary that the history of Judith should feature in an "approved" list that includes the Books of Judges, Kings, Joshua, Machabees and the Paralipomenon (201–05):

> If þat thee list in hem bayte [rest] thyn ye,
> More autentik thing shalt thow fynde noon
> Ne more pertinent to chiualrie. (206–08)

The redoubtable Judith epitomizes a public female challenge to military force that makes for an uneasy exemplarity. As slayer of Holofernes, whom she makes vulnerable through the controlled exercise of her sexuality, Judith is both an instrument of God, savior of her race, and an unsettling threat to masculine power, as Margarita Stocker has argued: "Precisely Judith's authorization by God for deceitful seduction and murder was what made her more terrifying than any mere villainess."[37] Chaucer's passing mentions of Judith feature her in somewhat piecemeal fashion, now as channel of God's grace, in the *Man of Law's Tale* (939–45), now as advice giver, in *Melibee* (1098), although the *Merchant's Tale* perhaps complicates the picture a little by linking her 'conseil' with her murder of Holofernes (1366–68). In the *Monk's Tale*, she appears as the instrument of a sexualized Fortune who plays wantonly with a Holofernes overproud of his ability as a warrior (2551–74).[38] Omission of the full story of Judith signals difficulties in accommodating it to normative moral commentary. In the *Regiment*, Holofernes's downfall is simply "dronkenesse," which suggests that Hoccleve is following Chaucer's practice in obscuring the narrative's complexity.[39] For Christine de Pizan, carefully rewriting her behavior toward Holofernes in terms of the utmost propriety, Judith is "a noble and valiant lady," whom Christine praises as "of exemplary virtue and chastity," a precursor of the Virgin Mary.[40]

Scriptural commentators, however, seem fully aware of the problems Judith's history presents. The Wycliffite Bible, for example, carefully notes her culpability in deceiving Holofernes, although it cites mitigating circumstances: "Vs nedith not to excuse Judith fro lesingis [lies] and tresoun to Olofernes, but we moun fauorably excuse hire for deedly synne in this doinge, for the greet loue that sche hadde to Goddis peple."[41] Nissé, with reference to this Wycliffite commentary, makes an interesting case that Hoccleve invokes Judith in his poem as a "female armed leader" as part of his reappropriation of scripture to counter Lollard reading practices, for the Wycliffite Bible has used her example to shame "proude werrioris" into fear of the Lord.[42] But this reading does not perhaps sufficiently interrogate the ambivalences of Hoccleve's invoking a female chivalric practice in the context of the terms of gendered heresy he has established, nor recognize the problems of interpretation mention of Judith raises. Hoccleve has no commentary on Judith in the poem, other than to insist twice on the text's authoritativeness (201, 208)—itself interesting in the light of the Wycliffite note that the book of Judith, as quasi-Apocryphal, is not fully "authorized."[43] Such an omission, along with the stress on authority, raises, and leaves hanging, questions of reader responsibility and of authorial license, and compounds the impression that Hoccleve half-recognizes and refuses his own ideological complicity in the representation of women, while displacing onto them his own writerly anxieties.

In the "Address," then, the spinning/domestic woman is open to unresolved nuances of interpretation, and her juxtaposition with the passing recommendation of the Book of Judith as suitable reading matter offers a no less confusing model for female—and male chivalric—behavior. The spinning woman and the militant woman are both part of the text's 'unraveling'; its language intimates a subtext that pulls against the poem's declared orthodoxies, but is not directly confronted. Ethan Knapp subtly traces, in the "Address," a critique of the iconographic terms on which the Lancastrian regime conducts its propaganda.[44] The poem's disjunctive invocation of women and their proper spheres of activity appears to work rhetorically on a similar, but more properly self-reflexive, level. The unarticulated links between 'unauthorized' women and the unclearly authorized male narrator concentrate issues of license and authority, and while these very links urge us to political and poetical analysis, it is the refusal to consider these links that in effect keeps the work together.

## *The Regiment of Princes*

The wry idiom "to have tow on one's distaff," features in *The Regiment of Princes*, a poem of good counsel that simultaneously interrogates the nature of advice giving and receiving, in a way that adumbrates marriage, women, sexuality, labor, and interpretation. It also refracts legitimacy, but in a different way from the presentation of female gossips in the "Address." The Hoccleve character, in conversation with the Old Man he meets by chance, preliminary to his penning his own work of advice for Prince Henry, outlines and considers his own condition, occupational, intellectual, social, and advisory. The Old Man's inquiries reveal a narrator agitatedly concerned with poverty, and with his situation as clerk at the office of the Privy Seal. There are some fine recent readings of the importance of the body as focus of anxiety in this poem, readings that consider in particular the sequence in which Hoccleve complains of the deleterious effects upon the body of the physical labor involved in writing (981–1029), and comment on Hoccleve's carefully modulated account of playfulness and control in the regulation of the body, on what he conveys of the human material cost of preserving the written word, and on the broader contexts of the dynamics and obligations of counsel.[45]

When the Old Man holds forth on the virtues of household economy, however, in recommendation of moderation, Hoccleve supplies a further image of regulation and pressure:

Tow on my distaf have I for to spynne
More, my fadir, than ye woot of yit,

> Which yee schal knowe or that I fro yow twynne,
> If your good lust be for to heren it. (1226–29)

This proves, in context, to be a coy reference to the narrator's married state—Charles Blyth, the *Regiment*'s latest editor, glosses the idiom as "domestic trouble."[46] In an *occupatio* of some three stanzas, Hoccleve tells the Old Man he does not wish to interrupt him with details of his burden, and we have to wait over 200 lines before Hoccleve reveals the reason he cannot take holy orders and so seek clerical advancement:

> "Than art thow, sone, a weddid man, par caas?
> [. . .]
> A sone, I have espyed and now se
> This is the tow that thow speek of right now!"
> "Now by the Rood, fadir, sooth seyn yee." (1449–59)

Why do both Hoccleve and his interlocutor and surrogate parent laboriously "mark" both this information and the idiom used to impart it? The curiously underlined exchange perhaps reassures the Hoccleve character that his counselor shares his register and understands him. The rueful idiom also aligns Hoccleve with other put-upon husbands such as Mak the sheep-stealer, who, in the *Towneley Second Shepherds' Play*, faking a premonitory dream of his wife's giving birth to yet another child to feed, laments:

> I haue tow on my rok [distaff]
> More then euer I had.[47]

In the *Regiment*, however, this amounts to more than a poor joke at the expense of Hoccleve's wife. From what follows, the "tow" idiom would appear to be a fairly provocative expression in need of defusing, as the Old Man goes on to probe the integrity of Hoccleve's motives for marriage, and to make certain that he acts out of "love" and not "lust" (1555–61). Even in a text marked by digression, Hoccleve's news disrupts the flow of the argument, leading to a prurient examination of Mr. and Mrs. Hoccleve's sexual practices (1555–96). Antony Hasler sees this as a "magnificently unmotivated" inquiry, serving primarily to expose the penitential mode as "a bizarre combination of epistemophilia and scopophilia."[48] But one may further understand this exposure of Hoccleve's personal life in terms of the *Regiment*'s complication of authorizing strategies, pertinent to which is Ethan Knapp's observation (already mentioned above), that the historical Hoccleve's marriage denies him any claim to literary clerical "authority." When Hoccleve admits to being married, the Old Man recommends having a wife because at least this saves him from clerical sexual hypocrisy

(1471–77). The Old Man moves on from this satirical aside, however, to insist on the spiritual importance, in sexual relations, of honest motive—and he also discourses at some length on the sins that tempt the married man as well as the supposedly celibate priest:[49]

> A Man may with his wyf do leccherie;
> Th'entente is al; be waar ay of folie. (1595–96)

Nicholas Perkins argues that in the first part of the *Regiment*, Hoccleve is constructing a personal *intentio auctoris* (which also draws on his life) as part of his advice-giving credentials, in which "entente," the evidence of good intention, is crucial.[50] If Hoccleve's declaration of his married state is a means of acknowledging his indeterminate status as advice-giver, but also of asserting his integrity—if not, perhaps, fully constructing an alternative idiosyncratic authority for himself—it also works, through reference to the difficulties of regulating the private life, to highlight the problems of ascertaining that same 'entente', and to remind us of the complexity of the conditions of human activity. Marriage is central to discussions of personal authority and integrity, but it is also a particularly fraught focus in a poem in which both marriage and gender relations play an important function in issues of interpretation and social stability (including, of course, the political stability of the realm, as the poem's good counsel culminates in the recommendation of a royal marriage as guarantor of peace).

In lieu of an unproblematic clerical 'authority', then, Hoccleve presents himself as embroiled in a continuing sexual and social dynamic, in the context of which his writing and advice giving must be both produced and understood. Emblematic of a duty that Hoccleve cannot avoid, and with intimations of a feminizing constraint, the "tow" both stands in for his absent wife—as the Old Man reads it metonymically—and suggests the labor Hoccleve has to undertake to support her, and so, by extension, the poetic work he has on hand, although it is not clear to what extent the domestic image, with its overtones of women's work, reflects comically on Hoccleve's authoring of the poem. Certainly, it shows that the work of advice giving cannot be divorced from the material (as well as the ethical) conditions that impel it. However, the idiom also carries other cultural baggage that tells us something more about the nature of Hoccleve's labor, and some of its dangers.

Perhaps the most well-known literary medieval character also described idiomatically as having work to do is Absolon, in his single-minded pursuit of vengeance upon the contemptuous Alison in the *Miller's Tale*, who, when he requests of the local smith the loan of a hot coulter, is described as having "moore tow on his distaf / Than Gerveys [the smith] knew" (3774–75).

There are surely resonances here (as in the *Regiment* Hoccleve's case) with the satirical image of the male spinner. Carter Revard, however, suggests a very specific link between the idiom as Chaucer uses it and a piece of Ricardian legislation (preserved in John Carpenter's *Liber Albus* of 1419), which records the punishment suitable to people guilty of crimes relating to sex and disorderliness, which was publicly to carry a distaff with tow on it to the public stocks:

> Item, si ascune homme ou femme soit atteint pur tensurere ou tensuresse, soit amesnez al thewe, ove un conoille ove lyn, appele *dystaf with towen*, en sa main, ovesques ministrallz, et mys sur icelle par certein temps, solonc discrecioun dez Maire et Aldermans.
>
> [Item, if any man or woman shall be attainted of being a brawler or a scold, let such person be taken unto the thew with a distaff [dressed] with flax (called "*distaff with towen*") in his or her hand, with minstrels, and be set thereon for a certain time, at the discretion of the Mayor and Aldermen.][51]

The record notes that sexual transgressors, including "comunes baudes et contenderesses" [common bawds and scolds] must be punished "a plaisance de Dieu, salvacioun de lour almes, et netture et honeste de la [. . .] citee" [to the pleasing of God, the salvation of their souls, and the cleanness and honesty of the [. . .] city].[52] The terms *tensurere* and *tensuresse* appear to have sexual connotations in this context, although the *Anglo-Norman Dictionary* interprets *tensurere* as 'quarreller, wrangler', and *tenceresse* as 'scold, shrew', which conforms to the meaning of Old French *tenceor/tenceresse*. Revard notes that Riley, in his printed text, glosses the Anglo-Norman words as 'procurer' and 'procuress', but that they appear in his full translation as 'brawler or scold'.[53]

More work needs to be done to establish how frequently this punishment was carried out in full in practice; some London cases of disorderliness Riley cites mention the pillory, but no details of a specific procession (although this might be taken as read). One Elizabeth, wife of Henry Moring, found guilty of being a procuress in July 1385, is judged to "be put upon the *thewe*, there to remain for one hour of the day, the cause thereof being publicly proclaimed," and then expelled from the city; in 1406, Richard Dod, a tailor, is found guilty of accepting money from William Langford, a chaplain, to procure his own wife for him, and punished with three hours at the pillory.[54] In an earlier case, from 1375, Alice Shether, indicted for being "a common scold," whose words inflicted "great damage" on local residents, is condemned to an hour at the thew.[55]

The Ricardian document makes an emblem of women's work a token of humiliation, in public correction of an offence that may be more 'verbal' than sexual. Strikingly for our interpretation of the *Regiment*, this later-medieval legislation punishes offenses against what the public defines as acceptable speech and legitimate sexual acts in apparently similar ways, but reserves for the "tensurere," the male quarreler/?procurer, the further feminizing refinement of humiliation by thew (the contraption the law reserved for women) rather than by pillory (the instrument of punishment for men). The *Regiment* also links verbal and sexual transgressions, when the Old Man complains of men who profit by flattery and pimping, and gain honor and praise thereby:

> But he that flatere can or be a baude,
> And by tho tweyne fressh array him gete,
> It holden is to him honour and laude. (547–49)

Sexual self-regulation, then, appears as a recommendation of verbal continence and honesty, and so the policing of Hoccleve's marriage is also tender of his good will as advisor. The crossover in sexual/professional identities we earlier saw implicitly at work in the ale-seller Garton's case is explicit here. If the Hoccleve persona is happy to place his marriage under scrutiny to prove his fitness as an advisor, the "tow" idiom nevertheless carries with it, in the light of legal practice, worries about the proper use of speech (What is the line between counsel and defamation, good advice and plain gossip?), and about the possible shame of self-publicity and authorial exposure.

The idiom of having tow on one's distaff may have gained further resonance from a literary motif to be found in tales as diverse as the romance of *Perceforest* and the story of *The Wright's Chaste Wife*, which latter is extant in a late-medieval London manuscript.[56] The bulky 'pre-Arthurian' early-fourteenth-century French romance and the *Gesta Romanorum*-derived fabliauesque tale have in common the trickery of high-status males by clever women who get their would-be seducers to spin rather than to satisfy their lusts. In the *Roman de Perceforest*, Margon, a knight in King Perceforest of Britain's service, has a beautiful wife who evades the ill will of two evil knights who, motivated by jealousy of her husband, seek to dishonor her.[57] She tricks them by promising her favors to each in turn, but shuts them up in a small room where they have no choice but to spin in order to earn their keep. Her success becomes proverbial; we learn that any lady who would thereafter discourage a knight's unwanted advances has only to warn him, "a gas ou a certes" [whether in jest or in earnest], to accept refusal gracefully, "qu'on ne vous apprenne a filler" [lest you be taught how to spin].[58] *The Wright's Chaste Wife* puts a similar story in an urban bourgeois setting. In this version, the clever carpenter's wife traps a lord, his steward, and a proctor, who seek to seduce her in her husband's absence, and forces them to overcome their shame through hunger, and to beat flax and to spin, "Mete and drynke ther-wyth to wynne."[59] For Barbara Hanawalt, the nature of the men's humiliation suggests female authorship.[60] Appealing as women might find the prospect of men working for their living, however, the other cultural evidence we have examined suggests that the shaming of men through association with women's work is not necessarily—certainly not uniquely—female devised. Hoccleve's tow image, with its overtones of sexual humiliation, functions as an intriguingly domestic displacement of worries over his motives for work, his work, and its reception.

Idiom, hermeneutic, and "autobiographical" narrative interact in the *Regiment*'s mention of tow and distaff, in a further literary echo. In *The Canterbury Tales*, the characters' quasi-confessional signaling of their marital troubles often marks the limits of their interpretive ability, as when the Host, in the *Prologue* to the *Monk's Tale*, responds to the story of the wisdom of Prudence, in *Melibee*, with a return to the literal, in his account of his less than prudent harridan wife, who berates her husband for his lack of manliness, whether in failing to defend perceived slights to her reputation, or in mismanagement of his workers:

> By corpus bones, I wol have thy knyf,
> And thou shalt have my distaf and go spynne! (1906–07)

The Merchant similarly, in his *Prologue*, seeks to confirm through autobiography the truth of the antifeminist troping in which he engages (1213–32). Thomas Hoccleve joins company with these pilgrims when he writes himself up autobiographically as an encumbered husband (as he does also in the *Dialogue*, in the *Series*, when he declines to speak of his private life, telling his Friend that his wife would only treat him with contempt were he to complain about their life together[61]). In the *Regiment*, Hoccleve constructs a female audience of interpretive resistance to his advice about wifely obedience—he imagines married women scolding him for not supporting their claims to equality (5104–09)—as a prelude to a sophisticated debate on the manipulation of gendered voices in (Chaucerian) advice literature.[62] The lack of serious consideration of women's political power, however, intimates that Hoccleve as married man cannot transcend the literalism of his situation, and his idiomatic way of encoding his condition then has a double function; it marks the limits of his own interpretive reach at the same time as it offers an 'alternative', and not wholly straightforward, model for his integrity as an advice giver.

I do not want to claim that the mention of "tow on one's distaff" automatically invokes sexual shame, public isolation and humiliation, and suspicion of verbal transgression, but I would suggest that the way Hoccleve refers to his domestic space summons up ghosts of public show and shame, drawing on the broader cultural resonances of a particular ideological discourse to highlight the problematic of his situation. His language marks how, as self-appointed counselor, he has continually to negotiate the value of his discourse, and to acknowledge that his own motives and behavior will be continually subject to public examination. Hoccleve's apparently innocent use of a familiar idiom may then be said, in its cultural and literary contexts, to adumbrate a series of anxieties and concerns; about how his marital status informs his masculinity, and what it contributes to or takes away from his status as authoritative advice giver; about the motives behind his advice giving, and the line between counsel and verbal disorderliness; about the nature of his intellectual labor, its interpretation and, perhaps, the dangers of its shaping in relation to the desired end of financial reward.

## Conclusion

Examination of the idiomatic essentializing of women's work reveals a complexity in medieval culture's ideological workings. Idioms both reflect and shape ideology; through the idioms and iconography of women and spinning, a masculine theorizing of women's fitness for a particular kind of work ignores the actualities of women's labor, and covers deeper social questions of women's economic value and significance. At the same time, the masculine culture so thoroughly internalizes this position that it may colonize what it has defined as women's space or women's work, by way of a parodic engagement (man as spinner) that reinforces, through reversal, the very terms by which it defines gender. It may also constitute, by means of such an engagement, a supplementary, "non-official" space for the projection and expression of masculine anxieties, and for the regulation of masculine behavior. Hoccleve's recourses to projection and parody in his brief and casual references to women's work and its instruments demonstrate the extent to which his writings belong to the dominant discourse, although he presents himself in some ways as an outsider. In conformity with his culture, the idioms of women's work are for him primarily in the service of masculine interests and anxieties.

## Notes

1. Albert B. Friedman, " 'When Adam Delved. . .': Contexts of an Historic Proverb," in *The Learned and the Lewed: Studies in Chaucer and Medieval Literature*, ed. Larry D. Benson (Cambridge, MA: Harvard University Press, 1974), pp. 213–30 (pp. 213–14; 222).

2. See, for example, Sylvia Resnikow, "The Cultural History of a Democratic Proverb," *Journal of English and Germanic Philology* 36 (1937): 391–405.
3. Paul Freedman, *Images of the Medieval Peasant* (Stanford: Stanford University Press, 1999), pp. 59–71 (p. 66).
4. J.K. Gibson-Graham, *The End of Capitalism (as we knew it): A Feminist Critique of Political Economy* (Maldon, MA: Blackwell, 1996), p. 102: "[. . .] as soon as we produce a dualism incorporating two related terms, gender may operate to sustain meanings of wholeness [. . .] dominance,[. . .] and subjectivity [. . .] for the first term and incompleteness [. . .] subordination [. . .] and objectification for the second." My thanks to the editors of this essay for directing me to this text and other bibliography that contributes to the theoretical underpinning of my argument.
5. Frances M. Biscoglio," 'Unspun' heroes: iconography of the spinning woman in the Middle Ages," *Journal of Medieval and Renaissance Studies* 25:2 (1995): 163–84 (163, 166).
6. Biscoglio," 'Unspun' Heroes," 175.
7. Laura F. Hodges, "Noe's Wife: Type of Eve and Wakefield Spinner," in *Equally in God's Image: Women in the Middle Ages*, ed. Julia Bolton Holloway, Constance S. Wright, and Joan Bechtold (New York: Peter Lang, 1990), pp. 30–39.
8. Gail McMurray Gibson, "The Thread of Life in the Hand of the Virgin," in ed. Holloway et al., *Equally in God's Image*, pp. 46–54.
9. Marbod of Rennes, *Liber Decem Capitulorum*, trans. C.W. Marx, in *Woman Defamed and Woman Defended: An Anthology of Medieval Texts*, ed. Alcuin Blamires with Karen Pratt and C.W. Marx (Oxford: Clarendon Press, 1992), pp. 228–32 (p. 230).
10. "The Wife of Bath's Prologue," in *The Riverside Chaucer*, general ed. Larry D. Benson (Oxford: Oxford University Press, 1988), ll. 401–02. Future references to Chaucer's works are to this edition, by line number, in the text.
11. The notes in the Riverside edition (p. 868) reveal that "many" manuscripts contain, as gloss to these lines, the Latin tag: "Lying and weeping, God gave unto woman," but the full version of the proverb is also current in Latin: "fallere, flere, nere, statuit deus in muliere." For Reason's defense of women, see Christine de Pizan, *The Book of the City of Ladies*, trans. Rosalind Brown-Grant (Harmondsworth: Penguin, 1999), pp. 26–28 (p. 28).
12. Slavoj Žižek, "How Did Marx Invent the Symptom?" in *Mapping Ideology*, ed. Slavoj Žižek (London: Verso, 1994), pp. 296–331 (p. 326).
13. Gibson-Graham, *The End of Capitalism*, p. 63.
14. David Herlihy gives a survey of women's contribution in these fields from the Carolingian to the late medieval period in his *Opera muliebria: Women and Work in Medieval Europe* (New York: McGraw-Hill, 1990), chapter four, "Spinners, Weavers, Dyers," pp. 75–102.
15. See Stephen Knight's survey of "The Voice of Labour in Fourteenth-Century English Literature," in *The Problem of Labour in Fourteenth-Century England*, ed. James Bothwell, P.J.P. Goldberg, and W.M. Ormrod (Woodbridge, UK: York Medieval Press, 2000), pp. 101–22.

16. Karma Lochrie, *Covert Operations: The Medieval Uses of Secrecy* (Philadelphia: University of Pennsylvania Press, 1999), pp. 153–57.
17. Cordelia Beattie, "Women's Work Identities in Post Black Death England," in ed. Bothwell, Goldberg, and Ormrod, *The Problem of Labour*, pp. 1–19 (p. 3).
18. Beattie, "Women's Work Identities," pp. 16–18.
19. Abelard, *Historia calamitatum*, in *The Letters of Abelard and Heloise*, trans. Betty Radice (Harmondsworth: Penguin, 1974), p. 71.
20. Biscoglio, " 'Unspun' Heroes," 164 (though she does offer one exception to this rule).
21. *Chronicle of the Third Crusade: A Translation of the* Itinerarium Peregrinorum et Gesta Regis Ricardi, trans. Helen J. Nicholson (Aldershot, UK: Ashgate, 1997), p. 48. The two essays in *Gendering the Crusades*, ed. Susan B. Edgington and Sarah Lambert (Cardiff: University of Wales Press, 2001), that cite this passage, contextualize it slightly differently, but both argue that it demonstrates how the text genders crusade as "male"; Sarah Lambert, "Crusading or Spinning," pp. 1–15 (pp. 3–4); Michael R. Evans, " 'Unfit to Bear Arms': The Gendering of Arms and Armour in Accounts of Women on Crusade," pp. 45–58 (p. 55).
22. See my "Hoccleve and. . . .Feminism? Negotiating Meaning in *The Regiment of Princes*," in *Essays on Thomas Hoccleve*, ed. Catherine Batt (Turnhout: Brepols, 1996), pp. 55–84.
23. For Oldcastle, see K.B. McFarlane, *John Wycliffe and the Beginnings of English Nonconformity* (London: English Universities Press, 1952), pp. 160–85. For a brief contextualization of Lollard activity in this period, see Jeremy Catto, "Religious Change under Henry V," in *Henry V: The Practice of* Kingship, ed. G.L. Harriss (Oxford: Oxford University Press, 1985), pp. 97–115. On the "Oldcastle Rebellion" 's relation to Lancastrian propaganda strategies, see Paul Strohm, *England's Empty Throne: Usurpation and the Language of Legitimation, 1399–1422* (New Haven: Yale University Press, 1998), pp. 65–86. On the interpretive implications of the timing of the poem's authorship, see Ethan Knapp, *The Bureaucratic Muse: Thomas Hoccleve and the Literature of Late Medieval England* (University Park: Pennsylvania State University Press, 2001), pp. 137–46.
24. Ruth Nissé, " 'Oure Fadres Olde and Modres': Gender, Heresy, and Hoccleve's Literary Politics," *Studies in the Age of Chaucer* 21 (1999): 275–99.
25. On the link between loose talk and sexuality, see Patricia Meyer Spacks, *Gossip* (New York: Alfred A. Knopf, 1985), especially pp. 40, 123.
26. "Address to Sir John Oldcastle," edited as "The Remonstrance Against Oldcastle" in *Selections from Hoccleve*, ed. M.C. Seymour (Oxford: Clarendon Press, 1981), pp. 61–74, ll. 145–49. Future references are by line number, in the text.
27. See Tertullian's advice to wives: "Keep your hands busy with spinning and stay at home, and you will be more pleasing than if you were adorned with gold." *Woman Defamed*, pp. 50–58 (p. 58).
28. Bodley MS 649, fol. 98r–v, reproduced in R.M. Haines, " 'Wilde wittes and wilfulnes': John Swetstock's attack on those 'poyswunmongeres', the Lollards,"

*Studies in Church History* 8 (1972): 143–53 (152). See also Margaret Aston's discussion, "Lollard Women Priests?", in her *Lollards and Reformers: Images and Literacy in Late Medieval Religion* (London: Hambledon Press, 1994), pp. 49–70 (p. 65). For the longevity of the "obedient woman spinner" trope in these contexts, see Keith A. Thomas, "Women and the Civil War Sects," *Past and Present* 13 (1958): 42–62 (52, 60–61, n. 70).

29. See Sylvia Federico's discussion of this passage, in the context of women's participation in the Uprising: "The Imaginary Society: Women in 1381," *Journal of British Studies* 40 (2000): 159–83 (174–77).

30. *The Book of Margery Kempe*, ed. Barry Windeatt (Harlow: Longman, 2000), pp. 258–59. Helen Barr, in her recent discussion of Hoccleve in *Socioliterary Practice in Late Medieval England* (Oxford: Oxford University Press, 2001), p. 30, also directs us to the *Margery Kempe* analogue, but for her, Hoccleve here (if anxiously) uncritically endorses and is complicit with, Lancastrian modes of legitimization: "There are no grey areas in this poem" (p. 31).

31. See also Karma Lochrie's note on this kind of women's work in *The Book of Margery Kempe* as "a metaphor for safety and security," p. 151.

32. Spacks, *Gossip*, p. 12.

33. On women's roles in their children's learning to read, see Susan Groag Bell, "Medieval Women Book Owners: Arbiters of Lay Piety and Ambassadors of Culture," in *Women and Power in the Middle Ages*, eds. Mary Erler and Maryanne Kowaleski (Athens: University of Georgia Press, 1988), pp. 149–87. On the difficulties of recovering specific evidence for women's writing, see V.M. O'Mara, "Female Scribal Ability and Scribal Activity in Late Medieval England: The Evidence?" *Leeds Studies in English* 27 (1996): 87–130.

34. Knapp, *The Bureaucratic Muse*, pp. 72–73.

35. Nicholas Watson, "Censorship and Cultural Change in Late-Medieval England: Vernacular Theology, the Oxford Translation debate, and Arundel's Constitutions of 1409," *Speculum* 70 (1995): 822–64 (849).

36. See my *Malory's* Morte Darthur: *Remaking Arthurian Tradition* (New York: Palgrave, 2002), pp. 131–32.

37. Margarita Stocker, *Judith, Sexual Warrior: Women and Power in Western Culture* (New Haven: Yale University Press, 1998), p. 15. Anne Squires examines how one Middle English author attempts to defuse the tensions inherent in representing "one who is redeemer by being seducer," and her implicit threat to male authority, in "The Treatment of the Figure of Judith in the Middle English Metrical Paraphrase of the Old Testament," *Neuphilologische Mitteilungen* 97 (1996): 187–200 (188). See also Leslie Abend Callahan, "Ambiguity and Appropriation: The Story of Judith in Medieval Narrative and Iconographic Traditions," in *Telling Tales: Medieval Narratives and the Folk Tradition*, ed. and intro. Francesca Sautman Canadé, Diana Conchado, and Giuseppe Carlo Di Scipio (New York: St. Martin's Press, 1998), pp. 79–93.

38. Stocker suggests that the omission of the "religious and patriotic" elements of the story are the only means by which the Monk can make Judith's story fit his "misogynist account of history" (*Judith*, p. 15).

39. Thomas Hoccleve, *The Regiment of Princes*, ed. Charles Blyth (Kalamazoo: Medieval Institute Publications, 1999), ll. 3858–59. Future references are by line number, in the text.
40. Christine de Pizan, *The Book of the City of Ladies*, pp. 131–32 (p. 131).
41. *The Holy Bible [. . .] Made from the Latin Vulgate by John Wycliffe and His Followers*, ed. Josiah Forshall and Frederic Madden, 4 vols. (Oxford: Oxford University Press, 1850), 1:35.
42. Nissé, " 'Oure Fadres Olde,' " 297–98.
43. Forshall and Madden, *The Holy Bible*, 1:35.
44. Knapp, *The Bureaucratic Muse*, pp. 137–46.
45. See, respectively, Antony J. Hasler, "Hoccleve's Unregimented Body," *Paragraph* 13 (1990): 164–83; Knapp, *The Bureaucratic Muse*, pp. 83–93; Nicholas Perkins, *Hoccleve's* Regiment of Princes: *Counsel and Constraint* (Cambridge, UK: Brewer, 2001), pp. 143–50.
46. For the proverb, see Bartlett Jere Whiting, *Proverbs, Sentences, and Proverbial Phrases From English Writings Mainly Before 1500* (Cambridge, MA: Belknap Press, Harvard University Press, 1968), entry T432. A version is still current in the Renaissance and later: Morris Palmer Tilley, *A Dictionary of the Proverbs in England in the Sixteenth and Seventeenth Centuries* (Ann Arbor: University of Michigan Press, 1950), entry T450.
47. *The Towneley Plays*, ed. Martin Stevens and A.C. Cawley, 2 vols. (Oxford: Oxford University Press, 1994), 1:142, ll. 562–63.
48. Hasler, "Hoccleve's unregimented body," 173.
49. The Old Man condemns adultery with another metaphor from spinning, to "spin a fair thread," ironically said of self-damaging behavior:

> Allas, this likerous, dampnable errour
> In this lond hath so large a threde ysponne
> That werse peple is noon undir the sonne. (1762–64)

50. Perkins, *Hoccleve's* Regiment of Princes, pp. 76–86 (pp. 81–82).
51. Henry Thomas Riley, *Munimenta Gildhallae Londoniensis*, Rolls Series 12, 3 vols. (London: Longman, Green, Longman, and Roberts, 1859–62), 1:459. Translation at 3:181. Carter Revard, "The Tow on Absalom's Distaff and the Punishment of Lechers in Medieval London," *English Language Notes* 17 (1980): 168–70 (168). See also Biscoglio, " 'Unspun' heroes," 174.
52. Riley, *Munimenta*, 1:457; 3:179.
53. Revard, "Tow," 169; *The Anglo-Norman Dictionary*, ed. William Rothwell, Louise W. Stone, and T.B.W. Reid (London: Modern Humanities Research Association, 1992), p. 778.
54. *Memorials of London and London Life in the XIIIth, XIVth, and XVth Centuries [. . .] A.D. 1276–1419*, trans. and ed. Henry Thomas Riley (London: Longmans, Green, 1868), pp. 484–86; 566.
55. Riley, *Memorials of London*, pp. 385–86.
56. On the late fifteenth-century manuscript, Lambeth MS 306, and for a historical contextualization of this story, see Barbara A. Hanawalt, "Separation

Anxieties in Late Medieval London: Gender in *The Wright's Chaste Wife,*" *Medieval Perspectives* 11 (1996): 23–41 (31).
57. *Perceforest: quatrième partie,* ed. Gilles Roussineau, 2 vols. (Droz: Geneva, 1987), 1: 327–85.
58. *Perceforest,* 1:385. Thanks to Sylvia Huot, whose talk on *Perceforest* at the King's College, London, conference on "Seeing Gender," January, 2002, drew my attention to the spinning motif in this romance.
59. *The Wright's Chaste Wife,* ed. Frederick J. Furnivall, EETS o.s. 12 (London: Kegan Paul, Trench, Trübner, 1865), l. 530.
60. Hanawalt, "Separation Anxieties," 36: "Males might well have felt the punishment was too threatening."
61. *Dialogue,* ll. 739–42, in *Thomas Hoccleve's Complaint and Dialogue,* ed. J.A. Burrow, EETS o.s. 313 (Oxford: Oxford University Press, 1999).
62. Batt, "Hoccleve and. . .Feminism?," 77–81.

CHAPTER 2

# "AS IF SHE WERE SINGLE": WORKING WIVES AND THE LATE MEDIEVAL ENGLISH *FEMME SOLE*

*Brian W. Gastle*

---

*This essay demonstrates how the legal term,* femme sole, *emerged and changed from the late thirteenth through early fifteenth centuries in England, and outlines the ways in which that classification disrupted medieval notions of marital obligation and equity associated with the marriage debt.*

---

*Let the husband render to his wife what is her due, and likewise the wife to her husband. A wife has no authority over her body, but her husband; likewise the husband has no authority over his body, but his wife.*

—*I Corinthians 7:3–6*

*And where a woman under the protection of a husband follows any craft within the said city by herself alone, with which the husband does not interfere, such a woman shall be charged as a single woman (*femme sole*) concerning everything which touches her said craft.*

—*Liber Albus, 1419*

*A married woman shall be deemed a* femme sole *so far as to enable her to carry on and transact business on her own account, to contract and be contracted with, to sue and be sued, and to enforce and have enforced against her property such judgments as may be rendered for or against her, and may sue and be sued at law or in equity, with or without her husband being joined as a party.*

—*Missouri Revised Statutes, Section 451.290, August 28, 1997*

Late medieval English urban communities, like contemporary cities, were centers of trade more than of manufacture, although it is somewhat anachronistic to assume modern notions of differentiation between the two. Production of goods—ale, cloth, clothing, virtually everything except agricultural products—took place primarily in the home, or in small shops which served both businesses and households, and the merchandising of these wares often took place directly between the manufacturer and the buyer. As this synthesis of production within the household and merchandising from the household grew, so too did the social power of these self-made merchants, thanks to the growing influence of English guilds. The population of a city like London, for example, consisted of a wide variety of professions, including full time civil servants (like Chaucer), a large contingent of clerical bureaucrats (like Langland), lawyers, students, and the like. But by far the major segment of the population consisted of its industrial, commercial, and service-oriented members: in other words, its merchant classes.[1] The birth of urban merchants in England gave rise to a form of post-partum depression, for while these merchants controlled a vast array of resources, their power was not institutionalized in the same ways as that of the aristocracy or of the clergy.

The genesis of merchants in English urban culture, like most births, was both bloody and productive, attended by the sounds of wailing and the promise of growth. The vigor of merchants created an economic power base upon which the government could, and did, rely to support national growth, in the form of economic prosperity and as a cache to fund military actions, both of which would eventually turn England into a major international power. However, such vigorous growth also caused consternation in an already declining medieval feudal hierarchy. This fourth estate—the merchant classes emerging among the traditional aristocratic, ecclesiastical, and peasant estates—given its access to and control of resources, did not fit into the traditional medieval tripartite estates system. And to further complicate the issue, the dissolution of a clear boundary between domestic and mercantile activities meant greater opportunity for all members of the domestic household, especially women, to participate in merchant activities. Among the most significant factors affecting late medieval merchants and the systems governing their social and cultural involvement were the opportunities afforded to women by trade and merchant activities. These opportunities included social advancement, economic stability and independence, as well as a growing freedom to critique current conditions while under the aegis of the very systems within which they operated.

A process of inscription therefore ensued, often in the form of contemporary legal dictates, to delineate mercantile power in general, and occasionally, female mercantile activity in particular; and in the texts negotiating mercantile and feminine mercantile boundaries, a peculiar issue emerged. Since mercantile activity was so closely associated with familial duty, the laws, writs, and statutes pertaining to labor and mercantile activity often transgressed the boundaries of public and domestic life and impinged upon the traditional sanctity of the marital union. The focus of this essay is to demonstrate how one such legal term, *femme sole*, emerged and changed in the late thirteenth through early fifteenth centuries, and to outline the ways in which that classification disrupted the medieval notions of marital obligation and equity associated with the marriage debt.

By the late fourteenth century, the concept of the *femme sole* had been firmly established in English common law and society. The term *femme sole*, simply put, referred to women who conducted business on their own. But the term's application extended beyond its literal translation of 'woman alone' or 'single woman' to encompass the figures in whom I am most interested: married women who conducted their own businesses apart from their husbands.[2] The term was used to differentiate them from the typical assignation of *coverte de baron*,[3] or 'under the protection of the husband'. Legally, wives maintained the same rights as minors when it came to most common law activities, so that the husband, *le baroun*, was responsible legally and economically for the actions of the wife. This relationship was codified through a traditional (and by the late fourteenth century, somewhat outdated) feudal hierarchy, which positioned the husband as feudal lord (baron) to the wife, so that, for example, if a wife were to kill her husband, she committed an act of petty treason against the state, rather than mere murder. But wives who maintained their own mysteries, plied their own trades, followed their own crafts, taught their own apprentices, or marketed their own wares, could trade or act—at least in urban areas—as *femmes soles*. The term *femme sole* legitimized women's economic role to some extent within the medieval legal system, but it also resulted in establishing a different economic structure in the family, wherein the autonomy of women conducting business disrupted medieval ideas of marital and conjugal debt.

The role and definition of *femme sole* is relatively common knowledge among medievalists. It is interesting to note, however, a general lack of knowledge concerning the origins and social history of the emergence of that term, especially for England in the Middle Ages. Historian Kay Lacey, for example, points out that, because a married woman could not own chattel, she could not enter into contractual negotiations:

> The common law principle was that *femmes coverts* were unable to make contracts, or even buy goods without their husbands' prior assent.[4]

She goes on to say that the *femme sole* trader was active by the fifteenth century and covered urban wives conducting business.[5] Not every wife who conducted business was considered (or perhaps took advantage of) acting as a *femme sole* trader. Rarely, in Shrewsbury for example, did a married woman appear in court without her husband, which might be an indication, according to historian Diane Hutton, that *femme sole* status did not exist there, whereas it was common in places like London and Lincoln.[6] For the most part, analyses of *femme sole* status have been relegated to isolated historical moments. Historians like Lacey and Hutton identify *femme sole* activity as part of a broader historical milieu of women's work in medieval England, but there are no real studies devoted exclusively to the emergence of the term or its wider effects on medieval women's mercantile (and more widely social) activities in this time of labor flux.

Women's participation in mercantile activity in England, and indeed throughout Europe, seemed to increase after the middle of the fourteenth century, perhaps due to the general shortage of labor caused by the plague of 1348, and this participation seemed to remain at high levels through the middle of the next century. Women participating in mercantile and guild activities in London enjoyed special privileges from London's peculiar borough status and its position as a major city, port, and governmental seat; these advantages gave rise, however, to serious mercantile repercussions when the crown threatened to remove those civic offices and the wool staple—the market appointed for the sale of wool—to other coastal cities more central to export to the continent or to the war effort. Such political machinations most certainly affected all mercantile activity, and women engaged in market activities were, like men, bound by both common law and canon law.

While most legal activities that affected mercantile behavior were controlled by common law, canon law could impose upon many mercantile situations, especially those involving marriage, defamation, adultery, and perjury. Common law appeals were relatively rare, since most secular motions were covered by either borough customs or city ordinances, neither of which officially belonged to common law litigation. Common law's interest in women's activities was devoted primarily to their rights as either wives or widows, focusing on issues of dowry and property. When a woman married, her husband gained control of any real estate formerly in the wife's name, as well as any other property and assets she brought into the marriage; but she did not entirely forgo her interest in such material. In fact, she was still, legally, the owner of such property, but given the husband's legally dominating position, he had almost complete use and control of that property during the marriage.[7] In a real as well as legal sense, he became her guardian, just as if she were a minor; she was therefore generally subject to any of a number of actions against both her person and her goods, except where such actions were circumscribed by law. Such circumscription could be provided by legal *femme sole* status. Moreover, as I show later, *femme sole* status could affect a wife's position vis-à-vis her dower and dowry, and what degree of control she had over it. Whereas 'dowry' refers to property brought into a marriage by a wife, 'dower' referred to that portion of an estate that fell to the wife upon her husband's death, property legally hers in perpetuity or until such time as the widow remarried, thus turning her dower into a dowry. Issues of dower and dowry were important for both common and canon law, since marriages were performed privately as well as, as the Wife of Bath would put it, "at chirche dore."

One of canon law's main contributions to the legal status of wives was to accord them the right to make testament. A person's will was considered a common law action that expressed the desires of the person regarding real estate disbursement. A testament, on the other hand, was devoted to the disbursement of all other goods and chattels. Since she had a great deal of control over personal goods as opposed to real estate—especially remnants of dower—she could legally, under canon law, dispose of those goods as she saw fit. Marriage partners had considerable power to contract for their own marriage under canon law, even without the permission of their parents or lords,[8] which meant that the marriage contract was specifically internal; it focused primarily on the relationship between the husband and wife rather than on their individual relationships to parents or feudal lords. The significance of *femme sole* status was to obviate both a woman's need for her spouse's participation and agreement in mercantile contracts and her husband's liability when those contracts were not profitable. *Femme sole* status also allowed a wife to act as her husband's agent if he were not present. This status therefore granted wives significant power to act on their own, with or without their husbands, in both mercantile and legal realms, and as such it represents an extremely important historical moment in the history of women's power—not merely in the Middle Ages, but throughout social history (although that power was to be eventually erased by the return of women from a wide range of professions to almost exclusively domestic ones).[9] But that opportunity for women to conduct themselves as *femme sole* upset the traditional family economy characterized by the marriage debt and its implications of mutual financial dependence and ownership.

The study of the history of women in the Middle Ages—indeed, throughout history—could be characterized by the study of women's work, especially work within their families. Women played a considerable role in both production and merchandising in medieval urban (and to a lesser extent rural) environments, despite the fact that most laws and customs related to women's work were confining and oppressive, and focused primarily upon their role within a family. Then as now, there were occupations that were so dominated by women that they became considered women's occupations, and therefore perpetuated a matrilineal continuation of such seemingly gendered occupations. While many of these occupations were domestic in nature—the most recognizable is brewing, an occupation that was dominated by women and could be conducted at home along with more traditional housekeeping duties—virtually every profession had its female constituency. Historian Eileen Power states that these domestic professions, especially for married women, were necessary only for supplementary wages,[10] a statement supported by more recent analyses as well.[11] However, as the emergence of the *femme sole* attests, such merchant activity was more than merely supplemental to women's participation in contemporary life; it was essential to the construction of individual women's power in a firmly established system of patriarchal domination.

The documentary evidence concerning the urban *femme sole* is abundant, especially from the late fourteenth century to the middle fifteenth century. Though even as early as the thirteenth century, the institutionalization of a wife's power within the mercantile realm was beginning to emerge. For example, around 1230, the charters of Salford, Stockport, and Bolton all contain stipulations regarding the power of a wife to conduct familial business without her husband present:

> Item quilibet potest esse ad placitum pro sponsa sua et familia sua, et sponsa cujuslibet potest firmam suam reddere preposito faciente quod fieri debeat, et placitum sequi pro sponso suo si ipse forsan alibi fuerit.
>
> [Every burgess may stand in a plea for his wife and household and the wife of a burgess can pay the rent to the reeve and do all that is needful, and follow a plea for her husband if perchance he be absent.][12]

In all of these English towns, a wife did not merely have the ability to represent her husband but a clear legal responsibility to do so "if perchance he be absent." But insofar as her juridical power was present, that power still remained tied to her relationship with her husband, as *sponsa*—an unusual legal term for a wife probably derived from the promissory aspect (*spondeo*) of her familial relationship, a relationship that is linked to the urban nature of that marriage in this passage. Such changes in diction, in a formulaic legal language generally quite codified and regular, mark the disruptive force of wives conducting business, either on their own or on their husband's behalf; it is a clear change in juridical language in cases where a wife needs to be differentiated from other women. Later in the passage, the husband is referred to in the usual *sponsus suo* of legal documentation, but his role must initially be posited not as a 'potentate' of the town but rather as the mercantile lord of the household, a nomenclature that differentiates his domestic economic role from his socio-political role. This text, while never actually using such terms as *femme sole*—or more appropriately, given the language of the edicts, *uxor* or *mulier*—begins to articulate the legal institutionalization of women's power within both a domestic and public economy, but it does so against the overbearing force of the husband's power within both the marital and public spheres.

Whether or not a wife worked was often a good indication of the social status of a particular household economy. Women have always played a significant role in domestic economies, traditionally in agricultural economies, and the late Middle Ages was no different in its focus upon women's roles in spinning, carding, farming, raising children, brewing, and the like. However, the tenor of their position changed as market economies began to flourish in late medieval England. As sustenance living gave way to trade and mercantile activities, women's labor also began an often slow but inexorable movement into those spheres. As the Salford custumal shows, the official recognition of this movement began with the establishment of that role vis-à-vis the marital contract. When women tested the boundaries of such regulation, the fact that they

> may have begun to assert themselves in other spheres, frightening men, other women, and perhaps even themselves, portended the destruction of the traditional sex-gender system and the institutions based on it.[13]

The earliest forms of *femme sole* law seem to try to limit the conceptualization, if not the role, of such women to an association with a controlling husband. It is, of course, difficult to say whether or not people were really 'frightened' by such emergences of women's power, as Howell suggests, but the documentary history does offer evidence for not merely the desire to delineate that power, but to do so with interesting changes (in this case changes in diction) from the formulaic legal discourse of the period.

By the fourteenth century, the *femme sole* trope began to emerge as a regular part of mercantile legal documentation in England, but generally only in situations concerning wealthy or aristocratic families. As a holdover from earlier Anglo-Norman *feme seule*, the term had found a foothold in formulaic legal discourse of later law French, which had superseded the documentary privilege of Latin. The *Rotuli Parliamentorum* (for example), perhaps the most comprehensive set of historical legal documents available from the period, reflects the movement from Latin to law French in documentary history. Strachey's 1767 edition of the *Rotuli Parliamentorum*[14] offers a plethora of evidence still not fully explored by modern medievalists. The documents therein reflect a specifically urban climate; nowhere else do we see reflected the entire montage of medieval English urban culture, given the makeup of early English parliamentary convenes: lords and laymen, burgesses and borough representatives, knights, priests, merchants, aldermen, and officials from around the country. The early parliamentary rolls—prior to the move of parliamentary records from the treasury to the Chancery during the early years of Edward III's reign—are unfortunately less complete than subsequent records, but from 1339 to the end of the fourteenth century there are only five years for which we have no extant rolls.[15]

During the reign of Edward I, the *Rotuli Parliamentorum* contained predominantly Latin pleas, petitions, and parliamentary proceedings. As in the preceding Salford custumal, references to marital business affairs refer to the wife as *uxor* or, occasionally, *mulier*. In these early Latin references to wives conducting business, the wives' most common position was under the direct governance of the husband. The Salford custumal is distinctive in its changed nomenclature for the wife, but it is quite ordinary in its positioning of the wife within the legal confines of the husband, reinforcing the traditional relationship delineated by the marriage debt. As a passage from the *Rotuli Parliamentorum* of 1291 shows, in a case where a wife does not have a clearly defined default position as her husband's ward, the court is in something of a quandary to legislate her rights:

> Videtur etiam quod durum esset, et non juri consonum in casu isto, quod Uxor propter delictum viri pateretur exheredationem.
> [It will be seen however that the case was not an easy one, and there was no law suitable to that case, that a Wife should be disinherited on account of the disclosure of the crime of the husband.] [16]

Clearly, the crimes of the husband have a noticeable effect on the wife's position and goods. This particular case addresses the rights of a wife to keep control of what few material possessions she had in a marriage, such as her dower, when a husband has forfeited to the crown his rights to similar possessions. It is not until the late fourteenth century that parliament stipulates the disassociation of a wife from her husband's criminal activities. The wife of a felon is given legal claim to her dower and any accompanying settlement as long as she does not participate in or consent to her husband's felony. She is not, as of yet, *solus*, acting as if she were a single woman. Rather, her position is more closely akin to that of a widow and the subsequent control a widow would have over her dower and inheritance.

Such legal representations of women within marriages as this passage signifies have done a grave disservice to their historical representation. Modern popular conceptions of medieval marriages, especially arranged marriages, assume that these relationships were almost exclusively business contracts for the negotiation and transference of property, often viewing the wife as part of that property. However, canon law did state that the marriage should be based upon mutual consent of both parties, and those marriages not performed at the church door were supported by similar common law stipulations.[17] For my purposes here, the interesting aspect of dower was the control that institution gave women over land, despite the edicts preventing their sole ownership of such land. A wife, upon her husband's death, or in this case upon the legal removal of a felonious husband, was entitled to a third of her husband's share of property (along with her original dowry) as her dower, encumbering that land until she remarried. She was not in sole possession and control of such land, but held it until such time as she could use it as a reinvestment in the marriage market. More than popular conception gives her credit for, the wife had a voice in her position in the marriage and might well participate in the marriage economy apart from the men in her life. Whether accorded the title or not, she could become, in effect, *femme sole*, which set precedent for the legimatization of that status with the rise of the mercantile classes in England.

In approximately the same year as the *Rotuli Parliamentorum* passage concerning a felon's wife's dowry, the town of Ipswich was also concerned with the relationship between wife and her husband in criminal actions. In a case that foreshadows the development of legal *femme sole*, the Ipswich custumal disassociates the wife from her husband in matters of sole legal transgressions.

> Item usé est qu femme coverte de baroun seyt justicee par les baillifes de la dyte vyle a respoundre devaunt eux en play de trespas, où peyne d'enprisonement ou de juyse peot estre agardé solom ley e usage de meyme la vyle, auxi com ele sereyt justisee si ele fust sole saunz baroun, c'est a saver de soun personel trespas, mès qe le trespas ne tuche mye fraunk tenement.
>
> [It is custom that a woman protected by her husband (i.e., a wife) is brought to justice by the bailiffs of the said village in order to answer before them in a plea of trespass, where there is risk of imprisonment or punishment according to the law and custom of the same village, she may be dealt justice as if she were single without a husband, that is to say for her personal trespass, but not that trespass which touches a free tenement.][18]

Again, we can see the legal representation of the wife within the document closely aligned with that of the husband. She is not yet regarded as a woman acting as if she were single, or a 'woman alone'. Rather, she remains a wife acting without her husband; that which defines her in this document is her position as a husbandless wife, so the husband still remains the defining aspect of her legal representation merely through mention of his absence. The wife's role in this document is still subject to the husband's defining characteristic as her 'baroun', and although she is given a degree of theoretical autonomy, this is done in order to protect the husband's goods from her transgression, just as the London edict is meant to protect the wife's interests. As a document rhetorically linking one party to the other, it does not assign true autonomy to either party, in that either party must be defined by his or her relationship with the other. *Femme sole* status clearly developed largely if not entirely to protect the rights of men financially and legally from women's mercantile activities. So what we see in these 'origins' is a forced association; the wife as 'other' is defined only insofar as she can be delineated from her husband. What I suggest is that eventually that legal move to protect the husband (which might upset marital economics itself, if you are used to thinking of spouses as a corporate entity) will be subverted to the uses of the wife, perhaps to the ultimate consternation of the traditional *fraternite* of medieval labor systems.

What happens in the fourteenth century is a rhetorical movement in the legal documents, a movement away from this forced identification of the wife with her husband. The *sole* in *femme sole* still implies a relationship with the husband, as the wife must be classified as if she were single rather than married, but more and more the documents do not include the husband as part of the wife's nomenclature. This can clearly be seen in the *Rotuli Parliamentorum* by 1328:

> Richard, fitz Gilbert Talbot, et Elizabet sa femme, qe come ils eussent suy de faire venir devant le Consail nostre Seigneur le Roi a son darrein Parlement a Westminster, les transcritz des pietz des deus Fyns pur lesqueux Fyns Hugh le Despenser, le piere, & le fitz, avoient purchacez les Manoir de Payneswik & Chastell Godrich, de la dite Elizabet, tant come ele fuit sole; Et par enprisonement, et par duresces, et par cohercions, tant come ele demurra en dure prisone a Pursrich, fuit la dite Elizabet costreint a faire le reconissances des Fyns...
>
> [Richard, son of Gilbert Talbot, and his wife Elizabeth, who having been made to come before the Counsel of our Lord King to his most recent Parliament at Westminster, pray the dismissal of two fines for which Hugh acquired the Manor of Paineswich and Godrich Castle from the said Elizabeth as if she were single; and on account of imprisonment, duress, and coercion, during the time she dwelt in prison at Pursrich, was the said Elizabeth constrained to make recognizances of these fines...][19]

Apparently, Elizabeth Talbot was forced to acknowledge an agreement over the money owed (recognizance of fines) for the transference of certain properties, and was forced to do so without her husband. The transcripts acknowledging the fines are, according to Elizabeth and her family, null and void given the fact that those transcripts were made while she was imprisoned and under duress. Elizabeth's legal position as *femme sole* trader is somewhat ambiguous here. She is not actually working by herself for the transference of those lands or properties, but rather she is used as if she were such a woman. This is an important distinction, for it shows how, in the *femme sole* tradition, that positioning was both accepted and used. Elizabeth and Richard are clearly not members of the broadest class of merchant traders and craftsmen, given the fact that this case deals with the transfer of such substantial estates. Often women of the aristocracy were considered *femme sole* for purposes of property disbursement. In 1344, for example, the Queen of England was treated as a *femme sole* for purposes of property,[20] and that tradition had been established long since then.[21] Rather than being a clear case of the *femme sole*, Elizabeth's incarceration and subsequent legal proceedings touch upon the English common law and canon law doctrine of unity.

Simply put, the doctrine of unity stipulated that, under the eyes of the law, a husband and wife were but one person united under the name of marriage. Within such a situation, the husband, of course, retained clear superiority.[22] In the Talbot case, while Elizabeth is referred to as *sole*, it does so only in reference to the transgression against the unity of marriage, which the recognizances represent. These recognizances were acquired (*avoient purchacez*) from Elizabeth as if she were single (*tant come ele fuit sole*). She is not acting as a *femme sole* but is forced into a contract allowed only to *femme sole* women. We can, in this case, see the concept of the wife acting alone emerging, but only insofar as that concept reflects upon the power of the husband in the unity of the marriage. Subsequent cases, however, place that concept in the affirmative, proactive role of allowing for an institutionalization of power apart from the defining role of the husband—allowing a woman to be truly a *sole* trader.

Subsequent legal refutations of women acting as *femme sole* again emerge in aristocratic arenas before becoming more common among merchants themselves. One of the most famous of such cases is the series of errors assigned to judgments against Alice Perrers in 1378. Perrers had been, since the early 1360s, the mistress of Edward III. After Queen Philippa's death in 1369, Perrers exerted increasing control over both the king and the court, even securing from Edward an estate at Wendover, near the estates of John of Gaunt (with whom she also was rumored to have had "relations") and the Black Prince.[23] After Edward's death in 1377, Perrers fled the country, fearing the animosity she had incurred in the commons.[24] The *Rotuli Parliamentorum* account of the legal retribution against her includes a series of "Errors dans le jugement d'Alice Perrers":

> Alice fuist mise de respondre come femme sole, la ou a cele temps, et long temps devant, ele fuist la femme William de Windesore et covert de lui…
>
> [Alice made her response as a single woman, where at that time and for a long time before that she was the wife of William of Windsor and "covered" by him…][25]

In this account of the error assigned in a judgment against Perrers, that error is based upon the fact that she operated as *femme sole* but was actually still bound by her marriage to William of Windsor. The text goes to great lengths to differentiate her from the *femme sole* tradition by calling attention to her married status not once but twice; she is both "la femme William de Windesore" and "covert de lui." This redundancy is rather peculiar in such cases, especially in that both references foreground the position of her husband in the situation. Perrers' "crime" against the people was linked explicitly to her position as both wife and mistress. In order to make her a part of the legal textual arena, she needs to be re-associated with her marital lord and disassociated from the king, her clandestine partner. Within a month of her flight from England, the crown had seized property of Perrers worth £2,626 8s. 4d.[26] The *Rotuli Parliamentorum* record shows the extent to which Parliament was willing to control such actions and use the name of *femme sole* as both a defining and a retributive force.

By the end of the fourteenth century, *femme sole* wives had become almost commonplace; the textual environment delineating their position had become much more comfortable with the terms and diction necessary to differentiate their role both legally and in the burgeoning mercantile environs. One of the clearest examples of the facility that developed regarding *femme sole* adjudication occurs in the *Liber Albus* of London. The *Liber Albus* represents one of the most comprehensive collections of social and legal documents and archival material from the period. It was compiled in 1419 from a number of documents—most notably the *Proemium*—by John Carpenter, Town Clerk. In it can be seen both a history of how civic and governmental cases were handled throughout the fourteenth century and the dexterity with which compilers discussed such developing issues as the *femme sole*.

The *Liber Albus* is meticulous in its efforts to differentiate between types of women in medieval law and society. While it is a hodgepodge of law French, Latin, and Middle English, it negotiates among terms as fluidly as among languages. The following Latin regulation, dealing with the number of essoiners[27] required for a defendant, exemplifies the way in which terms were not haphazardly assigned to women, but followed rather strict guidelines with respect to their marital status and their position vis-à-vis mercantile concerns:

> Quaestio XI. Si vir et uxor petunt versus aliquem, qualiter ipse tenens debeat se essoniare versus eos, vel per unum essoniatorem vel per duos?
>
> Responsio. Responsum est quod per unum tantum.
>
> [Question XI. If a man and wife bring suit against someone, just as when in the same way essoin is held against them, should there be one essoiner or two?
>
> Response. The answer is that there ought only to be only one.][28]

"AS IF SHE WERE SINGLE" 53

By the fourteenth century, that role had been taken on by attorneys themselves, and essoiners had become professional witnesses in court.[29] The *Liber Albus*, in this case, uses the most traditional kind of legal diction to refer to the wife: *uxor*. But such is not always the case in the *Liber Albus*. The very next issue in the *Liber Albus* vacillates between *uxor* and *mulier* in a situation which refers, supposedly, to the selfsame female juridical subject. This case deals with the duties of a woman who holds free bench, and responsibilities regarding buildings on that free bench estate:

> Quaestio XII. Si mulier habens francum bancum suum, et aedificia corruant, quis ea debeat reparare vel sustentare, haeres vel mulier?
>
> Responsio. Responsum est, quod quae habet francum bancum suum et aedificium receperit in bono statu, in eodem statu illud sustinebit, ita quod pro defectu mulieris non decidat. Sed si aedificium vetus sit in morte viri sui paratum decidere, oportet quod in tali casu haeres, si habeat unde illud reparare faciat, et postea domina, illud sustinebit. Et si post mortem viri multa sint ibi aedificia in franco banco, et uxor defuncti omnia non possit vel noluerit sustinere, ea quae voluerit sustinere retineat et sustineat.
>
> [Question XII. If a woman holds her free bench, and buildings are in disrepair, who is it that ought to repair or maintain it, the owner or the woman?
>
> Response. The answer is, that whosoever is in possession of her free bench and the building is responsible to keep it in good repair, to maintain it in the same state, so that it not fall down because of the woman's dereliction. But if, at the time of the death of the husband himself, the building is very old and about ready to fall, it is proper that in such a case the owner (or heir) should maintain it, if he makes as if to repair it, and afterwards the Lady of the household. And if after the death of the husband there be many buildings in free bench, and the wife is not able or is unwilling to maintain all of them, she who wishes to sustain them may own and repair them.][30]

Free bench (*frank bank*) is a "dower of copyhold land held by a woman via dower."[31] A woman's property rights are restricted, but when she has land assigned to her dower, she does retain some kind of control, and therefore responsibility, over that land. Just as in villeinage a tenant did not hold land in his own name but in his lord's name, so in free bench a woman did not own the land in her own name, but could secure rights to that land by holding it through her own 'lord's' name, usually her husband—another clear example of the playing out of the *coverte de baron* tradition. A woman who 'holds free bench' therefore manages property through the intermediary name of her 'lord' but that land is primarily associated with her dower, and therefore remains with her even when she is not married or widowed. This case uses three different terms to refer to the woman holding free bench: *mulier*, *domina*, and *uxor*. The woman only becomes *uxor* when she is unable to act successfully independent of the landowner's ability (i.e., when she cannot maintain the property sufficiently). As *mulier*, she is responsible for maintenance of the property and the buildings on that property; but in a situation that is hampered by her inability to maintain the property, and is to the detriment of those buildings and people dependent upon that property, she is reinscribed into the marital contract and disassociated from the independence offered by control of her free bench. This document codifies her legal position by assigning a juridical nomenclature based on her ability to successfully manage her property. In some ways, the woman is always *domina* (lady of the household) in such situations. Regardless of her current marital status, she vacillates between *uxor* and *mulier* based upon the extent to which the legal system can depend upon her *ability* to maintain her independent position by maintaining her properties. It is this kind of adherence to strict legal assignment of terms that paves the way for one of the clearest statements of the *femme sole* in late medieval legal documentation.

While female ownership of property was restricted, giving rise to such convoluted dowry situations as the free bench issue, women operating businesses on their own and wholly separate from their husbands were not only allowed but expected in certain mercantile families. Women most vigorously participated in such situations, giving rise to the clear delineation of those roles in *Liber Albus* common law representations:

> Uxor Quae Sola Mercandizat. Et lou feme coverte de baroun usee ascun craft deinz la dite citee apar luy soule, dount le baroun se melle rienz, tiele femme serra chargee come femme soule de tout ceo qe touche soun dit craft. Et si le baroun et la femme soient empledez, en tiel cas la femme pledera come femme soule en courte de recorde, et avera sa ley et autres avaunteges par voy du pley come femme soule. Et si elle soit condempnee, elle serra commys a la prisoune tancqes elle eit fait gree; et le baroun ne ses biens ne serrount my en tiel cas chargez nenpeschez.

> [And where a wife (woman under the protection of a husband) follows any craft within the said city by herself alone, with which the husband does not interfere, such a woman shall be charged as a single woman concerning everything which touches her said craft. And if the husband and the wife are impleaded, in such a case the wife shall plead as a single woman in a court of record, and she shall have her law and other advantages by way of plea like a single woman. And if she is condemned, she shall be committed to prison until she makes appeasement; and neither the husband nor his goods shall be in such a case charged or impleaded.][32]

The attempt to control the roles and powers of women, especially within the mercantile realm, was a project of circumscription. But that did not mean that women could not use that attempt advantageously: not necessarily, in Audre Lorde's phrase, using the tools of the master to tear down the master's house, but rather using them to build a house of their own. Regardless of marital status, medieval businesswomen had 'sa ley' (her law), which made them autonomous and brought with it both 'advantages' and the threat of legal condemnation. This type of sovereignty was critical if women were to conduct business on their own and for themselves. The passage uses *coverte de baron*, 'protected by the husband', that by now very recognizable legal term for a wife, subjugating the wife's position to that of the husband's by identifying her as someone "covered (i.e., defined, supervised, or legally protected) by the husband." But the purpose of the passage is to define the wife's position as independent of her husband's protection, or more appropriately, independent of his goods. Women themselves could use such semantic and substantive conflicts to reinforce and affirm their economic authority.

By the time of the production of the *Liber Albus*, women's mercantile activity was sufficiently pronounced to have institutionalized their position in those documents. This trend of female mercantile activity was motivated by both the changing demands placed upon the workforce, depleted by such events as war and plague, and also by the restructuring of the relationship between merchant and state reflected in such events as the Peasants' Revolt and the Good Parliament. This is rather analogous to women's so-called liberation in the twentieth century; increasing legal rights for women were based in part not on protest or activism, but simply on economic demand: when the workforce needed more workers (as during the world wars, when men were fewer) and when the household required two incomes to maintain it, there was no easy alternative to 'letting' women work. Women's desire to work for pay meant little until men also wanted them to work for pay. Such an institutionalization, both medieval and modern, moved the power of the woman beyond the domestic into the public spheres; that is, if such terms can be used of the medieval period in which, first, domestic and public production seemed to go hand in hand, and in which, second, the patriarchal structure defining the home economy was affected both by women's entry into the workforce as individuals (*sole*) and by subsequent legal moves to protect husbands in such relationships. As a form of defense, *femme sole* status protected the husband from economic and legal repercussions of his wife's activities, but it also institutionalized her power outside the boundaries of patriarchal familial control, or perhaps, more accurately, moved such control from the dominance of the domestic patriarchy to that of the public patriarchy, the state.

Such legal protection was not, by the fourteenth century, specific to mercantile activities. *Femme sole* status, often considered a specifically mercantile construct, which must be registered for by the woman, had exceeded that definition and was being used in other instances that were not so specifically mercantile. In a suit of trespass, for example, the wife in the absence of her husband might sue, or be sued, as *femme sole*, even though she might not be officially a *femme sole* trader:

> Item, si pleinte de trespas soit fait devers un homme et sa femme de trespas fait par la femme soulement, adouncqes la femme respoundera soule sanz soun baroun, si le baroun ne viegne mye, et avera pley come femme soule.
>
> [Item, if a complaint of trespass is made against a man and his wife for a trespass made by only the wife, then the woman shall respond alone without the husband, if the husband does not appear, and she shall plea as a single woman.][33]

This article, like the *femme sole* regulation, clearly protects the husband from the wife's trespass, even if she was *sa femme*. Plaints of trespass could include many infractions, from felony beatings to minor misdemeanors. Originally conceived as a physical assault "with force and arms" (*vi et armis*) or "against the king's peace" (*contra pacem regis*), strict *vi et armis* trespass was abandoned by the 1360s, when Chancery clerks began to omit the term from writs of trespass, and all but capital cases could be turned into civil-style suits for remuneration.[34] Where a wife was solely at fault for the trespass (which need not necessarily be physical assault) she was bound to answer for herself *come femme soule*, as if she were a single woman, and the article protects the husband from such legal and economic retribution as the court might allow. Of course the logical legal development for such a case would hold the opposite true as well, if a man and wife are trespassed against, a situation with which the *Liber Albus* deals directly.

> Item, si pleinte de trespas soit faite par le baroun et sa femme de baterie faite a la femme, en tiel cas la femme serra resceu pur luy, et pur soun baroun de pursuir et recoverir ses damages devers le defendant, coment qe le baroun ne soit my present.
>
> [Item, if a plaint of trespass is made by a husband and his wife concerning battery made upon the wife, in such a case the wife shall come for herself, and for her husband in order to sue and recover such damages against the defendant, even when the husband is not present.][35]

Once again, the text refers to the wife in relation to her husband, as *sa femme*, but in this case it offers her the opportunity to speak exclusively for herself (*pur luy*) and for her husband (*et pur soun baroun*), one of the rare instances in which the wife is actually given this sort of autonomy. The social implications of this statement are considerable, given the traditional role of the wife as property of her husband/lord. The legal proceedings become *her* suit rather than *their* suit, and such recourse as she has in trespass law extends not merely to legal retaliation but to economic reprisals as well. By recovering damages for herself, she is positioned as a juridical subject with comparable legal rights to those of her husband, indeed of any man, in the late medieval English legal system. While legally viewed as one half (or less) of the marital corporate entity, or as her husband's ward or even his property, a woman was not treated as such a subject; this change in the law's recognition of women is considerable and significant.

Such autonomy also blurs the boundaries between single (*sole*) women and married women with respect to specifically mercantile issues. In other types of cases, where economic issues are not at stake, the husband regularly retains control, such as in suits against a battery that causes an abortion.[36] Even though women generally held the same legal position as minors, and were treated legally as such, exceptions initially occurred in clearly mercantile cases:

> Item accioun d'accompt est mayntenable par usages devers une femme sole et devers enfauntz dedinez age, s'ils soient marchauntz ou s'ils teignent comunes shopes de mestier et des merchaundises; et acciouns de dette en mesme le manere, de ceo qe touche lour mestier ou lour marchaundises.
>
> [An action of account is maintainable through custom against a single woman and against under-age children, if they are merchants or they hold common craft or trade shops; and actions of debt in the same manner, for everything that touches their craft or trade.][37]

So in this case, the nomenclature of *femme sole* (here linked with the more traditional position of woman as a minor in the legal system) only makes sense within a labor context; it is a term that is not commodified, but rather codified, within a system of economic exchange. Unlike much of the literature of the period—like that of Chaucer's *Wife of Bath* or the Host's wife in *Sir Gawain and the Green Knight*, for example—the *Liber Albus* does not link female autonomy and negotiating power to images of sexual aggression or promiscuity. It does, however, as such period literature does, closely link them to their relationships with men, especially their breaks from traditional forms of male dominance, such as the marriage contract. Eventually, such exchange systems made their way outside the boundaries of the mercantile classes and affected the upper echelons of society against whom those very merchants were attempting to define themselves, and for whom they were attempting a renegotiation of the marriage contract. *Femme sole* status became a tool of the aristocracy, not merely of the merchant classes.

In 1464 the *Rotuli parliamentorum* records an act allowing Ann, Duchess of Exeter, to act as a *femme sole* trader with respect to those gifts of the crown she received before, during, and after her marriage. Notice the force that the crown places upon the autonomy of *femme sole* status:

> 42. The Kyng, our Soverayne Lord, of grete zele and tendre affection which he hath unto his entierly welbiloved suster Anne, wyf to Henry late Duke of Excestre, graunteth of his grace especiall...that all his Letters Patentes, and all other Grauntes, Yeftes and Feoffementes, made to hir afore this tyme, or hereafter to be made to hir, duryng the life of hir seid Husbond, of eny Lordships, Maners, Londes, Tenementes, Possessions, Enheritamentz, Goodes or Catelles, be to hir self oonly available, good and effectuell, as if she had be or were woman soule, tymes of the makyng of the seid Letters Patentes Grauntes, Yeftes and Feoffementes, she to have and to hold theym as woman soule, oonly to hir owne use, withoute lette empechement or clayme of the Kyng or his heires, Shirrefs, Eschetours, or eny other the Kynges Officers or Mynistres...And also to be able by the seid auctorite, to sue in hir name soule, by Writtes, Billes or Playntes, for almaner Fermes, Rentes, Goodes, Catelles and Dettes...to have as a woman soule, she to have theym soule to hir owne use. And also to be able by the seid auctorite, to sue in her owne name soule, almaner of actions as the case shall require, for all things that to hir his hereaftyer shal be nedefull to sue ayenst eny persone, for or by reason of eny of the premisses or otherwise...And that all Releases, Feoffementes, Yiftes, Grauntes, Obligations, Acquittauncez, Leases, and all other things to be made hereafter by or to the seid Anne, duryng the life of her seid husbond, be of the same force and effect, as they shuld be if she were or had been soule woman at the tyme of the makyng of theym.[38]

When it is in the interest of the crown to do so, the crown will assign *femme sole* status. Whereas Alice Perrers' case denies her *femme sole* status, overturning previous rulings, the Duchess of Exeter's case repeatedly returns and reinforces that status. The properties and assets she is allowed, as sister to the king, would normally be included as part of her dower, and such possessions were, under common law and tradition, safe in that position. However, by the middle of the fifteenth century, *femme sole* status has emerged not as an adjunct to such positioning but as an integral part of the legal status of women's power. And this secular legal status at times infringed upon, or at least existed less than harmoniously beside, the union dictated by the sacrament of marriage.

The Apostle Paul's mandate in I Corinthians for mutual sexual obligation had a strong influence on the general notion of marital relationships and the legal stipulations regarding those relationships. The conjugal debt was explicitly characterized by mutual obligation, since neither party could withhold "payment" (i.e., sexual contact) without the consent of the partner. However, the realities of that mutuality are suspect, as we see in literary negotiations that resemble those described by Margery Kempe in bargaining with her husband for her chastity; her husband protests vehemently when (after fourteen children) she considers her conjugal debt paid, or wishes to pay it in coin other than sex. We rarely see women of this period, in literature or history, complaining successfully of their rights in their husbands' bodies. Despite the supposed mutuality of marriage, the real "rights" in the matter were often the husband's.

Whether or not the "marriage debt" was actually one of mutual obligation, however, it is easy to see how Paul's statement could be superimposed upon a wider, more mercantile arena, to include the *material* obligations of a husband and wife. Since the marriage contract was as much economic as personal, the personal debt of conjugal relations transferred its significance to the economic realm. Both husband and wife generally brought to the marriage some property of their own. In the city, a husband would have had a recognizable profession or trade, or the lease of certain properties, and a wife would possess some form of dowry; trades and properties alike were meant to prosper within the family economy as the family itself prospered. Marriage was closely linked to procreative ideals both in the sense of familial continuation through offspring and in the sense of mercantile concerns of property, trade, and ownership. Labor therefore was both material (goods and wares) and bodily (children), and this labor depended upon the equity of the marital union.

As I have already noted, however, practice of the equality of marital debt was far from ideal. St. Paul's admonition to render the marital debt served as the basis for early canon-law regulations of marriage, but the social discrepancies between the genders resulted in a less than perfect system, discrepancies crucial to modern debates surrounding the debt; conjugal relations were no more free from patriarchal dominance than economic and legal ones. Gratian's canon law compilation of 1140, the *Concordia discordantium canonum*, commonly referred to as the *Decretum*, discusses marriage and the marriage contract at length. It was in this work that the notions of mutual consent and sexual obligation became institutionalized in legal venues.[39] This notion of conjugal debt as a form of mutual equality, however, has recently come under serious scrutiny and criticism, especially by historians who focus on the pervasive social oppression and domination of women in the Middle Ages. Theologian Eleanor McLaughlin, in "Equality of Souls, Inequality of Sexes: Women in Medieval Theology,"[40] and historian Dyan Elliott, in *Spiritual Marriage*, both recognize the fact that the inequalities inherent in the gender systems of the Middle Ages meant a similar disparity in the way the marital "equality" benefited the husband and wife respectively. As Elliott states,

> the rhetoric of equality that surrounds medieval and modern discussions of the debt is only convincing if all awareness of social mores and biological

differences is suspended. It is impossible that the debt alone should be free from all inequalities built into the gender system.[41]

In the growing urban economies of English cities, the division of labor was just one such instance of this gender role differentiation. Modern culture's own predisposition towards "masculine" work and "feminine" work has a clear precedent in medieval society. What this predisposition meant for the medieval home economy and representative family narratives was that the husband and wife, where they maintained their own craft or trade, sometimes maintained relatively disparate ones for the benefit of the family economy:

> Whether or not they actually worked together, family members worked in the economic interest of the family. In peasant and artisan households, and in proletarian families, the household allocated the labor of family members. In all cases, decisions were made in the interest of the group, not the individual.[42]

Even though independent market participation may have contributed to the home economy, *femme sole* status disrupted the ideals of that relationship by diverting the woman's work, subcontracting it, if you will, out of the family. Relatively abruptly, the marriage changed from a metaphysical union of two, into a business partnership; within the partnership, each member might work for the benefit of the corporation of the family, but might also keep a level of autonomy and individuality separate from that union. This separation of a woman's individual responsibilities from her familial obligations began with the emergence of *femme sole* status in the late thirteenth century. If indeed women's option to operate as *femme sole* was "frightening" to those imbricated within it, we can easily see why. If it did not actively threaten the traditional dominance of patriarchy in the realm or in the home, it certainly had the potential to disrupt the theory or ideal upon which so much domestic power was based, that of marriage as a union in which the woman's identity, labor and property were entirely subsumed in those of the man. In legally recognizing women's labor and women's property as distinct from those of men, the *femme sole* term was almost bound to conflict with the marriage ideal, which stated explicitly that women's labor and property were identical to those of their husbands. The fact that a term so disruptive of the marriage economy may have originally appeared to protect men from the liability associated with women's labor offers a certain pleasing irony, but it is doubtful whether this would be of much comfort to men who might have felt both their ideal of marriage damaged and their actual legal power in the home lessened by *femme sole*.

The late medieval English *femme sole* operates, therefore, in several tangential spheres. As a legal category, it applies to both married women and single women. It can attest to both the power of the husband and the autonomy of the wife. It can even serve as an example of the way that autonomy mediates the concerns of the merchant classes as a whole. And the juridical subject represented by *femme sole* status is constrained in many ways by its texts. That does not mean, however, that the legal representation of women's power is not a concern of a variety of texts. Whereas the idea of the *femme sole* is manifest explicitly in the narrowly defined legal texts I have examined here, we may also see that term exhibited much more fully, although not as explicitly, in contemporary family narratives; we may see it in the marriage negotiations in the *Wife of Bath*'s Prologue and Tale, in the social and familial disruptions represented in the bourgeois fabliaux "The Wright's Chaste Wife," and perhaps even in the aristocratic criticisms of Langland's Lady Mede. The forces that intersect to characterize a woman as *femme sole* during the fourteenth and early fifteenth centuries emerge in a rich and varied textual environment; documentary evidence proves an attention to rhetorical and stylistic specificity that is mirrored in contemporary literary documents. Texts such as the *Rotuli Parliamentorum* and the *Liber Albus* are constrained by their genre, as are more traditionally literary texts such as the *Canterbury Tales, Piers Plowman*, or the *Book of Margery Kempe*; however, both historical and literary genres offer us glimpses into the problems and opportunities manifest in literary and historical figures of merchants and merchant marriages. Once gender and autonomy are introduced into the mercantile marriage equations of power, dominance, submission, equity, value, and debt, it becomes increasingly difficult to balance the familial books.

## Notes

I would like to thank James M. Dean for providing invaluable assistance formulating and developing this essay, as well as Scott Lightsey and R.F. Yeager for their help with passages from the *Rotuli Parliamentorum*.

1. In fact, the term 'merchant' itself, and its Middle English variants—*marchaundes, marchaundise, marchaundisen, marchaundising*, and so on—all enter the language between 1300 and 1450. MED M.2 163–67.
2. For a discussion of single women and widows operating as *femmes soles* see Amy M. Froide, "Marital Status as a Category in Early Modern England," in *Singlewomen in the European Past 1250–1800*, ed. Judith M. Bennett and Amy M. Froide (Philadelphia: University of Pennsylvania Press, 1999), pp. 246–48 [236–69].
3. Both of these terms, of course, exist in several orthographic and linguistic variants: *feme couvert, covert baroun, feme sole, woman soule*, and so on.

4. Kay E. Lacey, "Women and Work in Fourteenth and Fifteenth Century London," in *Women and Work in Pre-Industrial England*, ed. Lindsey Charles and Lorna Duffin (Dover, NH: Croom Helm, 1985), p. 41 [24–82].
5. Lacey, "Women and Work," pp. 41–43.
6. Diane Hutton, "Women in Fourteenth-Century Shrewsbury," *Women and Work in Pre-Industrial England*, ed. Lindsey Charles and Lorna Duffin (Dover, NH: Croom Helm, 1985), p. 86 [83–99].
7. For a discussion of such property rights of women, see Amy Louise Erickson, *Women and Property in Early Modern England* (New York: Routledge, 1993), pp. 24–30.
8. This consensual power derived mainly from a series of letters from Pope Alexander III focusing on the importance of the consent of the parties involved. For an extended discussion of the role of consent and the development of late medieval marriages, see Charles Donahue, Jr., "The Canon Law on the formation of Marriage and Social Practice in the Middle Ages," *Journal of Family History* 8.2 (1983): 144–58.
9. For a discussion of the decline in the variety of occupations generally held by women, see Ivy Pinchbeck, *Women Workers and the Industrial Revolution, 1750–1850* (New York: Crofts, 1930), p. 303.
10. Eileen Power, *Medieval Women* (New York: Cambridge University Press, 1975), p. 53.
11. See, e.g., Sheila Rowbatham, *Hidden From History: 300 Years of Women's Oppression and the Fight Against It* (London: Pluto Press, 1973), p. 2, who believes that such trades "related directly to the work of women in the household because at this stage domestic and industrial life were not clearly separate;" and Richard T. Vanne, "Toward a New Lifestyle: Women in Pre-Industrial Capitalism," in *Becoming Visible: Women in European History*, ed. Renate Bridenthal and Claudia Koonz (Boston: Houghton, 1979), p. 195 [192–216], who posits that since most women in the period married at some time their work necessarily becomes part of their married life.
12. *Borough Customs*, ed. and trans. Mary Bateson, Selden Society, (London: B. Quaritch, 1904–06), pp. 222–23. For other examples of urban mercantile women's legal positions from the *Borough Customs*, including examples from Lincoln, Northampton, Hastings, and London, see P.J.P. Goldberg, trans. and ed., *Women in England, 1275–1525: Documentary Sources* (Manchester: Manchester University Press, 1995), pp. 131–32, 196–97.
13. Martha Howell, *Women, Production, and Patriarchy in Late Medieval Cities* (Chicago: University of Chicago Press, 1986), p. 183.
14. *Rotuli Parliamentorum: ut et Petitiones, et Placita in Parliament* [*Rolls of Parliament*], ed. J. Strachey, 6 vols., vol. 2 (1326–77), vol. 3 (1377–1411), (London, 1767–77); henceforth, *RP*.
15. For an excellent disussion of the early history of parliament and its attendant documentary evidence, see A.L. Brown, "The Development of Parliament," in *The Governance of Late Medieval England 1272–1461* (London: Edward Arnold, 1989), pp. 157–76. See also the very thorough introduction to H.G. Richardson and George Sayle, *Rotuli Parliamentorum Hactenus Inediti*,

*1279–1373*, Camden Third Series, 51 (London: Camden Society, 1935), pp. vii–xiii.
16. 19 Edward I; *RP*, vol. 1, p. 67.
17. Pope Alexander III, in the late twelfth century, wrote a series of decrees outlining marriage rules, including present consent, future consent, and minimum age of consent. For a succinct but thorough investigation of the development of marriage law, see Charles Donahue, Jr., "The Canon Law on the Formation of Marriage and Social Practice in the Later Middle Ages," *Journal of Family History* 8.2 (1983): 144–58.
18. *Burough Customs*, trans. Bateson, pp. 223–24.
19. 2 Edw. III; *RP*, vol. 2, p. 22.
20. *Year Books of the Reign of King Edward the Third*, ed. and trans. Luke Owen Pike, 15 vols. (London: Longman, 1883–1911), 11: 430.
21. One of the first *femme sole* married women in England was Eleanor of Provence, wife of Henry III. Eleanor's great contribution to English *femme sole* history was to secure the right for herself and subsequent English queens in the Middle Ages to hold, manage, and administer their dower lands, or the equivalency, while they were married as if they were *femme sole*. Margaret Howell discusses some of the events leading up to this development in her biography of Eleanor, *Eleanor of Provence: Queenship in Thirteenth Century England* (Oxford, Blackwell, 1998), esp. pp. 189–91 and pp. 291–94. A more focused study of Eleanor's administration as a *femme sole* is the opening section of Ann Crawford's "The Queen's Council in the Middle Ages," *English Historical Review* 116.469 (2001): 1193–1211.
22. For an overview of the doctrine of unity in medieval English law, see John Hamilton Baker, *An Introduction to English Legal History* (Toronto: Butterworth, 1990), pp. 550–57.
23. George Kay, *Lady of the Sun: The Life and Times of Alice Perrers* (New York: Barnes and Noble, 1966), is an excellent study of Perrers, the social milieux in which she operated, and her effect upon the period.
24. Perrers had, supposedly, drawn £2,000 to £3000 a year from the royal coffers, presumably as funds to increase her position in court through bribery and favoritism.
25. 2 Ric. II; *RP*, vol. 3, pp. 41–42.
26. May McKisack, *The Fourteenth Century, 1307–1399* (Oxford: Clarendon Press, 1959), p. 403.
27. As early as 1200, an essoiner, or *excusator*, was a person hired to stand for the principles in a case in court, in the eventuality that those principles could not appear.
28. *Liber Albus*, ed. Henry Thomas Riley (London: Longman, Brown, Green, Longmans, and Roberts, 1859–62), p. 68.
29. Baker, *English Legal History*, 179.
30. *Liber Albus*, 68.
31. J.H. Baker, *Manual of Law French,* 2nd ed. (Brookfield, VT: Scholar Press, 1990), pp. 119–20.
32. *Liber Albus*, 204–205.

33. *Liber Albus*, 205.
34. Baker, *Legal History*, pp. 71–75.
35. *Liber Albus*, 205.
36. See, e.g., *Liber Albus* 98 and 103, for two such suits for abortion by battery, one by a woman, one by a man.
37. *Liber Albus*, 219.
38. 4 Edw. IV; *RP*, vol. 5, pp. 548–49.
39. See Elizabeth Makowski, "The Conjugal Debt and Medieval Canon Law," *Journal of Medieval History* 3 (1977): 99–114, and James A. Brundage, "Sexual Equality in Medieval Canon Law," in *Medieval Women and the Sources of Medieval History*, ed. Joel T. Rosenthal (Athens, GA: University of Georgia Press, 1990), pp. 66–79. Makowski and Brundage point towards the *Decretum* as a pivotal moment in the institutionalization of equality in the marital relationship. Medieval conjugality, for both Makowski and Brundage, was characterized by mutual obligations and was therefore a form of equality, since that debt could only be evaded through mutual consent.
40. Eleanor McLaughlin, "Equality of Souls, Inequality of Sexes: Woman in Medieval Theology," in *Religion and Sexism*, ed. Rosemary Reuther (New York: Simon and Schuster, 1974).
41. Dyan Elliott, *Spiritual Marriage: Sexual Abstinence in Medieval Wedlock* (Princeton: Princeton University Press, 1993), p. 148.
42. Louise Tilly and Joan W. Scott, *Women, Work, and Family* (NY: Holt, Rinehart, and Winston, 1978), p. 21.

PART 2

SPIRITUAL EMPLOYMENT

CHAPTER 3

"THE WORKMAN IS WORTH HIS MEDE": POVERTY, LABOR, AND CHARITY IN THE SERMON OF WILLIAM TAYLOR

*Kate Crassons*

> This essay argues that the Wycliffite sermon of William Taylor presents seemingly contradictory arguments about the role of poverty, work, and charity within Christian society. Taylor ultimately rejects poverty as a widespread Christian virtue and instead favors labor as the primary force that sanctifies the larger community in protecting it from material deprivation.

Delivering a sermon at St. Paul's Cross in 1406, William Taylor began his controversial career as a Wycliffite reformer and articulated a social and evangelical vision so troubling to the religious orthodoxy that he would eventually be charged with heresy and burnt at Smithfield in 1423.[1] The list of articles finally condemning the priest includes, among other charges, his views on clerical ownership and mendicancy—the major topics addressed in this early sermon given at St. Paul's.[2] Demonstrating that spiritual concerns are not exempt from the exigencies of material reality, Taylor complains in his oration that the church has disrupted the proper course of production and consumption in contemporary Christian society. In its excessive accumulation of material goods and its promotion of fraternal begging, the church, according to Taylor, has misused the community's resources and sparked a socioeconomic crisis of unparalleled proportions. Taylor conveys to his audience the gravity of the church's transgressions by offering a reading of Revelation 12:15, which recounts how a dragon attempts to capture a woman by casting a great flood from its mouth. Explaining that the woman is a figure for the church, Taylor argues that the devil has flooded the contemporary institution with material goods so "þat preestis ben þus drawun fro goostly lyuyng and prestly ocupacioun and ben acumbrid in wordly nedis."[3] Taylor laments the devil's success in luring the church away from its poor, apostolic origins. He specifically criticizes the clergy's "vnordynat loue [for] þe world" and complains that they "ben so fer fallun þat vnneþe þe more part of temporalities and fatte benefciis may fulfille her appetiit. . . ." (6/109–11).

Criticizing the church primarily as an appetitive and all-consuming force, Taylor proposes ecclesiastical and social reforms designed to remedy the problems caused by mendicancy and clerical possessions. As it addresses the legitimacy of begging, the correct practice of almsgiving, and the benefits of labor, Taylor's sermon stages a Wycliffite intervention into the wider cultural and theological debates around poverty, work, and charity in late medieval England.[4] I therefore want to explore Taylor's work in light of what critics have seen as a "shift of values" or a "newer ethos," which praised labor as one of the highest Christian virtues and associated poverty with idleness, vagrancy, and sin.[5] Specifically in fourteenth-century England, antifraternal polemic fused with an extensive body of labor legislation that not only criminalized able-bodied begging and the donation of alms to such beggars, but also affirmed a larger cultural suspicion about poverty both as a chosen religious practice and as an unavoidable economic state.[6] Because it is beyond the scope of this essay to produce a detailed account of these debates about poverty, I shall examine Taylor's work alongside of Richard FitzRalph's *Defensio Curatorum*, an earlier orthodox sermon that quite clearly conveys the major tenets of this new anti-poverty ethos.

Offering a massive critique of the fraternal orders, the *Defensio Curatorum* provides a useful counterpart to Taylor's sermon because it explicitly discusses poverty and labor within an ecclesiological framework.[7] FitzRalph's oration, furthermore, was one of the most widely disseminated works of antifraternalism in the late medieval period.[8] It is significant that FitzRalph's arguments in the *Defensio Curatorum* were widely known and that his work more generally was influential on later writers like Wyclif and, as we shall see, Taylor himself.[9] Considering some of the relations between these two sermons, I argue that Taylor's text occupies a unique position among the conflicts regarding poverty and labor because it advocates a return to the poor, apostolic church at the same time that it echoes the anti-poverty ethos found in the antifraternal writing of FitzRalph. Thus, while Taylor lobbies for the protection of the poor and the disendowment of the church, he nonetheless disregards the poor Christ tradition, advocates a strict model of discriminate charity, and exhorts the Christian community not to cultivate patient poverty, but to work so as to become "myȝty and sufficient in husbondderie and marchaundise" (18/572).

With its fascinating account of labor, mendicancy, and almsgiving, Taylor's sermon affirms Margaret Aston's observation that poverty is a "continuous theme—if not an obsession—in Lollard writings."[10] Taylor's discussion of charity in particular promotes a view of poverty that seems to oppose the ideological shift casting suspicion on the poor. As I discuss here, Taylor's arguments about the essential importance of almsgiving accord with critical views contending that poverty is a fundamental value within Wycliffite thought. Aston, for instance, has claimed that the Wycliffite movement possessed "a truly evangelical commitment to the poor";[11] and Michel Mollat has similarly argued that the Wycliffites retained

> the goal of. . .leading their listeners to renounce the wealth and vanities of this world and donate all their belongings to the poor.[12]

Indeed, as Taylor urges the Christian community to fulfill their charitable obligations, he displays a passionate concern for the poor and a suspicion of wealth if it is not properly distributed as alms. Taylor's sermon, then, at least initially, seems to oppose the emergent anti-poverty ethos as evident in FitzRalph's *Defensio Curatorum*, a text that clearly denounces need as a Christian virtue.

Turning more specifically to Taylor's sermon, we can see that he prioritizes the topic of charity as he devotes an entire section of his oration to the thesis that "almesdede is werk of greet charge" (12/342). Taylor emphasizes precisely how important charity is by explaining that almsgiving is a requisite for salvation. He states, "For, certeyn, for þat duly fulfillid or þurȝ necgligence left, Crist bihotiþ us blisse or peyne euerlastinge" (12/341–43). Issuing an implicit warning about the dangers of material wealth, Taylor turns to the gospel of Luke and cites specific passages in order to provide evidence for his claims about the significance of almsgiving within the larger scheme of salvation. He begins with the story of Dives and Lazar in Luke 16 and argues that God dooms those who strictly maintain their plenteous goods. Arguing that the failure to give alms constitutes a failure to show mercy, Taylor states:

> And bicause þat we shulden be war þat we be not vnmerciful, Crist techiþ us. . .what bitidde of an vnmericiful man, riche and glotoun, þat delicatly and shynyngly fede himsilf wiþ his owne goodis, not reckynge of þe

wrecchid Lazar ligginge at his ȝatis; and so þe riche man diede and was biried in helle.... (12/344–49)

Refusing to distribute his possessions to the needy man waiting at his very own gates, Dives becomes a figure of covetousness and gluttony who neglects the basic Christian duty to love his neighbor. While Taylor locates Dives' sinfulness in his unmerciful nature, the sermon's emphasis on the rich man's damnation nonetheless serves as a powerful reminder to Taylor's audience that unless the rich mercifully share their possessions with the poor, they too will go to hell.

As Taylor goes on to discuss in greater detail the precise cause of Dives' damnation, he once again focuses primarily on the issue of mercy. Describing Dives as an otherwise virtuous man, Taylor explains that he is at fault for turning his back on someone in need. He continues:

> Upon þis axiþ seint Austin þe cause of þe dampnyng of þis riche man, namely siþen þer is no mencioun maad in þe gospel þat he was a raueynour, wrongful chalenger and extorcioner, ne oppresser of fadirles and modirles children or of widowis, but he was riche. Wherof was he riche?—of his owne. What þanne was þe cause of þe dampnyng of him? Certeyn bicause þat he was vnmerciful, seynge þe mysese of his broþir and hauynge no mercy on him.... (12/349–56)

Although Taylor condemns Dives for a specific moral failure, it seems as if the rich man's sin is compounded by his abundant material wealth. After all, the distribution of Dives' worldly possessions is the very act that constitutes and confirms his willingness to be merciful. The story of Dives, furthermore, draws attention to the fact that one cannot simply accumulate possessions and expect to achieve salvation. Even though Taylor makes it clear that Dives has not committed theft or extortion, but has earned his wealth honestly, the rich man's possessions jeopardize his hopes for salvation unless they are distributed mercifully as alms. While Taylor aims to focus his discussion on Dives' spiritual disposition, his sermon displays an implicit anxiety about maintaining superfluous material possessions. This concern about wealth is evident when Taylor produces another bleak account of a rich man whose abundant material goods pose some kind of obstacle to his salvation.

After discussing the fate of Dives, Taylor turns once again to the gospel of Luke and continues to reflect on the ethical status of material accumulation. Specifically, Taylor recounts how the rich man in Luke 12 similarly faces damnation for failing to part with his possessions. In an exploration of how the fruits of labor are best employed in a Christian society, Taylor first summarizes the gospel account:

> Crist telliþ how 'þe feeld of a riche man brouȝt forþ plenteuous fruytis, and he seide wiþynne himsilf "What shal I do þat I haue not whidir to gedre my fruytis?" And he seide "þis shal I do: I shal stroye my bernes and I shal make grettere, and þidir shal I gedere all þingis þat ben growun to me and my goodis. And I shal seie to my soule, 'Soule, þou hast manye goodis putt up into ful manye ȝeeris; reste, ete, drinke and make feeste." Forsoþe, God seide to him "Fool! In þis nyȝt þei shulen take þi soule fro þee,' " þat is to seie þe deuel. (12–13/361–69)

Setting aside the explicit issue of mercy in this particular instance, Taylor presents the rich man as an avaricious figure who succumbs to the temptation simply to keep his justly earned wealth for himself. Taylor focuses particularly on the man's solipsistic accumulation and consumption of his worldly possessions. As he "ete[s], drinke[s], and make[s] feeste" for himself alone, the rich man completely ignores his charitable obligations and engages in the negligent and wasteful spending of his own goods.

Noting that this man and Dives both go to hell, Taylor demonstrates that the rich are particularly vulnerable to spiritual danger. He thus offers the scripture as a cautionary tale to those men in his own community who similarly "laboren to encreece her poscesciouns and richessis, and to fulfille bernes and shoppis and gedren bisily, and holden hem noȝt apayed wiþ her owne goodis. . . ." (13/373–75). As in his discussion of Dives and Lazar, however, Taylor does not condemn wealth in and of itself, but particularly repudiates the rich who obtain their goods "bi extorcioun, wilis of þe lawe and ouerledyng of poore men, bi false and gileful weiȝtis, wily wordis, vnriȝtwise mesuris, vsurie, symonye and ypocrisie and oþere vnleeful meenys" (13/374–77). Despite his attention here to the sinful attainment of wealth, it is nonetheless significant that Taylor more generally casts suspicion on rich people's "hertily bisynesse aboute þe world" (13/378). In his account of the gospel passages, it is clear that the accumulation of goods hardly serves as a mark of holiness, but rather functions as a spiritual liability.

Emphasizing the problems associated with worldly possessions, Taylor's sermon seems to work against the dramatic valuations of wealth in FitzRalph's *Defensio Curatorum*. In contrast to Taylor's guarded view of material possessions, FitzRalph believes that wealth is a sign of goodness that actually brings one closer to divinity. He therefore finds value in earthly prosperity and in the forms of labor that can bring about material gain. In his account of the creation, for instance, FitzRalph makes the astonishing claim that the primary purpose of mankind is to labor and cultivate worldly goods. Making this assertion within his larger arguments against mendicancy, the details of which I later discuss, FitzRalph promotes "what looks like a new work ethic"[13] when he declares

> in þe first ordynaunce of man God ordeyned hym so þat anoon as man was made, God put hym in Paradys for he schuld worche & kepe Paradys; so hit is writen in þe bygynnyng of Hooly Writ. Hit semeþ me þat þere God tauȝt þat bodilich werk, possessioun and plente of riches & vnmebles, & warde & keping þerof for mannes vse, schuld be sett to-fore beggerie; for god sett man in Paradys for he schuld worche.[14]

Reversing the commonplace belief that labor was actually the punishment for Adam's and Eve's sins, FitzRalph transforms work and material ownership into sacred rewards. FitzRalph thus locates sanctity in the accumulation of worldly goods and not necessarily in their dispersal. Exhibiting absolutely no anxiety about the cultivation of possessions, he associates prosperity with prelapsarian innocence and argues that man "schuld kepe Paradys as his owne & haue þere plente of good, & catel, meble & vnmeble. . . ." (71). FitzRalph also goes on to offer an even more explicit approbation of wealth when he describes affluence as a kind of divine condition. He confidently explains ". . .riches is good having & worþi to be loued of God, for he is richest of alle. . ." (80).

While FitzRalph upholds a vision that correlates wealth with sanctity and God himself, Taylor laments what he sees as the church's fall into worldly concerns and goods. For FitzRalph, the issue of clerical possessions is relevant only so far as the secular cleric seeks to prevent the friars from taking money that he thinks rightfully belongs to parish churches and the secular clergy. In other words, the orthodox priest is not concerned about the superfluity of the church's wealth; in fact, he seeks to protect it from the friars who, in his view, are not valid members of the ecclesiastical hierarchy.[15] In Taylor's view, however, if it is dangerous for an individual to possess riches, then it catastrophic for any facet of the church to be encumbered in material ownership. Throughout the sermon, Taylor objects to clerical possessions and complains, for instance, that the devil "haþ wiþdrawun þe clergie from preestly office and brouȝt it into so greet worldlynesse. . .þat vnneþe reckiþ now ony man of þe office of preesthood to þe puple" (5/85–7). In Taylor's account, the clergy have focused their energies so fervently on the satanic pursuit of earthly goods and activities that they have lost their very identity as priests and, more generally, as men of God.

Because Taylor thinks that the clergy, the very "stomack" of the church, have turned to worldliness, the entire institution languishes in corruption. The "weylynge chirche" speaks in the Wycliffite sermon and complains that it has been compromised by the clergy's involvement in commercial endeavors: "'Sones haue I norischid and enhaunsid, þei forsoþe han forsake me. þei han forsake me and defoulid me bi foul liif, foul wynnyng and foul marchaundise'" (8–9/177–79). The church's lament suggests that the clerics have abandoned their spiritual obligations and view their offices as little more than a source of economic opportunity. Accordingly, Taylor characterizes the contemporary church leadership as a figuration of Dives himself. He therefore laments that there are members of the clergy who, "not reckinge of þe heelþe of her owne soule neþir of oþeris þat ben bitakun to her cure, seien in effect þat... 'Blessid be God we ben maad riche', and lyuen as *delicatly* and *rechelesly* as þou3 þat þei weren in dispeir of liif to comynge" (8/209–13, my emphasis). Revealing the extent of its decline into temporal concerns, Taylor concludes that the church has been infiltrated by antichrist and infected with the "rootid scabbe" of hypocrisy (7/165).

The contemporary institution thus acts as a foil to its original, apostolic model, which, in Taylor's view, remained content with only the basic necessities. His proposed cure for the church is its disendowment, a proposition central to Wycliffite thought more generally.[16] Advocating the return of the church's possessions to secular lords, he writes:

> oure clerkis, and specialy þo þat ben deed to þe world...shulden be redy to delyuere up into þe hondis of seculer men alle her poscessiouns and tresours...and on þis wise releeue þe chirche of Engelond...at þe ensaumple of Crist and his apostlis. (9/234–40)

In Taylor's view, the withdrawal of the church's possessions functions in itself as a kind of charitable act. Thus, the purpose of disendowing the church is to "releeue" the contemporary institution and reorient it to the ideal of poverty practiced by Christ and the clergy of the evangelical church.

For Taylor, however, this vision is not an immediate possibility, and as he continues to censure the church for its covetousness, he most harshly condemns the institution for hoarding alms that he thinks rightfully belong to the poor; he especially deplores the church's misuse of money or alms donated by the poor themselves. According to Taylor, the church should use all of its donations to support those in need. In displaying such concern, Taylor's sermon once again seems to diverge from the *Defensio Curatorum*, which discusses poverty primarily in relation to fraternal mendicancy. In addressing the feigned neediness of the friars, FitzRalph's sermon does not really consider the existence of indigent lay people and the injustices that they may experience.[17] In the Wycliffite sermon, however, Taylor repeatedly speaks in defense of the needy and objects, in explicitly political language, to what he sees as the church's outright abuse of poor people. After asking how the clergy actually treat the poor, Taylor answers:

> Certeyn, as we seen aftir þe quantite of almes of poore men, þei multiplyen hem meynee as worldly as a temporal lord, and alle þe myʒtye of þe cuntree þei confederen to hem for to putte doun vndir foote þe poore, alwey bringing yn, in as moche as in hem is, newe bondage as Farao dide on þe children of Israel. And. . .þei han waastid þe bodyes of her sogetis, vsynge hem as beestis, and bi extorcioun haue take of her goodis and trauelis as moche as þei may. . .Oo! how fer ben þese vnmerciful from þe condiciouns of merciful Iesu and his apostilis. . .(15–16/474–82)

In this account, the clergy have not just become like temporal lords, but function as dictators who enslave the poor by taking advantage of their labor and negligible material possessions. Underscoring the physical suffering and the church's exploitation of those in need, Taylor reminds his listeners that the treatment of the poor is not merely an abstract issue, but a matter of life and death. He goes on to state, for example, that "summe of þese [clergy]. . .suffren pore men þat owen þese goodis to perisshe in body as we seen" (16/484–87). According to Taylor, the role of the church has been subverted because the institution has been overtaken by covetousness and hypocrisy; rather than functioning as the steward of the poor, the church now steals directly from them and, in some cases, causes their death. Indeed, much of Taylor's anticlerical sentiment stems from the fact that he sees holy church as an insatiable force of consumption that "swolow[s] up," with disastrous consequences, "þe substance of almes due bi Cristis wille to poore men" (19/596).

In its exhortations to give alms and its criticisms of the church's wealth, Taylor's sermon certainly displays a commitment to the ideal of the apostolic church and passionately lobbies for the protection and just treatment of the poor. In this sense, the Wycliffite text diverges from FitzRalph's sermon, which does not give much attention to the poor themselves, and which correlates wealth with Christian sanctity. Furthermore, given FitzRalph's status as a secular cleric, the *Defensio Curatorum* does not have any interest in the church's disendowment and seeks to reform the fraternal orders alone. Despite these differences, the two sermons nonetheless begin to look rather similar when we investigate Taylor's particular version of the apostolic church and, more specifically, his representation of Christ. As we see, the Wycliffite ultimately stops far short of making poverty into an essential Christian virtue. Rather, Taylor begins to sound a lot like FitzRalph, and he ultimately promotes a socioeconomic ideal that prioritizes labor as the most important virtue in both the evangelical community and contemporary Christian society.

In Taylor's vision of the apostolic church, poverty is not a value in and of itself; in fact, Taylor's sermon seems to follow the *Defensio Curatorum* in emphasizing that the members of the primitive church sought to eradicate any form of need from within their community. FitzRalph, for instance, makes a central argument, among his many criticisms of the friars,[18] that mendicancy violates the basic principles of ecclesiastical law. Asserting that the church has always made provision for its different orders, FitzRalph insists that need cannot be a legitimate state for ordained members of the church. He says: "it is comyn lawe of holy cherche þat no man schulde fonge holy ordre, but he haue suffisaunt tytel to haue mete & drynke and cloþe" (66). In FitzRalph's logic, the office of priesthood and any other holy order entitles its members to the actual possession of basic material goods. In reference to Luke 10, FitzRalph goes on to emphasize that the clerical office is a form of labor, and he reminds the fraternal orders that "þe werkman is worþi his mede" (62). The friars, however, "makeþ [themselves] unable to þe office of prest & to ech holy ordre" (92) because they claim to renounce all ownership and refuse to acknowledge their rightful title to the necessities of the world. For FitzRalph, the friars are finally neither legitimate beggars nor a valid ecclesiastical order since "hauyng riȝt to preche and to cristen men may nouȝt stonde wiþ sich a foundment of beggerie" (62).

When Taylor discusses the structure of the early institution, he follows FitzRalph's logic and similarly emphasizes that Christ "ordeynede sufficiently for his chirche" (16). While he mentions that Jesus, Peter, and Paul conferred "worldly lordship" on secular authorities, Taylor explains that these early church leaders nonetheless retained a legitimate claim to possess basic material goods. Reiterating FitzRalph's original point, Taylor casts the priestly office in terms of labor and says, "for þe clerkis Crist. . .ordeynede, enasumplynge hem and techynge hem to receyue þat þat was nedeful to liiflode bi title of þe gospel and not of beggyng, seiynge on þis wise 'þe werkman is worþi his meede' " (16/505–508). Through their spiritual labors, the early clergy earned "wagis ordeynede bi Crist" (18/556), or more specifically "necessarie liiflode and hilyng" (9/238). Significantly, Christ made provision for his priests so that they should not have to resort to mendicancy.

As productive laborers, the clergy of Taylor's apostolic church actively worked to dispel need within the community. Just as FitzRalph recalls God's command to his people that "a nedy man & begger schal nouȝt be among ȝow" (81), Taylor explains, "þe apostils. . .in whom was þer plente of perfeccioun of þe gospel. . .wiþ a comyn asent ordeyneden þat þer shulde be no needy man or womman amonge hem, for it was departid to euery as it was neede" (17/529–32). While these kinds of statements may simply seem like an affirmation of the early church's commitment to charity, Taylor makes it clear that he is focusing on the institution's denial that poverty is a legitimate Christian state. Asserting that Christ and the apostles rejected begging as an acceptable means of livelihood, Taylor makes them affirm the ideology of contemporary antifraternal rhetoric. He says, for example, "þe cause whi þat Crist and his apostlis woulde no beggeris be may resonably be þe greuouse synnes þat comunly suen customable beggeris, as ypocrisie, flateringe, lyinge, enuye, drunkenesse and leccherie. . . ." (18/581–84).[19] Based on this assertion, Christ apparently provides for the poor not just to relieve their need, but in order to prevent them from lapsing into the 'sinful' practice of mendicancy.

Taylor's hostile view of begging conforms with FitzRalph's foundational argument that voluntary poverty is not a legitimate pursuit for anyone because it sinfully perpetuates the mere illusion of need. Specifically, FitzRalph contends that true neediness cannot be experienced by anyone who is capable of justly procuring the necessities of life for him or herself. Refuting the claim that Jesus was a mendicant, FitzRalph explains, "ʒif Crist beggide wilfullich he was a verrey ypocryte, semyng a begger, & was no verrey begger, for Crist was neuer a verrey begger, for no man þat may haue y-nowʒ at his wille, is a verrey begger, þouʒ he begge. But he is a verrey faytour, & he þat beggeþ wilfullich may haue y-nowʒ at hys wille" (84). As Wendy Scase has remarked, FitzRalph here makes an extraordinary claim in attempting "to establish that voluntary need [is] *by definition* impossible; anyone who [is] voluntarily needy by definition [has] the wherewithal to avoid need, and [is] thus not a true beggar, but a false one."[20]

FitzRalph, then, sets a precedent for Taylor's view of begging as a sinful activity that explicitly violates some of God's most central commandments. FitzRalph, for instance, insists that mendicancy opposes the fundamental Christian precept to love one's neighbor as oneself since "he þat axeþ of his neiʒbore vnskilfullich his neiʒbores goode wiþ-out nede, greueþ his neiʒbore" (82). Mendicancy, furthermore, disrupts charitable social relations because, in FitzRalph's view, it makes covetousness the central force that binds the Christian community together. The voluntary beggar "axeþ &. . .desireþ his neiʒbores þynge" and therefore "wilfullich doþ aʒenus Goddes heeste þat seiþ: 'þou schalt nouʒt coueite þi neiʒbores hous, noþer desire his wif, noþer his seruaunt man, noþer womman, noþer his oxe, noþer his asse, noþer any þyng þat is his' " (80–81). As a practice rooted in sin, mendicancy does not have a beneficial function in FitzRalph's vision of community. In fact, FitzRalph ultimately defines voluntary begging in terms that exactly oppose Francis' earlier estimation of mendicancy as a virtuous Christian pursuit. Francis, for instance, maintained that mendicancy was not a shameful activity but a kind of holy practice recalling

Christ's own neediness:

> The friars should be delighted to follow the lowliness and poverty of our Lord Jesus Christ, remembering that of the whole world we must own nothing. . . .If [the friars] are in want, they should not be ashamed to beg alms, remembering that our Lord Jesus Christ, the son of the living, all-powerful God. . .was not ashamed.[21]

FitzRalph, however, overturns Francis' valorization of mendicancy in asserting, "willful beggerie is nouȝt meedeful for oþer þing þan for schame; for þe beggar haþ but schame, for hit is a lowe dede and greuous by cause of kyndelich schame þat longeþ þerto" (85).

Offering such strident critiques of mendicancy, the *Defensio Curatorum* is clearly interested in refuting the friars' arguments that Christ chose a life of poverty and was a beggar himself.[22] This particular objection becomes a central component of Taylor's sermon as well, and the two preachers, as we shall see, make similar claims against theories of Christ's neediness. Like FitzRalph, Taylor, for instance, insists that Jesus could not have practiced mendicancy. Drawing on arguments that FitzRalph elaborates more fully outside of the *Defensio Curatorum*,[23] Taylor raises the question of Christ's dominion. Specifically, he goes on to explain that it was impossible for Christ to be a beggar not simply because he was able-bodied, but because the multifaceted nature of his dominion granted him use of anything that he might have needed. Taylor insists that Christ could not have begged "for þre causis:"

> First for Crist is God, wherfore he hadde ful lordship uppon alle creaturis bi title of creacioun. Bi title also of innocense he hadde as Adam ful lordship of alle þingis þat nediden to mannys vse. And þe þridde skile is for he was a trewe preest and bisshop to the Iewis, doynge duly his office to þe puple, þerfore he myȝte, as he dide bi title of þe gospel, receyue þat þat was needeful to hym in execucioun of his office. (21–22/700–707)

Taylor concludes that as God, the second Adam, and a priest, Christ, by his very nature, possessed varying degrees of lordship that prevented him from ever experiencing true need and living as a beggar. His different titles granted him dominion not only over "alle creaturis" but also over "alle thinges þat nediden to mannys vse" and everything "þat was needful to hym in execucioun of his office."

When Taylor and FitzRalph turn more specifically to the gospels for scriptural evidence of Jesus' self-sufficiency, they are both insistent on characterizing Christ as a laborer and an agent of charity. Claiming that "Crist neuer loued pouert for hit-self aloon," FitzRalph, for instance, argues that Jesus was a carpenter and, like Joseph, "gat his liflode sometyme wiþ trauail and wiþ his hond werk"(87). Making the very same point, Taylor contends that Jesus followed "Iosephis craft" because "þe Iewis calliden him not oonly carpenteris sone, but also þei calliden hym Iesu þe carpenter, as it is writun in Markis gospel" (21/679–81). In addition to emphasizing the 'ordinary' dimensions of Jesus' existence as a tradesman, the preachers also draw attention to moments in the gospel when Christ is a powerful and productive figure who works to sustain the community both materially and spiritually. FitzRalph, for instance, discusses the story of the fish and loaves in John 6, the biblical text that is the gospel reading for Taylor's own sermon. Discussing the scripture, FitzRalph asks, perhaps not unreasonably "how schuld [Jesus] feede foure þousand men by myracle & may nouȝt fynde hym silf mete?" (83).

Taylor similarly emphasizes Christ's generous nature, and he marshals an array of examples to present a version of Christ very different from the poor and meek persona often associated with the Franciscan tradition. Taylor's sermon strikingly transforms Christ into a commanding figure who is *never* in need of alms. Even when Christ is ostensibly asking for sustenance or lodging, the sermon casts Jesus as the ultimate almsgiver who is always offering to others some form of charity. By looking at a few examples, we can see how Taylor distinctively glosses the gospels to create a fundamentally powerful and charitable Christ. Directly engaging with fraternal arguments about Christ's poverty, Taylor discusses John 4 and explains, "for to coloure her vngroundid beggyng [mendicants] putten upon Crist þat he shulde haue beggid of þe womman of Samarie, whanne he seide to hir 'Womman ȝyue me drinke' " (19/607–10). Taylor rejects the friars' claim on two counts. First, he emphasizes Christ's power by explaining that Jesus "seide not in begginge maner but on comaundinge maner, 'Womman, ȝyue me drynke' " (19/615–16). After underscoring Christ's authoritative tone, Taylor then interprets the story allegorically to argue "it was not bodily watir þat Crist princiaply axide of þe womman, but watir of sorewe for synne and of feiþ" (19/617–18). In this reading, Christ does not merely beg or even command a glass or water; instead, he actually *gives* the Samaritan woman the opportunity to ask for Jesus' forgiveness and receive his mercy.

Taylor's refusal in this instance to acknowledge the possibility of Christ's neediness carries over into his subsequent discussion of other biblical passages relevant to the mendicant debates. Taylor, for instance, turns to the story of Jesus' exchange with Zaccheus to refute the friars' insistence that "oure Iesu shulde haue beggid an hous of Zachee, whanne Crist, seynge Zachee upon þe tree, seide to him 'Zachee, hastynge come doun, for þis day I moste dwelle in þyn hous'" (20/647–50). Rejecting this particular claim in virtually the same way that he deals with the case of the Samaritan woman, Taylor insists upon Christ's godly authority by declaring that he spoke "as a lord commandynge and not as a nedy man begginge" (20/650–51). Taylor goes beyond this specific claim, however, and, in a strategic act of exegesis, he then recasts the story to make Christ into a kind of almsgiver, who aids the sinful Zaccheus. Taylor explains, for example, not how Jesus benefits from Zaccheus' hospitality, but how Zaccheus actually benefits from being selected by God. He writes:

> And Crist þat tyme hadde about hym a greet noumbre of puple, as þe gospel seiþ, and eche of hem desiride þe presence of Crist as Zachee dide; and þei þat weren myȝty wolden haue had him to her placis, and þerfore þei grucchiden þat Crist ȝede forþ wiþ Zachee. þanne nedide not Crist for to begge an hous. *For Zachees profiit þanne, for to turne him to þe feiþ, and not for his owne neede*, maistirfully he lymytide to himsilf Zacheis hous, and comaundide him to go doun for to receyue him into his hous. (20/651–58, my emphasis)

In Taylor's interpretation of the biblical passage, Christ does not really ask for housing at all. He is instead offering his divine presence to the "myȝty" people praying that Christ will choose them as worthy recipients of his spiritual gifts. For Taylor, Jesus is unequivocally a "lord commaundynge:" he authoritatively selects Zaccheus, and those who are not chosen are left grumbling about their missed opportunity to be with Christ. Jesus clearly, then, does not beg for anything but works for Zaccheus' 'profit' and "maistirfully" grants him the gift of faith.

In addition to presenting a version of Christ who seems virtually incapable of receiving alms, Taylor promotes a work ethic perhaps even more extreme than FitzRalph's strenuous commendations of labor. Remarkably, Taylor emphasizes not only that Christ himself worked, but that his mission was to make others labor as well. Presenting labor as a virtue that mitigates against poverty, he generates the astonishing argument that Christ healed the sick so that they could be put to work. Commenting on Mark 10:46, Luke 18:35, and John 9:8, Taylor discusses "clamorous beggeris," or lifelong mendicants who "weren nedid to sitte at ȝatis and biside weies, and crye and begge." He then recounts what he sees as Christ's categorical repudiation of this activity: "And in tokenynge þat Crist loþide sich begging, he heelide siche men not oonly in soule but also in body, þat þei myȝten gete þat hem nedide bi her bodily labour" (19/589–92). Taylor's shocking assertion implies that Christ and his miraculous works do not primarily serve as a demonstration of divine love and grace; rather they function to increase economic productivity. This vision of Christ thus accords with FitzRalph's contention that "man is y-bore to travail," not to practice patient poverty. Furthermore, Taylor's position suggests that Christ's role is virtually no different from agents like the violent and coercive figure of Hunger in *Piers Plowman*: both achieve the final goal of putting the idle to work.[24]

Given his particular portrayal of Christ and the apostolic community, we can see that Taylor's call to return to the primitive church does not necessarily imply a return to the ideal of poverty. While Taylor, as we have seen, condemns the clergy for taking advantage of the poor, he more harshly reproves the church for actually making men poor, for turning able-bodied men into beggars, for draining the financial resources of the lay community. Emphasizing that absolute poverty violates God's decrees, Taylor argues that the clergy's usurpation of alms "constreyen[s] þe nedy puple to begge aȝeen þe lawe of God" (16/498). Arguing that the presence of beggars is a sign that society has violated Christian law, Taylor implicitly confirms FitzRalph's definition of poverty as "þe effect of sin" (80). As the corollary to his own view that wealth is a kind of sacred entity, FitzRalph claims that material need is actually a result of the fall. Accordingly, he explains that "ȝif oure forme fader & moder hadde neuer y-synned, schuld neuer haue be pore man of oure kynde" (80). As Taylor goes on to outline his vision for the reformation of the community as a whole, he echoes FitzRalph's sentiments about poverty and characterizes it as a condition that opposes Christian sanctity.

In his criticism of the contemporary church, we have seen how Taylor objects to the clergy's abuse of charity in hoarding alms that rightfully belong to the poor. The Wycliffite's complaints about the church and almsgiving, however, extend beyond his concern for the needy and involve a more central anxiety about the economic security of the lay community. Because it has covetously accumulated temporal possessions for itself, the church, according to Taylor, threatens to impoverish the whole of medieval society. He therefore complains that the church's insatiable desire for goods has forced otherwise self-sufficient people into need and has generated the increased demand for charitable collections. Taylor remarks that if the "blessid rule, ordynaunce or pollicie of Crist and his apostlis had be kept for to now, we shulden not haue fallun into so manye inconuenyentis as we ben now, ne þer shulde not haue ben sich a grucching and rumour for vitaylis amonge þe puple vnpayed, and gaderingis or quyletis maad as we now heeren" (17/540–45). Taylor consistently reiterates this anxiety about the community's diminishing funds, and later in the sermon, he deplores the fact that poverty has infiltrated all facets of society as a result of the church's increasingly acquisitive nature. He declares, "now, for þe wiþdrawing of þe ordynaunce and þe pollicie of Crist and his apostlis, we ben fallun into so greet a defaute and into a maner wrecchidnesse þat euery astaat pleyneþ of pouerte and defaute" (18/576–79). In rejecting Christ's laws, the entire community has compromised its ethical status, with the result that it now languishes in the "wrecchidnesse" of poverty.

While the church should disavow temporal possessions and extricate itself from "foul wynning and marchandise" (9/179), the rejection of material wealth, according to Taylor, should not be a goal for the community at large. Suddenly, involvement in commercial endeavors and material production becomes a central Christian duty as Taylor wistfully explains that if the "ordynaunce of Crist and his apostlis hadde be kept, þe comyntee of þe puple shulde haue be myȝty and sufficient in husbondderie and marchaundise to susteyne hemsilf, to paye þe lordis her rentis and oþere þingis þat ben due to hem, and to susteyne þe clergie in her office, and wiþ. . .þe chirche to bere þe charge of fyndyng of þo þat moun no lengere traueile" (18/570–76). Taylor's comment recalls FitzRalph's praise of productivity and material accumulation as activities that are both sanctioned and commanded by God. In Taylor's view, Christ *primarily* obliges the community to work and make money; the average Christian should be responsible for having enough wealth to support himself, to pay his lord, and to make donations to the church.[25] Indeed, Taylor explains that during his own life, Christ himself "conferm[ed] [the community's] iust labour, partynge wiþ hem of her goodis" (16/510). In the sermon, Christ clearly does not call his followers to patient poverty but endorses the secular community's business ventures. Christ, furthermore, is a figure who willingly partakes of the profits and goods that such endeavors produce. It thus seems as if throughout Taylor's arguments we can hear the echo of FitzRalph insisting, "riches is good having & worþi to be loued of God, for he is richest of alle" (80).

Seeking to recapture the prosperity that has been lost in the community's deviation from apostolic virtues, Taylor draws on FitzRalph's arguments to advocate a strict form of discriminate charity that promotes labor within society and ideally redirects alms only to those people who are "truly" needy. While certain theological and biblical writings mandate the practice of non-selective almsgiving,[26] FitzRalph and Taylor completely oppose this theory of charity. Their sermons thus reject arguments like that of Richard Maidstone who sees discriminate almsgiving as a 'diabolical' practice.[27] Turning to the *Defensio Curatorum*, we can see that FitzRalph makes the argument that only those who cannot work rightfully deserve alms. In FitzRalph's opinion, the individuals righteously following God's divine call to labor should not waste their hard-won goods on able-bodied beggars who feign poverty and willfully reject the virtue of work. Indeed, voluntary poverty remains such a problem for FitzRalph because he views it as a deliberate rejection of labor—as a deceitful and slothful means of acquiring others' justly earned possessions. In reference to the friars' procurement of certain clerical offices, FitzRalph maintains, for instance, that there is not "an esyere wey, more sly3 & wyly to gadre riches, þan by þe foreseide priuyleges wiþ þe obligacioun of beggerie"(72).

Seeking to disqualify such beggars as legitimate recipients of alms, FitzRalph cites Luke 14 and discusses Christ's command to invite specific people to the feast: " 'Whanne þou makest a feest clepe þou þerto pore men, halt & blynde, & þou shalt be blessed, for þei haueþ no3t wherof þie mowe quyte hit to þee' " (88).[28] FitzRalph goes on to gloss Christ's words to make it clear that "halt & blynde" function as adjectives modifying "pore men"; thus, Christ is commanding not that the poor, halt, and lame be invited, but rather the poor who are halt and lame. He continues with an exacting explication of the scripture: "þanne pore men þat beþ stalworþe and stronge schulde nou3t be cleped to þe feeste of beggers, for þei mowe quyte hit wiþ her trauail. Noþer riche feble men, noþer riche halt men, noþer riche blynde men schuld be cleped to þe feeste of beggers, for þei mowe quyte hit wiþ her catel" (88). Sketching out a brief taxonomy of those deserving alms, FitzRalph disqualifies both the able-bodied poor, who can help themselves by working, and the ailing rich, who can live off their own wealth. The lame, weak, and blind indigent remain as the rightful recipients of charity because they alone need to work, but are physically unable to labor.

Taylor exactly follows FitzRalph's line of thought on almsgiving. Offering the same interpretation of the Luke 14 passage, Taylor eliminates "the poor" as an autonomous group that should be invited to the feast. He first quotes Christ's command from the gospel: " 'Whanne þou makist þe feest of pitee calle poore feble, lame and blynde and þou shalt be blessid; for þei han not wherwiþ for to rewarde þee, it shal be rewardid þee in þe rewardyng of ri3twise men' " (15/452–54). Like FitzRalph, Taylor then glosses the text in order to assert that only the poor who are feeble, lame, and blind should be called to the feast.[29] Taking FitzRalph's arguments even further, however, Taylor makes this model of discriminate charity more extreme by actually specifying the appropriate causes of the deserving poor's disabilities. Taylor explains:

> For þe vndirstondyng of þis text Crist techiþ and specifieþ here þre bodily mysesis þat vnabliþ a man to gete his liiflode bi his labour, þat is to seie feblenesse *bi age or siiknesse*, lamenesse þat is depryuyng of mannys lymes *bi birþe, hap or violence as bi prysonyng*, and þe þridde is blyndnesse. (15/455–59, my emphasis)

As if physical disability alone is not a fully legitimizing factor for Taylor, he makes sure to detail the acceptable ways in which the poor become disabled and therefore worthy of alms. Despite his attention to the beggars' disabilities and the causes of them, Taylor is nonetheless emphatic that the beggars deserve charity not primarily because they are "mysesid," but because these specific "mysesis" "vndisposiþ a man to labore" (15/459).

Taylor's sermon makes it clear that all other individuals who fall outside of this category must work for the moral and material benefit of the community. Emphasizing the far-reaching range of this compulsion to labor, Taylor raises the question of gender. Specifically, he discusses the story of Clement from the *Legenda Aurea* and highlights Peter's insistence that Clement's mother should not beg. For example, he explains that Peter "blamyde Clementis modir for hir begging and seide þat she shulde traueile wiþ hir hondis" (17/527–28). This allusion to Clement's mother reinforces the importance of labor within the apostolic community and suggests that women are in no way excused from having to work. Continuing to address the issue of women as laborers, Taylor juxtaposes this discussion of Clement's mother with a consideration of the socioeconomic position of widows. Fearing that this group might drain all of the church's charitable resources, Taylor mandates that widows should also work. He thus invokes Paul who "in þe firste pistle to Tymothe. . .techiþ þat a widewe shulde not be chosun to lyue on þe almes of þe chirche bifore sixty wyntir, but þat she shulde laboure in trewe mennys housis, getynge her owne lyuyng, þat þe chirche shulde not be ouerchargid and vnsufficient for verry widowis" (17/523–26). In its hyperbolic supposition that the population of widows alone is likely to bankrupt the church, Taylor's statement works to demonstrate his relentless prioritization of labor for any person who does not possess a "legitimate" claim to alms.

Taylor seeks to limit those who are dependent on charity to such a small group of people because he, like FitzRalph, is insistent that poverty should not be a widespread goal for the Christian community. However, Taylor affirms the traditional view that Christ commanded that the poor should always be present in society because they allow the rich to have the opportunity of giving alms.[30] Taylor makes it clear, though, that he wants to keep this indigent population to an absolute minimum so that the wealthy are not overburdened by their charitable obligations. He is especially anxious to ensure that poverty does not subvert the knightly estate. In his lamentations about the contemporary socioeconomic situation in England, Taylor finally expresses greatest concern neither for those living at the level of mere subsistence, nor even for those few whom he perceives as worthy beggars. The poor themselves noticeably fade from the picture as Taylor deplores the "poverty" of knights. He declares, for instance, that if society had followed Christ's rule, then "temporal lordis shulden haue be sufficient in rentis and possessiouns for to defende hemsilf and þe rewme, and for to auaunce her children, where now…so manye temporaltees bi þe foly 3yuyng of temporal lordis ben 3ouun to vnprofitable puple to God and man þat vnneþe is left wherwiþ þat fortraueilid kny3tis sones may be releeued" (17–18/545–51).

Afraid that the estates model is on the verge of collapse, Taylor makes an important departure from FitzRalph by protesting not that the friars usurp the secular clergy's property, but that the entire church appropriates the wealth of secular lords. Taylor thus adapts FitzRalph's anti-poverty ideology to his larger concern for the landowning classes. In this regard, Taylor is clearly not troubled by the church's accumulation of goods due to the poor, but censures the institution's claims to the wealth of knights. Offering an implicit critique of FitzRalph's logical position, Taylor insists that members of the clergy, and indeed secular clerics like FitzRalph himself, threaten to undermine the integrity of the knightly estate as they "reioycen hem to be callid lordis and kingis in her owne" (6/110). The social order has now been dangerously reversed, and Taylor characterizes the sons of knights as wretched laborers who are "fortraueilid" and desperately in need of material relief. In Taylor's ideal vision, only the disabled would receive alms and all others would be forced to work for the moral and material benefit of the community, or in this case, for the economic security of the knightly class.

While there are instances in which Taylor seems to revere poverty as a Christian value and to exhibit some genuine concern for the poor, his overarching project of church and social reform clearly rejects the idealizations of poverty that can be found, for instance, at the root of Franciscan thought. Maintaining a rigorous distinction between the church leadership and the lay community, Taylor sanctions poverty as a way of life for the clergy alone. Even this endorsement, however, comes with the strict precaution that the church not fall into abject poverty or extreme forms of need that could lead to mendicancy. In regard to the lay community, Taylor's sermon conforms with the major arguments of FitzRalph's *Defensio Curatorum*, which contends that the righteous Christian society follows Christ by working. Through its labor, the wider community must amass enough wealth so as to support themselves and the church. Seeking to minimize the presence of need in the community, the non-clerical population should thus be 'mighty', 'sufficient', and zealous in their commercial pursuits.[31]

To return, then, to the observations of critics such as Aston and Mollat, it is clear from Taylor's sermon that poverty is not necessarily a fundamental value in this particular instantiation of Wycliffite ideology. Rather, Taylor prioritizes labor as a Christ-like activity that ensures the stability and distinct identity of the three estates. In his discussion of the church, Taylor suggests that the spiritual labor of priests, friars, and other religious leaders entitles the clergy to the basic material provision that keeps the church committed to poverty but that prevents it from lapsing into the sinful practice of mendicancy. The labor of the commons is also integral to Taylor's social ideal: it supplies the church with alms and therein ensures the wealth of knights by leaving them free to undertake the suitable "work" of defending the realm and maintaining their substantial material endowment. Whatever their specific social status may be, knights, priests, and commoners are somehow alike in their role as workmen who are worthy of their meed. Confirming society's adherence to Christ's rule and the apostolic ideal, labor thus serves as the central force that unites, preserves, and sanctifies the Wycliffite vision of community in the sermon of William Taylor.

## Notes

1. Giving an overview of Taylor's career, Anne Hudson notes that in 1406 Archbishop Arundel initiated a series of attempts to charge Taylor for his heterodox beliefs. He was excommunicated in 1407 for failing to appear before Arundel after delivering the sermon under discussion. Taylor was subsequently investigated for other occasions of heretical preaching by Archbishop Chichele and the prior of Worcester, John de Fordham (acting on behalf of the Bishop of Worcester). After a series of abjurations and additional investigations, Taylor was finally condemned as a relapsed heretic. For a more detailed account of Taylor's life and his persecution as a Wycliffite, see Hudson's introduction to *Two Wycliffite Texts*, EETS o.s. 301 (Oxford: Oxford University Press, 1993), pp. xvii–xxv [xi–lxii].
2. Hudson notes that of the five heretical articles ascribed to Taylor by Richard Flemyng, Bishop of Lincoln, "two opinions. . .are traceable" in his 1406 sermon: "on the incompatibility of civil dominion with clerical status. . .and on the culpability of fraternal begging. . . .," *Two Wycliffite Texts*, p. xxiv.
3. "The Sermon of William Taylor," *Two Wycliffite Texts*, pp. 4–5 [3–23], ll. 64–66. All subsequent quotations of Taylor will be cited parenthetically with reference to page and line number.
4. As scholars have demonstrated, medieval debates about poverty originated in the mendicancy conflicts of the mid-thirteenth and early fourteenth centuries. William of St. Amour, for instance, launched an attack against the friars by arguing that they falsely claimed to follow Jesus and the apostles in practicing mendicancy. For an account of William's understanding of Christ's poverty and his role in the mendicant controversy at the University of Paris, see James Doyne Dawson, "William of Saint-Amour and the Apostolic Tradition," *Medieval Studies* 70 (1978): 223–38; and Penn Szittya, *The Antifraternal Tradition in Medieval Literature* (Princeton, NJ: Princeton University Press, 1986), pp. 11–61. In the fourteenth century, Pope John XXII took steps to undermine the notion of poverty espoused by the Franciscan order. Issuing a series of bulls, he renounced papal dominion over the holdings of the

Franciscan order and declared the doctrine of Christ's poverty heretical. See his Ad conditorem canonum (1323), Cum internonnullos (1323), Quia quorundam mentes (1324) and Quia vir reprobus (1329). For an extended discussion of this papal legislation and the conflicts between John XXII and the friars, see Gordon Leff, *Heresy in the Middle Ages*, 2 vols. (Manchester: Manchester University Press), 1:163–66, 238–55; and Malcolm Lambert, *Franciscan Poverty: the Doctrine of the Absolute Poverty of Christ and the Apostles in the Franciscan Order, 1210–1323* (St. Bonaventure, NY: Franciscan Institute, 1998), chapter 10.

5. Maria Moisa calls the elevation of labor a "shift of values." See "Fourteenth-Century Preachers' Views of the Poor," in *Culture, Ideology, Politics*, ed. Raphael Samuel and Gareth Jones (London: Routledge and Kegan Paul, 1983), p. 166 [160–75]. David Aers similarly sees changing attitudes toward poverty and labor as forming a "newer ethos." See "Piers Plowman: Poverty, Work, and Community," in *Community, Gender, and Individual Identity: English Writing 1360–1430* (London and New York: Routledge, 1988), pp. 41–49 [20–72]. For additional summaries of this cultural shift, see Miri Rubin, *Charity and Community in Medieval Cambridge* (Cambridge, UK: Cambridge University Press, 1987), pp. 71–74; and Michel Mollat, *The Poor in the Middle Ages*, trans. Arthur Goldhammer (New Haven, CT: Yale University Press, 1986), pp. 251–94.

6. See in particular the Statute of Labourers (1351), the Vagrancy Petition (1376), and the Cambridge Statute of Labourers (1388). Miri Rubin succinctly explains this fusion of religious and civil concerns about begging: "As hostile attitudes toward labourers, and subsequently toward those deemed to be shirkers—the able-bodied beggars—hardened, the polemic on religious poverty was increasingly couched in terms current in labour legislation. Thus, poverty was divorced from its association with voluntary denunciation of goods...it came to be seen as a form of begging, of living off the hard-won earnings of others" (*Charity and Community*, p. 72). For further discussions of the relations between antifraternal ideology and English labor legislation, see Aers, "Poverty, Work, and Community"; Anne Middleton, "Acts of Vagrancy: The C Version 'Autobiography' and the Statute of 1388," in *Written Work: Langland, Labor, and Authorship*, ed. Steven Justice and Kathryn Kerby-Fulton (Philadelphia, PA: University of Pennsylvania Press, 1997), pp. 208–317; Moisa, "Fourteenth-Century Preachers' Views of the Poor," pp. 168–71; and Wendy Scase, *Piers Plowman and the New Anti-clericalism* (Cambridge, UK: Cambridge University Press, 1989), pp. 70–75, 144–45.

7. In response to charges levied by the friars that he had preached erroneously against them, FitzRalph delivered the *Defensio Curatorum* before the papal curia at Avignon in 1357. In the sermon, he defended his status as a secular cleric and launched another attack on the legitimacy of the fraternal orders. For a full account of the events surrounding FitzRalph's appearance at the papal court and his role in the mendicancy conflicts more generally, see Katherine Walsh, *Richard FitzRalph in Oxford, Avignon, and Armagh* (Oxford: Clarendon Press, 1981), esp. pp. 406–45; Szittya, *The Antifraternal Tradition*,

pp. 123–51; and James Doyne Dawson, "Richard FitzRalph and Fourteenth-Century Poverty Controversies," *Journal of Ecclesiastical History* 34 (1983): 315–44. I have chosen to use John Trevisa's translation of the *Defensio Curatorum* because Trevisa's interest in translating religious texts into English suggests a possible correspondence with Taylor's and the wider Wycliffite insistence on using the vernacular. Since Trevisa was perhaps sympathetic to some of Wyclif's reformist beliefs, his translation of FitzRalph may share certain parallels with the arguments and objectives of Taylor's own Wycliffite sermon. For a discussion of Trevisa's career, his interest in translation, and his possible associations with Wycliffism, see David C. Fowler, *The Life and Times of John Trevisa, Medieval Scholar* (Seattle: University of Washington Press, 1995), esp. pp. 82, 118–234.
8. Walsh notes that the *Defensio Curatorum* exists in eighty-four different manuscripts, and she argues "manuscript circulation and early printings reveal [the *Defensio Curatorum*] to have been the most influential piece of antimendicant polemic published during the later middle ages," (*FitzRalph*, p. 469, p. 413).
9. In his *De domino divino*, Wyclif, for instance, recapitulated much of FitzRalph's *De pauperie salvatoris*, which deals with the vexed questions of property, dominion, right of use, and possessions. In the work, FitzRalph presents the theory of dominion by grace and argues that an individual is stripped of a right or privilege if he abuses it or uses it in a state of sin. Following FitzRalph's logic, Wyclif adopted this theory but took the arguments of the hierarchically minded secular cleric to new extremes that would eventually be deemed heretical. Noting the influence of these arguments on Wyclif, Poole prints the first four books of *De pauperie salvatoris* as well as a table of contents for the last three books in John Wyclif, *De domino divino*, ed. R.L. Poole (London: Wyclif Society, 1890), pp. 273–476, 264–72. Wyclif and other Lollard writers also showed their approval of FitzRalph's teaching by consistently referring to the priest as "sanctus Ricardus," "sanctus Armachamus", or "Seint Richart." For these kinds of references, see, for example, Wyclif's *De Blasphemia*, ed. Michael Dziewicki (London: Wyclif Society, 1893), p. 232; "Nicholas of Hereford's Ascension day sermon," *Medieval Studies* 51 (1989): 205–41; and "De Blasphemia Contra Fratres," in *Select English Works of John Wyclif*, ed. Thomas Arnold, 3 vols. (Oxford: Clarendon Press, 1871), 3:412.
10. Margaret Aston, " 'Caim's Castles': Poverty, Politics, and Disendowment," in *Church, Politics, and Patronage in the Fifteenth Century*, ed. Barrie Dobson (New York: St Martin's Press, 1984), p. 61 [46–81].
11. Aston, "Caim's Castles," p. 67.
12. Mollat, *The Poor in the Middle Ages*, p. 260.
13. Aers, "Poverty, Work, and Community," p. 25. Aers also cites the following quotation from FitzRalph.
14. "Defensio Curatorum," *Trevisa's Dialogus*, ed. John Perry, EETS o.s. 167 (Cambridge, UK: Cambridge University Press, 1925), p. 71. All subsequent quotations of the *Defensio Curatorum* are cited parenthetically by page number.

15. Because papal privilege has exempted the friars from episcopal control, FitzRalph complains that they exist outside of the church hierarchy and have usurped the roles of the secular clergy, particularly in the offices of confession, preaching, and burial. As FitzRalph repeatedly argues, the friars' covetous usurpation of the clergy's privileges has negative consequences for the valid members of the church hierarchy. He objects in particular to the increasing wealth of the fraternal orders, which, in his view, comes directly at the expense of the secular clergy: in begging alms, the friars "steal" money and other goods that Christians would ordinarily donate to their parish churches. He curses the friars for taking such goods: "it semeþ no dowte, by Goddes owne lawe, þat teþinges of byqueestes & of fre ȝiftes is detty, & dewe to parische chirches, & to curatours þerof. . .þanne alle freres þat bynmeþ parische chirches þe teþinge of þat is y-ȝeue hem oþer biqueþe, beþ acursed" (44).

16. See, for instance, the "Lollard Disendowment Bill" in *Selections from English Wycliffite Writings*, ed. Anne Hudson (1978; repr. Toronto: University of Toronto Press, 1997). For further discussion of disendowment in Wycliffite thought, see Anne Hudson, *The Premature Reformation: Wycliffite Texts and Lollard History* (Oxford: Oxford University Press, 1988), pp. 337–42; and Aston, " 'Caim's Castles'. "

17. When he is not speaking explicitly about the friars, FitzRalph only refers to poor people abstractly and does not seem to advocate for them in the way that Taylor does. Rather, he makes statements that seem to support his general argument that poverty should be scorned. For instance, at one point in the *Defensio Curatorum*, he declares that "þe pore schal be hated of his neiȝbore" (83).

18. In addition to arguing that the fraternal orders exist outside of the church hierarchy, FitzRalph repudiates the friars for violating their vow of poverty and performing spiritual duties for profit. He, for instance, complains that the friars hear confession and perform burials of the rich in order to get money. See, for example, p. 47, ll.7–10.

19. In his mention of "customable" beggars, Taylor alludes to a larger taxonomy of begging that runs throughout the sermon. Customable beggars are those who habitually beg in order to make a living. Associated with these are clamorous beggars whose livelihood similarly consists of active and permanent begging. Opposed to these related categories, is the "constreyned" beggar, who is forced into mendicancy only by circumstantial factors. See Hudson, *Two Wycliffite Texts*, p. 103 n. 672. This basic taxonomic model can be found in other Wycliffite writings. See Aston, " 'Caim's Castles,' " p. 56.

20. Scase, *Piers Plowman and the New Anticlericalism*, p. 67.

21. *The Writings of St. Francis of Assisi*, trans. Benen Fahy (Chicago: Franciscan Herald Press, 1964), p. 39.

22. FitzRalph explicitly draws attention to his particular claims about Christ's rejection of poverty. In the opening of the *Defensio Curatorum*, FitzRalph explains that he has preached seven or eight sermons in London against the

friars. He then summarizes the major arguments of those sermons as well as of the *Defensio Curatorum*. Of the nine conclusions he lists, the following deal explicitly with the nature of Christ's poverty: "Oure Lord Ihesus, in his conuersacioun of manhed, alwey was pore, nouȝt for he wolde & loued pouert by-cause of hitsilf"; "Oure Lord Ihesus neuer beggide wilfulliche" "Crist neuer tauȝt wilfulliche to begge"; "Oure Lord Ihesus tauȝte þat no man schuld wilfulliche begge" (*Defensio Curatorum*, pp. 39–40).
23. Addressing the friars' professed emulation of Christ's poverty, FitzRalph argues in Book VI of *De Pauperie Salvatoris* that Christ and the apostles renounced civil lordship but retained original dominion entitling them to the common possession of necessary goods. See Russell Oliver Brock, "An Edition of Richard FitzRalph's *De Pauperie Salvatoris*: Books V, VI, and VII," diss., University of Colorado, 1953.
24. Langland's description of Hunger's "healing" effects on idlers and wasters puts Taylor's perception of Christ in an interesting perspective. After everyone begins working on the half-acre "for fere of Hunger," Langland explains that "Blynde and broke-legged [Hunger] botened a thousand / And lame men he lechede with longes of bestes," *Piers Plowman: the C-text*, ed. Derek Pearshall (Exeter: University of Exeter Press, 1994), VIII, 189–92.
25. Taylor's emphasis on the laity's commercial obligations also corresponds with what Aers sees as Wyclif's own prioritization of secular business and power. See "John Wyclif's Understanding of Christian Discipleship," in *Faith Ethics and Church: Writing in England 1360–1409* (Cambridge: D.S. Brewer, 2000), pp. 130–48 [119–48].
26. See, for instance, Jesus' command in Luke 6:30, "Give to everyone that asketh thee: and of him that taketh away thy goods, ask them not again" (Douay Bible). John Chrysostom also determined, "In hospitalitate autem non est habendus delectus personarum, sed indifferenter quibuscumque sufficimus hospitales nos exhibere debemus." [In hospitality there ought not to be discrimination between people, but we must act hospitably without difference to any one however we can.] *Decretum* D. 42 *dictum post* C.I. This passage and the accompanying translation are quoted in Rubin, *Charity and Community*, p. 68.
27. In an extreme denunciation of selective almsgiving, the Carmelite friar argues ". . . curiosa perscrutatio et discussio in hac materia est non solum peremptoria, immo diabolica. . ." [. . . painstaking inquisitiveness and consideration in this business is not only deadly—on the contrary, it is diabolical. . .] ("Protectorium Pauperis," ed. Arnold Williams, *Carmelus* 5 [1958]: 141 [132–80]).
28. Scase discusses the importance of this passage in the late medieval poverty conflicts in *Piers Plowman and the New Anticlericalism*, pp. 63–64.
29. Aston notes that this biblical interpretation was not only a "focus" for Wyclif, but also a *locus classicus* for the Lollards more generally. See " 'Caim's Castles,' " p. 49.
30. Taylor writes: "But 'Poore men', Crist seiþ 'alwey shulen we haue wiþ us', for ellis riche men shulden be bareyn. . . not hauynge whom þei shulde

releeue wiþ to moche abundaunce and superfluytee of her goodis" (17/537–40).

31. Of course it is often difficult to get a precise sense of the relationship between the church and lay society in Wycliffite thought. Some Lollards such as Hawisia Moone claimed "every man and woman beyng in good lyf oute of synne is as gode prest and hath as much poer of God in al thynges as ony prest ordred" (Hudson, *Selections from English Wycliffite Writings,* p. 35/57–61). From statements like Moone's it is not clear how the church and the clergy itself would be distinct from the community at large and the "priesthood of all believers." Taylor's sermon, however, works against such accounts and presents the church as a discrete institution that is separate from (and indeed subservient to) the lay population. This vision of the church is similar to Wyclif's rigorous split between the Christian laity and clerics, who alone must follow strict evangelical precepts. See Aers, "Christian Discipleship," pp. 130–48.

CHAPTER 4

THE NAKED AND THE DEAD: THE CARPENTERS' COMPANY AND LAY SPIRITUALITY IN LATE MEDIEVAL ENGLAND

Mark Addison Amos

> The imagined and enacted cultural identity of the Carpenters' Company melds rational self-interest and altruism to offer its communal body as a hedge against bodily and ghostly deprivations. This essay maps this middling economic guild's dynamic, complex, and often self-contradictory negotiations among its social aspirations, collective identity, and artisanal and religious interests as it confects disciplinary parameters of fellowship, sympathy, charity, and cooperation.

> An Haberdasshere and a Carpenter,
> A Webbe, a Dyere, and a Tapycer—
> And they were clothed alle in o lyveree
> Of a solemne and a greet fraternitee.[1]
>
> —The Canterbury Tales

It is suggestive that perhaps the most distinctive feature of the five guildsmen on pilgrimage in Chaucer's *Canterbury Tales* is their lack of distinction: telling no tales and figured in none of the poem's links, they remain unindividuated, existing only as members of a "greet fraternitee," a parish guild which itself remains unnamed.[2] Though their wives seek to be "ycleped 'madame' " and the naive narrator declares each "shaply for to been an alderman," civic records offer scant evidence to support that hopeful assessment for members of such middling guilds. In the poem, their individual craft brotherhood remains unremarked-upon, and the guildsmen are distinguished only by their fine dress—"Ful fress and newe hir geere apiked was"—and fine accouterment, attire more appropriate for a guild dinner than a pious pilgrimage. Yet in these few lines Chaucer figures the negotiation of several interests central to guild life in the later Middle Ages: social aspirations, collective identity, and artisanal and religious affiliations.

Guildsmen such as Chaucer's five were common in the later Middle Ages, for the guild structure pervaded the nation: Gervase Rosser estimates upwards of 30,000 guilds in the country.[3] Within the three general categories of guilds—craft, parish, and merchant—individual guilds encompassed a range of memberships and forms, their variety interrogating and, at times, invalidating those broad categories. The provenance and power of particular guilds varied similarly, from local craft guilds exerting little authority beyond the practitioners in their immediate locale to parish guilds wielding great political power in their communities, to powerful international merchant guilds influencing English national economic policies. The purposes and meanings of these guilds were distributed along a similar spectrum, concentrating their efforts on social, religious, political, or economic goals. Furthermore, even this acknowledgment of variations is insufficient to describe the range, for guilds ought properly be understood as dynamic structures that were formed and dissolved, split or combined, shaped and reshaped to anticipate and respond to altering private and collective concerns.[4] Still, unifying the variety of interests is the omnipresence of an ostensibly religious purpose.

While the authenticity and symbolic function of guilds' religious missions is open to historical debate,[5] it is less disputable that guilds mediated powerfully between the individual and the overarching institutions of city and church, and that their institutional weighing of the political, economic, and spiritual interests behind that mediation—a negotiation averred by the relative ambiguity of Chaucer's guildsmen's spiritual and occupational goals—was a profoundly self-conscious process. This is particularly true for the occupational guilds,[6] which—negotiating among civic, fraternal, and economic paradigms—used a variety of discursive media to define and legislate the lay spirituality of their members. This essay seeks to map the interplay between the religious systems of a craft guild and its economic and professional interests by examining the imagined and enacted cultural protocols of the Carpenters' Company,[7] a collective whose records and activities exemplify the complex and often self-contradictory processing of these elements into disciplinary parameters of fellowship, sympathy, charity, and cooperation. In large part it is the economic paradigm that drives this entire process, as investments in capital and labor appreciate and generate the profits of disposable monies and leisure time, which enable a craft guild's active participation in civic ceremonials and charitable works, as well as enable its cultivation of the sacral and spiritual well being of its members. Examining its participation in the economies of charity highlights an analogous melding of rational self-interest and altruism underlying the guild's institutional identity: corporate charitable outreach assumes the possibility of the donor's own individual misfortune; and guild membership itself is conceived as a hedge against deprivations both material and spiritual, bodily and ghostly.

Founded as early as 1271, recording ordinances by 1333, and incorporated in 1477, the Carpenters were a long-lived but vulnerable guild. Doubtless one constraint on their success was the nature of the craft itself: as a small-scale, mobile craft requiring only easily available and affordable tools, the Carpenters suffered from outside competition. (Even, and perhaps, especially, during periods of high building activities that should have enriched their coffers, they faced an influx of foreign workers, "forrens," and were likely to suffer impressment for Crown building projects.) Unrecognized by their peers, unlikely to hold important civic office—despite the readiness of Chaucer's Guildsmen's wives and his naive narrator for such an occurrence—unsuccessful in their petitions and litigations, and unremarkable in their finances and charity,[8] the Carpenters, given their doggedly middling status, are particularly useful subjects for understanding the mediating function of lay, corporate piety in constructing religious attitudes, both those in the guild structure and those in London itself.

Like parish guilds and most other occupational guilds, the religiosity of the Carpenters was orthodox in theology and conservative in practice. Their public enactments of lay religiosity included donating to their parish and supporting its clergy,[9] celebrating their patron saint's feast day,[10] attending mass, and maintaining lights, a commitment central enough to their purpose that guild fines could be paid either in money or in wax. Another organizing set of concerns was the institutional enactment of the church's corporal acts of mercy, especially as envisioned by Henry VII:

> And forasmuch as we inwardly consider that the seven works of Charity and Mercy be most profitable, due, and necessary, for the salvation of man's soul, and that the same seven works stand most commonly in six of them, that is to say, in visiting the sick, ministering meat and drink and clothing to the needy, lodging of the miserable poor, and burying of the dead bodies of Christian people.[11]

Organized in ways analogous to the church, the Carpenters' Company enacted a regulatory and paternalistic charity toward its members and its neighbors, and, until the Reformation, actively supported the theology of purgatory and the efficacy of prayers for the dead. Yet even given this range of traditional social activities we should not understand the Carpenters, or occupational guilds in general, as 'traditional institutions' in Weber's sense—that is, as institutions drawing their authority from the past.[12] Though accountable to both church and the civic order, the guilds were subservient to neither: their control was local, self-contracted, and—in many matters—consensual. Further, these externally directed activities of the guild offered internal benefits. Ultimately the guild's attempts to manage (urban) alienation and anonomie necessarily involve it in sophisticated forms of identity making.

The Carpenters emphasized their company's effective status as a unitary, legal entity constituted by voluntary contract through statutes, and, most significantly, through oath taking. Those seeking to be recognized as freemen in the Carpenters' Company would present themselves before the Master and Wardens and swear to obey the "rules and ordinances and all other rules and ordinances concernyng the said crafte," a set of organizing principles, customs and mores, which contributed to the solidarity and promotion of the group and the self.[13] To emphasize the solemnity of the guild's mutual rights and obligations, such incorporating practices are ritualized: at every level of promotion within a guild, a brother would swear anew his fealty to the fraternity. Though crucial in solemnifying a member's loyalty to the group and to its tenets—and thereby important to establishing the social, economic, fraternal, and spiritual elements of a guild identity—a guild's interest in sacralizing this process was not necessarily a wise pragmatic strategy relative to the outside world, for it threatened to put them at odds with both church and civil authorities: ecclesiastical authorities objected to the non-Christian elements of guild rites and saw the danger of perjury in swearing loyalty to a secular group; secular rulers accused guildsmen of sworn conspiracy. (This hegemonic unease with sworn oaths of allegiance lingers throughout the Middle Ages: a fifteenth-century example from the *Great Chronicle of London* describing guild rioters expresses the fear of false allegiance behind the statement that "eythir of theym was sworn unto othir, That noon of theym shuld dyscovyr othyrs Counsayll."[14]) Thus the hegemonic powers recognized that while most guild statutes offered a reassuring emphasis on their encouragement of positive civic virtues to support the common good, a guild's interest in solidarity and horizontal interdependence was inherently self-directed.

In its most potent form, attained in the later Middle Ages, the guild was nothing less than the central context through which its members defined, understood and lived their lives. Economic corporations in particular held virtually absolute jurisdiction over their members' livelihood: dictating daily schedules, prices, pay, interests, contracts, working conditions, and the acceptance and training of apprentices. Perhaps even more interesting, though, is the process, noted by Otto Gierke and Emile Durkheim, by which these specific controls helped define the collective and even moral consciousness of the members.[15] These influences extended beyond these boundaries into many other aspects of their members' lives: regulating attendance at mass, prescribing civic participation, mandating group dining, and controlling a variety of other activities. It is not surprising that guild statutes sought to forfend the perception of the group as based on unregulated self-interest and instead emphasized its status as a fellowship in which members worked together for the common good. But beyond this—in a way that went well beyond each guild's obvious need to curry favor with church and civil authorities—the brotherhood itself was conceived *as* a moral agent: the duties of the Master and the Wardens as delineated in the ordinances of 1487 included meeting weekly "for to have convercacion as well for the support and continuance of the good rules and ordering of the said crafte as for the reformation repressyng and punyshment of Rebellious or Mysdoers agenst the same Rules and ordering of any of them."[16] The other side of punishing the rebellious is rewarding the deserving. The only notable exception to the responsibilities to extend charity and fellowship to a fellow member is if the member himself is guilty of moral failure: expulsion is prescribed for any member who "became of evil name."[17] The company thereby assures both itself and the civic authorities that its members will fulfill their moral function and contribute to the common good, thus guaranteeing the moral nature of the entire guild.

Not only did the Carpenters join many guilds in setting watches and "ridyng ayenst" the sovereign—providing persons, cloth, banners, barges, and food whenever the king or another important figure visited London—they engaged in civic activities more specifically involving their craft: they filled the posts of the Office of the King's Carpenter and Surveyor of the King's Works, and, as noted above, were subject to impressment for royal building projects. For the Carpenters in particular the mutual self-conceptions as visible good citizen and internally sanctioning unit were doubly crucial, for much of their sense of civic responsibility was derived not from principled abstractions but from the regular practice of their craft. Most significantly, from as early as 1271 the Carpenters and the Masons formed the Office of City Viewers, a post which carried with it the responsibility "to make just consideration concerning the boundaries of Lands, ruined and divisible walls & gutters, and other matters touching their office in the city & suburbs of London, whensoever they shall be required.[18] Technical and metaphoric conceptions of responsibility are jostling in this language, and over time there appears a yet more burdened sense of moral responsibility—along with a stronger impulse toward self-promotion—in the brotherhood's ordinances. Empowered in their ordinance of 1455 to "make search in all places within the limits" of London, this already-wide claim is presented in their 1607 ordinance as ensuring that "neither the King's majesty, nor any his loving subjects be not deceived nor endangered through evil workmanship or insufficient building."[19]

Similar ordinances demonstrate that the Carpenters' moral language was not restricted to statements of Christian belief and charity, as they argue that these "evil" workmen act "of their inordinate covetous mindes for their owne private profitt to the great hurt and destruccion of the comonwealth," "abuseing the comonwealth with their defective & false measured timber."[20] Warrants from the Recorder of London issued against those so charged echo this language as they define the accused, who are "refractory and refuse to obey the orders and ordinances of the said Company [the Carpenters], and stand out in contempt of government, contrary to the lawdable custome of the Citty of London aforesaid; to the evill example of others in the like kinde offending, and against the publique peace."[21] Unsurprisingly, the Carpenters are imagined as standing on the other side of this bipolar presentation, intervening "for the generall good of the comonwelth."[22] Such morally charged language is unarguably formulaic; however, its rhetoric emphasizes the vital, practical nature of the Carpenters' civic role as it simultaneously assigns a transcendent purpose to their service to the city and to the practice of the craft itself. Such an overlaying of common civic utility with a moral doctrine defines the craft of Carpentry itself as a specific moral good.

The contrasting of the evil scofflaws with the honesty of the masters imbues the Carpenters' professional judgment with God's moral judgment, conflating vastly different concepts of justice. Fittingly, those fines collected in the completion of the Carpenters' service to the common good were themselves divided between the guild itself and the common good, with half going to the guild and half to the common fund of the city. Linked to the authority of God, the guild and the civic authorities legitimize each other and suggest that, like the antiphonal call-and-response of the liturgy, the condemnation of corrupting and self-serving influences is a bilateral and workaday concern.

Thus the Carpenters' code prompts some expansion of sociological formulations on guild objectives, from two directions. Gervase Rosser argues that the main thrust of such moral thinking and language—a defining aspect of guild membership—is the consolidation of an honorable group identity from which one can draw the respectable individual reputation necessary to secure loans, establish accounts, and generally to break into an occupational field: group credibility translates to individual credit, on a very practical and fiscal level.[23] To be sure, the Carpenters' language establishes them as a collective of honest men whose work can be trusted.[24] Yet such language also needs to be read in the wider context of belief that enables highly symbolic, and even quasi-typological, justifications of the craft itself.[25] The series of four paintings discovered in the Carpenters' London guildhall—of Noah building the Ark, of King Josiah ordering the repair of the Temple, of Joseph engaged in carpentry while Jesus collects wood chips in a basket, and of the young Jesus teaching in the temple, with the caption "Is not this the carpenter's son"[26]—clearly encourages a sense of pride that not only draws from an occupationally based understanding of sacred text and liturgy, but flows back into that understanding.

By the same token, whereas scholars such as Unwin see the impetus of a guild's religious purpose as primarily directed toward worshipping their saint, the interpretation and practical expression of that abstract purpose, for the Carpenters at least, was far more complex. Through its oaths, its social fellowship, and its religious activities, the company defined its communality as centered on the *substantive* good of mutual support—in life and in death—and it sought to inculcate a sense of group identity based on members' concrete contributions to the health of the collective. The many recorded cases of intraguild squabbling notwithstanding, the Carpenters' documents and activities show them to have consciously defined themselves in accord with a communitarian philosophy—envisioning and enacting the politics of the common weal, in ways consonant with the model of community as body.[27] This is given expression most directly in the company's repeated commitments to the care of sick members and to the spiritual well being of deceased members: two modes of attending to the health of the corporate body. More subtly, even as these ordinances worked to define the guild itself from above, they also defined its more mundane, regulatory functions, extending the model of the corporate body to the custodianship and disciplining of its members' bodies and conflating the notions of physical, spiritual, and economic health.

Alford and Barker characterize the Carpenters' earliest ordinance as "almost solely concerned with the provision of charitable aid to members for the fellowship,"[28] emphasizing the seriousness with which the guild took its communitarian responsibilities. We can see this emphasis in the specificity of that first ordinance's language: here the Carpenters pledge to "pay to the helping of sick men which that fall in [to] disease, as by falling down of an house or hurting of any eye or other divers sicknesses, twelve pence by the year." Besides work-related injury, the statute extends to general illness: should any fellow carpenter fall into poverty through sickness, "he shall have. . .Fourteen pence a week during this poverty, after he hath lain sick for a fortnight."[29] The logic of contingency extends even further: should the collective's funds prove inadequate to cover these expenses, individual brothers would be called to aid through an extra collection, revealing the intertwining of physical and economic health and of individual and collective responsibility. But this principle goes beyond mere financing to a concern with the literal body that is allied with the commodification of labor in the later Middle Ages, for a sick member cannot participate in the economic structure which defines the guilds. Like the crippled bodies forbidden by statute from joining guilds, an ill body is a non-participatory, and thus an unprofitable, body, and it is the guild's responsibility to care for that body and bring it—along with the larger corporate body of which it is a member—back into physical and economic health.

The reach of the Carpenters' resolution to address the economic health of their corporate body extends far beyond the mere pragmatism noted by Alford and Baker. The Carpenters' documented commitment to extramural as well as intramural charity bespeaks the guild's deep and abiding concern with the needy in their greater society. Their financial outlay on such enterprises was exceeded only by their expenses for fellowship at table (activities, as we see here, often combined).

Through thick and thin, the Carpenters maintained their needy fellows throughout the Middle Ages and beyond the early modern period: they drew from their general funds to feed the poor, to establish almshouses, and to educate poor students at Oxford and Cambridge—usually the sons of Carpenters, but occasionally children unrelated to the guild—and, in the seventeenth century, to found a hospital. Such corporal acts of mercy proceed from a sense of scripturally mandated distributive justice rather than from a 'progressive' economic model of reducing or eliminating poverty: guild policy assumes that the sum of all worldly goods is finite, limited, and already known, and emphasizes the redistribution of that sum for the common good.[30] Throughout, their records indicate the Carpenters' consistent and determined dedication to charitable causes: they increased their contributions when profits allowed—during one period of plenty increasing the meals they provided for the poor fourfold[31]—and resisted diminishing their largesse even in sustained economic downturns, trimming them as a last resort, and then only incrementally.[32] The interanimation of financing the guild structure and the guild structure's financing the needy is made explicit in their dedicating half of the payment for fines for refusal to serve in a high office to the poor;[33] this transference makes clear that, as with goods seized during the Carpenters' inspections, these disciplinary ordinances seek materially to maintain the moral and economic orders.

As I suggested above, the Carpenters supported not only brothers who became destitute but also the poor of their larger community, deploying their profits to support a variety of humanitarian causes outside their ranks, even seeking out methods of aiding their fellow man. In one exemplary instance, by taking up an extra collection when a particularly harsh winter threatened the needy, and in another, by redirecting their donations for Elizabeth I's poor laws in response to their perception of the greatest need.[34] That feasting was itself one of the forms their charity took is unsurprising given the centrality of the feast to a guild's identity[35]: Jupp and Pocock note that at times half of the Carpenters' annual outlay was for feasting, with charitable expenses a consistent second.[36] In parish guilds it was common to integrate the feast of the patron saint with corporate charitable acts by inviting some number of the general poor to the feast and then donating the leftovers.[37] In the Carpenters' guild we see both this activity and its reverse, for each time its leadership went out to investigate their poorhouses and almshouses and the property that generated the income to support these charities, arrangements were made for a feast at these sites,[38] with the fare for such feasts ranging from sumptuous to spartan depending on the current finances of the Carpenters. This combination of internal fellowship and communing with a broader brotherhood must have appealed to them on a symbolic level.

The consonance between the charitable acts of the fraternity and its individual Carpenters—who at times shaped the entire guild's giving in important ways—is apparent from the narratives of specific donors, and demonstrates the interweaving of collective and individual identities. Frequently, bequests charged the guild's leaders with managing and overseeing lands producing wealth to be donated. For example, Robert Wyatt, thrice Master of the Carpenters, donated land stipulating that its rents would support thirteen poor women; in his will he left a fortune, £500, for building almshouses for ten men from differing parishes. He instructed his executors to choose the first set of men, but entrusted the governors of the Carpenters to select them thereafter. Just as testators provided wages for priests and other funereal services, Wyatt provided for the expenses to cover the annual visit from the governors. Unfortunately the revenues produced by these properties did not keep pace with expenses, and so the guild became responsible for making up the difference. For a time the maintenance of these almsmen represented the greatest expense of the guild[39] (the fact that these men were not of the guild makes such ongoing altruism more remarkable). Wyatt's wife later augmented the bequest to provide the almsmen with new coats every three years, and, in an interesting application of generosity and thriftiness, also provided a small stipend so the almsmen could expand their wardrobes by converting their discarded coats into waistcoats.

In 1650, another Carpenter, Mr. Reads, bequeathed leaseholds to a free school "for distribution among poor housekeepers," and offered his "messuages and tenements in Naked boy Alley in the parish of St. Olaves Southwark...to the Masters Wardens and Cominalty of the Mistery of freemen of the Carpentry of the City of London and their successors." Reads' intent is that the leadership will "out of the rents, issues, and profits thereof pay and perform [his] several legacies and bequests," distributing "ten shillings each and a dinner to ten poore godly men or women yearly being freemen or freemen's widows of the said company"; he also gives freemen's widows an annual gift for gloves or "dinner or a supper at their election for their care and pains." Additionally, he leaves money for a "godly poor schollar" and for a school "to teach all boys of the said parish to read write & cipher and the girls there to read."[40] This will defines the guild's role in negotiating the translation of the testator's individual economic capital into cultural and communitarian capital: from the profits on his land, Reads provides for the care of the poor and the widowed and supports scholars young and old. Reads is careful to compensate those responsible—the company's clerk and its beadle—for their work in executing his charitable contributions.

The relationship between guilds and the urban poor was not as straightforward as the simple redistribution of wealth suggests. Although the poor were restricted from joining guilds by the labor statutes of 1388 and 1406, each iteration of financial protections offered in the Carpenters' ordinances bespeaks the fear that a brother might become poor while a member of the guild. Similarly, each charitable act supporting the poor served as a reminder of the threat that members of the guild themselves might fall victim to the same forces. Although it might seem that only the lowliest of guildsmen would be vulnerable to such a threat, the documentary record validates a widespread anxiety about downward mobility as a threat to the corporate body. In 1460, William Goldington received payments from the common fund "in hys sykenes"; only a few yers later he is elected as one of the guild Wardens, a position requiring a good deal of capital. The fact that even a wealthy member could be economically endangered by bodily sickness marks the distance between wealth and poverty as all too easily traversed.

Thus, despite the medieval church's official theology praising the poor and marking poverty as a site for spiritual richness, such theological praise of poverty is overmatched by its economic undesirability and the energy dedicated to mollifying its deprivations. Although it is important to mark the difference between guildsmen and the poor, that distinction is, as we've seen, at best one of degree rather than kind. The guilds' distributive paradigm assumes that there exists a set of people who live in permanent poverty and, furthermore, that some of these working poor are active members of the guild. The ramifications of this situation are played out in ritual scripts, as, for example, the one mandated by the city for the participatory spectacle of King Henry VII's funeral. The mayor ordered guild fellowships, including the Carpenters, to provide four members "clothed in black gownes to the calfe of the legge, with narowe typetts, on horseback, ayenst the recyving of the corps of the right noble and excellent prince King Henry the vijth late kyng of Yngland into this citie. . .to stand and garnysshe in suche place as by the surveyers therfore assigned shalbe appointed," an unsurprising request given each guild's responsibility to participate in and support civic, especially royal, functions. As the king's body passes, the bodies of the guildsmen, garbed all alike, signify their position as workers and as members of the guild and the civic corporate bodies.

However, the guildsmen do not function as simple symbols of incorporation. Each guild is also commanded: "in lyke manner ye prepare (viij) poure men to be clothed in White gownes and howdes with Torches; And eury of them to have a payer of beds (beads) in his hand."[41] Here the poor signify the contested nature of poverty. Side by side with the other guildsmen they pay homage on behalf of their guild and their city, yet they are marked as both within the guild and without it, clothed as members of the corporate body but clothed distinctly. As the poor provide the opportunity for guilds to engage in corporate acts of charity, these poor bodies are themselves pressed into service as representations of those charitable acts, thereby signifying their support of the system that ensures their poverty: the poor are required to embody the spiritual benefits of poverty touted by the church on a theological level as they simultaneously figure their place on the margins of the economic system. Thus, strung out along the streets of London, the poor are made to figure at once as the object of the guilds' charitable activities and as the permanent threat that guildsmen might find themselves changing the color of their costumes in this theater of poverty.

Ritual convocations such as these also served purposes beyond the symbolic interests of the state and its political and economic necessities, and reflected motivations located within the guild. Seeking unity and control, guild hierarchies required attendance both at public events that affected the company's standing in the community, and also at many events located wholly within the corporation. The frequent social and religious activities engaged in by each guild's members—meetings, feasting, drinking, attending mass, supporting civic functions—forged links between its members and bound these individuals into a community with shared interests, and responsibilities beyond the professional and economic. Missing any of these ceremonies without excuse was considered a violation, and punishments ranged from fines for early infractions to imprisonment for repeated ones.

The voluntary and self-selecting nature of the guild is emphasized in ordinances, which require unanimous consent for entry and for a number of other guild actions. Though seen as essential to the communalist nature of the guild, common consent was no doubt honored more in the statutes than in the guildhall. One feature of this common consent widespread among guilds is the provision for an internal legal system, and the insistence that a member present himself to his guild court before venturing forth seeking other legal remedies. The guild's court would appoint "daysmen" to investigate and arbitrate intraguild disputes. Such a system not only shutters internal problems from the public eye (and courts) to better present a unified and peaceable image of the guild to the city, but also keeps guildsmen from incurring the often-weighty costs of prosecuting or defending a case in the courts of the realm. While it is striking that such broad juridical powers are relegated to the guilds, what is even more significant is that the agents of this legal oversight, the master and the wardens, are granted their authority only by ordinances and the consent of the fellowship as a whole. Less altruistically, these broad juridical powers argue that the guild is the seat of just power and arbitration.

Civic and guild regulations make it clear that the guild leadership had long had the power to fine and even imprison members for violating either guild regulations or professional codes of ethics. Abuses garnering punishment include "disobedience and vsing gaming," "pprophaning the Lords Sabboath," "coming home late and breaking...windows with Stones, abvsing the neighbours with bad behaviour, and with many other misdemeanours."[42] Order is maintained by disciplining the recalcitrant until they become pliable, or removing them from the corporate body entirely. The company's interest in imposing order and regulating the bodies of its members does not stop when those bodies die; in point of fact, the guild is as much interested in its dead brothers as in its living.

Nowhere do the elements of (external) charity and (internal) regulation interact more compellingly than in the guilds' death statutes. Guilds invested a good deal of financial and personnel resources in caring for their dead. The earliest ordinance of the Carpenters pledges to bury a needy member, even if fulfilling this obligation requires the guild to travel: "if any brother or sister die honest death out of London the distance of twelve miles, and he have naught whereof to be buried of his own, then shall the Wardens of the Brotherhood wend thither and bury him at the common cost of the Brotherhood."[43] The death benefits bestowed by a guild were a significant perquisite for all members, not merely for the destitute. Just as wealthy individuals provided for elaborate funeral ceremonies and anniversary masses to ease their suffering in the afterlife, guilds took an active role in these rites of purgatorial theology: all manner of guilds required of their membership attendance at their fellows' funerals, ensuring that each deceased brother would receive a sufficient number of mourners praying for his soul at his death, and again at anniversary masses and beadrolls guaranteeing the deceased's ongoing inclusion in prayers.[44] Individual members of the fellowship could provide the capital to fund such exchanges, hiring the services of the spiritual agents and investing in the presence of poor prayers or, if particularly wealthy, they could endow a fund to provide such services in perpetuity.

Reading the *Calendar of Wills*, Unwin notes that testators shifted the agents they entrusted to execute their obits properly: "Down to the middle of the 15th century, however, the wardens of crafts were most usually named, if at all, in the second place, to act in case others failed to do so. After that date it became increasingly common to entrust them with the duty in the first instance."[45] Dated 1477, the will of Thomas Warham, former Master of the Carpenters' Company, offers a view into the elaborate preparations required by those with the wealth and desire to provide for themselves a thorough funeral service. He stipulates that the "maister, wardeyns, and comynaltee" gather in the church "to be made solemply, devoutly and distinctly the Anniusary by note for my sowle, the sowles of my father, my mother, my kyndrede, frendes, and benefactours and all cristen sowles," designating the cloth and tapers to be displayed.[46] He arranges for masses in the evening and in the morning, and prescribes prayers for the churchmen to "devoutly and distinctly syng placebo and dirige with lawdes and full. . .In the customary way. . . .Syngyng thre this Response, libera me due, with other prayers for people passed to God in such caas vsed; and also sey this psalme De profundis with versicles and orisons for my sowle and the sowles afoseid." The Carpenters' responsibilities for the care and maintenance of Warham's soul are never-ending, for his will also provides for an anniversary mass "in tyme to come for euermore." Only after nearly a century, when parliament claimed all such payments for the crown, did the Carpenters cease their spiritual ministrations for their brother Warham.

Thus it makes sense that purgatorial and lay 'work' theology come together in the guild's requiring attendance at commemorative masses. The multi-day celebration of the Carpenter's feast day—a ritualistic and defining event for any guild—centered on a "dyner of the fealship of the said Crafte [to] be holde and kept by the hoole fealship." The Carpenters also displayed their corporate body within the wider community by attending masses *en masse*: "the Master Wardeyns and the fealship of the said Crafte assemble togider at the said halle in their livery of gowns and hoods and so conveniently goo to-gider to the said masse and at the same masses offre after their devotions." As the Carpenters earned for their deceased members remission from punishments, they then extended the profits generated by those communal prayers beyond the narrow community of the company in widening circles: the 1486 ordinance provides the next day for another mass "To be saide for the soules of all the Brethern Sistern Benefactors and ffrends of the said Crafte that been dede and all Xtian Soules." These procedures at the same time reiterated the disciplining process of their regulations and extended the commodification of prayers inherent in late-medieval purgatorial theology to a commodification of the fellowships members themselves, for the economy of guild funerals required them to embody their prayers for the deceased through their attendance. Missing the death rites of "obytt derege & masse" garnered stiff penalties, and remiss brothers were threatened with expulsion,[47] making explicit the exchange among sins and prayers, monies and brothers. The commemoration ends with a reintegration of the corporate body of the guild: "after the Masses so doone for to returne and come agiders to their said halle there takyng such repast as for them shalbe ordeigned by the said Master and Wardeyns of the said Crafte for the time being."[48] Although the Reformation suppressed and finally eliminated public articulations of the efficacy of prayers for the dead, brothers' funerals remained important to the Carpenters through the time of the Great Fire,[49] for, as was evident from the ordinance of two centuries earlier, there had always been more to a funeral than the outlawed 'superstitious' activities. Mixed in nature in a way similar to the tales told by Chaucer's pilgrims on their way to Canterbury, these funereal activities combine solemn commemoration and festive celebration, and mingle religious observance with social fraternity, altruism with self-interest.

Absent from Chaucer's presentation of his underdefined guildsmen, as the poet must have been aware, is a sense of moderate, institutional mediation where hard-nosed pragmatism is leavened by lay theology (and vice versa). Though such negotiations are pointed to by the ostentatious dress of the unnamed guildsmen of the *General Prologue*, by the Reeve's past as a carpenter and current dress, and by John the Carpenter's superstitious and incomplete understanding of biblical history in "The Miller's Tale," they may border on the literarily 'unrepresentable'. Only by plumbing the interplay of personal and institutional 'history', as narrativized in civic and guild documentary records, can we limn these dynamic crosscurrents. In the examination of the Carpenters company I hope to have shown that we need to move beyond a model that reads this melding of spiritual and secular interests only in terms of the economic and sociological sense it makes; we should also pay attention to the lived and imagined lives of these guildsmen on their own terms and examine the elaborate steps taken to develop a plausible lay theology through symbolic strategies revealed in discursive praxes such as bylaws, ordinance, civic statutes, and public spectacle.

In the Carpenters' guild, religious statutes and behaviors constitute and insist upon images of structures of work and modes of living requisite to a communitarian society, defining a common good located in the recognition of brotherhood and extending beyond economic viability to the support of the weak, both living and dead. In its documents the Carpenters—and the many similar guilds—tout ideals analogous to what Adam Smith describes as the perfection of human nature, which, he argues, demands that one move far beyond self-interest. However, as we've seen, the Carpenters have defined their own self-interests—both corporate and individual—as including the necessity of articulating sympathy through acts of benevolence and altruism.[50] As the Carpenters company seeks to impose order on the living and the dead, it expends its profits to participate in the economy of charitable redistribution—mending and maintaining its members and the poor of the larger community—and supports the economy of penitential theology—trading prayers for remission of punishment. Through this strategy guilds such as the Carpenters extend those economies outward in widening spheres of influence, offering their members the ability to channel individual economic elements toward individual salvation (through participation in the fellowship), to channel corporate economic elements toward corporate salvation (through obits and masses), and to channel craft economic elements toward civic salvation (through supporting the common weal).

In an economic world where scarcity at all times threatened perdition, the religious and social underpinnings of these occupational guilds not only provided the opportunity to ensure against one's own suffering and to succor others so victimized, but also offered a protocol for directing idealism and a longing for service through a collective, and mapped out a theological justification for one's work, one's craft, one's contribution to society writ both large and small. Such an affirmative theological judgment about craft activities allows guildsmen to develop a plausible theology of the lay world and a theology of work,[51] a system of signification that enables them to draw a clear connection between the guild's economic activities and its civic and spiritual responsibility. Without such a plausible theology of the benefits of secular work, the only choice for remaining in good faith is to opt out of an evil economic system—the apostolic direction taken by St. Francis in the beginning of the thirteenth century—or to agitate actively against it.

## Notes

1. *The Canterbury Tales*, in *The Riverside Chaucer*, ed. Larry D. Benson (Oxford: Oxford University Press, 1987), I (A) 361–64.
2. Britton J. Harwood argues that the shared guild of Chaucer's guildsmen must have been a parish guild in "The 'Fraternitee' of Chaucer's Guildsmen," *Review of English Studies* 39 (1988): 413–17. Carl Lindahl finds that the

Canterbury pilgrims form a fellowship similar to a late medieval parish guild in *Earnest Games: Folkloric Patterns in the Canterbury Tales* (Bloomington: Indiana University Press, 1987). David Wallace has recently modified this assertion, arguing that the pilgrims represent not only the personnel of such a guild but that, as a collective, they embody the affinities expressed in a parish guild in *Chaucerian Polity: Absolutist Lineages and Associational Forms in England and Italy* (Stanford: Stanford University Press, 1997).

3. Gervase Rosser, "Going to the Fraternity Feast: Commensality and Social Relations in Late Medieval England," *Journal of British Studies* 33 (1994): 431 [430–46]. Rosser bases his calculations on an estimate of 8,000 or 9,000 parishes in England, a figure consonant with that of Peter Heath's earlier study, *The English Parish Clergy on the Eve of the Reformation* (London: Routledge & Kegan Paul, 1969), p. 8.

4. For four among many excellent studies of the political influence of parish guilds, see Miri Rubin, *Charity and Community in Medieval Cambridge* (Cambridge: Cambridge University Press, 1987), esp. pp. 250–59; Gervase Rosser, *Medieval Westminster: 1100–1540* (Oxford: Clarendon Press, 1989), pp. 281–314; and Ben R. McRee, "Religious Guilds and Civic Order: The Case of Norwich in the Late Middle Ages," *Speculum* 67 (1992): 69–97. Studies of merchant guilds and their influence frequently locate themselves in relation to E.M. Carus-Wilson, *Medieval Merchant Venturers* (London: Methuen & Company, Limited, 1954; reprint, 1967); and Sylvia Thrupp, *The Merchant Class of Medieval London* (Ann Arbor: University of Michigan Press, 1948; reprint, with new introduction, 1962).

5. The seriousness and vigor with which individual guilds approached and enacted their religious purpose were as varied as the other elements of their identities: historians have alternately argued that these religious interests were merely vestiges of earlier, 'true' brotherhoods, that they were overshadowed in the pursuit of economic advantage, or that they served as a cynical symbolic apology for corporate self-interests. Sylvia Thrupp, "The Guilds," in *Cambridge Economic History, vol. 3, Economic Organization and Policies in the Middle Ages* (Cambridge: Cambridge University Press, 1963), argues that the guilds'"traditions of corporate charity and piety further attest that they were once genuine communities within the larger community, with a social and religious character transcending mere economic interest and struggle for power" (p. 230 [230–80]). George Unwin, *The Guilds and Companies of London*, 1908; fourth edition, with new intro. William F. Kahl (Watford: Frank Cass & Co. Ltd., 1963), declares: "The truth is that religious devotion had never supplied the primary motive for the establishment or maintenance of the craft guild. At first it may have the most prominent of the subsidiary motives, but in course of time as the social and charitable activities developed, it lost this relative position" (p. 202).

6. Gervase Rosser finds a strong correlation between crafts and their guilds by the time of the composition of the *Canterbury Tales*: "by the late fourteenth century there were few organized crafts which lacked a corresponding fraternity"; "Crafts, Guilds and Work in the Medieval Town," *Past and Present* 154 (1997): 21 [3–31].

7. The two most thorough studies of the records of the Carpenters' Company to date, and the ones I draw upon here, are Edward Basil Jupp's *Historical Account of the Worshipful Company of Carpenters* (London: William Pickering, 1848; second edition and supplement with W. Willmer Pocock [London: Pickering & Chatto, 1887]); and B.W.E. Alford and T.C. Barker's *A History of the Carpenters Company* (London: George Allen and Unwin, 1968).
8. Alford and Barker, *A History of the Carpenters Company*, note that when the Corporation drew up a list of the forty-seven trades and crafts in London, "the Carpenters were not important enough to be included among them"—though lesser guilds were—and in a similar list in 1488, Carpenters rank forty-eighth out of seventy (p. 19).
9. The Carpenters supported their local clergy, moving from compensating a priest for presiding at specific gatherings such as a mass or a dinner to providing an annual wage for a chaplain of their own. Unlike some favored parish guilds—and even a few occupational guilds—the Carpenters had no 'ghostly treasure' such as remissions, indulgences, or pardons with which to entice and reward members.
10. The Carpenters' patron saint cannot be definitively determined, but it seems likely that it was the Blessed Virgin Mary, both from their earliest ordinance book's dedication to her and to her son, from her marriage to a Carpenter (Jupp and Pocock, *Historical Account of the Worshipful Company of Carpenters*, p. 19), and from the fact that Mary is the patron of almost one-third of all guilds; see Barbara Hanawalt, "Keepers of the Lights: Late Medieval English Parish Guilds," *Journal of Medieval and Renaissance Studies* 14 (1984): 26 [21–37].
11. Henry VII's will, as quoted in Jupp and Pocock, *Historical Account of the Worshipful Company of Carpenters*, footnote to p. 44.
12. Max Weber, *The Theory of Social and Economic Organization*, trans. A. M. Henderson and Talcott Parsons (New York: Free Press, 1957), defines a 'traditional' authoritative structure as one in which "legitimacy is claimed for it and believed in on the basis that the sanctity of the order and the attendant powers of control as they have been handed down from the past 'have always existed' " (p. 341).
13. Unwin sees all guilds as privatized, self-defining and regulating institutions founded on religious underpinnings, with loyalties confirmed by oath and centering on the immediate grouping, p. 92. The paradigms undergirding Unwin's views have been examined by Julia Stapleton in "English Pluralism as Cultural Definition: The Social and Political Thought of George Unwin," *Journal of the History of Ideas* 52 (1991): 665–84.
14. *The Great Chronicle of London*, ed. A.H. Thomas and I.D. Thornley (London: George W. Jones, 1938), p. 348.
15. Antony Black and, more recently, David Wallace treat the unambiguously positive interpretations Gierke and Durkheim offer of the functions of guilds. For Antony Black, see *Guilds and Civil Society in European Political Thought from the Twelfth Century to the Present* (Ithaca, NY: Cornell University Press, 1984), esp. pp. 223–36. For Wallace, see esp. pp. 76–79.
16. Jupp and Pocock, *Historical Account of the Worshipful Company of Carpenters*, p. 347.

17. Quoted in Alford and Barker, *A History of the Carpenters Company*, p. 17; abbreviations within medieval documents silently expanded.
18. Quoted in Jupp and Pocock, *A Historical Account of the Worshipful Company of Carpenters*, p. 186.
19. Quoted in Jupp and Pocock, *A Historical Account of the Worshipful Company of Carpenters*, p. 149.
20. Quoted in Jupp and Pocock, *A Historical Account of the Worshipful Company of Carpenters*, p. 156.
21. Quoted in Jupp and Pocock, *A Historical Account of the Worshipful Company of Carpenters*, p. 157.
22. Quoted in Jupp and Pocock, *A Historical Account of the Worshipful Company of Carpenters*, p. 152.
23. Gervase Rosser has argued that establishing a personal reputation is the focus of the moral language of the guilds in "Crafts, Guilds and Work," esp. pp. 10–11.
24. For a discussion of the function of books of manners in constructing just such a collective and respected identity, see Mark Addison Amos, " 'For maners make man': Bourdieu, de Certeau, and the Common Appropriation of Noble Manners in *The Book of Courtesy*," in *Medieval Conduct*, ed. Kathleen Ashley and Robert L. A. Clark (Minneapolis, MN: University of Minnesota Press, 2001), pp. 23–48.
25. Jacques Le Goff discusses such attempts to validate and elevate a 'theology of labor', and specifically notes its presence within John of Salisbury's image of the organic (body) conception of society in *Time, Work, and Culture in the Middle Ages*, trans. Arthur Goldhammer (Chicago: University of Chicago Press, 1980), pp. 114–16.
26. Jupp and Pocock discuss these paintings, and provide images of them, *Historical Account of the Worshipful Company of Carpenters*, pp. 235–42.
27. One of the most influential medieval expressions of this communitarian philosophy, and especially of its figuration as the body of a living creature, is in John of Salisbury's *Policraticus*, completed in 1159. See *Ioannis Saresberiensis Episcopi Carnotensis Policratici*, ed. Clemens C.I. Webb, 2 vols. (Frankfurt: Minerva, 1965). English-language readers may see a masterful translation in *Policraticus*, ed. and trans. Cary J. Nederman (Cambridge: Cambridge University Press, 1990).
28. Alford and Barker, *A History of the Carpenters Company*, p. 16.
29. Quoted in Alford and Barker, *A History of the Carpenters Company*, pp. 16, 17.
30. The relationship between work and the receipt of alms is explored extensively in Michel Mollat, *The Poor in the Middle Ages: An Essay in Social History*, trans. Arthur Goldhammer (New Haven, CT: Yale University Press, 1986).
31. Alford and Barker, *A History of the Carpenters Company*, p. 132.
32. An example of their increases appears in the orderbook entry for August 31, 1626–27: "It is likewise ordered that the sam poores pencon(ers) being at this tyme $x^d$ to each weekly, shallbe augmented and increased to $xx^d$ a

weeke to each one soe long as the Rents for that purpose hold out" (cited in Jupp and Pocock, *A Historical Account of the Worshipful Company of Carpenters*, p. 257). In 1743, a long period of unprofitability for the company caused them to cut back on their works of charity, but these cuts took the form of returning to levels of giving prescribed in their bylaws: eliminating gifts beyond those, and decreasing their education funds, rather than their habitual giving.

33. Summarized in Jupp and Pocock, *A Historical Account of the Worshipful Company of Carpenters*, p. 522.
34. Jupp and Pocock, *A Historical Account of the Worshipful Company of Carpenters*, pp. 127, 473.
35. Gervase Rosser sees the fraternity feast as itself a way for fraternity members of whatever degree to reclaim a moral authority officially denied to them by the canons of the church ("Going to the Feast," p. 433).
36. Jupp and Pocock, *A Historical Account of the Worshipful Company of Carpenters*, pp. 326, 535.
37. For examples, see H.F. Westlake, *The Parish Guilds of Medieval England* (London, New York: Macmillan Company, 1919), pp. 34, 160–62.
38. Jupp and Pocock record a letter in which the Masters of the Carpenters ask their agents to "provide a Dinner as usuall & a good Dish of ffish for the Gentlemen when they came down...To provide as usuall on the Company's going down to Visitt their Almshouses," *A Historical Account of the Worshipful Company of Carpenters* (p. 260).
39. Quoted in Alford and Barker, *A History of the Carpenters Company*, pp. 103–104.
40. Quoted in Jupp and Pocock, *A Historical Account of the Worshipful Company of Carpenters*, pp. 468–69.
41. Jupp, *A Historical Account of the Worshipful Company of Carpenters*, p. 45 n.
42. Collected and quoted in Jupp and Pocock, p. 158. The Carpenters' records also describe a number of instances where guildsmen were "commytted to ward," imprisoned, for offences as minor as missing an "Obyt Masse." While the offenders had been warned, Jupp and Pocock argue, "the explanation seems to be that neglect and small offences were often disregarded, until they grew to such a head that they could be borne with no longer" (pp. 380–81).
43. Quoted in Alford and Barker, *A History of the Carpenters Company*, pp. 16–17. Reading the *Calendar of Wills*, Unwin notes: "As the fraternities of the crafts gained a more assured corporate existence they began to compete with the rectors and churchwardens for this position of trusteeship," noting that after the mid-point of the fifteenth century, "it became increasingly common to entrust them with the duty in the first instance" (pp. 203–204).
44. Joelle Rollo-Koster clarifies that the bede roll served as a commemorative for the dead rather than as an administrative list; see "Death and the Fraternity: A Short Study on the Dead in Late Medieval Confraternities," *Confraternitas* 9 (1998): 3–12. A useful study focusing on England in particular is Virginia Bainbridge, *Guilds in the Medieval Countryside: Social and Religious*

*Changes in Cambridgeshire, 1350–1558* (Woodbrige: Boydell and Brewer, 1996).

45. Unwin, pp. 203–204. The varied and exacting payments specified in Warham's will, discussed above, provide further evidence of the commodified exchange among spiritual services and religious participants, prayers and bodies.
46. Warham's will is quoted in Jupp and Pocock, *A Historical Account of the Worshipful Company of Carpenters*, pp. 26–29. The *Plea and Memoranda Rolls* of London record numerous instances of similarly elaborate funerals.
47. Quoted in Jupp and Pocock, *A Historical Account of the Worshipful Company of Carpenters*, p. 384. Other examples of services the Carpenters provided their dead brothers discussed below.
48. Quoted in Jupp and Pocock, *A Historical Account of the Worshipful Company of Carpenters*, pp. 344–45.
49. The Carpenters' continuance of 'semi-public funerals' is noted in Jupp and Pocock, *A Historical Account of the Worshipful Company of Carpenters*, pp. 539–40.
50. Adam Smith, *The Theory of Moral Sentiments* (Oxford: Clarendon Press, 1976), pt. 3, ch. 1. Irving Kristol disagrees, arguing that the pursuit of self-interest was always tempered by natural, self-correcting limits; see "Adam Smith and the Spirit of Capitalism," in *The Great Ideas Today 1976* (Chicago: Encyclopedia Britannica, 1976), p. 289.
51. Max Weber discusses the impact of the Reformation on issues of work and asceticism in *The Protestant Ethic* (Allen and Unwin, 1930; rpt. London; New York: Routledge, 2001).

PART 3

LABOR AND THE LAW

# CHAPTER 5

# RECONSTRUCTING ENGLISH LABOR LAWS: A MEDIEVAL PERSPECTIVE

*Anthony Musson*

> As a means toward understanding the genesis of the English labor laws, this paper assesses the attitudes behind and arising from their enforcement in the later Middle Ages. It emphasizes that in spite of national legislation and governmental enforcement, many individuals initiated suits and sought private law remedies. It also highlights how problems of labor were acknowledged and accomodated both formally within the legal system and through more informal methods of dispute resolution.

The first national labor laws in England were not a by-product of industrialisation, but a governmental response to the economic and demographic disaster brought about by the first wave of plagues that hit England in 1348.[1] The Statute of Laborers of 1351 (and its precursor, the Ordinance of Laborers of 1349), therefore, provides an obvious starting point for anyone wishing to construct a picture of the regulations governing employment in medieval England. The statutory provisions dictated the terms of service, wage rates, the formation of agreements, restrictions on the hiring of workers and proscribed penalties for non-observance.[2] A variety of occupations were encompassed by the scope of the legislation, shopkeepers and artisans as well as agricultural laborers and domestic servants. Even stipendiary clergy were placed under the interdict in 1362.[3] Promulgated in parliament, the labor laws represented a coordinated response at the national level to what might be called the "problem of labor" that emerged in social, economic, religious, and intellectual arenas in the wake of the Black Death.[4]

The setting and impact of the labor legislation has received much academic attention. The context in which it emerged and the extent to which there was a preexisting crisis in the economy of the early fourteenth century has been the subject of considerable debate.[5] The prime focus of discussion, however, has centered on the effect of the labor laws. Since there were clear efforts made at enforcing the various provisions, historians have tried to assess the necessary judicial and administrative changes,[6] measure the success of the policy on capping wages,[7] and take stock of the legislation's social impact.[8] As a means of understanding the genesis of the legislation and the reasons for the measures taken in subsequent years it is equally important to try and perceive the attitudes of all parties, be it royal government, employers, or employees.[9] To accomplish this it is necessary to look both at the people involved in forming and administering the provisions of the statutes and at the way that the problems of labor emerging in the later fourteenth century were acknowledged and accommodated both formally within the legal system and through more informal methods of dispute resolution.

The Ordinance and Statute of Laborers was the royal government's response to the immediate difficulties in labor relations perceived to stem from the demographic shortage arising out of the outbreak of plague.[10] Such was the perceived dangerousness of the conditions, the provisions of the Ordinance of 1349 were not in fact deliberated in parliament, as it was presumably felt to be inadvisable for representatives to meet. The onus for its formulation, therefore, fell on the king's council and in particular the royal judges and senior serjeants-at-law who, as members of the council, had responsibility for advising upon and drafting legislation. Given the need for a swift reaction it is likely that they turned to precedents with which they (and workers) were already familiar. In towns and cities there were already measures in place restricting prices and trading practices,[11] while village by-laws governing agricultural labor, particularly at harvest time, were in existence throughout the country.[12] The remarkable similarity between the provisions of the Ordinance and existing local regulations suggests that the framers were thus drawing upon their working knowledge of these models.[13] The Statute of Laborers issued two years later following the parliament of 1351 consolidated and extended the measures contained in the Ordinance, but was again primarily inspired by the lawyers on the king's council.[14] Unlike much other legislation of the period, the mid-fourteenth century labor laws did not derive from detailed petitions from the Commons.[15] Indeed, the regulation of labor was on the agenda set in Chief Justice Shareshull's opening speech to the assembly and thus preempted the petitioning process.[16] The labor laws were clearly a political priority, one underpinned by legal opinion, though it was far from clear in that first decade that the legislation itself would be permanent.[17]

Significantly, in producing parliamentary legislation the government was trying to impose a national framework of regulation. The legal and political impulse to control working practices at a national level was not confined to the period of the first outbreak of the Black Death. A further thirty pieces of legislation were drafted or adopted as law in the century after June 1349. Indeed, as Given-Wilson has indicated, there was a preoccupation with labor issues to the extent that "more than a third of the seventy-seven parliaments held between 1351 and 1420 passed legislation relating to labor, and further acts were passed in the mid-1440s and again in the 1490s."[18] While these initiatives were obviously influenced to an extent by successive outbreaks of plague (occurring, for instance, in the years 1361–62, 1368–69, 1371, and 1375) the numerous statutes confirming, modifying or extending the initial measures show how the desire to legislate nationally on economic and labor-related issues gained impetus during the later fourteenth and early fifteenth centuries. The medium for formulating control, parliamentary legislation, embodies the extent to which the later statutes represent (and were themselves the product of) not only new initiatives, but also dialogue and disagreements within parliament over the scope and direction of labor law. The confirmation of provisions and the frequent issue of labor legislation does not, however, signify that these measures were necessarily a failure or wholly inadequate. In fact they point toward labor law as being a live concern, one being constantly debated, and to the shifting attitudes among the governing classes.[19] While the provisions may have derived from norms and practices adopted by communities of their own free will, when enshrined in statutory language arguably they took on a different form. When proclaimed in the market place and other public places, the statutes and ordinances (especially their preambles) set a particular tone and agenda. Couched in hyperbolic rhetoric with criminal allusions (referring, for example, to "the malice of servants" and laborers "giving themselves to idleness and vice, and sometimes to theft and other abominations") the royal government drew on the psychological power of words as a means of reinforcing its desire for control.[20]

The shift in direct control of working practices from being purely within seigneurial and civic cognizance to being within the purview of royal government not only rationalized them, but in many ways altered the focus and broadened the scope of their enforcement. In the first instance, following the Ordinance of Laborers, royal commissions with responsibility for the upholding of its provisions were issued to the justices of the peace, the agents increasingly at the forefront of the local administration of justice.[21] This policy was continued briefly after the Statute of Laborers was promulgated, when a new set of peace commissions was issued,[22] but thereafter in the decade, the task was ostensibly separated from the duties of the justices of the peace and entrusted to special commissioners of laborers.[23] It would appear that in terms of the administration of justice, the need to enforce the mid-fourteenth-century labor legislation led to a brief period of experimentation as to how this should be achieved with attempts to ascertain the personnel best entrusted with the task. In reality, while there was clearly some experimentation, the issuing of two sets of commissions should not be regarded as a significant divergence in policy: the parallel commissions covered complementary areas of jurisdiction.[24] Not only were the commissions to enforce the Statute of Laborers issued on the same day as, and thus in tandem with, those for holding peace sessions, but also there was a marked overlap of personnel.[25]

At first blush, the commissioners of laborers were in most counties identifiable as the justices of the peace merely without the "quorum" provided by the assize justices. For example, the commission concerning the Statute of Laborers for the county of Essex issued on June 3, 1353 included the same persons (with the exception of Henry Green and William Notton, justices of assize) as the commission of the peace of the same date. Similarly, the nine members of the commission for laborers in the West Riding of Yorkshire sent out on July 8, 1353 duplicated that of the peace commission of the same date with the exception of the assize justices (Basset, Fencotes, and Seaton) and the substitution of William Plumpton for Master William Fenton.[26] The issue was a practical one: it was unnecessary for the assize justices to be present as there were a considerable number of what amounted to trivial cases. There was no need for the determining of felonies and thus the requirement for the "quorum" (mandatory in peace sessions) did not apply. The assize justices could continue with their other tasks (hearing land pleas and trying prisoners accused of criminal offences) unhindered by having to attend all trials concerned with breach of the labor laws, which in some counties spread over as many as ten days at a time.[27] Interestingly, it is observable that by and large (as far as it is possible to tell from the surviving records) there was a considerable degree of variance over the dates when labor sessions were held.[28] In the decade following its promulgation in many counties, therefore, the periods for holding peace (and labor) sessions designated in 1351 by the Statute of Laborers were largely ignored.[29]

When the standing commissions were withdrawn in 1359, the justices of the peace resumed their role in enforcing the labor laws in an *ad hoc* fashion until their specific inclusion in the legislation and commissions of 1361–62.[30] Permanent jurisdiction was confirmed in 1368.[31] Their responsibility for the labor legislation was paralleled by the inclusion within their purview of measures intended to regulate trade and the economy. Enforcement of the standard weights and measures, which was included within the purview of the justices of labor,[32] was formally added to the peace commissions in 1361 and went hand in hand with the power to hear cases of forestalling (i.e., traders selling goods before the appropriate market hour) included in 1364. The administration of the chapters of the labor legislation was therefore part of a wider concern for rationalizing the work of *ad hoc* commissions and entrusting economic-related offences to judicial tribunals operating at shire level.[33]

The commissions to justices of laborers added another tier, but did not substantially alter the mechanisms for dealing with economic regulation and labor-related cases. Even though the sessions held under royal commissions were the intended forum for enforcement of the labor laws,[34] the central courts of common pleas and King's Bench entertained numerous actions arising under the labor statutes. The latter in particular heard labor-related cases when it periodically visited the shires as occurred, for example, during sessions held at Bury St. Edmunds and Thetford in 1379.[35] Indeed, the cases coming before the highest courts in the land from the 1360s to the end of the fourteenth century were such that they gave rise to at least thirty-eight points of law (judging from cases included in Fitzherbert's "Grand Abridgement").[36] Similarly, the local courts (both manorial and borough) had previously (after the Ordinance and Statute of Laborers) continued to play an important part in dealing with such litigation. As Clark's research found, "By the mid-fourteenth century labor disputes [we]re no longer exceptional among the general run of lawsuits in local courts." Although the manorial court rolls she examined rarely mention the statute itself, there are many examples relating to the contract clause and the payment of wages, while the preponderance of labor-related cases in towns were for breach of covenant or "trespass against the statute."[37] Various types of court within the legal hierarchy, therefore, exercised concurrent jurisdiction over the labor laws. The vitality of the local courts in the later fourteenth and fifteenth centuries indicates that the national labor legislation was not a purely centralizing phenomenon. Elements of private justice still pertained and the law continued to receive definition from below (from the customs and practices in the localities) as well as from above (in the rulings of royal justices).

Given this eclectic field, was there in administrative terms an essential difference in the type of personnel enforcing the labor legislation at the different jurisdictional levels, and following its "nationalisation"? Historians have highlighted the role played by the justices of the peace in this respect, arguing that in jurisdictional terms the policy adopted by the Crown in the decade or so following the plague (at its first appearance in 1348–49 and once the implications of its return in 1362 and 1368 had been felt) signaled a watershed in their development. It brought government recognition of their importance within the hierarchy of the legal system and at the same time (it has been argued) enabled them to exert control over the lower classes through their presidency of the peace (and labor) sessions.[38] The Crown's apparent embrace of the desire espoused by the parliamentary Commons for inclusion in the charmed judicial ambit and the rather sinister implications of their dual position as justices of labor and as landowners (with vested interests within the urban and rural communities) should not, however, be overdrawn.[39]

An examination of the personnel of the commissions to justices of the peace and of laborers reveals continuities in the type of person hearing labor-related cases and overlaps among the different areas of jurisdiction in terms of the personnel acting as justices within the hierarchy of courts. In other words, through personnel there remained links between what was happening at the manorial or town level and the county, and between the localities and the central courts. A number of the justices of the peace and justices of laborers were also stewards of lords and so had responsibility for the administration of their estates (which included presiding over the lord's courts).[40] John Coningsby, for example, justice of the peace and justice of laborers for Warwickshire was steward to John de Peyto at Stratford upon Avon in the 1350s.[41] John Roches, his counterpart in Wiltshire, was variously steward of the abbot of Malmesbury, Roger Beauchamp's local steward at Devizes and William la Zouche of Harringworth's steward at Calne in Wiltshire.[42] Special commissions of laborers were issued for various towns (such as Coventry, Scarborough, Retford and Kingston-upon-Hull), whose members (as in the case of Walter Whitwebbe, mayor of Coventry) held official civic positions.[43] Where there was no specific commission for a town, the county panel of justices sometimes included a civic representative, as in the case of William Horewode, mayor of Cambridge.[44] Magnates, such as Thomas Beauchamp, earl of Warwick, and Richard FitzAlan, earl of Arundel, were occasionally commissioned for certain (single) counties, providing political and social weight to a panel.[45] Ecclesiastical landowners were also represented on the commissions. Walter at Bergh was steward of the bishop of Salisbury and a member of the panel of commissioners for Wiltshire,[46] while John Sparry, who sat as a justice of laborers in Warwickshire, was steward of the abbot of Stoneleigh.[47]

The fact the people who presided as justices of laborers (and justices of the peace) were themselves part of the elite or representatives of landowners does not mean that we should automatically assume that they enforced the law solely in their own personal or class interests. As had become familiar from a range of *ad hoc* judicial commissions, it was assumed and intended that the king's justices in the localities should represent the upper levels of county society and be selected from those who already bore the brunt of government in the provinces. The inclusion of members of the gentry in peace commissions was certainly not designed specifically for the purpose of oppressing the lower orders. Moreover, there is evidence from Wiltshire that the bulk of the work at labor sessions was carried out in advance by deputies of the justices, presumably of a slightly lower social standing.[48] While we should be careful not to idealize the integrity of medieval justice, it should be remembered that the vast majority of people who came before the justices of the peace were men and women of low status whose business was uncontentious to the political elite. In the case of the labor laws it is true that the employer (usually bringing the case) was normally of higher social status than the employee (the defendant). But even here, however, the idea of blatant class conflict being worked out through litigation tends to be undermined by the fact that a significant body of employers seeking redress under the Statute of Laborers were themselves of peasant status. As a parliamentary petition of 1368 indicated, it was lesser landholders and employers (including many leaseholders within the upper ranks of the peasantry) who really encountered problems in securing and retaining household servants and agricultural laborers.[49]

Moreover, it should not be imagined that the labor sessions were totally devoid of input from central court justices. The extent of the Crown's (or central court lawyers') involvement in the labor commissions has largely been overlooked. In addition to the supervision afforded by the itinerant court of king's bench in the 1350s,[50] a number of royal judges and serjeants-at-law (some of them newly created),—men who adjudicated on or acted as legal counsel in trials involving labor issues in the courts of common pleas and king's bench, were in fact appointed to these commissions. Some assize justices were included in the commissions for their circuit,[51] some were appointed to counties outside their circuit.[52] Royal justices such as Robert Sadington and Robert Teye received commissions, as also did existing serjeants such as Peter Richmond, Hugh Sadlingstanes and serjeants of the future, John Cavendish and Thomas Moriz.[53] John Claymond, William Fifhide, William Finchdean, Nicholas Gower, Thomas Ingleby, John Knyvet and Illard Usflet, called to the order in 1354, were all named on commissions of laborers for various counties in 1354.[54] While it is difficult to ascertain the degree to which they actually acted since few records of sessions exist,[55] their inclusion suggests that the government was signaling that the enforcement of the Statute of Laborers was being taken seriously even if participation by central court judges was in reality necessarily limited.

The integration of the labor commissions into the overall plan for the administration of justice and their close association with the peace commissions during the 1350s is important to remember. Equally, the supervision of sessions by central court lawyers ensured (where possible) that consistency and equanimity were not overlooked. The paucity of surviving records of sessions held under the commissions to justices of laborers (and later peace sessions) means it is not possible to get a countrywide view of the efficiency of the statute's enforcement, though comparison of the length of sessions and the numbers of people appearing at them points toward some stark variations between the counties. This may reflect variations in the records themselves,[56] but also suggests the effectiveness of enforcement itself may have been relative to particular regions.[57] The Crown's tacit acknowledgment of the realities of local law enforcement can be seen in the fact that in 1390 the justices of the peace were empowered to fix wages according to the relative scarcity of labor within their localities (although apparently the concession was not applied with any regularity until the 1420s).[58]

The labor legislation offered an ongoing formal method of dealing with disputes concerning the workforce, but it does not provide the whole story, nor were the regulations the sole elements comprising English labor law. The Statutes of Laborers should be viewed in a wider context than is normally the case, as also should the ambit of rules governing employment and relations in the workplace. First, it is necessary to consider the limitations of the statutes and the legal ramifications and problems arising from their enforcement. Second, it is important to examine the wider spectrum of labor regulation in late medieval England and thus the "private" law elements that shaped labor disputes and the remedies that were available to parties. Third, we should be aware of the different jurisdictions that entertained cases involving work-related disputes and how this offered a wider choice to litigants than immediately envisaged by the statute or under the commissions of laborers. Fourth, attention should be given to the more informal methods of settling disputes and particularly to the private domain in which employment relations sometimes operated. Fifth and Last, an assessment should be made of some of the ideological facets of the labor legislation, especially its more sinister or paternalistic aspects with regard to exclusion and social control.

The limitations on the substantive regulations and the practicalities of administering the labor laws affected the nature and extent of their enforcement. The labor legislation covered a worker leaving employment before the period of his or her contract expired (without good cause) or not turning up at all once retained, but it appears that its ambit stretched only to periods of six months or greater (usually one year). Hiring for a shorter term, sometimes the case even with agricultural laborers, meant any breach was outside the scope of the statute and had to be pursued in the other courts. There was also the rather entertaining argument that chaplains owed their allegiance to a heavenly authority and were servants of God, rather than man.[59] The large number of defendants fined for taking excess wages, and the system introduced in the early 1350s to utilize the profits from sessions has given rise to the accusation that the justices were enforcing the penalties rather than the legislation. There was indeed an incentive to generate revenue, as during the first decade of the legislation the justices were allowed to collect wages from the profits of their sessions and (down to 1354) tax collectors were allowed to offset the burden of royal subsidies with the remainder.[60] Clearly also a number of employers were ignoring the legislation and ensuring a supply of labor for themselves and their estates by paying over the odds. The low pecuniary penalty was considered worth paying to secure service and labor, in turn suggesting the level at which it was set was not sufficient deterrent.

The practicalities of enforcement also served to undermine the effectiveness of the statutes. In addition to monetary fines, imprisonment was used as a punishment for recalcitrant laborers. Given the inadequacy of many jails for housing vast numbers of prisoners in terms of size and security conditions, it is unlikely that prison was a serious or long-term option for the justices.[61] The statute also required those outlawed at labor sessions to be branded on the forehead, though perhaps significantly there is no evidence that this punishment was ever ordered or indeed carried out.[62] In social terms the enforcement led to confrontations at the local level as a result of the stipulation that domestic servants and wage laborers make regular oaths before the constables and bailiffs of their vills obliging them to observe the legislation. The surviving records portray a culture of violent reaction to local law enforcement officers while they were trying to carry out their duties, whether it was arresting offenders or attempting to obtain oaths from laborers.[63] This in turn put the local officials in a difficult position, stretching their loyalties to king and community in different directions.[64] With the demands of the Statute of Laborers, the advent of poll taxes and searching judicial inquiries it is not surprising that many of the leaders of the peasant movements in 1381 were those who held authority as constables and bailiffs.[65] For whatever reasons, it is noticeable that the thousands of cases appearing in labor/peace sessions in the 1350s decreased significantly during the 1360s and 1370s to a mere trickle in the early fifteenth century.[66]

It is tempting to view medieval laws governing employment practices solely in terms of the labor legislation and its enforcement through the sessions of justices of laborers or justices of the peace. There were several actions available in the local courts and at common law, however, which could be brought by employers or employees in order to remedy problems arising out of contractual situations. Aside from covenant, which by the fourteenth century had declined in popularity as a remedy owing to its requirement for the formalities of a sealed written document, the action of debt together with the rapidly expanding categories of trespass were the main forms used in contractual contexts.[67] A debt action was available if the claim (usually for non-payment of wages) was for a specific sum of money. The plaintiff claiming non-payment for a job done (or indeed a job he or she was ready and willing to do) needed to show that the outstanding sum had been fixed in a contract, or could be extrapolated by reference to a contract, was settled by custom, or could be identified as the amount payable to laborers as set out in a regulation (either civic or guild) or as laid down in the Statute of Laborers.[68] The master/servant relationship was frequently explored, however, through the action of trespass, where interference with servants and the economic interests of the employer were usually in issue. The common law writ "per quod servitium amisit" governing the forcible abduction of servants gave an employer a right to sue (even though he was not the injured party) and remained an option in spite of the consolidation of this area under the Statute of Laborers. Although there was an apparent requirement for violence as the *vi et armis* (by force and arms) wording suggests, in fact the writ covered cases of enticement where the servant had not suffered any independent wrong. In some such cases it was claimed by the defendant that the servant had been found wandering and was not seemingly employed or that negotiations concerning employment had taken place between them.[69] Servants who left employment during the term of the contract had a good defence if they could show that they had been harshly treated, either through unreasonable corporal punishment or lack of provision of the necessities of life.[70]

Remedies for failure to honour obligations or satisfy customers were not provided under the Statute of Laborers. If an individual suffered loss as a result of negligent workmanship or some other form of contractual negligence by persons in a variety of occupations (doctors, lawyers, builders, carriers, shepherds, cloth-workers, and the like) and an undertaking had previously been given, it was possible to bring an action against them in what later became known as "assumpsit". In other words, the worker could be held liable if they had undertaken to perform the relevant task in a satisfactory manner, but had not exercised sufficient skill or care, carrying it out imprudently, incautiously, or carelessly or with the result that it did not turn out as envisaged under the contract.[71] Similarly, the action of trespass on the case could also be occupation based, but was generally used where, indirectly or as consequence of his or her actions, an individual's wrongdoing caused injury to someone else or damage to their property.[72] Although cases analogous to assumpsit and trespass on the case had appeared in the local courts prior to the Black Death,[73] the provision of special writs (and the acceptance of lawyers' arguments using technically non-admissible writs) added an extra dimension and enabled responsibility for the quality of work and services (and a higher level of damages) to be apportioned.[74]

The plea rolls do not suggest there was an overwhelming body of litigants suing on writs of assumpsit in the late fourteenth and early fifteenth centuries, but alongside the continued use of the local courts as a forum for such incidents and occasional cases involving "quality control" brought at peace sessions, they represent a further body of "private" law complementing, but existing outside of the framework of national legislation embodied in the Statute of Laborers.[75] The extent to which problems surrounding employment or service became the subject of litigation at all social levels and thus helped to shape labor law can be seen in the cases coming into the court of chancery in the fifteenth century. Johanna Rawe, for example, petitioned the chancellor that he might grant a writ of *corpus cum causa* so that the reason for her arrest upon an action of trespass brought by her sometime employer John Holme of London, mercer, could be aired in chancery and "right and conscience" prevail. She rehearsed the nature of the contract between them (she having agreed to be his servant on a yearly contract for a certain salary) and alleged that she had received only meat and drink and not the wages as covenanted. Although he had forbidden her to leave his service, she eventually departed as she had not received any payment or any kind of reward.[76] William Gregory of London admitted that he had paid his servant Alice Shevnington "divers payments as much to her wages came to [16s per annum] and more above," but claimed that she had wilfully absented herself from his employ "divers and many days and weeks" and then brought a feigned action of debt against him in the Sheriffs' Court. He requested a writ of *certiorari* to remove the case to the chancellor's jurisdiction.[77] The chancery bills frequently claim that a "fayned playnt of trespass" has been made against the petitioner and wish their cause to be considered "before the king in his equity." While the court of chancery clearly offered the opportunity for laborers (such as William Maye)[78] and particularly women (such as Aleynor Jane, widow of the late William Jane)[79] to put their case at the highest levels without having the expense of going to the court of common pleas or king's bench, it is possible that these cases, essentially involving a breach of covenant, in fact represent a cunning procedural ploy to enable the case to be heard in the royal courts. In chancery, the normal common law requirement for documentary evidence of the covenant did not apply. If it could be rehearsed as part of (and leading directly to) a wider issue, the judgment would in fairness have to consider the situation existing under the contract.

Aside from the sort of control exercised by the royal courts, more informal systems or methods of enforcement existed at lower levels in the hierarchy. In towns and cities some form of regulation of labor was carried out through the wardmote system. Depending upon the size of the borough or city there might be several wards, which formed administrative districts. The jurors within these areas reported on the "articles of the wardmote" to a civic official (or alderman) by means of an indenture and were thus responsible for much of the grassroots opinion and day-to-day organization. The householders, who made up the juries, were expected to attend the wardmoot as also were all (male) residents of age, including the hired servants in the ward.[80] The "articles of the wardmote" for London in the early thirteenth century regulated the quality of building (so as to avoid risk of fire in the city) and there were also regulations concerning those working on buildings and their hired servants (a group that included masons, carpenters, daubers, tilers, and plasterers). The civic ordinances of the mid-fourteenth century in fact exceeded the requirements of the labor legislation in their regulation of wages and they were still in effect nearly seventy years later when around 1419 it was specifically stipulated that ward jurors were to investigate the payment of wages to craftsmen and laborers above the rates prescribed by "the Assize" and concerning bargains that were usurious.[81]

The ward system often overlapped with other forms of control or governance: not only with the most intimate grouping of the household, but with the bonds founded on master/servant, master craftsmen/apprentice and employer/employee relationships. Informal pressure towards compromise and conformity were employed behind the closed doors of the craft guild and the household. The Pepperers' Fraternity of St. Antonin, for example, placed pressure on members not to submit disputes against fellow members to a public court (unless a serious crime had been committed) and established their own private court within the trade, to which differences could be brought.[82] Guild ordinances regulated the hiring terms of servants and the payment of wages. While the content of the regulations may initially have followed existing royal legislation and had to be registered before the mayor and bailiffs of the town, the growing status of craft guilds and an increasing government flexibility allowing for delegation of the setting of wage-rates made for differences in the scope of guild ordinances. By the fifteenth century, fines for infringements of trading laws were shared between the civic authority and the craft.[83] The household, similarly, was a place where a master craftsman exercised control over the servants and apprentices (as well as his own children) under his roof. He may have regulated his laborers in an informal way and often had a moral responsibility for them as well as forestalling any behavior that might have led to accusations being brought in public courts.[84]

Labor regulations were not aimed solely at the adult population; children too came within the legal framework. It can be inferred from the tenor of various statutes, in other words what they were legislating against, that children under twelve years old were working on the land and then were taking up a trade or craft. Parents were also apparently putting their children into an apprenticeship of sorts or some form of urban-based occupation.[85] The salary paid to working children seems to have been collected by their parents and put toward the general family reserves. The parents remained liable for damage to the employer's property or for breach of contract if, for instance, they decided to return home before the end of the agreed term. The parents were, however, able to sue those employers who maltreated their children, either through lack of provision of proper food or harsh physical treatment. Sometimes the contractual relations were forged between members of the immediate family: fathers hired their own sons and daughters. Occasionally this relationship produced an overlap between the control usually exercised within the family and the demands of the law. In 1407, for example, a father brought a suit in the Nottingham Borough Court against his son, who he claimed had (in spite of his agreement of apprenticeship) absented himself from work one day during August, leaving around midday and not returning home until after dark. The boy admitted his wrongdoing and was ordered to pay 6d. in damages to his father. But the son was also adjudged to pay a further 20d. (at least a couple of days' wages) for offending against the Statute of Laborers. While resorting to the courts might seem a strange or rather drastic measure, it may well not have been the first time this had happened and the father was, therefore, perhaps trying to discipline his son or teach him a lesson. When it came to law suits, one of the advantages of fathers employing their own children appears to have lain in the way decisions were normally made in their favour, especially where their offspring had allegedly been enticed into another's employ.[86]

The labor laws of medieval England focused primarily on the contracts made between employers and employees and the nature of the obligations arising under those contracts. The labor legislation was thus in many ways a vehicle for controlling the employment of agricultural workers, servants, and those in other occupations (largely by economic means) and spawned a substantial volume of litigation that tested, remoulded, readjusted, or reinforced the traditional obligations and the nature of work relationships. If its enforcement was not a straightforward exploitation or oppression of the lower classes, since it impacted equally on employers of peasant status and heightened competition between trades and groups of workers, by the later fourteenth century it had nevertheless gained a sinister edge. The scope of the legislation issued during the late fourteenth and early fifteenth centuries broadened and part of its focus narrowed to concentrate on those who were landless, unemployed, or who preferred short-term contracts. The fear of vagrants and vagabonds, which had been implicit in the trailbaston commissions of the early fourteenth century, was magnified in legislation compelling them to find pledges for good behaviour and extended in its definition to include those who refused to serve a particular master. Even itinerant preachers were identified with migrant laborers in the fight against Lollardy (itself a term used to denote "idle layabouts").[87] Although often prosperous and fairly settled, journeymen were discouraged from forming households and excluded from guilds, creating an artifically constructed group of unattached workers existing outside of (in received wisdom) the stable world of the household. On the one hand, therefore, the legislation attacked the real poor and unconnected, but also those who were willing and able to work, whose life choice to assume a more mobile existence in turn became stigmatized in the culture of work and employment regulation.[88]

This chapter has tried to assess the attitudes behind, and arising from, the enforcement of labor legislation in the fourteenth and fifteenth centuries. Naturally it has focused to some extent on the Statute of Laborers and related royal commissions, but it has also stressed the multiplicity of employment practices across the whole social spectrum and the variety of legal remedies sought both within and outside the hierarchy of courts. The precursors at both local and national levels had an important bearing on the ideology of the laws, how they were conceived, and in turn how they were received. In presenting a holistic view of labor regulation, my study has sought to dispel the myth that this was an area essentially governed by nationally promulgated public law prosecuted by the Crown. In many ways it was in fact disputed and upheld through the working out of personal suits in the arena of private law. The choice of venue and the counter-suits brought in different fora suggests that issues concerning employment, as with other areas of the law, were vigorously disputed by ordinary people. In turn it demonstrates not only a willingness to use the framework offered by the courts, but also a consciousness of obligations and legal rights from which we at the safe distance of the twenty-first century can reconstruct a perspective on use and abuse of the medieval labor laws.

## Notes

1. W.M. Ormrod, "The Politics of Pestilence: Government in England after the Black Death," in *The Black Death in England*, ed. W.M. Ormrod and

P.G. Lindley (Stanford: Stanford University Press, 1996), pp. 155–57; R.C. Palmer, *English Law in the Age of the Black Death, 1348–1381. A Transformation of Governance and Law* (Chapel Hill, NC: University of North Carolina Press, 1993), pp. 14–17. The plague was a Europe-wide phenomenon and other states similarly issued ordinances regulating labor: R.S. Gottfried, *The Black Death* (London: Free Press, 1983), p. 95; J.N. Hillgarth, *The Spanish Kingdoms 1250–1516*, 2 vols. (Oxford: Oxford University Press, 1976–78), vol. 2, pp. 4–5.

2. 23 Edward III; 25 Edward III, st. 2 (*Statutes of the Realm [SR]*, 11 vols. (1810–28), vol. 1, pp. 307–308, 311–13).

3. B.H. Putnam, "Maximum Wage-Laws for Priests after the Black Death," *American Historical Review* 21 (1915–16): 12–32.

4. For an interdisciplinary consideration of some of the issues see the collection of papers in *The Problem of Labour in Fourteenth-Century England*, ed. J. Bothwell, P.J.P. Goldberg and W.M. Ormrod (Woodbridge: Boydell and Brewer, 2000).

5. For some recent views, see R.H. Britnell, *The Commercialisation of English Society, 1000–1500* (Cambridge, UK: Cambridge University Press, 1993); B.M.S. Campbell, ed., *Before the Black Death: Studies in the "Crisis" of the Early Fourteenth Century* (Manchester, 1991); C. Dyer, *Standards of Living in the Later Middle Ages, C. 1200–1520*, rev. edn. (Cambridge, UK: Cambridge University Press, 1998).

6. B.H. Putnam, *The Enforcement of the Statute of Labourers during the First Decade after the Black Death, 1349–59*, Columbia University Studies in History, Economics, and Public Law 32 (New York: Columbia University Press, 1908); Palmer, *English Law in the Age of the Black Death* (Chapel Hill, NC: University of North Carolina Press, 1993), pp. 23–24; A. Musson and W.M. Ormrod, *The Evolution of English Justice: Law Politics and Society in the Fourteenth Century* (Basingstoke: Macmillan, 1998), pp. 52–53, 90–96.

7. S.A.C. Penn and C. Dyer, "Wages and Earnings in Late Medieval England: Evidence from the Enforcement of the Labour Laws," *Economic History Review*, 2nd ser. 43 (1990): 356–76; J. Hatcher, "England in the Aftermath of the Black Death," *Past and Present* 144 (1994): 3–35.

8. L.R. Poos, "The Social Context of Statute of Labourers Enforcement," *Law and History Review* 1 (1983): 27–52; M.K. McIntosh, *Controlling Misbehaviour in England, 1370–1600* (Cambridge, UK: Cambridge University Press, 1998).

9. W.M. Ormrod, "The English Government and the Black Death of 1348–49," in *England in the Fourteenth Century: Proceedings of the 1985 Harlaxton Symposium*, ed. W.M. Ormrod (Woodbridge: Boydell Press, 1986), pp. 175–88; Ormrod, "Politics of Pestilence," pp. 147–67; C. Dyer, "Work Ethics in the Fourteenth Century," in *Problem of Labour*, ed. Bothwell, Goldberg, and Ormrod (York: University of York/York Medieval Press, 2000), pp. 21–41; S. Knight, "The Voice of Labour in Fourteenth-Century English Literature," in *Problem of Labour*, pp. 101–22.

10. Modern historical scholarship is circumspect about the extent of the economic crisis in the 1350s, suggesting that in fact it was in the 1370s, two

decades later (following harvest failures and further bouts of plague), that the economic and social problems began to bite. See A.R. Bridbury, "The Black Death," *Economic History Review*, 2nd series 26 (1973): 577–92 and Hatcher, "Aftermath of the Black Death."

11. For example: *Calendar of Early Mayors' Court Rolls, 1298–1307*, ed. A.H. Thomas (Cambridge, UK: Cambridge University Press, 1924), pp. 59–64; M. Kowaleski, *Local Markets and Regional Trade in Medieval Exeter* (Cambridge, UK: Cambridge University Press, 1995), pp. 183–90; S. Rees-Jones, "York's Civic Administration, 1354–1464," in *The Government of Medieval York: Essays in Commemoration of the 1396 Royal Charter*, ed. S. Rees-Jones, Borthwick Studies in History, 3 (York: Borthwick Institute of Historical Research, 1997), pp. 126–27; Putnam, *Enforcement*, p. 156.

12. W.O. Ault, "Some Early Village By-laws," *English Historical Review* 45 (1930): 209, 211–12; W.O. Ault, "Open Field Husbandry," *Transactions of the American Philosophical Society*, n.s. 55 (1965).

13. For more detailed discussion see A. Musson, "New Labor Laws, New Remedies? Legal Reaction to the Black Death 'Crisis'," in *Fourteenth Century England I*, ed. N. Saul (Woodbridge: Boydell Press, 2000), pp. 75–79.

14. B.H. Putnam, "Chief Justice Shareshull and the Economic and Legal Codes of 1351–52," *University of Toronto Law Journal* 5 (1943–4): 251–81.

15. The only petition connected with the new Statute of Laborers simply recommended that the profits of the labor sessions be used to relieve the burden of a new direct tax, which was granted in that parliament (*Rotuli Parliamentorum, 1278–1503 [RP]*, 6 vols. [London, 1783–1832], vol. 2, p. 228).

16. B.H. Putnam, *The Place in Legal History of Sir William Shareshull* (Cambridge: Cambridge University Press, 1950), p. 54; Musson and Ormrod, *Evolution*, pp. 153–54. For Shareshull's speech to parliament see *RP*, vol. 2, p. 225.

17. Ormrod, "Politics of Pestilence," p. 156.

18. C. Given-Wilson, "The Problem of Labour in the Context of English Government, c. 1350–1450," in *Problem of Labour*, ed. Bothwell, Goldberg and Ormrod, p. 85.

19. Given-Wilson, "Problem of Labour," pp. 86–89.

20. J.A. Doig, "Political Propaganda and Royal Proclamations in Late Medieval England," *Historical Research* 71 (1998): 259–60; A. Musson, *Medieval Law in Context: The Growth of Legal Consciousness from Magna Carta to the Peasants' Revolt* (Manchester: Manchester University Press, 2001), pp. 225–30.

21. *Calendar of Patent Rolls [CPR] 1348–50*, pp. 526–27.

22. *CPR 1350–54*, pp. 85–91.

23. See for example commissions issued in 1353 and 1354 (*CPR 1350–54*, p. 451; *CPR 1354–58*, pp. 58–61).

24. E. Powell, "The Administration of Criminal Justice in Late-Medieval England: Peace Sessions and Assizes," in *The Political Context of Law*, ed. R. Eales and D. Sullivan (London: Hambledon Press, 1987), pp. 52, 56.

25. See for example: *CPR 1350–54*, pp. 449–52, 508–509; *CPR 1354–58*, pp. 58–62, 120–25.

26. *CPR 1350–54*, pp. 450–51.
27. See for example: Public Record Office [PRO], Justice Itinerant, Assize Rolls, Eyre Rolls, etc., JUST 1/125 mm4–5, 6–7, 7d–8 (Cornwall).
28. For example, sessions held in Herefordshire in November (JUST 1/313 m1d, 3d) and in Derbyshire and Cornwall in December (170 m3, 125 m4) outside the octave of Michaelmas (September 29–October 6) stipulated in the statute.
29. Musson, *Medieval Law in Context*, pp. 147–48.
30. *Some Sessions of the Peace in Lincolnshire, 1360–75*, ed. R. Sillem, Lincoln Record Society, 30 (Hereford: Lincoln Record Society, 1936), pp. xlv–xlvii; *Yorkshire Sessions of the Peace, 1361–64*, ed. B.H. Putnam, Yorkshire Archaeological Society Record Series, 100 (Leeds: Yorkshire Record Society, 1939), p. xiv; Powell, "Criminal Justice," pp. 52–53. The peace commissions of 1361–62 did not formally include the assize justices.
31. 42 Edward III c.6; *SR*, vol.1, p. 388.
32. JUST 1/1019 m3, 125 m1.
33. For some *ad hoc* commissions enforcing economic offences, see *CPR 1350–54*, pp. 332, 509 (forestalling), *CPR 1354–58*, p. 120 (forestalling), p. 121 (measures).
34. See the comment to this effect made during a judgment by Robert Thorpe in 1367 (Sir Anthony Fitzherbert, *La graunde abridgement. . .dernierment conferre avesque la copy escript, et per ceo correct* [London: Richard Tottell, 1565], vol. 1, fol. 89 pl. 30).
35. *Select Cases of Trespass from the King's Courts, 1307–1399*, ed. M.S. Arnold, Selden Society 100 (London: Selden Society, 1985), vol. 1, pp. xl, xliv (see footnotes for references); C. Dyer, *Everyday Life in Medieval England* (London: Hambledon Press, 1994), pp. 230–31. For the king's bench in the 1350s, see Putnam, "Shareshull and Economic Legal Codes," pp. 262–64.
36. Fitzherbert, *La graunde abridgement*, vol. 1, fols 87v–91r.
37. E. Clark, "Medieval Labor Law and English Local Courts," *American Journal of Legal History* 27 (1983): 332–37 (quotation at p. 335).
38. B.H. Putnam, "Transformation of the Keepers of the Peace into the Justices of the Peace, 1327–1380," *Transactions of the Royal Historical Society*, 4th ser. 12 (1329): 19–48; R.W. Kaeuper, *War, Justice and Public Order: England and France in the Later Middle Ages* (Oxford: Clarendon Press, 1988), pp. 174–83, 386–87; Palmer, *English Law*, pp. 9–27, 54–56; Ormrod, "Politics of Pestilence," p. 157.
39. Musson and Ormrod, *Evolution*, pp. 176, 178–80.
40. The references to stewards are gleaned from a perusal of the Gaol Delivery Rolls for the period 1350–75.
41. JUST 1/971 m3, 3d; PRO, Justices Itinerant, Gaol Delivery Rolls, JUST 3/140 m4.
42. JUST 1/1019 mm2, 3; JUST 3/147 m2, 151 m3d, 156 m5d.
43. *CPR 1354–58*, pp. 59, 60; JUST 3/140 m1.
44. *CPR 1350–54*, pp. 92, 508–509.
45. *CPR 1350–54*, p. 451 (Beauchamp—Worcs); *CPR 1343–58*, p. 59 (FitzAlan—Sussex). There are no rolls surviving that might have offered

evidence as to whether they actually sat as justices at the labor sessions. There is, however, a possibility that Beauchamp acted, as he is known to have done so in his capacity as a JP in the 1370s (JUST 3/166 mm7–8d, 10d, 12d).
46. JUST 3/147 m3d.
47. JUST 1/971 mm1–2d; JUST 3/140 m2.
48. See for example in 1352: JUST 1/1018 (printed in E.M. Thompson, "Offenders against the Statute of Laborers in Wiltshire, A.D. 1349," *Wiltshire Archaeological and Natural History Magazine* 33 [1903–1904]: 384–409) and 1355: PRO, Court of King's Bench, Ancient Indictments, KB 9/131.
49. *RP*, vol. 2, p. 296; Musson and Ormrod, *Evolution*, p. 95.
50. Putnam, *Shareshull*, pp. 72–73; Ormrod, "English Government and the Black Death," p. 179.
51. For example: *CPR 1354–58*, p. 62 (Shareshull, Burton, Stowford—Somerset; Basset, Seaton, Fencotes, Blakestone—York).
52. For example: *CPR 1354–58*, pp. 59–60 (Green—Northants; Notton—Yorks, Burton—Surrey).
53. *CPR 1354–58*, pp. 59–62, 125; *The Order of Serjeants at Law*, ed. J. H. Baker, Selden Society Supplementary Series 5 (London: Selden Society, 1984), pp. 156–57, 159. Moriz and Cavendish were called in 1362.
54. *CPR 1354–58*, pp. 59–62, 124–25: Knyvet (Northants), Claymond (Lincoln), Finchdean, Gower, Ingelby, and Usflet (East and West Ridings, Yorks), Fifhide (Sussex and Hants).
55. For example: JUST 1/731 (a commission to five men which includes assize justices Skipworth and Mowbray). The roll of presentments and indictments for Surrey 1351–52 includes the assize justice Richard Burton in the list of three presiding judges (JUST 1/907 mm1, 2). Future sergeant-at-law, Robert Belknap (called 1362), heard pleas concerning laborers within the liberty of Battle in 1351 (ibid., m5).
56. This includes what they were recording and for whose benefit.
57. Compare, for instance, sessions in Herefordshire (JUST 1/313) with those for Somerset (773).
58. 13 Richard II, st. 1, c.8; B.H. Putnam, *Proceedings before the Justices of the Peace in the Fourteenth and Fifteenth Centuries* (London: Spottiswoode, Ballantyne & Co. Ltd., 1938), pp. cviii–cix; Poos, "Social Context," p. 30.
59. D.J. Ibbetson, *A Historical Introduction to the Law of Obligations* (Oxford: Oxford University Press, 1999), p. 38; *Putnam, Enforcement*, pp. 187–89.
60. Ormrod, "English Government," p. 179.
61. R.B. Pugh, *Imprisonment in Medieval England* (Cambridge: Cambridge University Press, 1968), pp. 38–39, 169, 208–209, 366–67.
62. Putnam, *Yorkshire Sessions of the Peace*, p. xxvii.
63. *Sessions of the Peace for Bedfordshire, 1355–1359, 1363–1364*, ed. E.G. Kimball, Bedfordshire Historical Record Society, 48 (London: H.M.S.O., 1969), pp. 34, 47–48, 73–75; Poos, "Social Context," pp. 31–33.
64. For a more general discussion, see A. Musson, "Sub-keepers and Constables: the Role of Local Officials in Keeping the Peace in Fourteenth-Century England," *English Historical Review* 117 (2002): 1–24.

65. C. Dyer, "The Social and Economic Background to the Rural Revolt of 1381," in *The English Rising of 1381*, ed. R.H. Hilton and T. Aston (Cambridge: Cambridge University Press, 1984), pp. 17–19; M.J. Hettinger, "The Role of the Statute of Laborers in the Social and Economic Background to the Great Revolt in East Anglia," unpublished Ph.D thesis, University of Indiana, 1987, pp. 154–58, 192.
66. Penn and Dyer, "Wages and Earnings," pp. 356, 358–9.
67. Ibbetson, *Law of Obligations*, pp. 21–22, 24–31.
68. Ibbetson, *Law of Obligations*, pp. 31–33, 38, 75. Cases giving authority for the acceptance of non-performance but a willingness to do a job as remediable in debt come from the reign of Henry VI. Sickness or injury preventing performance of the contract was usually construed by masters as demonstrating the servant was "unable and unwilling" to work (Clark, "Medieval Labor Law," p. 340).
69. G.H. Jones, "Per Quod Servitium Amisit," *Law Quarterly Review* 44 (1958): 39–45; Ibbetson, *Law of Obligations*, p. 66; Arnold, *Select Cases of Trespass*, vol. 1, p. xliv.
70. Arnold, *Select Cases of Trespass*, vol. 1, p. xl; Clark, "Medieval Labor Law," p. 343.
71. Palmer, *English Law*, pp. 169–210.
72. Palmer, *English Law*, p. 228. See generally A. Kirafly, *The Action on the Case* (London: Sweet & Maxwell, 1951).
73. See the evidence presented in Musson, "New Labour Laws," pp. 79–81.
74. S.F.C. Milsom, *Historical Foundations of the Common Law*, 2nd. edn. (London: Butterworths, 1981), pp. 289–95, 305, 318–20; Palmer, *English Law*, pp. 164–227, 296–300.
75. Musson, "New Labour Laws," pp. 81–86.
76. PRO, Chancery, Early Chancery Proceedings, C 1/46/117.
77. C 1/66/264.
78. C 1/66/53.
79. C 1/66/52.
80. C.M. Barron, "Lay Solidarities: the Wards of Medieval London," in *Law, Laity and Solidarities: Essays in Honour of Susan Reynolds*, ed. P. Safford, J.L. Nelson and J. Martindale (Manchester: Manchester University Press, 2001), pp. 218–25; S. Rees Jones, "The Regulation of Labor in Medieval English Towns," in *Problem of Labor*, ed. Bothwell, Goldberg, and Ormrod, pp. 132–42.
81. Rees Jones, "Regulation of Labour," pp. 138–39; Barron, "Wards of Medieval London," pp. 223–24; see for example: *Liber Albus*, ed. H.T. Riley, Rolls Series (London: R. Griffin, 1861), pp. 334, 338.
82. P. Nightingale, *A Medieval Merchant Community. The Grocers' Company and the Politics and Trade of London, 1000–1485* (New Haven and London: Yale University Press, 1995), p. 179. See also B.R. McRee, "Religious Gilds and Regulation of Behaviour in Medieval Towns," in *People, Politics and Community in the Later Middle Ages*, ed. J. Rosenthal and C. Richmond (Gloucester: A. Suttton, 1987), pp. 108–22.

83. Rees Jones, "Regulation of Labour," pp. 148–49.
84. Rees Jones, "Regulation of Labour," pp. 144–45.
85. See statutes of 1388 and 1406: Given-Wilson, "Labour in the Context of English Government," p. 88.
86. Clark, "Medieval Labor Law," pp. 344–46 (drawing upon local court rolls from Nottingham, Ipswich, Wymondham (Norf), Sherburne (Yorks) and Great Yarmouth).
87. A. Harding, "Early Trailbaston Proceedings from the Lincoln Roll of 1305," in *Medieval Legal Records Edited in Memory of C.A.F. Meekings*, ed. R.F. Hunnisett and J.B. Post (London: HMSO, 1978), pp. 143–68; Given-Wilson, "Labour in the Context of English Government," pp. 88–94, 97.
88. Rees Jones, "Regulation of Labour," pp. 149–53.

CHAPTER 6

BRANDING AND THE TECHNOLOGIES
OF LABOR REGULATION

*Kellie Robertson*

> This chapter looks at records of labor violations from both secular and ecclesiastical courts as well as images of laboring bodies to argue that new strategies of enforcement made bodies available to be read as symbols by authorities eager to "textualize" and thereby "fix" laboring identities.

In 1350, Oxfordshire justices who had assembled to hear labor violations were attacked near Eynsham Abbey. The attackers (behaving like "madmen and men possessed by an evil spirit") besieged the presiding justice in the abbey and threatened to burn him alive if he failed to surrender all indictments and accusations in his possession.[1] The king later dispatched William Shareshull, chief justice of the king's bench, to investigate this so-called rebellion and punish its perpetrators. This incident must have been fresh in Shareshull's mind when he made the opening speech to parliament in February of 1351 (the first time parliament had met in three years due to outbreaks of plague). He used the occasion to lament the two greatest problems facing the kingdom—failure to keep the peace and the severe disruption caused by laborers' unwillingness to serve despite the 1349 ordinance—precisely the two failures evident in the Eynsham incident.[2]

Bertha Putnam calls the period between June 1349 (the date of the initial conciliar ordinance of laborers) and February 1351 (the date of the Westminster parliament that issued the first statute of laborers) a "period of various administrative experiments."[3] If this earliest phase of labor regulation was seen as an experiment, it was generally thought to be a highly unsuccessful one. The 1349 ordinance had made service compulsory for all landless, able-bodied workers under the age of sixty; it had additionally stipulated that wages were not to exceed those paid before the plague. The chronicler Henry Knighton claimed that the 1349 ordinance was simply ignored by workers who were so "arrogant and contrary-minded" [elati et contrariosi] as to allow the crops to rot in the field if their "arrogant and greedy demands" [elatam et cupidam uoluntatem] went unmet.[4] While the commons' hopes must have been high for the new legislation, the 1351 statute was (again according to Knighton) no more successful than its predecessor. Never the laborers' friend, Knighton lamented that, from the moment of the 1351 statute's enactment, laborers "served their masters worse than ever before."[5]

If the 1351 statute appeared unsuccessful in the eyes of the fourteenth-century landed classes, it cannot be denied that it was certainly a very different kind of experiment. Not merely a reenactment of the 1349 ordinance, the 1351 statute actually stipulated the wages to be taken and the prices to be charged for goods. Moreover, it made several innovations both in the regulation of the labor market and in punishment of offending laborers, innovations that all codified unprecedented levels of worker visibility. In terms of the labor market, the new statute mandated that all agricultural laborers bring their tools to the market square so that they could be hired publicly rather than in private (this provision presumably circumvented special deals being made by unscrupulous landowners willing to pay the workers' "arrogant and greedy demands"). Next, the statute required that, twice a year, all workers and artisans had to swear before local officials that they would abide by the provisions of the statutes.[6] In terms of punishment, the new statute required that offending manual laborers be placed in stocks (including those who refused to swear to obey the statutes). The statute additionally required that stocks be erected in every town for this purpose.

All of these innovations contributed to a new sense that workers' physical bodies were available for scrutiny to a much greater extent than in the pre-plague years. The process of contracting work (which had hitherto fore been agreements, customary or otherwise, between individuals) was now transformed into a public exercise subject to surveillance by both local and itinerant royal justices. This same surveillance is present in the clauses concerning punishment in stocks. The Commons had petitioned the king for corporal punishment to replace the 1349 ordinance's earlier (and presumably ineffectual) stipulation that laborers should be punished by either fine or imprisonment. One rationale for this petition may be that corporal punishment was seen to be more of a detriment than fines and imprisonment, though another, more persuasive rationale can be inferred: open display in stocks insured that employers would know where to find their AWOL workers in a way that fines or imprisonment in a jail (punishments that were essentially invisible to the community at large) would not.[7]

In analyzing how the 1351 statute changed the status of laborers, it is necessary to recall that post-plague labor practices and regulation still had much in common with pre-plague ones. Legal historians rightly remind us that the central provisions of the 1349 ordinance—requiring the able-bodied to work, fixing wages, and limiting worker mobility—had analogues in pre-plague manorial regulation; similarly, local courts had taken it upon themselves to enforce terms of service for manual workers and servants before the plague.[8] These continuities make the 1351 innovations all the more striking as they seem to express a newer, more acute sense that labor needed to be visible to the community that benefited from it. Legislated corporal punishment, public penance, and written records of labor misconduct all attempted to render labor offenses visible within fourteenth-century communities and thus more amenable to the control of both local and national authorities. In seeking to correlate available legal and textual identities with actual working bodies in the second half of the fourteenth century, this chapter charts how the successive reissuances of labor legislation introduced new uses of literacy and new ways of textualizing identities (whether by writing "on the body" itself or by issuing letters patent to travelling workers). Labor regulation not only deployed reading and writing as a means of enforcement, the statutes also foregrounded, in innovative ways, the tendency to consider laboring bodies as symbols "to be read"; in the wake of this statute, bodies effectively became texts. In this way, the labor laws become a significant site for discussing questions about the materiality of the medieval body as the laws give conflicting signals about what is precisely being read: the body itself? the work produced by this body? or, even, the obligation to work? Through textual and physical coercion, labor regulation attempted not only to produce an individualized, "political technology of the body" (as Foucault would have it) but also to regulate the larger social body—the common profit of the realm—through the laborer's individual body.

### Bad Bodies I: Branding and the Economies of the Visible

Like 1351, 1361 was another plague year, and, unsurprisingly, parliament again revisited the question of labor, reaffirming the earlier provisions of the labor statutes, and, once again, introducing new penalties for rebellious laborers. The 1361 statute stipulated that laborers and artificers who left their locale (presumably in search of higher wages) should be returned to their native village to face imprisonment and possibly the additional penalty of branding. The statute reads: "for his falsity [*fauxine*] he shall be burned in the forehead with [a brand] made of iron and formed into the shape of the letter 'F' as a sign of Falsity."[9] Like the 1351 statute that stipulated open display in stocks, this penal innovation attempted to legislate an exact identity between the laborer's body and the work that it performed (or failed to perform). Like stocks, branding would insure that renegade laborers could be identified for more vigilant surveillance. In these ways, stocks and branding were both technologies of labor visibility insofar as they were designed to render bad labor evident and, therefore, manageable by both masters and municipal authorities.

But penal branding went far beyond open display in stocks in both its physical severity and its coercive use of literacy. In licensing the branding of a presumably illiterate peasant with the first letter of a word he couldn't read, in a language he didn't speak (the statute was originally in French and then later enrolled in Latin), the 1361 statute appears Kafka-esque to modern eyes in its literal equation of body with crime. Contrary to our modern fantasy of the "darkness" of the Middle Ages, penal branding was not common at this time, and the 1361 statute appears to be solely responsible for reviving (or according to some historians, actually originating) the practice in Britain. According to the social historian John Bellamy, penalties of the body were relatively rare during the high Middle Ages when compared with either the preceding Norman or the proceeding Tudor periods.[10] Apparently, the Norman practices of penal body mutilation (castration and blinding in connection with rape and felonious wounding) mostly died out in the thirteenth century. Only when we reach the late fifteenth and early sixteenth centuries do we find the occasional record of a branded heretic,[11] and we have to wait until the end of the sixteenth century to find penalties of the body again in common usage. Holinshed, amidst a cheerful recitation of the whipping of vagabonds, burning of witches, and ducking of adulterers, mentions that perjurers and thieves claiming benefit of clergy are branded so that if they relapse they can be readily identified for more severe punishments.[12] The mid-fourteenth century labor statutes thus appear as a relative anomaly insofar as it was one of the few statutes that mandated corporal punishment for a judicial offense during the fourteenth and early fifteenth centuries.

The movement towards corporal punishment for labor violators not only tells us about changing social anxieties over the definition of "true labor," it also signifies the changing relation between the state and the medieval laboring body. A physical punishment like branding was more than just a mark of criminality and deviance; the branded body was intended to act as a permanent record of guilt and subjugation. Foucault explains how such a body can speak to its own social construction:

> [T]he body is...directly involved in a political field; power relations have an immediate hold upon it; they invest it, mark it, train it, torture it, force it to carry out tasks, to perform ceremonies, to emit signs.[13]

The framers of the 1361 legislation imagined the branded body of the renegade laborer as an articulation of the master's power over the worker, a surplus power in juridical terms. The symbolic nature of the brand asserted not only that a laborer was the equivalent of his or her badly performed work, but that it was permissible for the state to legislate a person's identity publicly in terms of his or her work. The body's surface was to become the page upon which a coercive, textualized identity was enacted.

Yet the statutes suggest more than just a Foucauldian relation between the state and a biopolitically inflected body. They raise the question of the materiality of both labor and the body since penal branding assumed identity was constituted through a person's outer behavior, and, therefore, it could be reconstituted on his or her skin in the form of a mark that identified a person in terms of his or her work. This assumption was necessitated by the fact that labor had to be connected to a specific laborer and that work itself, once performed, essentially becomes invisible. That the statute specifies the placement of the brand on the forehead was significant not only because it defied attempts at concealment but because the face was frequently viewed (at least since Augustine) as the reflection of one's personhood.[14] The threat of facial branding asserted the indelibility of identity: you are what you work. If definitions of "good" and "bad" labor were constructed through relations of power, these normative constraints not only regulate the laborer's body, they might be said to produce this body as well. The disciplinary norms of labor functioned in a performative fashion through the twin powers of iterability and visibility (performativity here being understood in Judith Butler's sense of this term as not "a singular or deliberate 'act,' but, rather, as the reiterative and citational practice by which discourse produces the effects that it names").[15] Peasant bodies must do the same things year in, year out, and be seen to be doing these same things in the same places: in the market square where they are hired, before local authorities affirming that they will comply with the laws, or in public stocks for noncompliance. In thinking about the materiality of sex in relation to acculturated gender norms, Butler asserts that there is no such thing as a "natural" material body that gets "inscribed" by culture; rather, language and culture specify the terms of the body's "prediscursive" materiality. There is no body prior to its interpretation since the act of performance creates the body. We might say, *mutatis mutandis*, that there is no laboring body before the act of regulation. The fact that we have no record of any labor violator being branded under the 1361 statute probably says less about either the ineffective enforcement of the laws or the paucity of the historical record and rather more about the social imaginary that created the labor laws. These laws were intent on producing not only a domain of regulated, and therefore, intelligible bodies but also a domain of counterfactual, unthinkable bodies: the branded bodies of labor violators. By threatening to brand bad labor, fourteenth-century authorities produced the cultural meanings of "true" as opposed to "false" labor through a dialectic of visibility and invisibility, materiality and immateriality.

If under the 1361 statute the renegade laborer had the potential to become a walking allegory for falsity, he was an allegory meant to be read by others. In addition to witnessing the power of a more centralized authority, the branded body also potentially voiced cultural scripts concerning the uses of literacy in relation to the mostly illiterate working classes. Such an enactment necessarily raises questions about the relations among labor, violence, and literacy: how does the branding of a presumably illiterate worker with the first letter of a word that he or she could not read function within the symbolic economy of those who could read and those who could not? In threatening to brand renegade laborers on the forehead with an 'F', the labor statutes literally advocated turning the peasant body into text, a text to be read by the land-owning authorities. In attempting to make bad labor legible, the 1361 statute marshals literacy as a coercive instrument of identity formation. That laborers understood literacy to be one of the oppressive handmaids of the labor laws became clear during the 1381 Rising—a rebellion fueled, in part, by resentment of the labor statutes—during which rebels seized and burned manorial charters and other documents that they claimed were responsible for oppressive forms of villeinage.[16] The threat of branding finds a less violent though no less coercive corollary in the 1388 labor statute that required migrating laborers to acquire letters patent from the local justice of the peace in order to travel from one village to the next. In this instance, illiterate workers were being issued travel letters, which they presumably could not read. These authorizing uses of literacy attested a desire not only to give a geographical fixity to the wandering bodies of vagrant workers but also to fix identity by textualizing it. The body is now made to speak the language of the law, which above all, is written. Whereas pre-plague laboring identity depended primarily on constant public recognition of identity through customary and remembered obligation, post-plague laboring identity meant that the body was—as a sign—iterable. Its meaning could be fixed outside the immediate community of laborers and masters that benefited from it. The danger of making the body a sign, however, is that the meaning of the sign was now open to negotiation in each subsequent iteration.[17]

The successive reissuances of the labor statutes witnessed the difficulty of this negotiation insofar as they gave voice to social anxieties not just about individual laboring bodies but about the unstable nature of the fourteenth-century master–servant relation. Changing penalties tell us much about the pressures brought to bear on this relation. The original 1349 ordinance stipulated two punishments: imprisonment in jail or fines for those paying or taking excess wages. In most cases, there was no standard fine, rather an "excess fee" was charged: the excess equaled the difference between legal and illegal wages taken by the laborer or paid by the employer.[18] In this arrangement, penal fines implicitly recognized the contractual nature of the work performed (it also implied a commodification of labor since quantities of wage were "exchanged" for quantities of labor). Excess fees were a distinct departure from the pre-1349 customs and by-laws that had treated the master–servant relation more like a feudal 'status'—that is, it was governed by certain privileges held by the master or lord.[19] The 1349 ordinance, on the other hand, reflected the changing economic climate that had to recognize this relation to be created by contract in the wake of the labor shortages.[20]

What we see in the 1351 and 1361 statutes is a movement toward corporal punishments and away from fines as a punishment. In 1351, the stocks provision was introduced in response to a commons' petition that specifically asked that corporal punishment be inflicted on bad laborers since fines and redemptions had proved largely ineffectual; likewise, the 1361 statute ordained that the previous statute of laborers should stand in all its provisions "except the pecuniar pain which from henceforth is accorded, that the laborers shall not be punished by fine and ransom"; instead, punishment should take the form of imprisonment and the threat of branding.[21] While fines continued to be levied, evidence suggests that stocks were regularly used post-1351, and their use gave rise to a culture of what might be called *furta labores*: numerous are the records of labor violators being liberated from stocks *vi et armis*. One 1351 Essex indictment describes a man who liberated a reaper and common laborer from the stocks with force and arms and against the king's peace "not wishing the said William to find security for staying in the said village to do his job according to the statutes." William's rescuer was most likely hoping to employ him.[22] Local quarter session records suggest that corporal punishment was used primarily for agricultural workers and domestic servants like William the reaper. Noting that the compulsory labor and length of contract clauses would refer only to this class of workers, Putnam concludes that, "for practical purposes it may be said that the justices of labourers were enforcing the law against manual laborers only."[23]

In ensuring that the punishment occurred in the realm of the physical and not merely the fiscal, the 1351 and 1361 statutes sought to reify the manual laborer's body and the work produced by this body. Under the 1351 and 1361 statutes, the authorities began to treat the master–servant relation again as one of 'status'—that is, closer to the older feudal mode of work and more similar to, say, a marriage contract insofar as the master had remedies available for breach of contract that went beyond those explicitly stated. In supplementing the fine system introduced in the initial 1349 ordinance with corporal punishments, the 1351 and 1361 legislations can be seen as retrograde insofar as they sought to reaffirm the feudal or tenurial nature of the laborer's obligation to work. Threats of corporal punishment such as branding and the stocks implicitly denied that peasant labor had a cash equivalent, preferring to see peasant labor as inhering within the peasant body. The problem of 'status' versus 'contract' seemed to be a concern of the 1381 rebels as well. According to the Anonimalle chronicler, one of the rebel demands presented to Richard II at Mile End was that "no one be required to serve unless it is of their own free will and according to a free contract" ["Que nulle ne deveroit servire ascune homme mes a sa volunte de mesme et par covenant taille"].[24] Apparently a reference to obligatory labor during corn harvest, this demand highlights the ways in which the labor statutes rendered the laborer's position ambiguous with regard to his master's rights over him; the rebels wanted this position clarified contractually.

The provisions for corporal punishment did not remain constant over the successive reissuances of the labor statutes, however. For example, in 1368, the commons gave up asking for more severe corporal punishments and instead petitioned for a two-fold increase in monetary penalties (an increase refused by the king).[25] These vacillations in punitive mindsets show that the 1351 and 1361 corporal punishment clauses were not just a matter of increased severity but evidence of a new way of thinking about labor: in making the punishment visible to the community that benefited from the work, the statutes articulated a view of work as public and communal. This legislation aimed to make laboring bodies visible to the communities that depended on them. Corporal punishments like stocks or the threat of branding not only functioned in the disciplinary realm, they performed in the hermeneutic realm as well. These punishments made the peasant body speak the conservative (even regressive) social transcript that saw the laboring relation as status rather than contract and that sanctioned extra-contractual remedies (like corporal punishment) for transgressors.

## Bad Bodies II: Archbishop Courtenay and Legislated Penance

Evidence for the materialization of the laborer's body—as well as an authorizing attempt to "read" this body—is to be found not just in the parliamentary legislation that regulated its practices, but also in the ecclesiastical penances imposed upon it. In the spring of 1390, the Archbishop of Canterbury, William Courtenay, summoned five of his feudal tenants to a tribunal to answer charges that they had failed to perform their customary duties of delivering cartloads of straw to his palace at Canterbury. Some straw had, in fact, been delivered to the palace by the tenants; however, Courtenay was angered that it had been done on foot and in sacks rather than on carts. For Courtenay, the tenant's method of delivery implied not only secrecy but contempt [vilipendium], suggesting that the men were not prepared to acknowledge openly the labor obligation customarily owed to him. When the tenants appeared before Courtenay, he imposed the following penance upon them: on the next Sunday, the penitents, walking single file and wearing neither hoods nor shoes, were to lead a procession around the collegiate church of Wingham, each carrying on his back a sack overflowing with straw and rubbish. They were to proceed with slow steps, full of humility and devotion [lentis incessibus procederent humiliter et devote].[26]

This episode raises several related questions as to the motivations of the Archbishop and the carters. The first is why Courtenay himself would be involved in the manorial minutiae of the administration of his estates. While the Archbishop was a territorial magnate in addition to his theological and executive responsibilities as head of the English church, matters involving laymen were usually left to his bailiffs. Courtenay had many (presumably more serious) problems occupying his attention that spring: Lollard heretics were active in a number of diocese (including his own); a heated controversy was brewing with one of his bishops over visitation rites; and the king was seeking to block payment of a papal subsidy. In the midst of these pressing problems, the fact that Courtenay took the time to summon and sentence six peasants from the small village of Wingham tells us that he viewed this labor problem as more than just an infringement on his clerical prerogative.[27]

If we consider the carters' possible motivations for resisting their customary duty, Courtenay's involvement starts to make more sense. The archiepiscopal register attributes the accused tenants' failure to perform their duties to "ignorance, mother of errors" [erroris mater ignorantia].[28] It is unlikely, however, that the carters were unaware of their duties; nor was it the case that the actual work was particularly onerous. Rather, their secret and partial fulfillment of the hay delivery was an act (correctly interpreted by Courtenay) of resistance to seigniorial dominance.[29] Kentish peasants had a history of resistance to labor obligations, a resistance most recently visible in Kent's leading role in the Rising of 1381. The 1381 rebels destroyed Latin records (rentals, muniments, and memoranda) that recorded customary labor obligations. Kentish rebels particularly targeted documents relating to labor services due to the archbishopric all over Kent including at the Archbishop's Lambeth Palace near London.[30] It was not only documents that were destroyed, however; one of the most gruesome acts of the Rising was the slaying of Courtenay's predecessor, Archbishop Sudbury, who was dragged from the Tower and beheaded by the rebels along with several royal servants. According to the Westminster chronicler, the victims' heads were then placed on poles with Sudbury's head "set in the middle and higher than the others and to make it specially recognizable among them they nailed on it a scarlet cap."[31] Courtenay's personal involvement with his tenants' labor violations is more understandable in this context: the archbishop insisted on his prerogative not simply out of abstract principle, but because resistance to labor obligations was feared to lead not only to dangerous social mobility but to outright rebellion against both secular and religious leaders.[32]

The final question this episode raises concerns the nature of the penance and its representation. The recalcitrant carters' sentence—to walk in the public square of Wingham with sacks of straw on their backs—seems to reverse usual penitential logic. If a murder was committed, the penance was rarely a literal or symbolic reenactment of murder; it was usually either a literal or ritual restitution. The carters, however, were asked to reenact bad work done secretly at the Archbishop's palace in Canterbury but now publicly in their own village of Wingham. Their penance was designed to make hitherto invisible bad labor visible to their own community. Since Wingham was one of the largest of the Archbishop's demesnes and possessed the most tenant land, this cautionary lesson about performing bad work was put on for the benefit of the Archbishop's other tenants.[33] In effect, the penitential logic of this scene mimics the visibility politics of the stocks and branding legislation. Medieval authorities "read" bad labor in working bodies and then staged this bad labor for the benefit of a local audience, an audience implicitly constituted as potential labor offenders for whom these penal and penitential dumb shows were supposed to be cautionary. These public, physical acts of punishment and penance therefore functioned much like stained glass windows were supposed to function in the great British cathedrals; they gave a largely illiterate audience legible models for behavior, whether cautionary or exemplary.

The penance of one of the accused carters is represented in a marginal sketch found next to the record of the proceedings in Archbishop Courtenay's register (still kept at Lambeth Palace in London) [figure 6.1]. While we cannot know if the Archbishop or the scribe copying the register was responsible for having the Wingham laborer drawn in the margins, the effect is the same: the drawing makes the unruly peasant laborer perpetually

# BRANDING AND LABOR REGULATION 143

6.1   A carter doing penance.
*Source*: Lambeth MS. Reg. Courtenay, f. 337v.

available to a Latin clerical reader. It reinscribes the workers' customary duties just as effectively as the Latin muniments that the rebels tried to burn in 1381. The drawing is also a symptom of how language difference—English-speaking peasants laboring for a Latin- or French-speaking elite—played a significant role in the enforcement of labor obligations when manorial magnates (like Courtenay) used Latin literacy as a way to enforce and survey workers, giving their labor a textual as well as a social body. Like branding or the issuance of letters patent for traveling laborers, the drawing in Archbishop Courtenay's register gave a textual body to the (potentially) badly laboring worker body that made it available to literate authorities. In all of these instances, bad labor is turned into text.

The labor violator was punished by being reduced to his body both in parliamentary juridical discourse (which stipulated corporal punishments in certain statutes) and in the ecclesiastical courts (through ritualized public penance). Both parliament and the church were increasingly endorsing a visibility politics of regulation for manual laborers. That penalizing labor violators found analogous practices in ecclesiastical and parliamentary settings is unsurprising since these institutions comprised the largest cumulative landholders. A body publicly penalized in stocks or branded on the forehead (rather than privately fined or imprisoned) speaks not only individual guilt but also the power of the state. This is not the modern, Kantian state but the 'common profit'—a state that saw itself as a body, a body composed of individual laboring bodies, which are sometimes made to speak even when silent.

## The Laborer's Two Bodies and the Medieval Body Politic

In his well-known study, *The King's Two Bodies*, Ernst Kantorowicz describes the paradoxical double body of the king: one body transitory, corruptible and subject to the laws which he himself enunciates and, at the same time, a body timeless, corporate, and touched by the divine. Kantorowicz traces the interplay between legal and theological discourses in molding medieval and early modern notions of kingship, stressing that kingship was 'liturgical' insofar as the king was imitating or impersonating Christ in his humanity.[34] Foucault, in his reading of Kantorowicz in *Discipline and Punish*, suggests that opposite the king's body is another double body: that of the condemned man who likewise "gives rise to his own ceremonial."[35] Rather than the generic condemned man, I would argue that, in fourteenth-century England, it was the laborer's body that occupied this oppositional position. Like the king's body, the laborer's body was twinned in its separate theological and juridical existences. While the idea of the good laborer was extolled in certain types of theological discourse that proclaimed the laborer's necessity to the social whole, actual workers' bodies were legally regulated as if they were all potentially walking labor violations, continuously threatened with corporal punishment. This doubleness of the laborer's body (again like the king's) was fundamental to the efficient operation of the medieval body politic.

Just as the king's body in its theological form was equated with the body politic, so too the good laborer's body in sermon and homiletic literature came to stand in for the smooth running of the commonwealth. Through biblical allusion, the ploughman had long been synonymous with the good Christian.[36] Medieval historians from Jacques Le Goff to Aaron Gurevich to (most recently) Paul Freedman have argued that as new agricultural technology developed from the ninth century onward, a new theology of idealized manual labor had to be developed by the church. This theology was articulated most clearly in the twelfth-century Cistercian ideal that saw in manual labor a medium for meditation and an antidote to the sin of sloth.[37] Labor was thus no longer seen exclusively as penance for Adam's fall; it was seen to have a potentially positive spiritual value as well. A new emphasis on the social value of labor can also be traced in the writings of twelfth- and thirteenth-century theologians who employed a trifunctional model of society. In this view, agricultural labor performed faithfully supported all orders of society and, though the lowest of vocations, was still seen as necessary to the proper functioning of society and therefore praiseworthy.[38]

Just as the king's body politic was invisible—it couldn't be touched or handled—the good laborer's body was also a disembodied ideal.[39] This de-materialization was to be found not only in sermons and homiletic treatises but in the vernacular literature of the period. Think of Chaucer's parson and his brother, the plowman, the "trewe swynkere" who both tilled and tithed. On the basis of their exemplary work, they are arguably the only two pilgrims who go unsatirized in the General Prologue to the *Canterbury Tales*; interestingly, neither are these pilgrims given a physical description. True work—allegorical work—is paradoxically work done without bodies. If ideal labor is often, paradoxically, performed without bodies, the corollary of this is that true labor also doesn't tell tales—the plowman doesn't get a tale in Chaucer's original frame nor does he get a portrait in the Ellesmere manuscript.[40] Chaucer's badly laboring bodies, on the other hand, are conspicuously visible and verbose. Think of the speaking bodies of the thieving Miller with his long 'nose thirles' and warts or the hypocritical Pardoner with his stringy blond hair and ambiguous sexual markers. As in juridical discourse, so too in poetry: the bad laborer is a narrativizing or narrativized body while good laboring bodies are either silent or invisible (or both).[41]

When the body of the good laborer *is* visible to medieval society—when it is depicted in stained glass or illuminated in manuscripts—it often has an idealized immateriality to it. Figure 6.2 is a well-known image of fourteenth-century peasants laboring in the margins of the Lutrell Psalter; the scene is one of several harvesting scenes that function as a marginal gloss for Psalm 95—"let the fields exult." As an image intended for the eyes

6.2 Plowing.
Source: Luttrell Psalter. British Library Additional MS. 42130, f. 170.

of the manorial lord who commissioned it, the scene is a fantasy of regulated labor. As one of the largest landowners in East Anglia, Geoffrey Luttrell had a vested interest in seeing laborers working his lands. But it was also a fantasy in the sense that decades of bad harvest and crop failures (along with pre-plague overpopulation) had lead to peasant unrest on Sir Geoffrey's lands.[42] In effect, this representation was an exercise in wish fulfillment. It is a peculiar kind of wish-fulfillment fantasy, however, where the figure of the peasant is represented in a way that simultaneously enables and negates the fantasy. Notice the clothes: they are not the usual undyed gray or brown wool that demesne workers wore but rather the multicolored garments with green linings that the fourteenth-century nobility favored. These peasants are playing dress-up. As the art historian Michael Camille has observed, not only are their clothes historically inaccurate, they would have been illegal according to contemporary sumptuary laws, which prohibited members of the lower orders from wearing the expensive fabrics of the upper estates.[43] Here, the *corpus mysticum* of the laborer (like that of the king) not only lacks individuation but is just as unnatural as the figures of monopods and cephalogi that inhabited the margins of contemporary *mappae mundi*.

If we compare this image of good labor to the image of the penalized carter found in Archbishop Courtenay's register [figure 6.1], the contrast between the two laboring bodies can be seen as emblematic of the doubleness of the laborer's body that developed in the fourteenth century.

Courtenay's carter is the 'body natural' of the peasant laborer. Unlike the Luttrell Psalter's 'peasants' who wear elegant purple hoods and gloves in addition to their rich clothing, Courtenay's carter is wearing what the sumptuary laws ordained for him: a simple tunic that looks to be made of "blanket and russet wole of [no more than] 12d." and is hitched up to reveal the "gyrdel of linnen" prescribed by the statutes (rather than the colored underclothing of the Luttrell Psalter's peasants).[44] Courtenay's carter is not only a negative example of bad labor, he is a positive example of conformity to the sumptuary laws. He is also an example of the ways in which statutes and court rolls attempted to legislate the laborer's "natural body" by specifying not only what this body could wear, but also what it could eat, what wages it could take for its work and what it could charge for the goods it produced.[45] If the Luttrell peasant is counterfactual, Courtenay's carter is hyperfactual.

The fourteenth century produced two separate but ubiquitous laboring bodies: one, theological and idealized—like that portrayed in the Luttrell Psalter and proclaimed from the pulpits—the other, juridically regulated and "naturalized"—like that prescribed by the laws and described in the records of labor violations such as those found in Courtenay's register. This comparison is not meant to suggest a teleological progression wherein the peasant body becomes more "realistic" or "material" over the course of the fourteenth century in response to the labor laws (and, indeed, the Courtenay register carter is hardly "realistic" in a narrow sense). The intent of these images is, after all, more constitutive than mimetic in relation to their subjects. Rather, my argument is that the two images existed side by side and were indivisible (just as the king's two bodies were indivisible), and that this binary was ideologically necessary—and became even more necessary over the course of the subsequent reissuances of the labor statutes. The indivisibility of the king's two bodies in medieval political theory insured continuity of the monarchy and served as a shield against any local infelicities that may have befallen the king's actual, material body.[46] This theory allowed Henry Derby (the future Henry IV) to dispose of Richard II and his two little boys in 1399 and still say the words "divine right of kings" with a straight face afterwards. Similarly, these two images of labor served to guard the wholeness of the commonwealth even in the face of unprecedented labor shortages in the wake of the plague, peasant resistance to work regulation, and outright rebellion in 1381. Like the king's two bodies, the laborer's two bodies were a mystification of the physical body in relation to the political economy, a body whose doubleness signified a nostalgia for feudal stabilities in the face of radical social changes (or as some historians believe, a nostalgia for nonexistent feudal stabilities). Like the two bodies of the king, the two bodies of the laborer were simultaneously indivisible yet incompatible insofar as they housed contradictory fantasies: the idle recalcitrant worker who was always already suspected of labor violations and therefore always already regulated, and the good laborer incapable of such violations.

The laborer, like the king, then was seen as the material yet intangible support of the community. The line between the laborer's sempiternity and his temporality, between his immaterial contribution to the symbolism of the body politic and his material contribution to the manorial and urban economies, was always present but also always subject to renegotiation. This placing of the material next to the immaterial was a usual scholastic application of dialectical understanding, just as, say, the Archbishop of Canterbury was seen to comprise the particular person occupying the office at any given moment and, simultaneously, the See of Canterbury. The laborer's body, like the king's, also gave rise to its own public ceremonies of submission; while the king's coronation oath swore that he would not alienate property belonging to the king's body corporate, the laborer had to swear publicly before the justices of laborers that his own labor could be alienated. Foucault claims that the body of the condemned man (as the antithesis of the king) does not reflect "the 'surplus power' possessed by the person of the sovereign," but rather "the 'lack of power' with which those subjected to punishment are marked."[47] So too the labor violator's body (potentially branded, left in stocks, or performing public penance) attested a lack on the part of labor power. Out of this laboring body—idealized in theological discourse, pejorized in legal discourse—rose the innovative bureaucratic strategies of control and new discourses about the good society.

## Notes

1. *Calendar of the Patent Rolls Preserved in the PRO, 1232–1509* [*CPR*], 52 vols. (London: HMSO, 1891–1916), vol. 8, p. 594. It is clear that villein services in this area were under significant stress from plague mortality as villeins renegotiated labor services with Eynsham Abbey in 1349; see *Eynsham Cartulary*, ed. H.E. Salter, 2 vols. (Oxford: Oxford Historical Society, 1907–1908), vol. 2, pp. 19–20.
2. *Rotuli Parliamentorum*, ed. J. Strachey, 6 vols. (London: 1783), vol. 2, pp. 225–27. Bertha Putnam, *The Place in Legal History of Sir William Shareshull, Chief Justice of the King's Bench, 1350–1361* (Cambridge: Cambridge University Press, 1950), speculates that the Oxford incident was "a factor in leading to the enactment of the more rigid statute of 1351" (p. 147).
3. Putnam, *The Enforcement of the Statutes of Labourers during the First Decade after the Black Plague* (New York: Columbia University Press, 1908), p. 10, 12. On the need for the 1351 parliament, see *RP*, vol. 2, p. 225.

4. *Knighton's Chronicle, 1337–1396*, ed. and trans. G.H. Martin (Oxford: Clarendon Press, 1995), pp. 102–103. All subsequent references refer to this edition.
5. *Knighton*, pp. 120–21. Contemporary historians have been kinder to the statute. W.M. Ormrod, "The English Government and the Black Death of 1348–49," in *England in the Fourteenth Century*, ed. W.M. Ormrod (Woodbridge, Suffolk: Boydell & Brewer, 1986), asserts that "the labour laws were a good deal more effective in the decade after the first outbreak of the Black Death than they came to be thereafter" (pp. 178–79).
6. For the text of the statutes, see *Statutes of the Realm [SR], 1101–1713*, ed. A. Luders et al., 11 vols. (London: 1810–28), vol. 1, pp. 311–13. For a list of offenses against the oath-taking provision, see Putnam, *Enforcement*, p. 76.
7. For the common's petition for corporal punishment, see *RP*, vol. 2, p. 227.
8. On the continuity of pre- and post-plague labor practices, see Anthony Musson, "New Labour Laws, New Remedies? Legal Reaction to the Black Death 'Crisis'," in *Fourteenth Century England I* ed. Nigel Saul (Woodbridge, Suffolk: Boydell & Brewer, 2000), esp. pp. 76–77. Musson's argument seeks to redress views like those put forward by R. C. Palmer who believes that the post-plague labor market was radically different from the pre-plague one (*English Law in the Age of the Black Death, 1348–1381: A Transformation of Governance and Law* [Chapel Hill, NC: University of North Carolina Press, 1993]). See also Musson's article in this volume, chapter 5.
9. 34 Edw. III, c. 10. *SR*, vol. 2, p. 367.
10. See John Bellamy, *Crime and Public Order in England in the Later Middle Ages* (London: Routledge & Kegan Paul, 1973), p. 182. For the pre-medieval history of branding, see C.P. Jones, "Stigma: Tattooing and Branding in Graeco-Roman Antiquity," *Journal of Roman Studies* 77 (1987): 139–55.
11. For example, eight heretics were branded at St. Paul's Cross in London in 1499. See *Chronicles of London*, ed. Charles Lethbridge Kingsford (1905; repr. Dursley, Gloucestershire: Alan Sutton, 1977), p. 226; Shannon McSheffrey, *Gender and Heresy: Women and Men in Lollard Communities, 1420-1530* (Philadelphia: University of Pennsylvannia Press, 1995), has documented sporadic instances of heretic branding in this time period (pp. 31, 73).
12. Raphael Holinshed, *Chronicles of England, Scotland and Ireland*, 6 vols. (1586; repr. New York: Ames Press, 1965), vol. 1, pp. 310–13. Several sixteenth-century examples of penal branding can be found during the reign of Edward VI: for example, the 1547 statute of vagabonds authorized the branding of a 'V' on the breast of a runaway slave; church brawlers were liable to be branded on the cheek with the letter 'F' for 'fraymaker'. Branding was only abolished as a form of punishment in Britian in 1829. See William Andrews, *Bygone Punishments* (London: William Andrews and Co., 1899), pp. 138–42.
13. Michel Foucault, *Discipline and Punish: The Birth of the Modern Prison*, trans. Alan Sheridan (New York: Random House, 1979), pp. 25–26.
14. The 1361 statute's stipulation that the labor violator was to be branded on the face can be compared to later branding practices that specify other parts

of the body; for example, in the sixteenth century, offenders who sought sanctuary and subsequently chose to abjure the realm were branded on the brawn of the thumb with an 'A'; see Bellamy, *Crime*, p. 112.

15. *Bodies that Matter: On the Discursive Limits of "Sex"* (New York: Routledge, 1993), p. 2.
16. Stephen Justice discusses the symbolic import of the rebels' document burning in *Writing and Rebellion: England in 1381* (Berkeley: University of California Press, 1994), esp. pp. 150–56. Such instances of peasant appropriation of documentary culture suggest that the field of knowledge constituted by the labor laws (and the power relations it represents) was not exclusively unidirectional.
17. On the problematic of iterability in language, see Jacques Derrida, "Signature Event Context," in *Margins of Philosophy*, trans. Alan Bass (Chicago: University of Chicago Press, 1982), pp. 307–30.
18. For the text of the 1349 ordinance, see *SR*, vol. 1, pp. 307–308: For a discussion of the penalties under this ordinance and particularly the system of excess fines, see Putnam, *Enforcement*, pp. 82–85. On difficulties in enforcing the ordinance, see L.R. Poos, "The Social Context of Statute of Labourers Enforcement," *Law and History Review* 1 (1983): 29–30 [27–52].
19. Legal historian S.F.C. Milsom, *Historical Foundations of the Common Law*, 2nd ed. (London: Butterworths, 1981), describes how the labor statutes created confusion over the difference between agricultural services as obligation/status and as contract: "The narrow concept of covenant was the product of a society in which most obligations were seen as flowing from tenure or status. This was obviously the case with agricultural services. The ploughman who did not plough would be summoned to his lord's court as a wrongdoer long before anyone would think of suing him as an equal in contract. . . .Grants had been precisely to create obligations for service, to plough or to fight; and the only common arrangement concerning land which has sounded in covenant was the term of years" (p. 325).
20. On the difference between the older customs and by-laws (which had treated the master–servant relation as a status) and the labor laws (which showed an ambivalent interest in the contractual nature of the relation), see William Holdsworth, *A History of English Law*, 16 vols. (1903; repr. London: Methuen, 1966), vol. 2, pp. 459–63.
21. In 1351, the commons petitioned the king for corporal punishment because laborers "ne ount regard a fynes ne a redemptions, mes fount de jour en autre pire ou pis" (*RP*, vol. 2, p. 227). On the 1361 statute, see 34 Edw. III, c. 9–10 (*SR*, vol. 2, pp. 366–67).
22. For the Essex case, see Elizabeth Furber, ed., *Essex Sessions of the Peace, 1351, 1377–1379*, Essex Archaeological Society, Occasional Publications 3 (Colchester: Essex Archaeological Society, 1953), p. 106. On the frequency of such liberation tactics, see Putnam, *Enforcement*, p. 181.
23. Putnam, *Enforcement*, p. 179.
24. *The Anonimalle Chronicle*, ed. V.H. Galbraith (Manchester: Manchester University Press, 1927), pp. 144–45.

25. *RP*, vol. 2, p. 296. On the effects of the 1368 legislation, see Bertha Putnam, *Proceedings before the Justices of the Peace, Edward III to Richard III* (London: Spottiswoode, Ballantyne and Co., 1938), p. xxv. That the third estate recognized this ambivalence about the difference between status and contractual labor (and that they saw corporal punishment as a symptom of the former) is witnessed by the 1381 rebels' demand that "there should be no law but the law of Winchester" (*Anonimalle*, p. 147). This judicial reform would have effectively repealed the 1361 statute that introduced the new provision of branding and the penalty of outlawery. On this rebel demand, see Alan Harding, "The Revolt Against the Justices," in *The English Rising of 1381*, ed. R.H. Hilton and T.H. Aston (Cambridge: Cambridge University Press, 1984), pp. 165–93.
26. This episode is described in Courtenay's register, Lambeth Palace Library, Reg. Courtenay, f. 337v.
27. This is the explanation offered by Joseph Dahmus, *William Courtenay, Archbishop of Canterbury 1381–1396* (University Park: Pennsylvania State University Press, 1966), p. 223. On the controversy with the Bishop of Salisbury over rights of visitation, see Dahmus, p. 149. On Courtenay's involvement (along with Arundel) in the dispute over the collection of a papal subsidy blocked by Richard II and Parliament, see Dahmus, p. 180.
28. Lambeth Palace Library, Reg. Courtenay, f. 337v.
29. R.A.L. Smith, *Canterbury Cathedral Priory: A Study in Monastic Administration* (Cambridge: Cambridge University Press, 1943), notes, "while many labor services (like ploughing or mowing) on Kentish manors in the fourteenth century could be commuted for money rents, the exception to this general rule was carrying services, however. This was seen to be an essential service since it brought food to the monks household and carried waste hence" (pp. 122–23).
30. See W.E. Flaherty, "The Great Rebellion in Kent of 1381," *Archaeologia Cantiana* III (1860): 90–96 [65–96].
31. "Sacratum capud archiepiscopi in medio et eminenciori loco fixerunt, et ut specialius a ceteris capitibus agnosceretur capellam rubeam super capud cum clavo fixerunt"; see *The Westminster Chronicle*, ed. and trans. L.C. Hector and Barbara F. Harvey (Oxford: Clarendon Press, 1982), pp. 6–7.
32. Courtenay's involvement therefore can be read as of a piece with his pursuit of Lollard heretics, especially since labor and heresy legislation intersected in important ways (particularly in their common view of the threat posed by unruly English-speaking peasants).
33. On labor obligations in Wingham, see F.R.H. Du Boulay, *The Lordship of Canterbury: An Essay on Medieval Society* (London: Thomas Nelson and Sons, 1966), p. 159.
34. Ernst Kantorowicz, *The King's Two Bodies: A Study in Medieval Political Theory* (Princeton, NJ: Princeton University Press, 1957), p. 87.
35. *Discipline and Punish*, p. 29.
36. On the symbolic significance of the plowman in the fourteenth-century manorial economy, see Michael Camille, *Mirror in Parchment: The Luttrell*

*Psalter and the Making of Medieval England* (Chicago: University of Chicago Press, 1998), p. 186. Late fourteenth-century preachers like Thomas Wimbledon frequently cited the parable of the vineyard (Matthew 20: 1–10), which equated positive labor with the good society. See *Wimbledon's Sermon: Redde Rationem Villicationis Tue*, ed. Ione Kemp Knight, Duquesne Studies, Philological Series 9 (Pittsburgh, PA: Duquesne University Press, 1967). For a discussion of the social benefits of manual labor in late medieval *florilegia* and *summa predicantium*, see G.R. Owst, *Literature and Pulpit in Medieval England* (Cambridge: Cambridge University Press, 1933), esp. 568–76.

37. For Jacques Le Goff's views, see *Time, Work, and Culture in the Middle Ages*, trans. Arthur Goldhammer (Chicago: University of Chicago Press, 1980), pp. 83–86. Aaron Gurevich discusses peasant labor in "Oral and Written Culture of the Middle Ages: Two 'Peasant Visions' of the Late Twelfth Centuries," in *Historical Anthropology of the Middle Ages*, ed. Jana Howlett (Chicago: University of Chicago Press, 1992), pp. 50–64; and in *Categories of Medieval Culture*, trans. G.L. Campbell (London: Routledge and Kegan Paul, 1985), pp. 264–65. Paul Freedman compares Le Goff and Gurevich on this subject in *Images of the Medieval Peasant* (Stanford: Stanford University Press, 1999), pp. 24–25.

38. The so-called Three Orders model of society was most commonly articulated as "those who pray, those who fight, and those who work." Freedman argues that the Three Orders scheme relied on a model of mutuality and that "implicit within the idea of mutuality is the notion that labor has a merit at least comparable to that of spiritual and physical protection" though "labor never lost its lowly representation as 'servile' " (*Images*, pp. 24–25). The foundational discusion of trifunctionality is found in Georges Duby, *The Three Orders: Feudal Society Imagined*, trans. Arthur Goldhammer (Chicago: University of Chicago Press, 1980). On the Three Orders as the result of the failure of the Cistercian ideal of monastic labor, see William Ovitt, *The Restoration of Perfection: Labor and Technology in Medieval Culture* (New Brunswick: Rutgers University Press, 1987), pp. 137–63.

39. For a discussion of how the king's body politic is 'angelic,' see Kantorowicz, *King's Two Bodies*, esp. pp. 7–9.

40. For the descriptions of the parson and the plowman, see *The Riverside Chaucer*, gen. ed. Larry Benson, 3rd ed. (Boston: Houghton Mifflin, 1987), I. 475–541. The plowman does not get a portrait until Caxton's second edition but there it only repeats the woodcut of the parson, his brother (see STC 5083). On this mix-up, see Betsy Bowden, "Visual Portraits of the Canterbury Pilgrims, 1484 (?)–1809," in *The Ellesmere Chaucer: Essays in Interpretation*, ed. Martin Stevens and Daniel Woodward (San Marino, CA: Huntington Library, 1995), pp. 171–204.

41. On the pardoner's speaking body, see Caroline Dinshaw, "Eunuch Hermeneutics," in *Chaucer's Sexual Poetics* (Madison, WI: University of

Wisconsin Press, 1989), pp. 156–84; and Glenn Burger, "Kissing the Pardoner," PMLA 107 (1992): 1143–56.

42. On the relation between the manuscript illumination and the material conditions of the Luttrell estate, see Camille, *Mirror*, pp. 198–99. For a helpful summary of arguments about dating the Luttrell Psalter, see Richard K. Emmerson and P.J.P. Goldberg," 'The Lord Geoffrey had me made': Lordship and Labour in the Luttrell Psalter" in *The Problem of Labour in Fourteenth-Century England*, eds. James Bothwell, P.J.P. Goldberg and W.M. Ormrod (York: York Medieval Press, 2000), pp. 346–48. Emmerson and Goldberg date the manuscript to the 1340s. For earlier discussions of the manuscript's genesis, see Eric G. Millar, *The Luttrell Psalter* (London: British Museum, 1932) and Janet Backhouse, *The Luttrell Psalter* (London: British Library, 1989).

43. Camille, *Mirror*, p. 184.

44. For a discussion of the sumptuary laws of 1363, see Frances Elizabeth Baldwin, *Sumptuary Legislation and Personal Regulation in England* (Baltimore: Johns Hopkins University Press, 1926), pp. 50–51. On the iconography of European peasant clothing, see Gerhard Jaritz, "The Material Culture of the Peasantry in the Late Middle Ages: 'Image' and 'Reality'," in *Agriculture in the Middle Ages: Technology, Practice and Representation*, ed. Del Sweeney (Philadelphia: University of Pennsylvania Press, 1995), pp. 163–91.

45. The materiality of the laboring peasant's body is also an issue in much post–1381 writing: see, for instance, Gower's *Vox Clamatis* where the poet describes rebel peasants no longer willing to till the fields—formerly men of reason—now transformed into asses (*The Major Latin Works of John Gower*, trans. Eric Stockton [Seattle: University of Washington Press, 1962], pp. 54–55). In Gower, as in juridical discourse, the unruly laboring body becomes material and visible in a way that it seldom is in ecclesiastical discourse about the honest laborer.

46. On the indivisibility of the king's two bodies, see Kantorowicz, *King's Two Bodies*, p. 9.

47. Foucault, *Discipline and Punish*, p. 29.

PART 4

PRODUCING POETICS

# CHAPTER 7

# THE DISPLACEMENT OF LABOR IN *WINNER AND WASTER*

*Britton J. Harwood*

> Winner and Waster *both alludes to and displaces contemporary interclass conflict (including episodes of civic unrest in Chester as well as the controversial policies associated with William Shareshull).*

Why does the first fitt of *Winner and Waster* switch back and forth between *chanson de geste* and satire? With the second of its three fitts, the poem takes the form of debate and stays with it.[1] Only the opening fitt shows the "shifting narrative focus and unstable perspective" that Stephanie Trigg imputes to the poem.[2] It was these shifts no doubt, following from its generic volatility, that led Constance Hieatt to place the poem as a whole at the "lower level of literary quality."[3] My working assumption here, however, will be Pierre Macherey's: "In narrative there is no continuity, but rather a constant disparity which is the form of its necessity and the possibility of its existence."[4] The critic's task, I take it, is not so much to deplore the lack of continuity, as if that were a corrigible flaw, but rather to explain it.

*Winner and Waster* begins as the romance *Sir Gawain and the Green Knight* does, once the later poem has surveyed the movement of the empire west: "Sythen that Bretayne was biggede. . ." (*Winner and Waster*, line 1);[5] "[a]nd quen þis Bretayn watz bigged. . . ."[6] *Gawain* goes on at once to mention the daring men who faced more marvels ("ferlyes") than have happened since and proceeds immediately to a particular adventure of Arthurian wonder. Like *Gawain*, the alliterative *Morte Arthure*, a *chanson de geste*, moves from invoking a splendid past to a specific instance of it:

> ȝe that liste has to lyth or luffes for to here
> Off elders of alde tym and of theire awke dedys,
> How they were lele in theire lawe and louede God Almyghty,
> Herkynes me heyndly and holdys ȝow styll
> And I sall tell ȝow a tale þat trewe es and nobyll
> Off the ryeall renkys of the Rownde Table. . . . [7]

By contrast, the "selcouthes" that the *Winner and Waster* poet takes up, immediately upon mentioning the founding of Britain, are not the "ferlyes" that challenged Arthurian pride but social climbing, the duplicity and vulgarity of a late age. When "boyes of blode"—which is to say, "no blood," "low fellows in lineage"[8]—marry above themselves, the reign of Antichrist is approaching (10–16). This lament for the passing of straightforwardness brings in the convention of complaint, as it will also appear, for instance, in *Piers Plowman*: "For nowe alle es witt and wyles that we with delyn, / Wyse wordes and slee and icheon wryeth othere" (5–6). So Dame Study observes that "[w]isdom and wit now is noȝt worþ a risshe / But it be carded wiþ coueitise as cloþeres don hir wolle." A regret that the sort of alliterative *gestour* who might once have sung a *chanson de geste* has been supplanted by an upstart, cherished because "he can jangle als a jaye and japes telle" (26), shares a satiric convention with *Piers*:

> Ac mynstralcie and murþe amonges men is nouþe
> Lecherie, losengerye and losels tales.[9]

As if to avoid struggles he himself has conjured, the narrator walks out into a lovely meadow, only to be delayed in falling asleep, as if disorder had come along with him. The thrushes, for instance, "threpen togedire," and the rough streams are "ruyde" (37, 42). When he finally sleeps, a dream returns him to the beginning of the *chanson de geste* and thus the beginning of the poem. Two opposing armies, in mail coats and helmets, their banners displayed, emerge from the woods at either end of an open field. So in laisses CCXV through CCXXXIV of the *Chanson de Roland*, the armies of Charlemagne and Baligant assemble themselves, until "Bien s'entreveident en mi la plaine tere" [They see each other very well across the plain].[10] In a kind of anachronism, the poem depicts an emerging fourteenth-century conflict as if, as Sidney Painter remarked about twelfth-century battles, it differed little from a tournament;[11] and Edward III is seated in a pavilion high on a cliff "to rewlyn the wrothe" (57) as Theseus will preside over the tournament in Chaucer's *Knight's Tale*. The poem does not depart from the conventions of *chanson de geste* when a knight, who first arms himself (109–18) as Charlemagne does (laisse CCXIV), is sent by Edward as messenger to the opposing hosts; or when the countries represented in these armies are identified ("Lorreyne,. . .Lumbardye,. . . Lawe Spayne," and so on). So the *Chanson* names the nationalities of Charles's divisions (Bavarians, Germans, Normans, and so on).

Then, however, dreamlike, the messenger, the *sandisman*, himself seems to substitute for the "wandrynge" narrator. He says, "Full wyde hafe I walked. . ." but has seen few sights like these armies (136–37)—or at least, we may say, like the first of them; for there are now few signs of "[h]arde hattes apppon hedes" (51). Rather, the headgear together with the heads themselves have been transferred to the banners displayed as very unusual heraldic devices: on the second banner the *sandisman* sees there are "thre hedis white-herede with howes one lofte, / Croked full craftyly and kembid in the nekke" (150–51)—and the reader has been returned to the terrain of satire.[12]

The pope is there, "ferse to the fighte" (148). The second division of the first army comprises lawyers and judges, and the "bende of grene" (149) on their banner may suggest the green wax of the seals on writs that made litigation expensive. The Franciscans, known by their banners that feature brown straps, are rested and ready to kill everyone. The narrator says of these mendicants, "I wote wele for wynnynge thay wentten fro home,/His purse weghethe full wele that wanne thaym all hedire" (161–62). Within the same conventions of satire, a Franciscan will tell the narrator of *Pierce the Ploughman's Crede*,

And myghtestou amenden vs with money of thyn owne,
Thou chuldest cnely [kneel] bifore Crist in compas of gold
In the wide windowe westwarde wel nighe in the myddell,
And seynt Fraunces himself schall folden the in his
  cope. . . .[13]

And so with the other four divisions of the first army, nominally Winner's.[14] Then, however, with the second army, "a sober, unostentatious military class,"[15] and the return of the *sandisman* from ironical narrator to royal agent ("Forthi I bid ȝow bothe that thaym hedir broghte / That ȝe wend with me are any wrake falle. . ." [197–98]), the poem reverts again to *chanson de geste*, and the first fitt ends. Why this oscillation?

There cannot be too many exceptions, I think, to the generalization that *chanson de geste* finds a society's enemy in another society, especially in those members of it who form part of a military aristocracy—an aristocracy unbounded, nonetheless, by any single country. The object of attack is, in some sense, external. By contrast, complaint and satire take aim at objects not only internal to the poet's society but socially inferior, usually, to the well born. The way the Franciscans lead "ledis of the lande. . .thurgh witt" (171) recalls the "witte and wyles" that "we" have to deal with these days and suggests an internal social corrosion.[16] Curiously, however, the opposing armies have come from elsewhere: the messenger tells them, ". . .ȝe knowe noghte this kythe ne the kynge ryche" (134). This puts the Franciscans, for instance, both inside and outside England and is part of the odd way that generic oscillation in the first fitt is attended by several puzzling shifts between external and internal.

As the narrator describes how the king is suitably clad, he sees that he wears a belt embroidered with ducks evidently trembling from fear of a falcon, and says that he thinks that the king will be riding "to the reuere. . .vmbestounde" (100)—as if the ducks internal to the belt will soon be external to it. The armies excusable because they don't know the English "vsage" for riding with banners displayed include, in fact, folk of "Ynglonde" (141). They get redescribed as "ledis of this londe" (152); and having been summoned to climb the cliff and appear before the king, readily agree, since "he clothes vs bothe / And hase vs fosterde and fedde this fyve and twenty wyntere" (205–206). As I have noted, the messenger knight, an actor in what the narrator observes, takes over description of the armies and then (195) reverts to actor. And the narrator, outside the action, sees the king call for wine, once everyone has mounted to the royal pavilion, and then goes inside the action to join them all in drinking it (215).

Textual disruptions, like generic instability, are the inevitable consequence of every writer's working within two histories at the same time. These disruptions happen because the *Winner and Waster* poet, like every writer, is doubly situated. Standing first within economic and political history because of how he identifies himself with particular groups, he writes with an "ideological imperative."[17] In this poem, it comes from the poet's identification with a military aristocracy and a sympathy with measures that it sees as necessary for maintaining its revenues.[18] Such an imperative, however, can be realized only as a "project of writing." "The possibility of such an undertaking" implies that he will adopt "the implements, the actual means of this practice"—forms such as the *chanson de geste* and the complaint, for example.[19] Thus, the *Winner and Waster* poet stands as well within the history of texts. The ruptures in the surface of his own text show how these means, having a history of their own, are adaptable to his purpose only imperfectly.

I want to propose that the poet cannot settle on a tradition in literary history within which to write because there is a problem in economic/political history that exerts pressure on him and that he in some sense cannot, and perhaps would not wish to, address directly. He cannot settle on a tradition because neither set of generic conventions—*chanson de geste* or satire—can accommodate the problem without rupture. The problem, I believe, is that of prospective peasant violence. Lazy peasants of course can be satirized within literary tradition, and Langland will do it. However, satire cannot show open rebellion by an army of direct producers because such a force is not to be defeated by tendentious jokes. The conventions of *chanson de geste* in their turn do not lend themselves to a military action by princes and dukes when their target is only their fellow countrymen, objecting to increased fees for plowing in the forest.

My thesis first is that the poem is born out of a history of relations between an exploiting class and the class of direct producers. This history, like a mass submerged in a stream, causes disruptions in the textual surface.[20] My thesis is also that the unknown poet wrote with an unconscious ideological imperative,[21] first to keep the prospect of interclass violence invisible by representing instead a war that confuses the issue of class; then to replace that first representation with intraclass debate; and finally, at the presumable end of the poem, as an act of containment, to strengthen Edward III by having him internalize both Winner and Waster as the variable tactics of a successful ruler. Something of an analogy to the path of the project occurs in two lines of somewhat unclear satire against lawyers and judges. They seem to mean that one is foolish to risk violence against an enemy when one can sue him before a subornable judge: "I holde hym bot a fole þat fightis whils flyttynge may helpe/When he hase founden his frende þat fayled hym neuer" (154–55). In the poem, an impending intraclass battle (displacing from the text prospective interclass violence) gives way to an intraclass "flyttynge." Any opposition is further softened when, toward the presumed conclusion, the king in effect displaces Winner and Waster from themselves.

Why think that the battle in the first fitt acts to keep distant from the poem the prospect of peasant violence? The representation of a battle that cannot be fought displaces a battle that cannot be represented. In the case of the represented battle, the reader is not led at first to suspect any imbalance of the two armies (50–54). When the narrator returns to them, however, there is incommensurability twice over. To the first, he devotes fifty-five lines, the first five of them about various west European "folke," not otherwise described except as "stuffede in stele" (142). In the remaining fifty lines, we hear nothing further of armor but only of coifs (150), sandals (157), belts, buckles, silk, and wool. In stark contrast to the long description of this militarily dubious collection, the second army gets two lines:

> And sekere one þat other syde are sadde men of armes,
> Bolde sqwyeres of blode, bowmen many. . .(193–94).[22]

The first army gets vastly more lines, but it is hard to imagine how an army of religious and merchants could withstand "sadde men of armes," much less the longbow that took the measure of France. All the soft clothing represented on the banners of the first army becomes by displacement a figure for the inconceivability of its defending itself successfully. This is a battle that could not have happened. It displaces from the text a battle that might happen, even one that has already happened, but nonetheless cannot be allowed as a possibility; cannot be represented. And the symptom of this suppression is the interest in banners, with the poet citing their treasonable display (52, 130–33) and then devoting virtually the entire description of the first army to the distinguishing insignia on its banners.

The impending battle in the first fitt is fantastic because it pits a recognizable army, "the nobility and the professional soldiers"[23] ("sadde men of armes, / Bolde sqwyeres of blode, bowmen many"), against an army composed entirely of the nongentle, as we know because none of their banners shows heritable arms. To the contrary, "sqwyeres" are "of blode" precisely because their forebears had been ennobled by the delivery of arms.[24] That their shields and tunics carry these would have gone without saying. We already know what these are like, of course, from the royal arms on the mantling of the "wodwyse" (71), whom we shall return to later, and the coat of arms ("[t]hre wynges inwith wroghte in the kynde / Vmbygon with a gold wyre") appearing on the front and back of the knight messenger's "jupown" (115–18). Those is the first army identified only by "merchandes merkes" nonetheless lived in symbiosis with the military aristocracy, just as the banners raised above lawyers and friars in the first army mark the ideological servants of the exploiting class. If in fact at the margins of the poem is prospective violence involving those to whom all arms will eventually be denied,[25] it has been replaced in the text by a supposititious contest between elements of the ruling class, some armigerous, some not. The displaced war would be too disturbing to be thought. The displacing one is too cozy to be true.

Are, then, the peasants, the producers of the surplus that Winner and Waster would consume in different ways, nowhere in the poem?[26] They show up just briefly, and serviceably when they do. In a poem about contests, the husbandman—the plowman with his fifteen or thirty acres—appears to ask for nothing. Winner tells Waster, "Teche thy men for to tille and tynen thyn feldes" (288). We see this same plowman at war, in the snapshot of the second army, supporting his masters with his longbow, as he did at Crécy (1356).[27] In describing the two armies, the poet stops just three staves short of not describing the second at all. If he had gone on to the last stave, moving the *coupure* to divide the squires from the bowmen, the whole exploiting class would have been lumped together, "sadde men of armes" and squires with the merchants, lawyers, and friars; and thus the longbows would have pointed at all those who cooperated to extract the surplus.[28] The very brevity of the second description is a kind of suturing, a sort of whistling past the graveyard, as if, should the poet have lingered there too long, the second army would have fallen apart.[29]

In the years leading up to the probable date of *Winner and Waster*, there were threats of peasant violence in 'westren' England where the narrator locates himself (7, 32).[30] That this is specifically Cheshire is suggested by the odd inclusion of "Ynglonde" among the countries represented in the troops that "knowe noghte this kythe" (134):

> For here es alle þe folke of Fraunce ferdede besyde
> Of Lorreyne, of Lumbardye and of Lawe Spayne,
> Wyes of Westwale þat in were duellen,
> Of Ynglonde, of Yrlonde, Estirlynges full many
> þat are stuffede in stele strokes to dele. (138–42)

The inclusion of "Ynglonde" might be simply a slip, or the poet might be thinking of English mercenaries or adventurers in an otherwise foreign force. It is also the case, however, since shortly after the Conquest, that Cheshire was a palatine earldom, with the earl of Chester—a count of the palace—exercising unlimited royal jurisdiction except for the rights of the king himself.[31] Created for defense against Wales, the earldom had been distinguished from the rest of England for a long while. Pleas to parliament from Cheshire as late as 1354 and 1355 refer to it as a "foreign" county.[32] Conversely, a Chester annalist had written at one point of Edward I that he had left Chester and returned to England; and in the Magna Carta of Cheshire, the earl's barons living on estates of his in other counties are called his "knights from England."[33] Edward III is king of "this kythe," Cheshire having merged with the rest of England and the earldom having escheated to the king in 1237. Yet there would be a long tradition in Cheshire of thinking of knights from other shires as foreign.

These threats of violence in Chester—what Freud might have called 'the exciting cause' of the poem—are what I am suggesting that the poem silences and repeatedly displaces.[34] But a rising that required the attention of a force led by the Black Prince, the duke of Lancaster, the earl of Warwick, and the earl of Stafford[35] might well have been known in London, if that is where the poet wrote; and from a metropolitan outlook, a fundamental struggle might well have been discernible that eventually brought peasant violence itself home to the capital.

Assuming that Lois Roney is right, that "the poet's central purpose" has to do with "economic conduct,"[36] we might consider what was characteristic and finally notable about "economic conduct" in Cheshire in 1353 and the years leading up to it. From a metropolitan and a local perspective both, Sir William Shareshull must have loomed very large.[37] He combined in himself executive, legislative, and judicial powers that in the modern world are presumed to be largely separate. Leaving the magnates aside, he was arguably the most powerful person in England in the early 1350s. With grievous results for Cheshire, he dealt effectively with two interrelated problems for the English ruling class: the need for revenue to support armies in France, in particular the Black Prince's; and the rise in labor prices that made it painful for landlords to pay the tenths and fifteenths that financed the war effort.[38]

Shareshull's speech from the throne in 1352, known to readers of *Winner and Waster* exclusively, I think, for its reference to "les destourburs de la Pees et meintenours des quereles et des riotes," went on to remind the commons of their previous advice to the king to "purchase allies" and of their promise of "additional aid." Commons was instructed to elect representatives to meet with the magnates and report by sunrise the next day. "The result was a grant of a new triennial subsidy, on condition that it be aided by the penalties under the labor legislation."[39] Tenths and fifteenths would be paid for three years, but the impact upon the ruling class would be greatly reduced by certain experiments of Shareshull's. The first, having to do with efficiency in enforcement of the Ordinance and Statute of Laborers (June and November 1349, 1352), was the commissioning of justices of laborers—residents whose only duty was labor cases, "with extra stipends for extra zeal in obtaining convictions."[40] The second, far more important, was the collection as a penalty from the worker of double whatever was received above the legal wage. This was then put towards the tax subsidy owed by the district. Only then was the difference collected from taxpayers, who were, of course, "for the most part, the owners of land and the employers of labor."[41] Throughout the kingdom, the wages confiscated from peasants defrayed the total tax bill by some ten percent. In some districts, however, the boon to the landlord class was much greater. The tenth levied upon Colchester amounted to only £26 2s. 9d., but £84 7s. 7d. was collected in penalties. The difference (£54 4s. 10d.) was then used to defray the subsidy in another community.[42]

This device of Shareshull's was demanded by the commons in January 1352 and then remorselessly enforced, not least by Shareshull himself as chief justice of the king's bench. Bertha Putnam has chronicled his tireless efforts over a long career on commissions of assize, as justice of common pleas and of the king's bench, and then chief justice, as an itinerant justice, as a member of the king's great council and of smaller councils, as chief baron of the exchequer, and on commissions of peace. Here, where we can focus on his judicial work in Cheshire, we must first note his association with Edward of Woodstock, the Black Prince, over some thirty years. Edward's council was "extraordinarily like the king's council in its activities," in Putnam's opinion,[43] and had oversight of his affairs in his duchy of Cornwall and of course in Cheshire; for it was the infant Edward who had been created earl of Chester in 1333. Not only was Shareshull a member of the council of the Black Prince; the work of it, Putnam believes, fell to him and to the prince's clerk, Peter Gildesburgh; and it obviously entailed raising money. Questions of extravagance aside, military action by the Black Prince meant Shareshull needed to increase revenue from Chester. As early as 1342, 1344, and 1345, he had obtained "enormous sums" for the king's exchequer through judicial proceedings in Suffolk.[44] In the county palatine of Chester, Shareshull's friend from youth and frequent associate on the bench, Sir Roger Hillary, had been appointed justice by the king and thus given charge of the entire administration.[45] As Suffolk had served for the king, so, it seemed, Chester was to serve for the prince.

Putnam cites a July 20, 1347 letter from the council to the prince: "We have appointed an oyer and terminer and sessions to be held soon, to your great profit." The Chester county court, convened on September 18, 1347 with Shareshull present,[46] came down particularly with heavy fines on people who had been asserting their holdings in the three forests in the county in accordance with a right granted, so they believed, in 1215 and confirmed by Edward I in 1300.[47] By August 1353, grievances not only over forest tenure but also over other customs that the Black Prince was seeking to limit—the pannage of swine, or the taking of housebote and haybote—clashed with the prince's need for income. An eyre, accordingly, was proclaimed for August 1353.

When Shareshull and Hillary were commissioned by the prince to bring justice to his palatinate (eyre being law French for *iter*, 'journey'), even districts with fewer grievances than Cheshire would have had reason for anxiety. Eyres so burdened a county or town that custom limited them—or so the assertion went—to once in seven years.[48] All Cheshire judicial business would have been transferred to the justices in eyre. These justices would have caused the selection of a jury of twelve knights from each hundred, who would then have been asked long lists of questions—about infringements over the past seven years of the prince's proprietary rights, about official corruption, about ordinary crimes that were less than felonies, and about fraud in the sale of wine and cloth. They would have heard accusations of trespass and felony, and heard plaintiffs who sought specific relief that could take the form only of monetary compensation assessed by justices or jurors.[49] Eyres flourished under Henry III, but ceased under Edward I, except for sporadic revivals. Chester was visited with one of the last.[50]

The rising that resisted it—the only one in the west of England between 1349 and 1365, according to John Scattergood—took the army led by the Black Prince himself and Henry, duke of Lancaster, to crush it.[51] For calling off the eyre, the prince exacted an immense fine of some £3375, to be spread over the four following years. But then, when the people of Cheshire

> believed that they were quit, and altogether free, the justices began a new session of trailbaston, and raised money beyond measure, and took many lands and tenements into the prince's hands, and levied fines almost innumerable.[52]

In other words, after the people of Cheshire had bought off the eyre, the prince turned around and, "doubtless at Shareshull's advice," commissioned Shareshull and others as justices of laborers to hear and determine.[53]

This is the 'economic conduct' that I believe to be at the edges of *Winner and Waster*, kept invisible by the text at the price of disturbance. The one likeliest symptom of it, it may be objected, Shareshull, appears not in the first fitt but well into the second, when the course of the poem has begun to run smoothly in debate. He is cursed by Waster, who wishes

> thies beryns one the bynches with bonets one lofte
> That bene knowen and kydde for clerkes of the beste,
> Als gude als Arestotle or Austyn the wyse,
> That alle schent were those schalkes and Scharshull
>     itwiste
> þat saide I prikkede with powere his pese to distourbe. (314–18)

Waster, Winner complains, is inclined to "boste with his brande and braundesche hym ofte" (241)—to be in short, a "meintenour des quereles et des riotes." Moreover, Shareshull appears here not as the tough administrator for the Plantagenets who conceived of justices of laborers, but rather as someone disliked by unruly knights. In fact, he was.[54]

But a leading, perhaps the chief, meaning of "waster" in the fourteenth century is 'an idle or unproductive consumer,' the lazy peasant given a voice by Langland:

> "I was noȝt wont to werche," quod Wastour, "now wol I noȝt
>     bigynne!"
> And leet liȝt of þe lawe and lasse of þe knyȝte,
> And sette Piers at a pese and his plowȝ boþe,
> And manaced hym and his men if þei mette eftsoone.[55]

This is a rowdy version of, say, Thomas Boney, who was fined 40d. by a justice of laborers at Chester because "noluit servire."[56] Although Thomas probably did not ride a horse to do it, he might well have been among those who rose up against Shareshull in 1353, "his pese to distourbe." I suggest, in short, that one waster and disturbance in conjunction with Shareshull suppresses another one. This waster is a landlord, drinks wine, and flashes florins. But not far beneath his good times in the tavern ("Then es there bott 'fille in' and 'feche forthe,'. . ./ 'Wee hee' and 'worthe vp' wordes ynewe" [281–82]) are those who "holpen ere þe half acre wiþ 'how trolly lolly.'"[57]

The 'economic conduct' of Shareshull, in service to the Black Prince, is at the center of the threat of the class violence lying just beyond the borders of the poem. The two other identifiable figures are connected with the prince also—his father, of course, but also the knight messenger, Sir John Wingfield, who had held land in Cheshire since his youth,[58] whose arms ("Thre wynges inwith wroghte in the kynde") Elizabeth Salter identified, and whose "rising importance in the Black Prince's household" she called attention to some years ago.[59] He and Shareshull sat together on the Black Prince's council, where Wingfield was chief under the earl of Suffolk, who was often away. As the single steward of the Black Prince for all of his counties, Wingfield would have been 'mainly peripatetic', at least if he had been like Edward's earlier stewards; and as such might have been a likely candidate for 'sandisman'. Moreover, since, in 1359, Edward will bind himself to repay Wingfield and others as much as 20,000 marks, in earlier years the prince might also have had to borrow from him. And thus Wingfield might have had an interest in the success of the funds-raising judicial processes on the prince's behalf that I have described.[60]

It would not be too much, I think, to say the poem is haunted by the prince, who may even be literally there; after all, the first individual the poet sees is festively disguised "as a wodwyse, alle in wrethyn lokkes" (71). The mantling that falls from the back of the helmet on this figure to cover his neck carries the royal arms of England. He wears a hat above the helmet, and on that

> ane hattfull beste,
> A lighte lebarde and a long lokande full kene
> ȝarked alle of ȝalowe golde in full ȝape wyse. (73–75)

This description, Salter observed, "could be precisely illustrated by the helm, cap, and crest of the Black Prince, still to be seen among his funeral achievements in Canterbury Cathedral."[61]

As the second fitt begins, the knight messenger has brought the leader from each side before the king, who says he will make a judgment. Although the two have led the armies here (197), they have only a tenuous connection with either army. While Waster may be a man of arms (238–41), he is hardly a sober one. If Winner were a merchant, as has sometimes been suggested,[62] he might have had a place in the first army. But like Waster, he is a landlord. If he were a merchant, he would take the current oversupply of wheat into account in what he paid for it and have no particular reason to worry. To the contrary, Winner despairs over "þe poure plenté of corne," in Waster's view (370), because he must have fixed or even rising costs in producing it. In expectation of poor weather at last, he is caught unprepared for yet another bountiful harvest (437–38). Again, the tenuousness of the connection is not, I think, some failure of the poet's craft but rather the result of the discrete demands of narrative convention and ideological imperative. Interclass warfare had been signified in the first fitt by the very representations that concealed it. The banners of the nonmilitary elements of the ruling class had faced off against coats of arms.

Now the second fitt acts to resignify that battle. It displaces yet again the kind of cases that had come before Shareshull—cases that could be heard only with a large armed force keeping the peace—with a case before the king himself and the prospect of trial by battle, still an avenue of appeal before the King's Bench:[63] "Forthi, comely kynge," says Waster, "that oure case heris, / Late vs swythe with oure swerdes swyngen togedirs. . . ." (319–20). The second and third fitts displace with yet another layer of representation a fundamental struggle within feudalism that cannot be acknowledged.

The impending battle at the beginning of the poem had substituted for that interclass violence a battle between the nongentle and gentle strata of the exploiting class. The new substitute in fitts 2 and 3 is not only nonviolent ("I holde hym bot a fole þat fightis whils flyttynge may helpe" [154]); it resituates the dispute entirely within the gentle stratum, the military aristocracy, where for a moment the impending battle in the first fitt seemed to have been located ("In aythere holte was ane here in hawberkes full brighte. . ." [50]). Perhaps ninety percent of the income of Western Europe when the poem was written rested on agriculture,[64] and military aristocrats like Winner and Waster[65] owned much of the land that yielded the bulk of English wealth.[66] With this relocation, which has put interclass violence at a maximum distance, the poem can move smoothly and amusingly, its dislocations behind it.

Thomas Boney, who was fined because he did not want to work, was unproductive in one way. That kind of failure in productivity is reregistered for the aristocracy in a comic argument between a proponent of unproductive expenditures on the one hand and a proponent of productive ones on the other.[67] Unproductive expenditures are what Georges Bataille called *dépense*, "a group characterized by the fact that in each case the accent is placed on a *loss* that must be as great as possible in order for that activity to take on its true meaning."[68] Waster "wastes thurgh pryde," says Winner (230).[69] Exactly. Pride was the defining sentiment claimed by nobility, the class with which knights had long ago intermarried in Western Europe, and it rested on *dépense*—the generosity indispensable to *generositas*, 'prestige'.[70] "Although throughout the middle ages," Painter has observed, "there were sensible writers who limited the exercise of [*largesse*] as did Philip de Navarre, chivalric generosity tended to become more and more closely identified with reckless extravagance."[71] This notwithstanding, Jean Flori discerns an ideological movement from the eleventh century onward that caused the ethic of the protection of the weak to descend downward from kings until it became obligatory for knights, who thus gained their "lettres de noblesse."[72] And predictably enough, Waster demands of Winner, "Late the peple and the pore hafe part of thi siluere. . ." (256). "It es plesynge to the prynce þat paradyse wroghte," Waster will say a little later, "[w]hen Cristes peple hath parte" (296–97).[73]

Winner calls upon Waster to make expenditures surely enough—rebuilding his dovehouses, for instance (235). These outlays, however, would be consumption toward a return. And that is just what Winner embodies, "the use," in Bataille's words, "of the minimum necessary for. . .the continuation of individuals' productive activity in a given society."[74] It involves calculation; and so, for instance, Waster imagines Winner tormenting himself over whether he should have invested in larger barns (435–38). Waster, by contrast, spends money he does not have (268–72, 283–85, 392–97), and none of it, of course, for "the continuation of. . . productive activity." Rather, in the feasts he lays on for his retainers (332–35), the money he lays out for their gear (270–72) and his wife's (392–95, 407–14), he manifests the self-destructiveness of *largitas*, the evidence that he is under no external constraint. ("Why hase this cayteffe no care," asks Winner, "how men corne sellen?" [233]). Waster is Chaucer's Genghis Khan, come to dilapidation and pawnshops. Winner has been mistaken for a merchant because he has no compulsion towards *dépense*.

In short, the poem has narrowed its focus further. This argument is not simply between two landlords. The argument of the two has sometimes been interpreted as economic and, as such, vitally significant to the England contemporary with the poem;[75] but their economics actually seems to hark back to an earlier time, when gift exchange, or a generalized prestation, was an economic alternative to trade more important than trade itself.[76] The argument has sometimes been interpreted as moral, with the vice of greed squaring off against the related vices of prodigality and pride;[77] but *generositas* had its own ethical force within chivalry and nobility before its appropriation by Christianity.[78] Rather, the argument, not simply between two landlords, is closer to the psychological.[79] If one were literal about that, one might think of Freud's distinction, in the fourth chapter of his *Ego and the Id*, between a serviceable fusion of the drives (Winner) and a defusion of them (Waster). It is a struggle between an impulse to productive expenditure on the one hand and an impulse to *dépense* on the other.

Here we are already at a great distance from the indolent Boney and the energized Shareshull. The poem, however, has one further displacement. Edward III will act to separate Winner and Waster from each other and from themselves. Whatever the original conflict, conflict in itself is obviated so far as Winner and Waster are never again to be in the same place at the same time (468–71). And each is ordered to become something quite alien. While Winner is sent to the pope, who led the first of the armed divisions of what was nominally Winner's army, Winner will be lying in silk sheets (463), although he had complained of women who had dressed in clothing so fashionably slick that they were as hard "to handil in þe derne, / Als a cely symple wenche þat neuer silke wroghte" (413–14). Where Winner had complained of Waster's openhanded rewards to his retainers (270–72), Winner will wind up giving "giftes full grete of golde and of silver" to the "ledis" who had accompanied Edward in his French wars. Waster's fate is equally grim. He has, he had said, lived at no one's expense: what have our clothes cost you, he had asked Winner, after the latter had complained about them (425)? He pays what he owes. "…we vouchesafe þat þe siluer payen" (427). Now he is to become a parasite and a sponge. The "westren" man who hardly dares to send his son southward will discover to his chagrin that Waster has been waiting for him (474–89).

The poem breaks off with Edward's anticipation of his expeditions. The silent history present when the poem started had to do, I have suggested, with his son's expeditions, their associated costs, and Shareshull's efforts to defray those, not least with his justices of laborers and his eyre into Chester. That the beginning of the poem is unrecognizable in its conclusion is the result of a project of writing—the result of a constantly renewed containment and mediation.

### Notes

1. See esp. Thomas L. Reed, Jr., *Middle English Debate Poetry and the Aesthetics of Irresolution* (Columbia, MO, and London: University of Missouri Press, 1990). The poem was "largely written as a work of recreational irresolution" (269). Taking up the difference between the first fitt on the one hand and the second and third on the other, Thomas Bestul, author of the fullest commentary on the poem, makes the point in another way: "[t]he narrative scope of the poem, once narrowed, is never again broadened." *Satire and*

    *Allegory in Wynnere and Wastoure* (Lincoln: University of Nebraska Press, 1974), p. 40.
2. Ed., Stephanie Trigg, *Wynnere and Wastoure*, EETS o. s. 297 (Oxford: Oxford University Press, 1990), p. xlvii. In *Satire and Allegory*, Bestul points to "discontinuity," because "each component of the poem is so starkly individuated. . . .The parts are by no means homogeneous in nature" (99). By "parts," however, Bestul is not referring to the three fitts.
3. "*Winner and Waster* and the Parliament of the Three Ages," *American Notes and Queries* 4 (1966): 101. There are, of course, opposing judgments of the poem's literary quality. "The poem is a *tour de force* of rich and controlled skills. . .": Derek Pearsall, *Old English and Middle English Poetry* (London, Henley, Boston: Routledge & Kegan Paul, 1977), p. 160.
4. Pierre Macherey, *A Theory of Literary Production* (1966), tr. Geoffrey Wall (London: Routledge & Kegan Paul, 1978), p. 36. For a fuller statement and example of the critical procedures I am using here, see my "Plot of *Piers Plowman* and the Contradictions of Feudalism," in *Speaking Two Languages: Traditional Disciplines and Contemporary Theory in Medieval Studies*, ed. A.J. Frantzen (Albany: SUNY Press, 1991), pp. 91–112, 242–53.
5. *Winner and Waster* will be quoted throughout from Trigg's edn. and line references given parenthetically in the text. While the dating of *Winner and Waster* is still a matter of dispute, I believe no one has put it later than *Gawain*. By wide agreement, the *terminus a quo* is 1350, when William Shareshull (see line 317) became chief justice of the King's Bench, or 1352, when Edward III had reigned for twenty-five years (see line 206). That the *terminus ad quem* may be as late 1361, the year of Shareshull's resignation as chief justice, or even 1366, the year of his last service on a commission of the peace, is not crucial to my argument. On the date, see esp. J.R. Hulbert, "The Problems of Authorship and Date of *Wynnere and Wastoure*," *Modern Philology* 18 (1920): 31–40; J.M. Steadman, Jr., "The Date of *Winnere and Wastoure*," *Modern Philology* 19 (1921): 211–19; and Elizabeth Salter, "The Timeliness of *Wynnere and Wastoure*," *Medium Ævum* 47 (1978): 40–65.
6. *Sir Gawain and the Green Knight*, 2nd edn., ed. J.R.R. Tolkien and E.V. Gordon, rev. Norman Davis (Oxford: Clarendon, 1967), l. 20.
7. Ed. Mary Hamel (New York and London: Garland, 1984), ll. 13–17.
8. Thorlac Turville-Petre, "The Prologue of *Wynnere and Wastoure*," *Leeds Studies in English* 18 (1987): 20.
9. *Piers Plowman: The B Version*, ed. George Kane and E. Talbot Donaldson (London: Athlone Press, 1975): 17–18, 49–50.
10. Ed. T. A Jenkins, rev. edn. (Boston: Heath, 1924), l. 3294.
11. See *French Chivalry* (Ithaca and London: Cornell University Press, 1940), p. 47. Maura Nolan has now linked "the tournament setting" to a resemblance of trial by battle in the Court of Chivalry. Nolan is arguing in part that the poem shows chivalry, like other "systems of representation," to be "inadequate to historical change." See " 'With tresone withinn': *Wynnere and Wastoure*, Chivalric Self-Representation, and the Law," *Journal of Medieval and Early Modern Studies* 26 (1996): 14, 22.

12. Cf. Bestul: "In the descriptions of the banners of the pope, the friars, the lawyers, and the merchants are most of the principal objects of encyclopedic satire. . . . " (72).
13. *The Piers Plowman Tradition*, ed. Helen Barr (London: Dent; Rutland, VT: Charles Tuttle, 1993), ll. 123–26.
14. N.R. Havely notes that in the case of the Dominicans, the fourth division, irony "is signaled not by obvious reference to defects but by exaggerated deference to their pretensions. . .": "The Dominicans and Their Banner in *Wynnere and Wastour*," *Notes and Queries* 228 (1983): 209 [207–9].
15. Nicholas Jacobs, "The Typology of Debate and the Interpretation of *Wynnere and Wastour*," *Review of English Studies* n. s. 36 (1985): 488.
16. Cf. ". . .now is no frenchipe in fere bot fayntnesse of hert, / Wyse [i.e., wily] wordes withinn . . . . " (21–22).
17. "Something *to say*. . ., in other words something that must not be said," Macherey, *Literary Production*, p. 91, his emphasis. Cf. esp. 90–95, 114–17, 132–33.
18. His portraits of the identifiable aristocrats are better than uncritical: Edward III is "[o]ne of the louelyeste ledis whoso loueth hym in hert / That euer segge vnder sonn sawe with his eghne" (89). The *sandisman* is probably a Wingfield (see Salter, "Timeliness," pp. 52–53), with Sir John Wingfield (d. 1361)—partly, perhaps, for reasons I suggest below—the leading candidate. On this see Thorlac Turville-Petre, "*Wynnere and Wastoure*: When and Where?," in *Loyal Letters: Studies on Mediæval Alliterative Poetry and Prose*, ed. L.A.J.R. Houwen and A.A. MacDonald (Groningen: Forsten, 1994), p. 161. The poet calls the *sandisman* "[o]ne of the ferlyeste frekes" who never failed the king (102). Moreover, as Salter remarks, the questions put by Waster to Winner—"Woldeste þou hafe lordis to lyfe as laddes on fote . . . ?," and "Schold not a ladde be in londe a lorde for to serue?" (375, 388)—should not be read simply as deliberate attempts to give us unfavorable insights into Wastoure's 'ethic'. They are orthodox elements in medieval social philosophy—harsh, hierarchical, but, for the period, 'just'. ("Timeliness," p. 44).
19. Macherey, *Literary Production*, p. 91. V.J. Scattergood has remarked "an unfortunate polarizing effect on responses to the poem. It has been treated either precisely as historical source material, or it has been assessed more generally in literary terms, but rarely as both." ("*Winner and Waster* and the Mid-Fourteenth-Century Economy," in *The Writer As Witness: Literature As Historical Evidence*, ed. Tom Dunne [Cork: Cork University Press, 1987], 41). Macherey's critical procedures seem to make it possible exactly to do both.
20. Thus, the text "entertains a specific. . .relation with history," but "history beyond its edge, encroaching on those edges." History is not to be stuck on to the work, but shows up as "a sort of splitting" there, a contradiction that reflects history only so far as that, too, is split with contradiction: Macherey, *Literary Production*, p. 94.
21. As "unconscious," it is what Fredric Jameson called "the political unconscious," which is to say, a political preconscious, descriptively but not

dynamically unconscious. For the difference between the two, see my "Psychoanalytic Politics: Chaucer and Two Peasants," *ELH* 68 (2001): 18 n. 3.
22. Lois Roney assumes that the poet is competent and therefore that "this major imbalance" must result from the loss of some 35 lines describing Waster's army, "perhaps...appropriate Cheapside groups...but also gold- and silversmiths," etc. See "*Winner and Waster*'s 'Wyse Wordes': Teaching Economics and Nationalism in Fourteenth-Century England," *Speculum* 69 (1994): 1093, 1094. She entertains, and then rejects, the possibility that someone inserted thirty-five lines of satiric description into the first army (1093). On the disparate lengths, see also Jacobs, "Typology," 488.
23. Thorlac Turville-Petre, *The Alliterative Revival* (Cambridge: Brewer; Totowa, NJ: Rowman and Littlefield, 1977), p. 2.
24. See Maurice Keen, *Chivalry* (New Haven and London: Yale University Press, 1984), p. 164.
25. See *Statutes of the Realm* (1101–1713), ed. A. Luders, T.E. Tomlins, J. Raithby et al., 11 vols. (London, 1810–28), vol. 2, p. 57.
26. "...Where Langland included artisans, minstrels, agricultural laborers, beggars, and hermits, these groups are appropriately absent from *Wynnere and Wastoure*, for if one is designated as either a winner or a waster, the availability of surplus wealth must be supposed" (Bestul, *Satire and Allegory*, p. 4).
27. C.W.C. Oman, *The Art of War in the Middle Ages* (1885), rev. and ed. John H. Beeler (Ithaca and London: Cornell University Press, 1953), pp. 116–37. The peasant population otherwise is represented only by its least militant elements, the most impoverished, the landless or cottars, perhaps, whom Waster mentions, "Thou scholdeste reme for rewthe in siche ryfe [quantity] bene the pore" (l. 258) and who may, he says, get something from wasters by trickledown (ll. 294–98). Other mentions of the poor, however, have only to do with a landlord's retainers (l. 382), aristocrats who have lived beyond their means (l. 393), and those who are voluntarily poor (ll. 420–22).
28. Of course he has not gone on. "'Diverting attention' is to show without being seen, to prevent what is visible from being seen....Therefore everything happens as though the accent had been shifted." Macherey, *Literary Production*, p. 88. The accent, so to speak, has been shifted two staves back.
29. I owe this suggestion to Stephen Knight.
30. Most of the various conclusions on the location of the original dialect of the poem place it not very far from Chester, scene of events I discuss below. Angus McIntosh's placement of it near the place where the counties of Yorkshire, Lincolnshire, and Nottinghamshire come together is the one that puts the location furthest from Chester. See Trigg, ed., p. xxi.
31. See J.H. Baker, *An Introduction to English Legal History* (London: Butterworths, 1971), p. 16. Because the English king is not above the law, there had been speculation that, in extreme cases, "the earl of Chester as count of the palace [might]...have some coercive power over the king." See Frederick Pollock and Frederic William Maitland, *The History of English Law Before the Time of Edward I*, 2nd ed., 2 vols. (Cambridge: Cambridge University Press, 1898), 1: 182.

32. See *Rotuli Parliamentorum*, ed. J. Strachey, 6 vols. (London, 1767–77), 2: 259, 266.
33. See H.J. Hewitt, *Medieval Cheshire* (Mancheser: Manchester University Press, 1929), p. 7.
34. Scattergood refers to the 1353 uprising in Chester provoked by the proclamation of an eyre for Chester and Flint at which Shareshull was to preside. See "*Winner and Waster* and the Mid-Fourteenth-Century Economy," 51. Turville-Petre mentions this eyre and points out the association of Sir John Wingfield and Shareshull on the council of the Black Prince and thus, presumably, Cheshire business. "*Wynnere and Wastoure:* When and Where?" pp. 161, 166.
35. See Henry Knighton, *Chronicon*, ed. J.R. Lumby, Rolls Series 92, 2 vols. (London, 1889–95), 2: 75.
36. "Wyse Wordes," p. 1071.
37. Criticism has connected "Scharshull" (317) with *Winner and Waster* mostly in relation to the Statute of Treasons, passed by Parliament in 1352, when, as he did from 1351–55, Shareshull opened parliament with a speech—made, in effect, the speech from the throne. However, it is not at all clear that the 1352 narrowing of treason is reflected in the poem. Salter considers this thoroughly in "Timeliness," pp. 41–45.
38. I summarize here and below, of course, some of Bertha Haven Putnam's work on Shareshull, both in *The Enforcement of the Statutes of Labourers* (New York: Columbia University Press, 1908), and *The Place in Legal History of Sir William Shareshull* (Cambridge: Cambridge University Press, 1950).
39. Putnam, *Shareshull*, p. 53.
40. Putnam, *Shareshull*, p. 71. Separate commissions for justices of laborers were issued from December 1352, even though it was not until the September 1353 meeting of the great council that they were provided for, as part of the statute of victualers.
41. Putnam, *Enforcement*, p. 99.
42. Putnam, *Enforcement*, pp. 106–31. This second experiment of Shareshull's did not originate in 1352. He had already secured additional revenue through penalties imposed in court in several areas (including Chester in 1347) when the November 1349 ordinance of laborers ordered the subsidy collectors to levy on laborers the difference between the legal wage and their actual wage and to put the difference towards the subsidy. See Putnam, *Shareshull*, p. 68.
43. *Enforcement*, p. 38.
44. See Putnam, *Shareshull*, p. 78.
45. See Hewitt, p. 8.
46. See Putnam, *Shareshull*, pp. 67–68.
47. See Hewitt, pp. 11, 16.
48. Pollock and Maitland, 1: 202.
49. Anne Reiber DeWindt and Edwin Brezette De Windt, *Royal Justice and the Medieval English Countryside*, 2 vols. (Toronto: PIMS, 1981), 1: 4–7; Pollock and Maitland, 2: 520–27.

50. See DeWindt and DeWindt, 1: 8.
51. Scattergood, p. 51.
52. *Knighton's Chronicle, 1337–1396*, ed. and trans. G.H. Martin (Oxford: Clarendon, 1995), p. 123:

    Cumque se crederent esse quietos et liberatos in toto, iusticiarii sederunt de nouo super Traylbastons, et leuauerunt pecuniam ultra mensuram, et multe terre et tenementa seisita in manus principis, et fines multas fecerunt quasi sine numero.

53. Putnam, *Shareshull*, p. 73.
54. Putnam, *Shareshull*, p. 148.
55. *Piers Plowman,* B.6.167–70.
56. See Putnam, *Enforcement,* p. 145.★
57. *Piers Plowman*, B.6.116.
58. See T.F. Tout, *Chapters in the Administrative History of Medieval England*, 6 vols. (Manchester: Manchester University Press, 1920–33), 5: 387 n.6.
59. "Timeliness," 52–53. His brother, Sir Thomas Wingfield, was a justice of laborers in Sussex in 1354 (Putnam, *Enforcement*, p. 138★).
60. See Tout, *Chapters*, 5: 385 n.4, 386–88, 317, 364 n.3. In 1358, as "governor of the prince's business," Wingfield received 10s. a day, the largest daily wage of any of the prince's ministers (387–88). Of Wingfield, Tout remarks "his name was of itself authoritative." *Chapters*, 5: 388.
61. "Timeliness," 48.
62. See Bestul, *Satire and Allegory*, p. 49; Scattergood 50; Trigg, ed., p. xlvii. Roney, however, points out that "Winner is characterized specifically as a landholder" (p. 1093). There is nothing obviously mercantile in Winner's upbraiding Waster for planning to see off his heritage and letting go the old aristocratic ways: "ʒour forfadirs were fayne when any frende come / For to schake to þe schawe and schewe hym þe estres. . . . " (ll. 402–403).
63. See Putnam, *Shareshull*, p. 132.
64. See M.M. Postan, "The Economic Foundations of Medieval Society" (1951), in *Essays on Medieval Agriculture and General Problems of the Medieval Economy* (Cambridge: Cambridge University Press, 1973), p. 22.
65. They are called "lordes" (54).
66. There were some seventy noble families in England at the time of the poem and some 1000 to 1500 knights at the beginning of the century. See Chris Given-Wilson, *The English Nobility in the Late Middle Ages* (London: Routledge, 1987), pp. 65–66, 70.
67. That Waster is simply unproductive in Thomas Boney's way survives in the poem in one of Winner's first charges against Waster: "His londes liggen alle ley, his lomes [tools, looms] aren solde. . ." (l. 234).
68. "The Notion of Expenditure" (1933), in *Visions of Excess: Selected Writings, 1927–1939*), ed. Allan Stoekl, trans. Allan Stoekl et al., Theory and History of Literature, Vol. 14 (Minneapolis: University of Minneapolis Press, 1985), p. 118; his emphasis. In *Satire and Allegory*, Bestul has pointed out that Waster, like Raison in the *Roman de la Rose*, affirms "the aristocratic

principle that expenditure is necessary to maintain honor and reputation. . ." (pp. 35–36).
69. See also ll. 237, 267, 433–34.
70. *Mediae Latinitatis Lexicon Minus*, comp. J.F. Niermeyer, 11 fascicles to date (Leiden: Brill, 1954———). On the eventual intermarriage of nobles and knights—those who had been simply armed *ministeriales*, 'retainers,' unrecognized in law as a distinct class—see Léopold Genicot, *L'économie rurale namuroise au bas moyen âge*, 2 vols. (Louvain: Centre belge d'histoire rurale, 1974–75), 2: 55, 77, 80, 83, 112, 129. On the place of *generositas* within another alliterative poem, see my "*Gawain* and the Gift," PMLA 106 (1991): 483–99. On the possibility of the noble gift, see also now Jacques Derrida, *Given Time: 1. Counterfeit Money* (1991), trans. Peggy Kamuf (Chicago and London: University of Chicago Press, 1992). Waster's references to charity for the poor (ll. 255–62) and to the usefulness of gifts in binding the loyalty of retainers (l. 388) attempt to back away from, to sanitize, his radical self-destructiveness and the centrality of that as a class ethic.
71. *French Chivalry*, p. 32. Cf. Bestul, who, having cited the *Roman de la Rose*, points out that "both Raison and Waster affirm the aristocratic principle that expenditure is necessary to maintain honor and reputation" (*Satire and Allegory*, pp. 35–36).
72. *L'essor de la chevalerie, XIe-XIIe siècles* (Geneva: Droz, 1986) p. 141; see also pp. 150, 162, 256.
73. Richard Meyer believed that such alms had a *kaufmännisch*, 'commercial' character (because of the purchase of heavenly reward) not present in the primitive gift: "Zur Geschichte des Schenkens," *Zeitschrift für Kulturgeschichte* 5 (1898): 24. Similarly, Waster's gifts to his retainers, binding them to him (e.g., ll. 270–72), are also only a decayed form of the *Pflichtgeschenks*, 'obligatory gift' (Meyer 26–27).
74. Thus, Lois Roney appears to be in error in saying of Winner that "he refuses to consume," "Wyse Wordes," 1091.
75. See, e.g., Roney esp. 1071–72, 1077–78, 1090–91. Cf. Pearsall 159.
76. See Philip Grierson, "Commerce in the Dark Ages: A Critique of the Evidence," *Transactions of the Royal Historical Society*, 5th series, 9 (1959): 137–40. Nicholas Jacobs may be making something of a similar point when he suggests that the poet is idealizing "a distributive society" as against a new and "acquisitive" one. "Typology," 496.
77. See Bestul, *Satire and Allegory*, pp. 13–18 et passim. David Starkey has brought Waster and Winner into relation with two Aristotelian virtues, *megalopsychia* or *magnanimitas* (in its Roman translation) and *phronesis* or prudence, and has written interestingly of their connection to the two separate compartments of the noble household, the chamberlain's and the steward's. See "The Age of the Household: Politics, Society, and the Arts, *ca.* 1350–*ca.* 1550," in *The Later Middle Ages*, ed. Stephen Medcalf (London: Methuen, 1981), pp. 253–57.
78. It is interesting to speculate that *generositas* was given an eleemosynary force coincident with the use of an Aristotelian ethics to resituate "largesce" as

a golden mean between avarice on the one hand and "fole largesce" on the other. John Scattergood quotes from *Li Libres du Gouvernement des Rois*, a fourteenth-century version of the *De Regimine Principum* of Aegidius Romanus: "il covient avoir une vertu meeine entre avarice et fole laresce, et cele vertu est apelee largesce et liberalite. . . ." (p. 47). In other words, in the Christianizing strategy, *dépense*, "largesse," is resignified as a species of madness: *fole* (or *fol* or *foux*), largesse. Bataille would not, I think, have resisted this. "The madness that insinuates itself even into Mauss's text," writes Derrida, "is a certain excess of the gift" (p. 45).

79. Cf. John Speirs, *Medieval English Poetry: The Non-Chaucerian Tradition* (London: Faber and Faber, 1957): "Winner and Waster could be aspects of the same person" (p. 289). Or Jacobs: "a balanced debate between two opposed tendencies." "Typology," 494.

# CHAPTER 8

# SCRIBAL HERMENEUTICS AND THE GENRES OF SOCIAL ORGANIZATION IN *PIERS PLOWMAN*

*Andrew Cole*

> This essay argues that critics too often assume that William Langland's allegorical practice is immaterial. On the contrary, Langland deploys allegorical models here that are thoroughly material—affiliated, as they are, with contemporary genres that memorialize, archive, and legislate labor in lists, guild ordinances, and statutes.

## The Work of *Piers Plowman*

Frederick Furnivall, founder of the Early English Text Society, and patron of the first modern critical edition of William Langland's *Piers Plowman*, was, like so many of his contemporaries, fascinated with this poem "because of its sketch of working men in the fourteenth century."[1] This poem remains the obvious choice for discussions about medieval labor. To my mind, it's a *locus classicus* for such discussions not for its purported realism or the vividness of its labors, but rather, because the poem itself enacts contemporary methods of memorializing labor in legal, scribal culture. We shall be exploring that claim in two parts, each of which details the themes conjoined in my title.

In part one, I elaborate upon the ways in which Langland finds the topic of labor generative—a rubric under which to articulate names, occupations, foibles, sins, social ideals, and Trinitarian theology—an occasion for, simply, more poetry. Particularly, I argue that Langland uses the genre of the list at the end of the Prologue to *Piers Plowman* to *produce* allegorical effects—the forgetting of the particular for the sake of the universal—a process conducive to the formal effort of ending, of closure, much like a pull-back shot in a film makes for a good end while the credits roll. But why the list? And why this emphasis on allegorical effect, rather than allegory? The larger critical point, and one that I believe is transposable across a variety of medieval writing, from alliterative works such as *Winner and Waster* and *Sir Gawain and the Green Knight*, to Chaucer's *Knight's Tale* and Gower's *Vox Clamantis*, is that allegorical effects not only signal this underappreciated form, the list, but point to an entire literary historical phenomenon, whereby after the early fourteenth century, archival genres concerned with labor, materials, and productive processes enter into new quarters of late medieval writing, and offer new ways of reading traditional materials.[2] Though this literary phenomenon is too wide ranging to be thoroughly described here, it can be illustrated very well by taking a close look at *Piers Plowman*, in which these allegorical effects, particularly lists, appear intermingled with other traditions and genres. In a telling move, Langland turns away from conventional sources and models, such as the Augustinian principles of allegorical reading and writing, the *forma tractandi* of Ciceronian, rhetorical copiousness, the Boethian invention of topics, and the sermonological enumeration of sins, and instead draws his lists from London legal sources, many of which are now contained in the PRO.[3] We shall read Langland's list and endeavor to understand how 'scribal hermeneutics,' as I'd like to call it, are imagined through it; and in the process, we shall test the limits of allegorical criticism and then pinpoint a source to his list, a labor ordinance—the presence of which verifies the particular yet newer tradition in which the poet writes.

In part two, I discuss one of the most memorable, and commented upon, passages in *Piers Plowman*—the plowing of the half-acre in passus 6. Langland derives his sense of social organization through clerical genres that will provide us yet another angle from which to view the intersections among archival forms, literary practice, and social history. Indeed, this argument concerns political history more than in the first part. My task is to look at the so-called 'problem of labor' in literary, historical, and legal discourse both before and after the tumultuous event that was the Peasants' Rebellion, so as to discern what clerical forms were available to Langland and his contemporaries in imagining labor dysfunction and revolt. For his part, Langland in passus 6 imagines a dystopia of striking workers or, more simply, a community of failing workers and, in so doing, assigns to Piers a role resembling that of a guild 'over-seer', whose task is to expect and attend to labor dysfunction. Langland's view of labor here is, in short, very London—in its characterization of Piers, in its conceptualization of social space, and in its use of scripture as a legal imperative. This claim, which brings us to the London letter books, as well as to the guild returns of 1389 that record these established tasks of labor management, will bring us to a final comment on allegory and scriptural form, particularly the ways in which the injunctions for "measurable hire" in the gospel of Matthew are in these legal documents and in *Piers Plowman* not prompts for an abstractive allegory but rather a rationale for a very material, economic concern.

## Part I: Scribal Hermeneutics

### Overseeing Allegory

> Barons and burgeises and bondemen als
> I seigh in this assemblee, as ye shul here after;
> Baksteres and brewesteres and bochiers manye,
> Wollen webbesters and weveres of lynnen,
> Taillours and tynkers and tollers in markettes,
> Masons and mynours and many othere craftes:
> Of alle kynne lybbynge laborers lopen forth somme
> As dykeres and delveres that doon hire dedes ille
> And dryveth forth the longe day with 'Dieu save Dame Emme!'
> Cokes and hires knaves cryden, 'Hote pies, hote!
> Goode gees and grys! Go we dyne, go we!'
> Taverners until hem tolden the same:
> 'Whit wyn of Oseye and wyn of Goscoigne,
> Of the Ryn and of the Rochel, the roost to defie!'
> Al this I seigh slepyng, and seven sythes more. (B Prol., lines 217–31)[4]

Thus ends the Prologue to *Piers Plowman*, but here begins a poem of extraordinary complexity with matter ranging from political satire to passion narrative. Not only can the prologue—which portrays the 'working men' and women of whom Furnivall speaks—be metonymically referred to as the "field ful of folk," but the entire poem might be usefully described in this way, concerned, as it is, with reconciling the work of salvation with the work of the world.

Elizabeth Salter has hitherto supplied the most sustained analysis of the passage in question, finding it not only to be a prime example of Langland's allegorical craft, but as a ripe occasion on which to challenge a host of critical views about *Piers Plowman*, views that had yet to shed some patently nineteenth-century notions about the poem as something of a realist text exhibiting a lucidity that seems anything but allegorical. She writes:

> And as in Bosch's picture [*The Haywain*] the eye falls from the over-all spiritual patterning of God's purpose for man to the detailed illustration of man's ugly resistance to that purpose, so in *Piers Plowman* we soon leave one mode

of allegory for another: we come down to the Field Full of Folk. For in Langland's ruthless examination of the way of the world we have not left allegory. The realism which contributes vividly to the general effect of the Prologue must not be mistaken for complete literalism. This is now allegory in a lower key, but like the central panel in Bosch's *Haywain*, it is not offered simply as a piece of documentary drawing from life in fourteenth-century England. All these figures and groups of figures, reviewed rapidly by poet and painter, make up, and *mean* Man-on-earth; they *mean* good and evil in the human state. Neither artist intends us to forget this, just as neither intends that we forget the rays of light leading the scene back to Heaven, and the tower of truth dominating over the plain.[5]

To put this comment in its critical context is to understand that Salter takes up a renewed understanding of allegory apart from the universalist approach of Robertson and Huppé, but conducive to formalist approaches wholly indifferent to the Robertsonian program, such as Robert Worth Frank's, *Piers Plowman and the Scheme of Salvation*.[6] Salter's emphasis is, instead, to speak of shifting modes of allegory within the poem that, in turn, solicit an ever-adjusting practice of close reading.[7] What for Salter marks a change in allegorical mode at the end of the Prologue and elsewhere in the poem, is precisely the seeming realism, the details, the very literal letter of *Piers Plowman*. Details, accordingly, must be *forgotten* at the urging of a generality beyond them, which we are *not* to forget, as Salter's final sentence indicates. So to be certain that we don't mistake these lines 'for complete literalism', we must do away—it is sad to say—with "Hot Pies, Hot!," because it is really quite impossible to render these words into any kind of 'particular sense'. "Hot Pies, Hot!"? So what? Augustine, in his prescriptions for reading Christian doctrine, was ready to supply ways of dealing with the salacious letter or anything contrarious in scripture that might uncharitably detract from the Christian message. But he had no grasp of the senseless detail. Indeed, these lines seem so senseless as to have us ponder what is really so conclusive about them. Why end the Prologue, here, now? Why not keep going? Nor, finally, could we even begin to discern why Langland revised this passage in his last version of the poem by adding just one more detail to line 228, "Tauerners 'a tast for nouht' tolden the same."[8] If A.V.C. Schmidt (following E.T. Donaldson[9]) is right in saying that Langland, as a reviser, favors the "non-repetition of inessentials"[10] for the sake of the allegorically necessary physical details, perhaps we can call these inessentials essential, or at least worthy of note. They are worthy of note because Langland is not asking for these details to be read allegorically, since exegesis proper begins not at the end of the Prologue but at the beginning of passus 1, where commences the explanation of what "this...bymeneth" (B.1.1) by none other than Holy Church herself.[11] Yet Langland still needs these details, and we shall be asking why and how.

But before proceeding, let me say that my assertion about inessential essentials is itself an argument. Most critics follow Salter, usually forgetting the details of *Piers Plowman* so as to remember something else—if anything, the lesson that every passage in the poem is allegory of *some kind*, a lower or higher register, such that there is hardly a sustainable moment of literalism in the poem. This point about details is, again, a question of labor—the work of writing and the writing of work. Criticism of formalist, historicist, and theological varieties are surprisingly at one when dealing with this passage, and passages like it. Each moves from the details about labor (its types, its processes, its songs, its deviance) to some immaterial generality. Each separates the material from the allegorical in the broadest sense of the term. There are many examples of this tendency from David Aers' fine early work on allegory in 1975—"here the visionary poet concentrates attention on the material basis of society. . .The rejection of the standard allegorical methods provides something of a shock"[12]— to Charles Muscatine's honest thoughts, "But artistic logic fades as one scene reels and melts into the next, as characters—sometimes whole troops of them—appear and disappear or are forgotten. . .there may be a kind of allegorical logic" but really "only confusion, a heaping and piling of images"[13]; to Malcolm Godden's introduction to *Piers Plowman*, "[the prologue] collapses back into uncertainty with the final, kaleidoscopic list of ranks and trades. The cries of the street traders seem far removed from the stern questions of Truth and Wrong associated with *tour* and *donjon*"[14]; to Kathleen Hewitt-Smith's very recent essays on *Piers Plowman*: "Langland's concrete representations of working. . .frustrate the success of allegorical interpretation by forcing our attention to an historically immediate material world"; "Langland's representations of the working poverty on the half-acre resist complete allegorical sublimation and disrupt the authoritative allegorical framework of the scene."[15] Where there's work, there's no allegory, only "the materiality of allegory's 'other' "— to cite another example.[16] And where there's poverty, there's the "de-stabilization of allegory."[17] As valuable as these commentaries are, the invocation of a limit to allegory in *Piers Plowman* often turns out to be a bar to the expansion of what allegory is and can be made to mean. We might do better to adjust our readings to suit Langland's particular formalism, seeking (in such sources as legal documents) new genres and indeed, new modes of allegory to explain such phenomena as the detail and the list.[18]

## *Dreaming of Enumeration*

Derek Pearsall has made a striking observation about the lines in question, writing, "When the 'feld ful of folk' dissolves into a blur of crowded impressions and a chorus of street cries at the end of the Prologue, both agricultural and urban workers are referred to, but the latter predominate."[19] Indeed, Pearsall sees the "blur," indicating, again, the extent to which the details here seem beyond account. However, he does discern some other details, the classifiably different kinds of worker presented here—the urban and the agricultural. What Pearsall sees, however, is not so much different kinds of worker, than different kinds themselves—genres:

> Barons and burgeises and bondemen als
> I seigh in this assemblee, as ye shul here after;
> Baksteres and brewesteres and bochiers manye,
> Wollen webbesters and weveres of lynnen,
> Taillours and tynkers and tollers in markettes,
> Masons and mynours and many othere craftes. . . .(Lines 217–22)

Here, I think, is an example of where Langland's poetry at points touches upon other sociopolitical discourses that are not at all working within Christian allegorical models, yet are still trying to represent the material—labor, work—within its appropriate forms. For instance, legal texts contemporary with Langland, such as ordinances, statutes, guild returns, and inquisitions, show that the enumeration of workers is a form of accounting for labor that aspires to supply a total view of work in a given community, or at least the *feeling* of a total view. For example, "the whole community. . .[of]. . .all the craftsmen ["artifices"] of the town of Beverley" is imagined as follows: "mercers and drapers ("tannatores"), masons, skynners, taillours, goldsmyths, smyths, plummers, bollers, tornours, girdelers, cutlers, latoners, brochemakers, horners, sponers, sadilers, furburs, websters, walkers, coverlid weavers, cartwrightes, coupars, fletchers, bowers, cordwaners, baksters, fleshhewers, fysshers, chaundelers, barburs, vytners, sadilers, rapers, hayrers, shipmen, glovers and [. . .] werkmen."[20] This form of enumeration is all over medieval law, and the records of legal proceedings, including the seemingly endless membership lists of guilds.[21] There's no stopping the form, nor predicting its uses, whether in an inquisition depicting the illicit supporters of the erstwhile mayor of London, John of Northampton—"Armurers Girdeleres Lorimers Pynners Wyrdraweres Cardmakeres Curreours Horneres Tileres Smythes Dygheres Fullers Shermen Haberdasshers Cordewaneres," and other mysteries;[22] or in the Letter-Books detailing "the misteries summoned and present" at licit assemblies,

> Grossers, Mercers, Pessoners, Drapiers, Vytners, Orfeyvrers, Taillours, Pelters, Sellers, Cordewaners, Seynturers, Ismongeres, Armurers, Broydurers, Tapicers, Tysters, Teynturers, Fullers, Joygnours, Peautrers, Wexchandelers, Talghchandelers, Salteres, Sporiers, Bowyers, Hornerers, Curreours, Haberdassheres,

Cotillers, Foundours, Bochers, Letherselleres, Brasbeyers, Plomers, Feveres, Hurers, Peyntours, Lorymers, Toundours, Wodemongeres, Tanneres.[23]

More examples of this form are not necessary. Perhaps fewer, indeed even one, would have sufficiently communicated this genre's capacity for sheer enumeration, and its fantasy that the laboring social body can be accounted for by enumerations in finer and finer distinctions that somehow maintain their differences.[24] Such a fantasy no doubt is primarily a legal one, seeing as well publicized laws like the 1351 Statute of Laborers, which addresses the realm of workers, uses the familiar form: "carters, ploughmen, leaders of the plough, shepherds, swineherds, domestic and all other servants," "carpenters, masons, tilers, and other roofers of houses," "cordwainers and shoemakers"[25] and so on—with repetition itself conveying, as if by cadence, the imperative of law. But why are laborers typically the subjects of lists and whence this fantasy of accounting? The partial evidence I present here from registers, inquisitions, and statutes are different in kind and purpose, but nonetheless might best be viewed as extensions and embellishments of generic habits beginning in the early thirteenth century and continuing right into the fourteenth and beyond—the task of listing exampled both in taxation rolls (which account for the number of laborers and animals and the value of equipment on estates) and in estates rolls—registers of recognizances of debts, rents, and farms.[26] So what's significant about Langland's usage?

### *Item Time*

What's primarily significant, and what's most obvious, is that Langland is also a lister of labor, inscribing within his poem this genre's working obsessions *to register*, a compulsion to repeat that's all the more felt by its very cessation, a stopping that only reminds one of the potential to list more. Moreover, Langland knows this, as Will says in the last line, "All this I saw sleeping, and seven times more."[27] Plenty of potential, in other words. Yet Langland, I now suggest, evokes the genre's time signature, its temporality so to speak, *as* the closing moment in the Prologue, availing himself of the genre's prescriptions for reading, checking, and considering details, item by item—a reading whose tempo is slower than the time signatures of allegory, which in *Piers Plowman* criticism speeds up, over, and above details, *especially* material details. Think of my suggestion as a recasting of Anne Middleton's serviceable thesis about how and why *Piers Plowman* continuously stops and starts again. Rather, the poem slows down and speeds up, I suggest, over a shifting generic terrain.[28] This point about genre, and the time signature of genre, is not a question of legal citation—what Langland knows of late medieval law; nor is it one of legal vocabulary. Instead, we are looking at how legal genres prescribe different modes of reading, signaling a scribal hermeneutic sufficient, in Langland's mind, to effect closure, yet generate particular meaning. Such a generic understanding requires that we consider clerical composition, the processes that go into constructing (and reading) lists, accounts, registers, and so forth—a process probably very familiar to Langland, whose clerical background has never really been in much dispute (save the question of *what kind* of clerical work he did).

According to these forms of composition, items or entries accumulate in lists but lists of course never follow the unfolding logics of narrative or allegory; even so, we still do learn something about writing and recording—the memorial and accumulative practices of scribal culture. A scribe, charged to enter into the books names of persons, their occupations, their debts and settlements, might pile up several pieces of paper or vellum scraps of these details before copying them down all at once[29], knowing that a detail by detail, item by item, entry would be a waste of time, excruciating, unnecessary, and sometimes impossible.[30] Yet a scribe-recorder of pleas and debts could not but help to add items as time warrants, one day after the next. He could accumulate entries but never get ahead of himself, because that would mean getting ahead of time and routine, which would mean making things up—that is, fabricating a legal document, not entirely uncommon and not always forgery of course, but rarely done with this particular genre.[31]

But when it is done, the results are fascinating. For instance, a clerk in Wiltshire in 1432 stands out for special notice, since he was "given to literary flourishes," writing in the right-hand column of a parliamentary return a list as a sentence, temporalizing it as a fiction, and fabricating names for missing initials: "Adam, Belle, Clyme, Ocluw, Willyam, Cloudesle, Robyn, hode, Inne, Grenewode, Stode, Godeman, was, hee, lytel, Joon, Muchette, Millersson, Scathelok, Reynoldyn."[32] Of course, these literary inventions, which are also interventions, run afoul of the wisdom and mythology of scribal culture, the exhortation that memoranda are not to be messed with: according to one statute for scriveners, "no attorney [should] sit...among the clerks nor meddle with the rolls or other memoranda."[33] Even erasure fails as a form of forgetting, here, and loses to the interests of permanence: items are typically crossed out with a line, so as to be recalled, rather than erased.[34] Such are the sublime and sublimated requirements of archiving that a scribe at all costs is to resist omissions and eye-skipping and instead, as one manual exhorts, be "lynx-eyed" to avoid mistakes ['oculi lincei necessarii essent ne erraret'],[35] to "note down everything,"[36] never to oversee or to forget every detail that matters.[37] The task itself is raised to a sworn duty ("Et qe vous ne lerrez" [and that you shall not omit]).³⁸ Here we can think of Thomas Hoccleve at work in the Privy Seal, bracing his pained back and refocusing his strained eyes.

Perhaps it's because Langland can't mess with the memoranda that we have *Piers Plowman*, for indeed, the kinds of literary invention witnessed by the Wiltshire scribe are evident in this poem in its odd and very unallegorical appellations, such as "Tomme Trewe-tonge-tel-me-no-tales / Ne lesynge-to-laughen-of-for-I-loved-hym-nevere" (4.18–19), or the names of Piers' wife, daughter, and son—respectively, "Dame Werch-whan-tyme-is" (6.78), "Do-right-so-or-thi-dame-shal-thee-bete" (79–80), and "Suffre-thi-Sovereyns-to-haven–hir-wille:/Deme-hem-nought-for-if-thow-shalt-it-deere-abugge" (80–81). These names are sentences, needless to say, and within the generic confines of the list, are excesses, marginal matter insinuating itself, appropriating the energies of listing and channeling them in the direction of the syntagmatic.

Scribal literary invention—to typify this practice so—is even more, or at least differently, evident in the list at the end of the Prologue. There, according to scribal habits of memory, Langland presents a passage where the task is to interpret details as details, to record them in our minds as carefully as would a guild's secretary or recorder, or the mayor's clerk. This is scribal hermeneutics, in so far as Langland understands which genres can slow the poem down and, in this case, effect closure—item by item: he makes us actually read the list, rather than permitting us to resort to allegory as an excuse to skip it, or rubrics and indices as a means to organize it. As we reread this list, we can now fully describe its operations, especially where the logic of the list meets narrative. We find that Langland begins this ending by listing in the first six lines, and then by allowing the list to assemble into a syntax, into sentences—as if the names come to life from the margin—having "lopen forth"—and as if the list confronts the reality it seeks to organize. Muscatine's "characters—sometimes whole troops of them—appear and disappear or are forgotten," and therefore, describe a logic not of narrative or plot but rather of the page, of the list.

Furthermore, our reading the list item by item produces a source for us, and reasserts the relevance of legal citation right at the center of deviance. The "Taverners," who shout that "Whit wyn of Oseye and wyn of Goscoigne, / Of the Ryn and of the Rochel" are conveniently sold in one stall, are voicing a regulation for taverners, which rules that, on the contrary, "no white wine of Gascoigne, of La Rochel, of Spain. . .shall be laid in taverns where Rhenish wine is for sale."³⁹ This ordinance is all over the London Letterbooks, so it's a wonder the great editor and annotator, Skeat, didn't catch this parallel to *Piers Plowman*.⁴⁰ No one has, so far as I know, perhaps because of the allegorical effects of forgetting, perhaps because we wouldn't think Langland would invest significance here in the poem. Yet when these effects are properly understood as deriving from the list, from memorial practices, we then can follow the scribal imagination all the way into the archive, broadly conceived, and look for correspondences between legal sources, as is the custom in clerical culture itself. Indeed, while Langland has all kinds of things to say, prescriptively and proscriptively, about clerks, he nonetheless betrays a clerical sense of genre in the very performance of his poem.[41]

To conclude this part of my paper: one of the twentieth century's most important Langlandians, Morton Bloomfield, made an off-hand remark that now circulates widely in criticism, since it seems to hit the nail on the head in describing the many twists and turns of *Piers Plowman*. He said, simply, that the poem reads "like a commentary on an unknown text." I believe, however, that we can often replace Bloomfield's comment with an earlier statement by the now obscure Jean Jusserand. In 1893, he thought that *Piers Plowman*, "which would almost seem a commentary on the Rolls of Parliament, resembles still more closely the Book of Statutes, or even the 'Liber Albus,' wherein are recorded the municipal regulations of London,"[42] and wherein, I might add, we find many lists. *Piers Plowman* is a commentary on a culture of writing whose relevance to late medieval literature we are only now beginning to understand. Indeed, Langland's lists allow for a permeability between the poem and this culture of writing, such that we momentarily leave not only the "field ful of folk" but rather the poem itself and, as if in some intergeneric fashion, enter into another writing altogether. This is, finally, the more interesting historical claim to be made about *Piers Plowman*, and one that itself revises our sense of its historicity. It's not only that, as one important critic put it, Langland's is an "outstanding imaginative response to the teeming energies of his society" of "new economic forces, and newly emergent social groups."[43] Such places in the poem also evince a history of memory, a history of thinking about writing, and memorializing labor through the ingathering of legal genres.[44] This, I believe, is a history we cannot forget, as we explore further the relations between late medieval writing and scribal hermeneutics.

## Part II: The Genres of Social Organization

There's another kind of list at work in *Piers Plowman*, signaled by the term "assemblee" (218)—what Langland in fact calls that entire group of workers at the end of the Prologue. By way of contrast: elsewhere, he uses the term in tandem with a list not exclusive to laborers, so as to describe Lady

Meed's full wily retinue:

> Of alle manere of men, the meene and the riche,
> To marien this mayde was many man assembled,
> As of knyghtes and of clerkes and oother commune peple,
> As sisours and somonours, sherreves and hire clerkes,
> Bedelles and bailiffs and brocours of chaffare,
> Forgoers and vitaillers and vokettes of the Arches;
> I kan noght rekene the route that ran aboute Mede. (2.56–62)

"I kan noght rekene the route that ran aboute Mede" means that cessation delimits and defines this genre of registration. There are many in the company of Meed. Even the customary listers are listed, clerks, bailiffs, beadles—perhaps available for the presentation of False's charter (2.69–114), which follows immediately and which features another list, an entry of witnesses:

> In witnesse of which thyng Wrong was the firste,
> And Piers the Pardoner of Paulynes doctrine
> Bette the Bedel of Bokynghamshire,
> Reynald the Reve of Rutland Sokene,
> Munde the Millere—and many mo othere. (2.108–12)

Cessation here—"and many mo othere"—is generically necessary, seeing as the listing itself draws in the narrator as a witness to witnessing, as a potential witness, himself authenticating the charter while testifying to the impossible—that is, validating the truth claims of False's charter. The narrator must stop.

The point here is that lists and 'assemblies' are two sides of the same coin and, as such, are often imagined as having political motivations. In all kinds of late medieval writing, the 'assemblee' frequently appears as a list out of hand, a list come alive—the seriated individuals ordering themselves into a dangerous group. From the late 1370s to the mid 1380s, the 'assemblee', as a term for social organization, came to look distinctly less neutral (as the *MED* might lead one to believe) and more of an antitype to regulated associations between laborers—the 'corporation' or 'fraternity' or guild that so distinguishes the late fourteenth century as a period of collectivities.[45] In England, both before and after the momentous occasion that was the Peasants' Rebellion of 1381, the 'assemblee' came to represent crowds in their most potentially threatening version for the clerical gaze. The author of *The Anonimalle Chronicle* writes of 1381: "les comunes del pais et les comunes de Londres assemblerount a treshidous proiar al nombre de c mille et plusours."[46] And Austin canon, Henry Knighton, recalls 1381 this way:

> Then others and still others joined them [sibi associauerunt], and each sent word to his friends and kin, and so from town to town, and country to country,

asking and requiring them without delay to lend their counsel and aid to those endeavours that the common good and necessity urgently demanded. Who, rejoicing in their fashion, began with the greatest triumph to assemble their multitudes, glad that the day was come in which they could look to each other for relief from such oppressive need. . . . And thus they assembled [congregati sunt] on Blackheath, where amidst so many [pre multitudine] they forgot themselves, and no longer content with their first purpose, nor satisfied merely by minor crimes, they ruthlessly contemplated greater and unspeakable evils, nor would they be ready to desist from their wicked plans until all the lords and the great men of the kingdom had been utterly destroyed.[47]

However, we'd be mistaken to think that these accounts are unusual in their claims, or particularly new to post-1381 England. Indeed, what's interesting about the chronicle accounts are not only their potential echoes of peasant intent and strategy, which has been discussed by scholars[48], but also the genres these historians share and derive from the very medieval laws they read, sometimes compile, and always echo. We can appreciate, in other words, that in the post-1381 context the archive is activated in new ways, that history is the occasion for, among other things, new methods of genre gathering. Old genres (and their respective subjects and problems) are reoriented toward new themes that don't, it must be emphasized, *appear* as old themes. On the one hand, chroniclers would animate, unwittingly, and ever more rigorously and unanimously, the pre-1381 legal themes about riots and large illegal assemblies such as we see above—themes prevalent since at least the time of Edward III through to the frustrated petitions of 1377 regarding "villeins and tenants" who "have made confederation and alliance together."[49] On the other hand, lawmakers themselves would not only diligently legislate against vagrants, idle servants, and the usual lot of peasants leaving their lord's land for higher wages, à la the ordinance of June 18, 1349 and the Statutes of 1351,[50] but also against the potential for those individuals to form a collective, their separate agencies becoming one in a far more dangerous and challenging maneuver.

To lawmakers, these are not the seriated laborers that occupy the rolls, membership lists, and other legal documents, in which the enumeration itself presupposes managed restrictions on the behalf of land owners. Rather, these are the very 'assemblies' imagined in the 1383 Ricardian enactment—"noman make none congraciouns, conuenticules, ne assembles of poeple, in priue nen apert, ne no more than other men, with oute leue of the Mair; ne ouer more in none manere ne make alliances, confederacies, conspiracies, ne obligaciouns, forto bynde men to gidre, forto susteyne eny quereles in lyuingge and deyengge to gidre; upon peyne of enprisonement."[51] When the mayor and aldermen in the chamber of Guildhall, London brought charges against the Cordwainers in 1387, they cited this enactment: "serving men of said trade of Cordwainers . . . brought together a great congregation of men like unto themselves, and there did conspire and confederate to hold together; to the damage of the commonality, and the prejudice of the trade before mentioned and in rebellion against the overseers."[52] The 1383 enactment not only seems to have been a point of necessary reference in Thomas Usk's successful appeal against John of Northampton,[53] but also informed the petitions in the Cambridge Parliament of 1388,[54] where all previous Statutes of Laborers were reinforced yet again, and where guilds were mandated to account for their wealth and doings, including of course their 'assemblies', occasions when the "Fraternite schul assemble to-gydere in the chirche" on the guild's respective Saint's feast day.[55] The king's writ of 1388 (which produced the 1389 returns) asks the guild masters and wardens to detail in their returns "de mode and de forma sacramentorum, congregacionum, conuiuiarum, assembliarum" [the manner and form of their rites, congregations, discussions, and assemblies]—perhaps to ensure to the authorities that there are no ulterior or clandestine motives in meeting, no post-1381 conspiracies afoot among workers who have organized themselves into groups that already serve their own interests.[56] There can't be any happenings like those in the entry from *The Anonimalle Chronicle* (above), nothing like the experience of 1381 all over again.

From the legal and literate perspective, then, it's hard to look upon a group of workers without projecting onto it a great design. But the problem is, really, the legal and literate perspective, which frames peasant rebellion in the ordered and organizing terms of assemblies and congregations—licit forms of social organization that appear regularly in guild ordinances, regal proclamations, inquisitions, and memoranda and that occasionally irrupt in the record as antitypes, not as disorder but *bad* order. These were all the more horrific because they invert the licit processes by which "honest and discreet men," often assemble in the face of "clamour" and "tumults" that often beleaguer council.[57] There's certainly no concealing the affective associations between the rebellion of 1381 and the smaller and intermittent dissensions and strife imagined to be right in your very hall or neighborhood. Order goes awry right at the very center of the literate fantasy about social control. Which explains why chroniclers can't illustrate 1381 in the way they do other riots (similar to those between northerners and southerners at the universities, or between town and gown) in the terms of melee.[58] They imagine 1381 as the worst of the law come alive—its pathologies and stereotypes. The law becomes what it is, comes to flaunt the knowledge of what it disallows, comes to destroy itself.

We can think of Langland's ending, the cessation of the Prologue at a particular moment—the moment of listing that could ceaselessly continue—as a way of denying collective agency to seriated individuals, a way of looking away, as if the looking itself brings agency to those who will rise against you. We can recall here John Gower's clerical speaker in *Vox Clamantis*: "Yet from a distance I observed how they made their mutual arrangements.... The more I saw them, the more I judged I ought to be afraid of them, not knowing what sort of end would be bound to come" (1.9 [66]). It is as if looking makes matters worse; it is as if looking draws Gower into the very materialist phenomenology that Jean-Paul Sartre was trying to articulate centuries later in examples such as this: "they are both manual workers, and they are both from the country; they differ from each other less than they differ from me and, in the last analysis, their reciprocal negation is, for me, a kind of deep complicity. A complicity against me."[59] Will's look at labor is different, of course: he is not looking at 1381, as it were, but he is looking at seriated individuals gathering into a collective, 'the assemblee' (218), a social formation elaborated here as laborers—"Barons and burgeises *and bondemen als / I seigh in this assemblee*, as ye shul here after"—excluding the "Barons."[60] The final point here is that Langland, like his literary, historical, and legal contemporaries since the 1370s, places upon the 'assemblee' the *burden* of subversive collective action, a burden that has a recursive effect in the likes of a need, the need to look away or, as in this case, to effect formal closure, as at the end of the Prologue. But whatever action is suppressed here is reexpressed elsewhere—passus 6, that scene of local labor rebellion in *Piers Plowman*, where Piers cannot look away. He must look at labor and rebellion. For he is an 'over-seer'.

### Piers as 'Over-Seer'

In so far as the "ordering of the folk of the field is the initial challenge of the poem," such that "their periodic reentries test the ability of each genre to better the ordering"[61], we can confirm that, in passus 6, the 'assemblee' of the Prologue reappears to realize the "dedes ille" in ever more poignant ways. Piers watches the crowd work and then rebel with their mocking songs:

> At heigh prime Piers leet the plough stonde,
> To oversen hem hymself; whoso best wroughte,
> He sholde be hired therafter, whan hervest tyme come
> Thanne seten somme and songen atte nale,
> And holpen ere this half acre with "How trolly lolly!" (6.112-16; 8.119-21)

What resources does Piers have here to deal with this mess? Or, better, what forms and conventions does Langland use here to depict Piers' role in managing the folk? Let's make an imaginative leap, for a moment, and run with Pearsall's idea that a "distinction between agricultural and urban workers cannot be strictly maintained."[62] Let's, that is, look to urban forms of labor management to determine whether Langland means to characterize Piers, the agrarian, as something of a "surveyour," whose task is indeed "To oversen hem hymself; whoso best wroughte." For so doing may give these clerical perspectives of labor more historical specificity, such that even the gaze itself will emerge from a material basis.

We go to London and the Letterbooks, in which the 'overseer' is a veritable office of labor management, held by a person typically elected to the post by the guild itself. The guild aspires to choose "men of the most loyal and befitting of the said trade" to present "defaults" to the Mayor and Aldermen "without sparing any one for friendship or for hatred."[63] In turn, these officials "shall oversee that all those who work by the day shall take for their hire according as they are skilled, and may deserve for their work, and not outrageously"; moreover, "said overseers shall have so reasonably set such journeymen at his value. . .until he shall have learned to deserve more."[64] These expressions run throughout the guild ordinances and are really formulae for labor management and quality control.[65] They are important because they presuppose that labor in collective contexts and confined spaces always threatens to cease and devolve into unregulated, atomized, and internecine efforts. And so a formula, or better, a genre, appears to match the circumstances: as he is imagined, the overseer is obliged to make order out of disorder and, more importantly, to look for what is *already* wrong.

Enter Piers and the multitude, "a thousand of men tho thrungen togideres" (B.5.510; 624), crammed onto his excruciatingly small half-acre (6.4), and we can begin to appreciate some of the strictures of co-ordinating collective and diverse tasks within confined spaces. Langland's spatial imagination here itself *remains* urban in rendering the half-acre about the size of a city block in London, which itself would be mapped out, and distinguished from the next block, according to laboring processes—who works where.[66] The half-acre is thus a suitably tight environment for Piers' work of oversight, which initially aspires to collect somehow all idealized human endeavors befitting to most estates (knights, women, laborers) but which soon finds its task reduced to one—tilling and surveying tilling.[67] One space, one work: "Now is Perkyn [Piers] and thise pilgrimes to the plow faren / To erie this half-acre holpen hym manye" (B.6.105–6).[68] Accordingly, Piers, however much he is ostensibly characterized as an agricultural team leader, finds himself with responsibilities not unlike that of the urban guild 'over-seer'. It's not only for lexical reasons ("To oversen hem hymself") that this is the case, but rather because the ordering of "folk," "this folk" specifically (B.6.2), many of whom were those yelling Londoners who close out the Prologue, is Piers' charge here in Passus 6. Imagine Piers' task framed by the language of the guild over-seer, and we begin to see where urban and rural languages blur. Doubtless himself a "most loyal" worker, he must "oversen hem hymself...whoso best wroughte"; he must assess the laborers' worth and qualifications for future employment, who "sholde be hired therafter, whan hervest tyme come." He must, in short, "oversee that all those who work by the day shall take for their hire according as they are skilled, and may deserve for their work, and not outrageously"—setting each worker "at his value...until he shall have learned to deserve more." There perhaps could be no more appropriate language to describe what Piers is doing at the half-acre.

None of it helps, however. The workers become wasters—or more properly, the wasters make their presence known among the other workers. They are compelled to return to work through the fear of impending hunger: Hunger, "hir maister, ther wolde noon of hem chide" (6.318). Piers experiences what other over-seers experienced before, "rebellion against the overseers."[69] In other words, for Piers, things have *already* fallen apart at the half-acre.[70] Langland seems to want Piers to fail insofar as he imputes to him an office that deals directly with labor dysfunction, and which is typically the first office to be apprized, as it were, of said rebellion.

The historical point here, besides the one that such passages imagine the very history of problems leading up to 1381, is that this rebellion, this problem of labor, should be quite familiar to anyone having to do with official literate culture in London. It's a rebellion already expected and accommodated for in the Letterbooks.

Of course, Langland has his reasons for this chaos. The poem must go on, other resources and perspectives must be presented and tested. Piers' abandonment of the plow, for instance, must be understood in this context of failed labor; the only terms with which even to speak of labor as a condition, and an end in itself rather than a means, are through failure: " 'I shal cessen of my sowyng,' quod Piers, 'and swynke nought so harde' " (7.118). Piers' words are remarkable, because his admission that plowing is "harde" labor, which he will forgo for a less laborious form of life that involves nonetheless a different kind of pain—penance, challenges the very viability of "harde" work first seen by Will in the Prologue: "Somme putten hem to the plough, pleiden ful selde, / In settynge and sowynge swonken *ful harde,* / And wonnen that thise wastours with glotonye destruyeth" (Prol. 20–22, my emphasis). We find there the distinct opposition between "ful harde" work and "thise wastours." Piers, in giving up work, however, potentially collapses the distinction between himself and his employees, impinging on the very speech and acts of the wasters: "I was noght wont to werche...and now wol I noght bigynne!" (6.167); "And tho wolde Wastour noght werche, but wandren aboute" (6.302; 241).[71] This is not to say that Piers becomes a waster, though Piers can easily recognize that these rascals are "my blody bretheren" (6.207)—a recognition that in ideal circumstances must be foreclosed, since the over-seer operates "without sparing any one for friendship or for hatred."[72] It's to point out how limited are the terms by which to express the failure of work. There is no clear justification for why work isn't theologically appropriate in the end; there are only the injunctions that one should work. The declaration that work won't work, a material exclamation in the strictest sense, is a theme all too present in the medieval legal record. Langland expresses these limitations through the figure of Piers, who consolidates the law's demands for labor organization and its counter-tendencies to depict the dissolution of labor—all in the same place.

Now to a final point about allegory: Piers' tasks at the half-acre are specified in terms that combine all at once the problems of freemen, day-labor, the demands of labor statutes, and the difficulties of setting wages at regulated levels—problems that critics traditionally see at work here but have not understood to be *all* collected in Piers' administrative task but rather in a diversity of sources that critics themselves must gather, negotiate, and read into Piers—biblical, medieval, and critical. This gathering of traditions is not entirely necessary, even though it remains illuminating, for when Langland explains that "[Piers was proud therof], and putte hem to werke / And yaf hem mete as he myghte aforthe and mesurable hyre" (6.197–98; see also 3.70–80 and 14.136–53), he is citing scriptural passages contained in the germane ordinances for the over-seers in London, ordinances that already enfold the injunctions in Matthew 6: 5 and 20: 1–18: "two-pence a day, or his food, shall be given to the collector; for (it is wisely said), 'the laborer is worthy of his hire and food'."[73] The scriptural citations in these texts are not a prompt for Christian allegory nor an abstraction away from the matters of routine and work. Instead, the scriptural citation itself becomes a legal formula, a literal thing, directing us right back to its inscriptions in ordinances. So too, does Langland's half-acre draw from surrounding legal texts, not only from whatever "statut" (6.319) we believe is operative there, but rather, and perhaps more capaciously, from the methods of memorializing labor in which allegories are *institutional* allegories where the insistence is always upon the material, the matters of labor and law.

### More Work

Several reflective, associated points are in order. Langland does not value labor by *one*, all-encompassing version but a mixture of versions deriving from theological, literary, legal, and allegorical sources. He typically demarcates each source generically in ways suggestive of the modern insights into reader response; that is, for Langland, each genre not only signals its respective 'kind' but rather, and more complexly, prescribes a way of reading fitting to the institutions whence Langland derives them. This means that many times, Langland's ideas about labor proceed from generic necessity, as at the end of the Prologue, as much as from an interest in any contemporary debate about labor or, more broadly, from the limits of an ideological climate. Any look at the criticism will show how common it is to read medieval labor in light of the successive enactments of statutes regarding bondsmen, harvesters, and others, but often critics, as if at the urging of such laws (let alone the biblical thematics of farm work Langland often evokes), spend more time thinking about agricultural forms of work and social organization, and their literary expressions, to the relative exclusion of urban forms, or to the guild organizations that join the two together. Urban guilds imagine their own community with respect to "trewe tyliers and men of craft," since the most wealthy guilds have tenements (typically absconded into mortmain).[74] These are hybrid forms of social organization, and they appear, as I have tried to show, in *Piers Plowman*. Yet chroniclers also hybridize these forms. They characterize masses of rebelling agricultural workers (and their London peers) in terms that involve some of the issues and problems of mass organization endemic to guilds and especially urban craft guilds—both before and after 1381.[75] Obviously, it makes good sense to interpret representations of labor rebellion in light of 1381 (and its after-effects in the literate imagination), but any look at the court records and guild ordinances will show that labor rebellion and violence between guilds and workers in the urban and rural setting were perennial, or at least well legislated against. Which means an author or chronicler would have ready-to-hand forms by which to characterize rebellion or, as is probably likely, contextualize, so as to mollify and understand, their own shock of the event of 1381. Indeed, the Rising is recollected through a past of local rebellions, disputes, and subversions—through, ironically, the very terms that seek to maintain order, from the procedural practices of the assemblies to the detailed lists that are imagined to make work work licitly and collectively. But, of course, we can acknowledge that local practices, and working social organizations, never would look the same after 1381.

## Notes

I am grateful to Maura Nolan and Fiona Somerset, who supplied me terrific commentaries on this paper.

1. William Benzie, *Frederick James Furnivall (1825–1910): Victorian Scholar Adventurer* (Norman, OK: Pilgrim Books, 1983), p. 52.

2. My sense of this phenomenon, as it relates to *Piers Plowman*, is gathered from a variety of scholarly work, which I cite in full below, by John Alford, Michael Clanchy, Andrew Galloway, Steven Justice, Anne Middleton, and Paul Strohm. Emily Steiner's, "Langland's Documents," and Bruce Holsinger's reply, are both interesting and certainly relevant; see, respectively, *Yearbook of Langland Studies* 14 (2000): 95–107, 110–13.
3. On second and third traditions, see Ann W. Astell, "Response to Clopper's 'Langland and Allegory: A Proposition,' " *Yearbook of Langland Studies* 15 (2001): 43–46; on the fourth, see Morton Bloomfield, *The Seven Deadly Sins* (East Lansing: Michigan State University Press, 1952; rpt. 1967).
4. By passus and line, I cite *The Vision of Piers Plowman: A Complete Edition of the B-Text*, ed. A.V.C. Schmidt (London: Everyman's Library, 1991).
5. Elizabeth Salter, *Piers Plowman: An Introduction*, 2nd ed. (1962; Oxford: Basil Blackwell, 1969), pp. 71–72. I believe it's right to see Salter's study as a response to the kinds of criticism instanced not only by D.W. Robertson and Bernard F. Huppé, *Piers Plowman and Scriptural Tradition* (Princeton: Princeton University Press, 1951), but also by Rosemary Woolf, "Some Non-medieval Qualities of *Piers Plowman*," *Essays in Criticism* 12 (1962); George Kane, "The Vision of *Piers Plowman*," in his *Middle English Literature: A Critical Study of the Romances, the Religious Lyrics, Piers Plowman* (London: Metheun, 1951); and Charles Muscatine, *Poetry and Crisis in the Age of Chaucer* (Notre Dame: University of Notre Dame Press, 1972), a book of lectures delivered in 1969, virtually coterminous with the second edition of Salter's study.
6. Robert Worth Frank, *Piers Plowman and the Scheme of Salvation* (New Haven: Yale University Press, 1957). Specifically, Salter's point here is like Robert Worth Frank's of "man working in this world toward eternal punishment or reward" (p. 19).
7. The fruits of such a close reading, one that continuously and cautiously mediates Langland's images with their purported scriptural and exegetical significances, are clearly born out in David Aers' *Piers Plowman and Christian Allegory* (New York: St. Martin's Press, 1975).
8. Walter W. Skeat, ed. *The Vision of William Concerning Piers the Plowman in Three Parallel Texts*, 2 vols. (Oxford: Oxford University Press, 1924), C. Prol., 228. Cf. *Piers Plowman by William Langland: An Edition of the C-text*, ed. Derek Pearsall (Berkeley and Los Angeles: University of California Press, 1978), C. Prol. 230–31.
9. E.T. Donaldson, *Piers Plowman: The C-Text and Its Poet* (New Haven: Yale University Press, 1949).
10. A.V.C. Schmidt, "Langland's Visions and Revisions," *Yearbook of Langland Studies* 14 (2000): 21–22; 16–17 [5–28]. My remarks on useless details are in dialogue with Roland Barthes' wonderful essay, "The Reality Effect," *French Literary Theory Today: A Reader*, ed. Tzvetan Todorov, trans. R. Carter (Cambridge: Cambridge University Press, 1982.), pp. 11–17.
11. Cf. James Simpson, *Piers Plowman: An Introduction to the B-text* (London and New York: Longman, 1990), p. 21.

12. Aers, *Christian Allegory*, p. 114; see also pp. 117, 121.
13. See Charles Muscatine, *Medieval Literature, Style, and Culture: Essays by Charles Muscatine* (Columbia: University of South Carolina Press, 1999), p. 123.
14. Malcolm Godden, *The Making of Piers Plowman* (London: Longman, 1990), p. 32.
15. Hewett-Smith, "Allegory on the Half-Acre: The Demands of History," *Yearbook of Langland Studies* 10 (1996): 4 [1–22]. See also Simpson, "Spirituality and Economics in Passus 1–7 of the B Text," *Yearbook of Langland Studies* 1 (1987): 99–102 [83–103].
16. Citing here the title to chapter two, "Piers the Plowman and the Materiality of Allegory's 'Other'," in Claire Marshall, *William Langland, Piers Plowman* (Horndon, Tavistock, Devon: Northcote House, 2001), pp. 49–79.
17. Hewett-Smith, " 'Nede ne hath no lawe': Poverty and the De-stabilization of Allegory in the Final Visions of *Piers Plowman*," in *William Langland's Piers Plowman: A Book of Essays*, ed. Hewett-Smith (New York: Routledge, 2001), pp. 233–53.
18. Even Steven Justice, who had broached this interesting question of "shifting generic commitments" in the poem, cannot but help to treat genre as Christian allegory by another name; see "The Genres of *Piers Plowman*," *Viator* 19 (1988): 292 [291–306]. For examples as to where Justice subsumes genre into allegory, see 298, 300–304, as well as his blunt claim about passus 6: "Its genre is Bible; more specifically, it is exodus [sic]" (301). James Simpson briefly discusses Langland's genres as "discourse"—"the claims to power made by a given genre," "the authoritative claims made by a given way of writing" (*Introduction to the B-text*, p. 15). On the interesting notion of "self-conscious genre performance," however, see Anne Middleton, "Acts of Vagrancy," 256–58; especially 258.
19. "Langland's London," in *Written Work: Langland, Labor, and Authorship*, ed. Steven Justice and Kathryn Kerby-Fulton (Philadelphia: University of Pennsylvania Press, 1997), p. 186. The title to this section is taken from Allen Ginsberg, "A Supermarket in California":

    What thoughts I have of you tonight, Walt Whitman, for I walked down the sidestreets under the trees with a headache self-conscious looking at the full moon.

    In my hungry fatigue, and shopping for images, I went into the neon fruit supermarket, dreaming of your enumerations!

    What peaches and what penumbras! Whole families shopping at night! Aisles full of husbands! Wives in the avocados, babies in the tomatoes!—and you, García Lorca, what were you doing down by the watermelons? (*Howl and Other Poems* [San Francisco: City Lights Books, 1959])

20. *Royal Commission on Historical Manuscripts: Report on the Manuscripts of the Corporation of Beverley* (London: H.M. Stationery Office [Mackie], 1900), p. 65. A more extensive and slightly different example concerning Beverley

as well is in the *Calendar of Patent Rolls: Richard II, 1381–85* (London: PRO, 1897), 146; item dated June 16, 1382, which lists persons and their trades. For the contexts, see R.B. Dobson, "The Risings in York, Beverley, and Scarborough, 1380–81," in *The English Rising of 1381*, ed. Rodney Hilton and T.H. Aston (Cambridge, 1984). There is here, I should note, no escape from the material or urban such as that literally enacted by Petrarch: "Arise, come, hasten, let us abandon the city to merchants, attorneys, brokers, usurers, tax-gatherers, scriveners, doctors, perfumers, butchers, cooks, bakers and tailors, alchemists, fullers, artisans, weavers, architects, statuaries, painters, mimes, dancers, lute-players, quacks, panderers, thieves, criminals, adulterers, parasites, foreigners, swindlers and jesters, gluttons who with scent alert catch the odor of the marketplace, for whom that is their only bliss, where mouths are agape for that alone. For on the mountains there is no smell of cookery" (*De Vita Solitaria*, trans. Jacob Zeitlen, *The Life of Solitude*, 312. Cited and discussed by David Wallace, *Chaucerian Polity: Absolutist Lineages and Associational Forms in Late Medieval England and Italy* [Stanford: Stanford University Press, 1997], pp. 272–73).

21. See Caroline M. Barron, "The London Middle English Guild Certificates of 1388-9: I. Historical Introduction," *Nottingham Medieval Studies* 39 (1995): 111. For a somewhat accessible example of this relatively and understandably unavailable sort of text, see *The Register of the Freemen of the City of York from the City Records, vol. 1, 1272–1558*. The Surtees Society 96 (1896) (Durham: Andrew's and Co., 1897). More recently, see *Parish Fraternity Register, Fraternity of the Holy Trinity and SS Fabian and Sebastian in the Parish of St Botolph without Aldersgate*, ed. Patricia Basing, London Record Society (London, 1982); and Patricia Basing, *Trades and Crafts in Medieval Manuscripts* (New York: New Amsterdam, 1990). For an example of the overlap of these genres, see Riley, *Memorials*, p. 571.

22. *The Peasants' Rising and the Lollards*, ed. Edgar Powell and G.M. Trevelyan (London: Longmans, Green, and Co., 1899), p. 27. Paul Strohm identifies this text as "a point-for-point recasting of (Thomas Usk's) 'Appeal' into Latin." See "The Textual Vicissitudes of Usk's 'Appeal,'" *Hochon's Arrow: The Social Imagination of Fourteenth-Century Texts*, with an appendix by A.J. Prescott (Princeton: Princeton University Press, 1992), p. 154 [145–60]; Strohm refers to the PRO document itself, E163 5/28 number 12, and not to this edition. More on Usk below.

23. *Calendar of Letter-Books. . .of the City of London: Letter-Book H*, p. 41; see pp. 42–44, 107.

24. Cf. Wallace's remark about Chaucer's collection of pilgrims: "Work is as natural and unique to human beings as language; the necessity of work and language argues that humankind is a political animal, not an aggregate of atomized individuals" (*Chaucerian Polity*, p. 68).

25. R.B. Dobson, ed., *The Peasant's Revolt of 1381*, 2nd ed. (London: Macmillan Press, 1983), pp. 64–66. There are surrounding yet more localized ordinances of the same, regarding "masons, carpenters, plasterers, tilers, and all kind of laborers" who take more than is desired (see also *Memorials of London and*

*London Life in the XIIIth, XIVth, and XVth Centuries, A.D. 1276–1419*, ed. H.T. Riley [London, 1868], pp. 253–58 [dated 1350]).

26. For examples and discussion on various kinds of lists and their purposes, see M.T. Clanchy, *From Memory to Written Record: England 1066–1307* (London: Edward Arnold, 1979), pp. 31–32, 51, and plates 9, 10, and 15.

27. An example in passus 5 is conspicuous, where the list approaches the carnivalesque (See Aers, *Chaucer, Langland, and the Creative Imagination* [London: Routledge & Kegan Paul, 1980]):

> Thanne goth Gloton in, and grete othes after.
> Cesse the Souteresse sat on the benche,
> Watte the Warner and his wife bothe,
> Tymme the Tynkere and tweyne of his [knav]es
> Hikke the Hakeneyman and Hugh the Nedlere,
> Clarice of Cokkeslane and the Clerk of the chirche
> Sire Piers of Pridie and Pernele of Flaundres,
> Dawe the Dykere, and a dozeyne othere—
> A Ribibour, a Ratoner, a Rakiere of Chepe,
> A Ropere, a Redyngkyng, and Rose the Dysshere,
> Godefray of Garlekhithe and Griffyn the Walshe,
> And [of] upholderes an heep, erly by the morwe,
> Geve Gloton with glad chere good ale to hanselle.
> Clement the Cobelere caste of his cloke,
> And at the newe feire nempned it to selle.
> Hikke the Hakeneyman hitte his hood after,
> And bad Bette the Bocher ben on his syde. (5.307–23)

28. Anne Middleton, "Narration and the Invention of Experience: Episodic Form in *Piers Plowman*," *The Wisdom of Poetry: Essays in Early English Literature in Honor of Morton W. Bloomfield*, ed. Larry D. Benson and Siegfried Wenzel (Kalamazoo: Medieval Institute, 1982), 91–122; and "William Langland's 'Kynde Name': Authorial Signature and Social Identity in Late Fourteenth-Century England," *Literary Practice and Social Change in Britain, 1380–1530*, ed. Lee Patterson (Berkeley: University of California Press, 1990)—essays which propel forward Kane's earlier assertions that the poem makes "false starts and changes of direction, frequent pauses, anxieties, hesitations, and impatience" (244). For a renewed and thoroughly thought-provoking inquiry into these actions of starting, see D. Vance Smith, *The Book of the Incipit: Beginnings in the Fourteenth Century* (Minneapolis: University of Minnesota Press, 2001).

29. See, for instance, Chamber's and Daunt's introduction to "The Brewer's First Book," *A Book of London English, 1384–1425*, ed. R.W. Chambers and Marjorie Daunt (Oxford: Clarendon, 1967), pp. 138–40. See also Riley's introduction, *Memorials*, pp. vii–viii.

30. For an example of itemized tasks and payments, see *Book of London English*, pp. 147–48, 152–56, 168–70, 173–77; Riley, *Memorials*, p. 265; of itemized presents, 314. For an extraordinary list of fines against "labourers, artificers,

and servants," see *Calendar of Letter-Books. . .of the City of London: Letter-Book G, circa. 1352–1374*, ed. Reginald R. Sharpe (London: John Edward Francis, 1905), pp. 115–18; for a list of donations, pp. 171–73.

31. For cases involving forged bonds, see Riley, *Memorials*, pp. 401–402 (H.f. liv); pp. 412–14 (H. fol. lxv); forged letters, pp. 442–43 (H. fol. cxxv); for false indentures of apprenticeship, p. 397 (H. fol. xlii). Were there to be any fabrications of such documents, they would likely involve under-reporting to the Chancery or the Exchequer, especially if the accounts have to do with the wealth or possessions of an individual or guild. For a bill ordering a reassessment of subsidies "and the rolls," *Calendar of Letter-Books. . .of the City of London: Letter-Book H*, p. 163.
32. See J.C. Holt, *Robin Hood* (London: Thames and Hudson Ltd., 1982), p. 69.
33. *Calendar of Letter-Books. . .of the City of London: Letter-Book G*, p. 74.
34. See *Dialogus de Scaccario: The Course of the Exchequer by Richard Fitz Nigel*, ed. and trans. Charles Johnson (Oxford: Clarendon Press, 1983): "Cauendum autem est scriptori ne aliquid motu animi sui scribat in rotulo nisi quod thesaurario dictante didicerit. Quid si forte per negligentiam, uel alium quemlibet casum, contigerit eum errare in scriptura rotuli uel in nomine uel in numero uel in causa in quibus uis maior scripture consistit, non presumat abradere, set linea subtili subducta cancellet et scribat in serie quod oportet. Habet enim rotuli scriptura hoc commune cum cartis et aliis scriptis patentibus, quod abradi non debet et ob hoc cautum est ut de pellibus ouinis fiant, quia non facile nisi manifesto uito rasure cedunt" (p. 31); see also p. 28 See the crossed out membership list in *English Guilds*, ed. Joshua Toulmin. Smith and Lucy Toulmin Smith, EETS o.s. 40 (1870; repr. London: Oxford University Press, 1963), p. 96.
35. *Dialogus de Scaccario*, p. 18.
36. Clanchy, *From Memory to Written Record*, p. 76.
37. On memory and the archive, see Clanchy, *From Memory to Written Record*; specifically Clanchy's useful breakdown of "memoranda kept by institutions," pp. 70–82, which demonstrates the movability of the genre. See also Mary J. Carruthers, *The Book of Memory: A Study of Memory in Medieval Culture* (Cambridge, UK: Cambridge University Press, 1990). Expostulating on another kind of forgetting, and reading (briefly) the end of the Prologue, Smith writes: "Yet, because the everyday emerges along with the forgetting of the exceptional, it tends to appear on the borders of the pathological. The close of [the Prologue]. . ., for instance, represents the everyday as a splitting-off (or a running out of bounds) of the representative and the pathological (although "ill" here probably doesn't bear its modern somatic force). . . .The cacophony with which the [Prologue] ends suggests, also, that the everyday is intimately linked with pandemonium, with a lack of recursive structure" ("Irregular Histories: Forgetting Ourselves," *New Literary History* 28.2 [1997]: 163 [161–84]). I shall, however, emphasize the recursiveness of these lines, their archival effects, and their anti-pathology. All told, however, Smith offers a compatible assessment of memory and forgetting in writing and historiography, see pp. 170–73, especially.

38. At least for the city recorder and common clerk: "Et qe vous *ne lerrez*, pur doun, ne pur favoure, ne pur promesce, ne pur hayoure, qe owele leye et droiture frez as toutz maneres dez gentes, si bien as poverez come as richez" (*Liber Albus*, 308–309, my emphasis); see 311–12, where ironically, the editor writes, "The conclusion of this Oath has been omitted, probably by inadvertence" [312]). See also the ordinances for scriveners, Riley, *Memorials*, p. 372; G. fol. cccvii.
39. Riley, *Memorials*, p. 343 (G. fol. ccxliii; dated 1370). See also *Calendar of Letter-Books. . .of the City of London: Letter-Book G*, pp. 102, 124, 129–31, 149, 272; *Calendar of Letter-Books. . .of the City of London: Letter-Book H*, p. 145.
40. See Skeat, *Piers the Plowman in Three Parallel Texts*, 2.19–20.
41. See 4.149–50; 5.538; 8.20; 10.51–52, 69–70, 104–406, 112, 245–46, 284–85, 301–302; 12.68–69; 12.175–80, 216, 272–77; 13.431–32; 15.148–99; 19.462–65.
42. Morton Bloomfield, *Piers Plowman as a Fourteenth-Century Apocalypse* (New Brunswick, NJ: Rutgers University Press, 1962), p. 32; J.J. Jusserand, *Piers Plowman: A Contribution to the History of English Mysticism*, trans. M.E.R. (New York: Russell and Russell, Inc, 1965; 1893), p. 113.
43. Aers, *Chaucer, Langland and the Creative Imagination*, pp. 3–5.
44. Cf. Aers, *Chaucer, Langland, and the Creative Imagination*: "we are shown a mass of self-absorbed social practices in which there is no consciousness of any coherent order, organic unity or social telos, let alone a divine one. The participants, as in the Meed episode, appear to be discreet members of a mobile, fragmenting society revelling in processes of consumption and production which are an end in themselves" (p. 5).
45. See Wallace, *Chaucerian Polity*.
46. *The Anonimalle Chronicle, 1333–1381*, ed. V.H. Galbraith (London: Manchester University Press, 1927), p. 144: "the commons of the country and the commons of London assembled in fearful strength, to the number of a hundred thousand or more" (Dobson, *Peasants' Revolt*, p. 160).
47. *Knighton's Chronicle, 1337–1396*, ed. and trans. G.H. Martin (Oxford: Clarendon Press, 1995), pp. 209–11. See Dobson, *Peasant's Revolt*, p. 273; Thomas Walsingham, *Historia Anglicana*, 2 vols., ed. Henry Thomas Riley (London: Longman et al., 1863–64), 1.471.
48. See Strohm, " 'A Revelle': Chronicle Evidence and the Rebel Voice;" and Steven Justice, *Writing and Rebellion: England in 1381* (Berkeley: University of California Press, 1994).
49. Dobson, *Peasants' Revolt*, pp. 76–78; here, p. 76. The earlier such instances are represented by ordinances (Riley, *Memorials*, pp. 232; 242; 346; 360; 417), trade regulations (pp. 306–308; G. fol. xciii), proclamations in 1351 against carrying arms in London (pp. 268–69; F. fol. ccviii) and in 1353 against assemblies "for making covin, confederacy, or alliance" (pp. 272–73: G. fol. x), and this interesting instance in 1364: "And to this John answered that he was a tailor, but as to any design, he knew nothing about it; whereupon, the same Richard [Hay, a fuller] said to him that there were ten thousand men

in the said city, all of one alliance and of one agreement, that, at a certain time, such as should seem to them the best, they would all be ready and prepared with their arms,—those who have arms, and those who have none of their own, with such arms as they may get,—to slay all the best people, and the great folks and officers of said city [Havering at Bower]" (p. 315; G. fol. cxxxviii). See *Calendar of Letter-Books. . .of the City of London: Letter-Book H*, pp. 35–36, 99; for a bill ordering the mysteries to "put down conspiracies" and "maintain the King's peace," see p. 59. Portions of my argument here intersect with Andrew Galloway's, "Making History Legal: *Piers Plowman* and the Rebels of Fourteenth-Century England," in *William Langland's Piers Plowman: A Book of Essays*, pp. 7–39.

50. The latter legislation recapitulates the former; see Dobson, *Peasants' Revolt*, pp. 63–68. See also the proclamation against vagrants in 1359, Riley, *Memorials*, pp. 304–305; G. fol. lxxviii; and *Calendar of Letter-Books. . .of the City of London: Letter-Book G*, pp. 111, 208, 301; *Calendar of Letter-Books. . .of the City of London: Letter-Book H*, p. 110.

51. *Book of London English*, p. 31; the mayor of London issued the proclamation himself. This legislation revives the following Edwardian one: Riley, *Memorials*, pp. 480–81; here, 480. Much of this language about "conventicles" appears in canon law at least since the time of Innocent III. Also see the entry regarding Cheshire in 1381: "From the evidence of trustworthy men we have learnt that several of the villeins (*nativi*) of our beloved in Christ the abbot of Chester have made certain assemblies within the area of your jurisdiction, and they have gathered in secret confederacies within the woods and other hidden places in the said hundred. . . .everyone residing in your said hundred, of whatsoever estate or condition, should absolutely refrain from such assemblies and remain in peace" (Dobson, *Peasants' Revolt*, pp. 297, 298; also in Powell and Trevelyan, pp. 14–16).

52. This describes the formation of religious fraternities outside of the regulated guild; Riley, *Memorials*, p. 495. See also *Calendar of Letter-Books. . .of the City of London: Letter-Book H*, pp. 265, 274, 311.

53. Usk associates a lack of governance with the intent for workers to assemble and congregate for particular political purposes: "And, vpon al thys matirs be-forn seide, tho that John Norhampton atte tat tyme mair, John More, & Richard Norbury, & William Essex & otherwhile Adam Bame, seyen that the worthy persones wer drawe fro hem for willesful gouernaile & fiebel conseyl, & that they had made refus of hem to-forn tyme, tho *they drewe to hem many craftes & mochel smale poeple that konne non skyl of gouernance ne of gode conseyl & be confederacie, congregacion, & couyne, purposed & to-forn cast for to meigtene be myght thair fals & wykked menyng*, vnder colour of wordes of comun profit euer more [charg]ed the people fro day in to other to be redy to stonde be hem in that euel purposed matirs" ("The Appeal of Thomas Usk against John Northampton," *Book of London English*, p. 29, my emphasis) He continues with an admission: "And also the foreside John Norhampton, John More, Richard Norbury, & William Essex, so fer

forth wolden depraue the worthy men of towne that *the people was, & ys, the more enbolded to be rebel a-yeins thair gouernours that bien now, & that shul bien in tyme komyng, be her fals informacion & excitacion, couyns, & gadrynges, & confederacies atte that tyme maked & euer sithen continued, as it ys to-forn seyde; & so be hem, & be ther procurementy, & confederacies, & excitacions, the debates & the grete stryf*, that yet ys regnyng in the cite, ys komen jn principalich be John Norhampton, John More, Richard Norbury, & William Essex; so that ys in poynt to truble al the realme; & the cite hath stonde in grete doute & yet doth. To which euel menyng I was a ful helpere & promotour in al that euer I myght & koude, wher-for I ask grace & mercy of my lyge lord the kyng, & afterward of the mair, & of al the worthy aldermen, & of al the gode comunes of the town, as he that wol neuer more trespace a-yeins the town in no degre" (Ibid., 29–30, my emphasis). For more on Usk, see Barron, "Middle English Guild Certificates," 113; and Strohm, "Textual Vicissitudes of Usk's 'Appeal,'" in *Hochon's Arrow*, pp. 145–60. For a discussion of Langland's potential response in C.3.77–83; 90–97 to Northhampton's sought-for reforms, see James Simpson, "'After Craftes Conseil clotheth yow and fede': Langland and London City Politics," in *England in the Fourteenth Century: Proceedings of the 1991 Harlaxton Symposium*, ed. Nicholas Rogers, Harlaxton Medieval Studies 3 (Stamford, UK: Paul Watkins, 1993), pp. 109–27; esp. pp. 121–27.

54. *The Westminster Chronicle*, ed. and trans. L.C. Hector and Barbara F. Harvey (Oxford: Clarendon Press, 1982), pp. 356–57 (on guilds); pp. 355–69 (for the entire entry). Note that this entry is a summary of the petitions. The documents have been lost.

55. *Book of London English*, p. 48; see also pp. 50, 54, 56. On the Cambridge Parliament of 1388, part of which was to reenforce the 1351 Statute of Laborers, see Anthony Tuck, "The Cambridge Parliament, 1388," *English Historical Review* 84 (1969): 225–43. On this parliament's attempt to control the potentially subversive associations of unrelated persons between and among guilds, see Strohm, "'A Revelle!': Chronicle Evidence and the Rebel Voice," in *Hochon's Arrow*, pp. 58–63. Let it be noted that the "hostility of the Commons was directed at fraternities which had a common livery and promoted 'confederacy, maintenance [of judicial suits] and riots in hindrance of the law" (Barron, "London Middle English Guild Certificates," 108). On how the Ricardian mandate bespeaks post-1381 fears about laborers' conspiracies, see H.F. Westlake, *Parish Guilds of Medieval England* (1919), pp. 36–37; May McKisack, *The Fourteenth Century, 1307–1399* (Oxford: Oxford University Press, 1959), p. 373. For a recent overview, see William R. Jones, "English Religious Brotherhoods and Medieval Lay Piety: The Inquiry of 1388–89," *The Historian* 36 (1974): 646–79. The problem of holding "clandestine meetings" was, of course, longstanding; see George Unwin, *The Guilds and Companies of London* (London: George Allen & Unwin Ltd., 1938), pp. 41, 70. For examples of a guild whose ordinances deal with "oure brethren that is rebell," see Laura Wright, "The London Middle English Guild Certificates of

1388–9: II. The Texts," *Nottingham Medieval Studies* 39 (1995): 127, 128, 135, 144; on authorized assembly times, see 136, 137, 139.
56. *English Guilds*, p. 28, where the writ is recopied in a return. There are a variety of legislated assemblies and meetings, some compulsory; on the election of sheriffs, for which "soient les Mair, Recordour, Audermans, et Communes assemblez," see *Liber Albus*, p. 43; on the "Gyldeday pur terminer comune bosoignes," see p. 666; on folkmoots, see p. 118 ("Treis Folkemotz chiefs sunt en lan" [118]); also 310 and 323.
57. *Calendar of Letter-Books. . .of the City of London: Letter-Book H*, p. 227.
58. See *Calendar of Letter-Books. . .of the City of London: Letter-Book G, circa. 1352–1374*, ed. Reginald R. Sharpe (London: John Edward Francis, 1905), pp. 39, 271 (Edward III's proclamation against privy assemblies and rioters).
59. Jean-Paul Sartre, *Critique of Dialectical Reason*, vol. 1, trans. Alan Sheridan-Smith (New York: Verso, 1991), p. 103.
60. The term "assembly" can be added to John A. Alford's, *Piers Plowman: A Guide to the Quotations* (Binghamton, NY: Medieval and Renaissance Texts and Studies, 1992). Mistakenly or otherwise, I presently assume, as do most critics, that the B-text was written before 1381.
61. Justice, "The Genres of *Piers Plowman*," 297. I emphasize, again, however, that by "genre" Justice means allegory (rather than the distinct forms I describe here); Justice even orients the debate form toward exegesis of the traditional kind, as in his reading of the Meed episode (see 298).
62. "Langland's London," p. 186.
63. Riley, *Memorials*, pp. 232–34, here p. 233 (F. fol. cxxvi). Examples in *English Guilds* (see pp. 373, 393) show that "surveyour" translates literally as "overseer"; to "survey" is to "oversee."
64. Riley, *Memorials*, pp. 280–82, here, p. 282 (G. fol. xli); pp. 438–42, here p. 439 (H. fol. cxviii).
65. See Riley, *Memorials*, pp. 247–48 (F. fol. clxxiii); p. 292 (G. fol. cxxx); *Calendar of Letter-Books. . .of the City of London: Letter-Book H*, pp. 39, 162, 231, 235, 261, 336 (which records the 1388 call for guild returns), p. 397.
66. See the map of London in Unwin, *The Gilds and Companies of London*, p. 34.
67. For a discussion as to how Langland finds the late medieval "fraternity" "part of a system in which the existence of most brotherhoods was bound up with principles of exclusion and competitive display," which are antithetical to this poet's own understanding of an ideal community, see Aers, *Community, Gender, and Individual Identity*, pp. 69–70; here, p. 70. While Aers finds that the passage concerning Grace's distribution of crafts (B.19.250–51) "is a utopian negation of the present world where the poet has to separate his language of 'fraternity' from actually existing 'fraternities' " (p. 70), Simpson understands such utopian gestures as part of the poet's "interest. . .to imagine a context for the renovation of the Church, and to imagine a context in which intense trade rivalry of his London is resolved" ("After Craftes Conseil," p. 127).

68. Notice, too, that earlier Piers claims to perform rural labors but also know urban crafts—"Som tyme I sowe and sometyme I thresshe, / In taillours craft and tinkeris craft, what Truthe can devyse, / I weve and I wynde and do what Truthe hoteth" (5.546–48)—as a means to convey, in effect, that he represents work in the broadest sense possible. Of course, weaving and cloth-making are done at the half-acre (6.9; 13–14), but these are not cited as trades, as they are in the passage in question here or, indeed, in the examples from the registers or the Prologue mentioned earlier. Which explains why Piers, in turn, will qualify *any* kind of labor as plowing (see also 7.6–7).
69. Riley, *Memorials*, p. 495.
70. For accounts as to why the half-acre is set up for failure already, see Aers, *Chaucer, Langland and the Creative Imagination*; Britton J. Harwood, "The Plot of *Piers Plowman* and the Contradictions of Feudalism," in *Speaking Two Languages: Traditional Disciplines and Contemporary Theory in Medieval Studies*, ed. Allen J Frantzen (NY: SUNY Press, 1991), pp. 91–114; and Cole, "Trifunctionality and the Tree of Charity: Literary and Social Practice in *Piers Plowman*," *English Literary History* 62 (1995): 1–27.
71. For an alternative view of lines like these, see Godden, 54.
72. Riley, *Memorials*, pp. 232–34, here p. 233 (F. fol. cxxvi). This is also not to exclude the hypothetical of how Piers, now an unemployed, wandering plowman, seeking no more work, might appear to sheriffs seeking to enforce labor statutes.
73. *English Guilds*, p. 142.
74. *English Guilds*, p. 23.
75. See also Rodney Hilton, "Peasant Movements in England Before 1381," in *Class Conflict and the Crises of Feudalism: Essays in Medieval Social History* (London: Verso, 1990), pp. 49–65.

# PART 5

# BOOK WORK

# CHAPTER 9

# POETIC WORK AND SCRIBAL LABOR IN HOCCLEVE AND LANGLAND

*Ethan Knapp*

> This chapter isolates the category of scribal labor in the work of William Langland and Thomas Hoccleve and describes the unstable attempts made by each of these poets to forge a metaphorics of scribal labor that would distinguish it from more traditional depictions of agricultural and monastic work.

To what extent can the work associated with textuality and the professional manipulation of written language, the work of poets, scribes and clerks, be considered labor? What unites or separates such work from other forms of labor? These questions have a long history, one rooted in divergent and contradictory intellectual traditions and economic formations. The majority of this history, from the Greek distinction between *techne* and *episteme* to the modern industrial separation of labor and management, has insisted on a sharp distinction between craft practiced by hand and the sciences of the mind, a division bringing with it a consistent devaluation of labor and material existence. Running contrary to this division, however, we find also the persistent suspicion that this bifurcation is, fundamentally, an ideological fabrication, a suspicion revitalized most recently amongst Italian theorists of the problem of "Immaterial Labor." These theorists have argued that the social subjectivities formed in a post-industrial economy cannot be adequately understood through a blunt division between manual labor and other forms of work but must be thought of as the creation of value through an assemblage of creative and affective labors.[1]

Though these theorists scrupulously situate their work as an analysis of the culture of mass consumption, it is worth pointing out that the Middle Ages too had its own theories of Immaterial Labor. The most obvious and influential came from the monastic category of the *opus dei*, the work of god performed in prayer and liturgical service. Somewhat less prominent, but central to any understanding of literary culture in the period, was another kind of work which lay ambiguously at the crossroads of manual and intellectual labor: the work of poet/scribes such as Thomas Hoccleve, Thomas Usk, George Ashby, and John Capgrave. As has often been remarked, one of the signal distinctions between the notion of 'writing' in the medieval and modern eras is the greater physicality assumed in medieval usage. Whereas modern usage tends to associate the act of writing, particularly the creation of the literary artifact, with the immateriality of thought and the immediacy of inspiration, medieval usage tended to tie writing much more concretely to the craft, skills, and materials needed to produce a text as physical object. This association is particularly prominent in the case of those scribes and bureaucrats who come to prominence in the late fourteenth and early fifteenth centuries, but it is widespread throughout the corpus of Middle English poetry. Any student of late Middle English verse becomes quickly familiar with the pervasive hum of complaint running through these works calling attention to the dire physical labors involved in the production, compilation, and dissemination of texts. Even a brief survey of the topos would include Chaucer's reference to his daily work with "rekenynges," Capgrave's admiring fiction of the "grete labour" of the priest who had gathered together the materials of St. Katherine's life, Usk's petulant complaints that it is hard to write quickly enough to get all of Lady Philosophy's wisdom down, and, of course, Hoccleve's numerous invocations of his own labors.[2] Some of these labors would be separated by our retroactive categories into poetic, bureaucratic, and spiritual endeavors, but these potential conceptual differentiations should not obscure the fact that, for the cultural workers of the moment, the objective technical skills involved bound the works of production, compilation, and dissemination together into a closely associated constellation of labors.

In describing the status of these labors, such writers called attention to a series of striking ambiguities. Although we see a widespread emphasis on the physical travails of such work, these laments often go hand-in-hand with claims for the transcendent ends of the work, claims that were surely meant to refuse any demeaning identification with *mere* labor. Usk may complain that his hand is tired, but he still lays claim to a shadow of

Boethian *auctoritas* as he does so. Similarly, the period's distinct fondness for playing with the boundaries between orality and textuality testifies to an interest in blurring the distinctions between the laborious tedium of the scribe and the free immediacy of poetic inspiration and spiritual vision. Thus, within the world of strictly textual products, we see many versions of Chaucer's delight in establishing and then undermining simulacra of purely oral discourse. Even more distinctively, we see the textuality of the manuscript environment itself swept aside for moments by such conventions as the 'go little book' of an envoi, moments that fictively play with establishing an oral address to the now completed manuscript; here the product of textual labor simultaneously calls attention to the scene of its production while also aspiring to the freedom of a commodity fully dissevered from that scene.[3] Conversely, even cultural labor carefully removed from the tablets and vellum of the scribe, labor such as the recitation of the liturgy or the performance of sacramental action was at times described through terminology derived from the world of the text. For example, even as the bifurcation between *opus dei* and *opus manuum* served to distinguish the labor of the scriptorium from that of the liturgy, it served also to draw an insistent equation between the dignity and value of the two activities. Indeed, the terminological substitution of *opus* for *labore* surely serves to draw the manual and the spiritual into even greater proximity as the word *opus* carries with it both certain literary possibilities and also, even more significantly, an implicit commodification of labor, a sense that it is always engaged in objectifying itself within some final product.[4]

An analysis of the contemporary meaning of textual labor is thus made difficult by two distinct but related matters: first, the shifting boundaries between the labor of the writer and other manual labors; and, second, the tendency of discussions of textual labors to exist in an uneasy and often blurred contrast with theologically based categories of oral and liturgical labor. Many of the surviving descriptions of writerly labor in Middle English work through these contrastive categories in the attempt to craft distinct representations of the labor involved in making vernacular literary texts. For the purposes of the present essay, I will outline a preliminary sense of such representations by looking at the writings of two of the poets who produced the most explicit and detailed considerations of the nature of their own labors, Thomas Hoccleve and William Langland.

## Figural Tendencies: Agricultural Tropes and Scribal Bodies

As the editors of a recent historical collection on *The Problem of Labour in Fourteenth-Century England* have suggested, the shifting demographic realities of the fourteenth century seem to have produced a widespread sense of labor as a 'problem', a problem which revealed itself symptomatically in attempts at repressive legal control and in a surge of literary and imagistic representations of labor and laborers.[5] Of course, by 'labor' in this context most commentators, both medieval and modern, have in mind specifically agricultural labor. The need to think through and around the dominance of this category is one of the first challenges in considering other forms of medieval work. Given the overwhelming importance of agriculture in the medieval economy, the absorption of all varieties of labor into the omnipresent representations of agriculture and the peasant may at first be taken for the simple reflection of historical fact.[6] But the transfiguration of the abstract notion of labor into the figure of the peasant, the reliance on this metaphor as the starting point of so much medieval thought about labor, must also be recognized as a figurative habit that threatens to obscure in retrospect the complexity and diversity of medieval social structures and forms of labor.[7]

One of the results of this figural habit was a tendency for other sorts of labor to be considered always in comparative terms, with the agricultural labor of the peasant presumed as the natural basis of comparison. Consequently, in examining the work of poets and scribes we often find them describing their work through an oddly displaced comparison to agriculture. Indeed, the influence of this perennial metaphoric system (combined with the more immediate impact of the Statutes of Laborers) seems to have shaped what we might consider an autobiographical sub-genre: the *apologia pro vita sua* cast narrowly as an explanation for the refusal of agricultural labor. I look at two of the more prominent of these *apologias* with a single question in mind: if agricultural labor was taken to be the paradigm of manual labor *per se*, how did such writers reconfigure the metaphoric conventions of this paradigm to adapt it to discussions of textual labor?

Perhaps the best known of such considerations is the autobiographical passage occurring between the first and second visions of the C version of *Piers Plowman* (passus 5).[8] Here Langland famously describes his own choice of a clerical vocation. Waking "amonges lollares of londone and lewede Ermytes" (C.5.4) in harvest time and in good health, Will is challenged by Reason and Conscience to account for himself.[9] Reason asks whether he is capable of work in the field, and Langland responds:

> Sertes, y sayde, and so me god helpe,
> Y am to wayke to wurcche with sykel or with sythe
> And to long, lef me, lowe to stoupe,
> To wurche as a werkeman eny while to duyren. (C.5.22–5)

As Anne Middleton has demonstrated, this exchange is animated, even structured in its sequence of queries and responses, by the 1388 Statute of

Laborers.[10] Will is confronted as a suspicious layabout and questioned as to whether his idleness during harvest can be justified by any one of a set of very specific legal exemptions from such labor. In this context, the excuse given above is clearly meant to be ludicrously inadequate: as Middleton puts it, "the inconvenience of tall stature for stoop-labor is not likely to have convinced an enforcer of any version of the labor laws to exempt a healthy, strong, and youthful man from the imperative to work."[11] Pressed further by Reason on the only three possible legal exemptions, sufficient land, sufficient income, or actual physical incapability, Will sidesteps these questions completely and instead turns to an account of his education. In response to Reason's questions "Thenne hastow londes to lyue by. . .or lynage ryche. . .Or thow art broke, so may be, in body or in membre / Or ymaymed thorw som myshap whereby thow myhte be excused?" (C.5.26, 33–4), Will offers the following personal narrative:

> When y [ȝut] ȝong was, many ȝer hennes,
> My fader and my frendes foende me to scole
> Tyle y wyste witterly what holy writ menede
> And what is beste for the body, as the boek telleth,
> And sykerost for þe soule, by so y wol contenue.
> And foen[d y] nere, in fayth, seth my frendes deyede
> Lyf þat me [l]lykede but in this long clothes. (C.5.35–41)

Middleton makes the point that this change of topic indicates both a serious legal argument and a point of humor, as "it is momentarily comically ambiguous whether he means to cast his schooling as a kind of inheritance or as a 'myshap' that has maimed him."[12] Education does indeed stand as a sort of inheritance, as it is his clerical status, gained from patronage and schooling, that will be his final reason not to labor ("Me sholde constrayne no Cler[k] to no knaues werkes," C.5.54). Education also stands as a sort of mishap, since the micronarrative of Will's schooling comes to a climax with his loss of patronage—a misfortune that has indeed left him unfit for more respectable clerical labor. But, in addition to the points contained in Middleton's joke, there is another meaning to the dislocation here, another sense in which the slippage of topic from physical incapacity to education is meant to clarify the essence of Will's vocation.

The most unexpected, and overlooked, element of Will's explanation here is his insistence that his education has changed him in both mind and body. The condition of Will's body is a central issue throughout the opening of the passus, as the whole juridical dialogue with Reason presupposes the subject of a healthy vagrant. Moreover, as Kathryn Kerby-Fulton has pointed out, the genre of this interlude itself projects an expectation that

Will's body will be a central issue, as the physical portrait of the author was a typical element of the *apologia* derived from monastic precursors. As Kerby-Fulton puts it: "it is no accident that the most elaborate physical description of Langland occurs in the *apologia*."[13] Indeed, in this *apologia* Langland spins out an allegory positively Foucauldian in its transformations of the idealized object and actions of pedagogy into new productive capacities for the body. This allegorical transformation begins at line 38 with the neat syntactical and metric parallel between "what is beste for the body" and "sykerost for þe soule," a parallel that serves to dissever body and soul as separate and equally important pedagogical objects of "the boek." This separation seems to be almost instantly repaired as the body is covered by "this longe clothes" (l.41), the dress intended to provide the outward mark of his clerical vocation and to hierarchize the relation of body and soul by restricting the meaning of the body to an outward sign of inward spiritual vocation. But, as so often in Langland, this apparent solution merely provides grist for the mill of allegorical contradiction. The bookishly trained body is here figured as both perfectly integrated but also ruined, books having raised him up into "what is beste for the body" but also serving to explain to Reason how Will has become "ymaymed."

These contradictory claims are developed further as Langland immediately returns to the question of labor with which Reason had begun, now focused by his invocation of 'long clothes' and turned into an allegory of a pastoral vocation.

> Yf y be labour sholde lyuen and lyflode deseruen,
> That laboure þat y lerned beste þerwith lyuen y sholde:
> *In eadem vocacione qu[a] vocati estis [&c]*
> And so y leue in london and [vp] lond[on] bothe.
> The lomes þat y labore with and lyflode deserue
> Is paternoster and my primer, *placebo* and *dirige*
> And my sauter som tyme and my seuene p[s]almes. (C.5.42–48)

In justifying himself to Reason, Will claims that his education has given him the ability to practice an allegorical sort of labor, one in which his books have become "lomes," lambs to be shepherded.[14] To a large extent, of course, this allegory simply reflects the typological figure of the pastor as good shepherd, perhaps the single most widespread extension of an agricultural motif into the world of clerical labor. Significantly, however, Langland's version of this mini-allegory veers away from its type by construing the sheep not as souls to be saved but as the psalter and primer with which the cleric works. In his revision of the parable, the pastoral vocation is here redefined not as the care of souls but as the care of texts. There is evidence that contemporary readers may have found this passage disconcerting, or at least confusing. We find signficant scribal difficulties with two sections of the passage. First, line 45 is variously recorded as "upon londoun," "on londen," "by londoun," "in londone," "out of londone," "opelon," and "up þe londe" as scribes tried to make sense of this pastoral allegory by either imagining Langland justifying a parasitic existence living off the wealth of London (Skeat's preferred explanation), or, alternatively, by anticipating the shepherd metaphor in emphasizing Langland's dual residencies in both London and its rural environs (Pearsall's commentary).[15] This geographical muddle is, I think, itself a sign of a deeper concern, a reflection of the ethical difficulty raised by Langland's attempt to reshape the pastoral metaphor. Whereas the conventional image of the pastoral care of souls was so well worn as to render the agricultural vehicle of the metaphor virtually invisible (and thus the location of the labor easily transferable to an urban environment), the innovation of the pastoral care of books suddenly throws the analogy between clerical and agricultural labor back into sharp relief (and forces such labor to resituate itself again in the countryside). With this change, the accumulated ethical resonances of the abstracted pastoral also vanish, asking to be reconstructed now from a new foundation, a cure not of souls but of books. In effect, the justification he offers to Reason is that there is a labor with books that can draw its justification not from an ethical resemblance to the clerical/pastoral but from a physical act of toil resembling the agricultural/pastoral. Like so much in Langland, a challenging ethical proposition is drawn from a stubborn misapplication of a foundational trope. It seems likely that the scribal inventions witnessed in this much-botched line testify to an unease at Langland's destruction of the familiar pastoral metaphor.

There is a very similar ambiguity registered in the transcriptions of line 46, where we find the whole pastoral metaphor done away with in Harley 2376 by the substitution of "lymes" for "lomes." Harley 2376 (or N in both Skeat and Russell–Kane's classifications) is the famously disappointing manuscript Skeat had hoped to use but finally rejected as "utterly worthless" because of the apparent willingness of its scribe to revise and gloss the text, perfectly anticipating the editor's *durior lectio* by consistently simplifying Langland's more challenging poetic choices.[16] In the spirit of such simplification, the Harley scribe has altered the pastoral metaphor so that the texts are construed not as sheep but as the limbs with which Langland will tend to the sheep (whose identity is then unproblematically supplied in line 48 as the "soules of suche as me helpeth"). This alteration smoothes a difficult passage in several ways. First, the ethical shape of the allegory returns to a traditional pastoral mission, with the texts now figured subordinately as useful tools rather than the final goal of pastoral care.

Second, the strange syntax that had depicted Will "laboring with lambs" as though they were both tools and end wrapped together ("The lomes þat y labore with. . .") is resolved into a clear instrumentality by taking the objects in question to be the tools ("lymes") rather than the objects ("lomes") of the care.[17] Lastly, this interpolation also maintains the imagistic emphasis on Will's body that has been prepared in the preceding sections of the passus (and that will be continued in the passage immediately to follow on the link between clerical privilege and the tonsure—"Clerkes ycouned, of kynde vnderstondynge, / Sholde nother synke ne swete ne swerien at enquestes," C.5.56–7). Like the confusion over topography in line 54, this scribal revision attests to a difficulty in accomodating Langland's image of pastoral labor to received models.

I cite these scribal readings not, of course, to suggest that they testify to authoritative readings of these lines, but rather because they make explicit a key tension in Langland's description of his clerical labors, one which finally collapses the metaphoric construction. Will responds to Reason's interrogation by claiming to perform a new version of the cleric's pastoral role. He is not a vagrant, but a shepherd of texts. Unlike more conventional versions of this occupational allegory, Will's version emphasizes both his own physicality (the body shaped into the maimed and perfect shepherd) while also renewing the agricultural and rural roots of the allegory by offering the striking image of texts as sheep. Though it would be tempting to suggest some solution to the problem of representing the author's labor in this new metaphor, this moment seems rather to be one of those in which we see Langland's powers of diagnosis overrunning his capabilities, or tastes, for stable solutions. As we have seen, his metaphor seems to have baffled some of his scribes, and Will himself soon abandons this account, dropping this image of labor as a justification for his vagrancy. As the *apologia* comes to an end, Will returns to an earlier rationale, that anyone tonsured is simply to be exempted from labor *tout court*. Langland's *apologia*, then, seems to flirt with the possibility of representing the labor of books and prayers as an allegorically displaced version of agricultural labor but discards this possibility in the end in favor of a more traditional disidentification with such work. But this effort does demonstrate at least one inescapable fact about the depiction of the writer's labors, that one crux of the difficulty lies in establishing a distinct register through which to represent the writer's body.

Turning to Hoccleve, we find that the constitution of the writerly body is also the topic of a similar passage in his *Regiment of Princes*, one so similar that it should be added to the growing list of evidence for Hoccleve's close familiarity with Langland's work.[18] In the midst of the Prologue to the *Regiment*, Hoccleve breaks off his conversation with the Old Man in order to deliver a long complaint concerning the life of the writer. Hoccleve's explanation of this life is strikingly similar to Langland's in that he begins by explicitly contrasting his labor to that of the agricultural worker; but the account is also distinct in that Hoccleve begins by casting his inability to pursue this work as a liability, both in the sense that his incapacity is yet one more reason to fear eventual poverty and in the sense that this inability is caused not by the mishap of education but by a lack of education:

> Six marc yeerly and no more than that,
> Fadir, to me me thynkith is ful lyte,
> Considerynge how that I am nat
> In housbondrye lerned worth a myte;
> Scarsely kowde I charre away the kyte
> That me byreve wolde my pullaile,
> And more axith housbondly governaille.
>
> With plow can I nat medlen ne with harwe,
> Ne woot nat what lond good is for what corn,
> And for to lade a cart or fille a barwe,
> To which I never usid was toforn,
> My bak unbuxum hath swich thyng forsworn,
> At instaunce of wrytynge, his werreyour,
> That stowpynge hath him spilt with his labour. (ll. 981–87)[19]

Hoccleve's passage reads like the product of someone who had read Langland, understood his little joke about education and literacy as a mishap, but insisted on literalizing the joke. Where Langland plays with the acquisition of literacy as a humorous excuse for vagrancy, Hoccleve insists that it's no joke, that writing has literally broken his body. Moreover, where Langland had, in a traditional argument, associated learning with clerical privilege and a refusal of manual labor, Hoccleve here associates knowledge with just such labor, suggesting that the protection of livestock and the planting of fields were occupations requiring real knowledge, and coming near to implying that writing is what one is left with if one is unequipped with such knowledge.

As Hoccleve's *apologia* continues, he begins to defend writing as a form of labor, but the defense, rather than attempting to separate literary labors off into their own category, as Langland had done, produces a series of identifications between writer and laborer:

> Many men, fadir, weenen that wrytynge
> No travaille is; they holde it but a game;
> Aart hath no fo but swich folk unkonnynge.

> But whoso list desporte him in that same,
> Let him continue and he shal fynde it grame;
> It is wel gretter labour than it seemeth;
> The blynde man of colours al wrong deemeth.
>
> A wryter moot thre thynges to him knytte,
> And in tho may be no disseverance:
> Mynde, ye, and hand—noon may from othir flitte,
> But in hem moot be joynt continuance;
> The mynde al hool, withouten variaunce,
> On ye and hand awayte moot alway,
> And they two eek on hym, it is no nay. (ll. 988–1001)

Hoccleve begins here by expanding the range of knowledge and ignorance. There are those with practical knowledge of husbandry; they farm and assure themselves of some prosperity. Ranked below these are the writers, who know nothing about husbandry. (Their vulnerability is emphasized by the nicely threatening resonances of their inability to "charre away the kyte," or scare away the kite.) And yet below these are the "folk unkonnynge" who don't even understand the simple labor of writing, thinking it nothing but a "game." Elaborating upon the (often misunderstood) nature of this writing, we find that, in a move both surprising and consonant with Hoccleve's autobiographical concerns elsewhere, writing is here characterized as laborious less because of its tedium or physical demands (though these are acknowledged elsewhere) than because of its requirement that the writer be a model of self-discipline and concentration.

I have suggested elsewhere that the Prologue to the *Regiment* mounts an argument against the pretense of bureaucratic documents to embody an escape from the fallibility of memory and human mortality.[20] In brief, Hoccleve's descriptions of the ruinous physical effects of scribal labor portray the writer as a person prematurely aged and rendered into a collection of wrecked organs by his work. In other ways, however, particularly when read alongside Langland's *apologia* and alongside the self-divisions Hoccleve chronicles obsessively in his autobiographical complaints, this description of writing may also seem remarkably optimistic. Insofar as self-division seems the great fear of the Hoccleve persona elsewhere, writing would seem a potential cure in its ability to bring the subject together into coherence. Writing, amongst all labors, is, in a metaphor to which we return later, the labor which knits up the self. It is admittedly, as is typical of Hoccleve, a rather paranoiac unity, as the self remains unified only by spying on itself (the mind must watch the hand and eye, while eye and hand watch the mind, always—to paraphrase ll. 999–1001), but it is a unity nevertheless.

The cost of this unity, however, soon begins to surface as Hoccleve's description of the writer continues, with the stipulation that the writer, once he has bound mind, eye and hand together, must remain silent. It is with this paradox, the fact that the writer's labor with words removes the subject from the human community of linguistic contact, that Hoccleve's *apologia* reaches its climax:

> Whoso shal wryte, may nat holde a tale
> With him and him, ne synge this ne that;
> But al his wittes hoole, grete and smale,
> Ther muste appeere and holden hem therat;
> And syn he speke may ne synge nat,
> Bot bothe two he needes moot forbere,
> His labour to him is the elengere.
>
> Thise artificers see I day be day,
> In the hootteste of al hir bysynesse,
> Talken and synge and make game and play,
> And foorth hir labour passith with gladnesse;
> But we laboure in travaillous stilnesse;
> We stowpe and stare upon the sheepes skyn,
> And keepe moot our song and wordes yn. (ll. 1002–1015)

The writer is here locked into silence, unable to hold his wits together unless he forbears to speak or sing. This silence traps him within tedium and solitude, made bitter by the contrast to the "artificers" who "talken and synge and make game and play." But this solitude and tedium are only surface manifestation of a much deeper problem for the writer, one that bears directly on the shape of the writer's labor. First, this solitude is not all it seems, for though the writer is isolated by his silence, the writer is also construed, unusually, as a "we" ("we laboure," "we stowpe and stare"). Hoccleve's image here is of the writer as a member of the lonely crowd, surrounded by fellow workers, but isolated from them by the requirements of their joint labor. The second structural diagnosis lying beneath the complaint of silence is signalled by the persistent contrast between the activity of the artificers and the strange lethargy of the writer. The artificers' work is represented throughout as multiple and simultaneous activities, all moving forward loudly and productively, their surplus of activity represented in the kinetic figure of "the hootteste of al hir bysynesse." The writer on the other hand spends his labor on pure negation, on the effort to ensure that "mynde, ye, and hand—noon may from othir flitte" and that he "nat holde a tale" and "ne synge this ne that."

This syntax of negation reaches its apogee with Hoccleve's final summation: "We stowpe and stare upon the sheepes skyn / and keepe moote our song and wordes yn." Where Langland's semi-educated cleric had been "to long, lef me, lowe to stoupe," Hoccleve's writers are now perfectly adapted to stooping. In fact it is through stooping, the paradigmatic agricultural toil that Hoccleve has here transcoded as scribal labor, that the scribe has become unsuited to anything other than writing (cf. ll. 985–87 above). Moreover, stooping and staring have now become the sum total of their labor. The writer labors furiously, but labors to do nothing. And in the reduction of the writer's labor to stooping and staring we see the anxiety that the writer truly produces nothing. There is labor, there is stooping, but in place of the one product that should issue forth, words, there is only silence and the frozen contemplation of the page. And, as with Hoccleve's choice of the term stooping, the silence of the page is also represented with a backward glance to the world of agriculture, the "sheepes skyn" presented here as the dead emblem of the writer's purposelessness, the productivity of agricultural labor entirely vanished.

In looking at these two *apologias* side by side, then, we can see that both representations of clerkly, bookish work are haunted by the model of agricultural labor. Both Hoccleve and Langland try to work through this figure, but both surrender to it in the end, Langland perhaps because he is determined to maintain a final distinction between the essential natures of clergy and laborer and Hoccleve because the nature of writerly labor appears in the end to be a labor that may have no product, no value to counterpose to the work of the artificers. To say this is also to say that Hoccleve's effort is distinct in moving away from the attempt to define labor by beginning with a vocational category and toward a definition that begins with a yoked analysis of the labor performed and the commodity produced. Hoccleve thus shifts the contradictions that mark Langland's account of vocation to the level of the commodity itself. The attempt to read the significance of a form of labor backward through the nature of the commodity is a strategy that marks several of Hoccleve's meditations on the nature of poetic production. With this strategy in mind, I turn now to consider another of Hoccleve's representations of textual labor, one both more figural in its mode of representation and more optimistic in its conclusions.

### Prayer and Productivity: Hoccleve's "Story of the Monk Who Clad the Virgin"

The *apologia* from the Prologue to the *Regiment of Princes* is only one of three moments at which Hoccleve discusses the labor of writing. In addition to the *Regiment* he takes writing as a subject in the *Series'* and, I argue here, in his short Marian narrative, "The Story of the Monk Who Clad the Virgin by Singing Ave Maria." "The Story of the Monk Who Clad the Virgin" exists in three manuscripts, one the Huntington holograph (HM 744), one Trinity College, Cambridge MS. R.3.21, and, the other (a much-modified version) the Christ Church, Oxford manuscript of Chaucer's *Canterbury Tales* (MS 152), into which it has been interpolated as the spurious Ploughman's Tale.[21] Hoccleve's sources for this tale are obscure, but Beverly Boyd has demonstrated that the narrative belongs to a family of popular legends concerning the origin of "Our Lady's Psalter."[22]

The narrative of this poem is straightforward. It tells the story of a young monk, raised by his father to say the Ave Maria, who on a visit to his father's house is confronted by a vision of the Virgin in a sleeveless garment. When he asks about the condition of the garment, he is told that what exists has been woven by his prayers and that the garment will be completed by his continued custom in saying her Psalter, to be punctuated, according to her instruction, by the Pater Noster. The monk obeys this stipulation and is visited on the next holy day by the Virgin, now in a complete garment, who instructs him to take this ritual back to his monastery. He does so, and becomes both abbot and tutor to his abbey. The explicit moral of the poem is supplied in the last stanza, which reads:

> Tho yeeres past, his soule was betaght
> To God. He heuene had vnto his meede.
> Who serueth our lady, leesith right naght.
> Whe souffissantly qwytith euery deede.
> And now heeraftir the bettre to speede,
> And in hir grace cheerly for to stonde,
> Hir psalteer for to seye let vs fonde.[23]

The poem is thus an exercise in devotional pedagogy, meant to enact on its reader the central, reiterated, action of its plot, the instruction in the correct form of prayer to the Virgin which is passed from father to son, from Virgin to monk, and from monk (and abbot-to-be) to his brothers.

In addition to this devotional lesson, this poem also offers a depiction, in sharp distinction to the troubles of the *Regiment*, of the potential productivities to be gained in the production and reproduction of verbal artifacts. The central metaphor in the piece is, of course, the weaving of the garment and its sleeves out of the prayerful labor of the monk. The emphasis on productivity here is most evident when compared to its principle analogues. As Boyd has pointed out, there are a series of miracles of the Virgin, which draw on images of physical objects being created through prayer, the most widespread of which was the story of the Virgin weaving a garland out of the roses that fell from the lips of a monk when he said the Ave.[24] In the analogues, however, the objects created tend to be either liturgical or markedly aesthetic, such as this garland of roses. In Hoccleve's version, on the other hand, the object created is one both eminently practical and one central to the burgeoning economic power of late-fifteenth-century England, namely, woven textiles.

If we take this poem then as, in part, an allegory of the power of words to produce something of tangible value, we must notice the fact that this production seems to be traced through a surprisingly circuitous route. The Virgin's presentation of this miracle of production is itself straightforward. As she tells the young, unnamed, monk:

> And vnto him seide, 'Beholde now
> How good clothyng and how fressh apparaille
> That this wyke to me youen hast thow.
> Sleeues to my clothynge now nat faille,
> Thee thanke I, and ful wel for thy trauaille
> Shalt thow be qwit heer, in this lyf present,
> And in þat othir whan thow hens art went.' (ll. 92–98)

His work has created her clothes, and she thanks him, significantly, not so much for his devotion as for his "trauaille." But, despite the simplicity of this equation, the production of goods and the circulation of value all stemming from simple work, the course of the monk's work in the larger narrative is complicated by two oddly tangential paths in the narrative, one having to do with the physical setting of the story and the other concerning the complex circuit through which the monk's lesson must travel.

The narrative energy of this poem derives from a pedagogical circuit inscribing the transfer of a prayer from person to person, as the Ave Maria is given from the secular and noble father to monastic son, then corrected and given again by the Virgin to the monk, and then disseminated widely as the monk passes the corrected form on to his brethren. What we see inscribed in the shape of this circuit is not a linear transmission, but a peculiarly staggered progression, as the text moves from father to son, doubles back then from Virgin to monk and then moves out into a wider monastic transmission. What is the meaning of this structured passage? Within the narrative, the need for the Ave to be given first by the father and then again by Mary is explained by a need for correction. The prayer originally taught to the monk by his father is adequate to knit a partial garment for the Virgin, but when she appears to him she makes it clear that the garment can be completed only with an improved version of the prayer:

> His fadres lore to fulfille him hied,
> And L sythes with deuout corage
> Seide Aue Marie as was his vsage.
>
> And when þat he had endid his preyeere,
> Our lady, clothid in a garnement
> Sleeuelees, byfore him he sy appeere,
> Wherof the monk took good auisament,

Merueillynge hym what þat this mighte han ment,
And seide, "O goode lady, by your leeue,
What garnament is this, and hath no sleeue?"

And she answerde and seide, "This clothynge
Thow hast me youen, for thow euery day
L syth Aue Maria seyynge,
Honured hast me. Hensfoorth, I the pray
Vse to treble þat by any way,
And to euerby xthe Aue ioyne also
A Pater Noste. Do thow euen so." (ll. 47–63)

The circuit of verbal transmission in this narrative is governed in this narrative by a dynamic of correction, a process in which an original text is produced, disseminated, corrected, and then disseminated further. It is the process of correction that produces both value (in the difference between an original imperfect text and a second, more perfect, one) and the engine of dissemination (as this difference and its value provide the rationale for iteration). As the narrative continues, such correction becomes unnecessary with the achievement of the correct form of the prayer, but the initial fulfillment of the monk's liturgical duty is possible only through this process of corrective iteration.

Although the narrative's aspiration towards the eventual perfection of liturgical regularity may seem to suggest that it is concerned primarily with right ritual in a monastic context, I would argue that the central importance of this alternative model of corrective iteration in fact splits the narrative between two worlds of production, on the one hand, the monastic world of oral performance, and, on the other, the scribal world of bureaucratic textual dissemination. The corrective process of production, revision, and dissemination is exactly parallel to that depicted in another of Hoccleve's works, the *Series*, in which Hoccleve's translation of his first *Gesta Romanorum* tale, the "Tale of Jereslaus's Wife" is not allowed into circulation until his Friend revises it by adding its missing moralization, completing the work and authorizing the dissemination of the improved result. Like the monk who clad the Virgin, Hoccleve's own labors must be passed along in preliminary form, corrected, and then distributed. In the context of the *Series*, this collaborative labor seems a clear projection of the world of bureaucratic labor into the world of poetic composition.[25] The clerks worked in a distinctive textual universe in which documents were not original compositions but the products of successive revisions and disseminations, created as an original writ or letter travelled from office to office growing through a process of accretion as notes were attached and corrections made before it could be authoritatively recorded or disseminated.

As this world of collaborative labor shaped Hoccleve's representations of poetic composition in the *Series*, so, I would suggest, the narrative deflection of circulation into correction betrays the fact that it is this same world of bureaucratic textuality that undergirds the process of corrective iteration in "The Story of the Monk Who Clad the Virgin."

This likelihood is further reinforced by what is known of the context of its production and likely patronage. According to a marginal note in the holograph copy (Huntington manuscript HM 744), this poem was "feust faite a l'instance de T. Marleburgh."[26] This Thomas Marleburgh was a stationer and Warden of the Limners and Textwriters' Gild, an important figure in the London book trade, and, like Hoccleve, a member of that small circle of scribes and bookmen who seem to have been an important first audience for much of London's vernacular literary production.[27] The *ordinatio* of the holograph carefully separates the poem's prologue of dedication to the Virgin from the Miracle proper, and John Thompson has suggested that the placement of the the marginal note alongside the beginning of the prologue may indicate that Hoccleve was crediting Marleburgh specifically with encouraging Hoccleve to add a prologue to his story of the Miracle.[28] If correct, this would mean that Marleburgh was himself performing a revision exactly parallel to that made by the Friend in the *Series* and by the Virgin of "The Monk Who Clad the Virgin." In its marking out of the prologue as supplement, the holograph displays a textual analog to the Virgin's corrections within the poem. In addition to this parallel, the reference to Marleburgh also points to the social circles that formed at least one audience for the poem. Regardless of Marleburgh's exact role in the genesis of the work, we should note that he and the members of this circle would have felt an instant familiarity with a story in which a young aspirant finds success in being trained to produce and disseminate verbal artifacts out into an ever increasing spiral of circulation. The protagonist may have been a monk and the artifacts verbal, but they would have had no difficulty seeing their scribal world in this mirror.

I conclude by looking more briefly at the second structure of narrative deflection in this text, that concerned with its depiction of space and settings. As with the matter of textual circulation, it is, in essence, the apparently superfluous role of the monk's father that is at issue. As we saw the Ave Maria being traded back and forth between various personages, so the action of this poem shuttles back and forth from place to place, beginning at the home of the father, moving to the son's monastery, then returning to the home, where the young monk receives his vision in a private chapel his father has had built, only then to return again to the monastery to become abbot. What is the significance of these movements? Why should this staple of liturgical prayer be derived from a vision experienced not in the abbey, but rather in a visit back to his father's home, as though something absolutely central to monastic experience (as depicted here) had to be discovered back in a familial, domestic, secular, and noble space? In part, the desire to sacrilize a private chapel is certainly part of this poem's implicitly anti-Wycliffite stance. As Anne Hudson has pointed out, both the emphasis on Mary's intervention and the praise of Latin devotional practices provides a direct counter to Wycliffite urgings that the "Our Father" be said in English without Mary's mediation.[29] The reverence given to a private chapel seems a consonant part of this anti-Wycliffite stance, attaching the appeal of private aristocratic practices of worship to specifically Marian (and monastic) devotions.

In addition, however, the importance given to this private extra-monastic space also helps shape the poem's treatment of textual production. Secular and monastic spaces are here suggestively depicted as spatial supplements to each other, and as the locations of mutually reinforcing textual activities. The Ave Maria is first generated in the monk's home, but its value is realized only in reiterative performance of this text at his monastery. The accrued value is revealed only upon his return home, where he then receives a new version of the text to put into circulation at the monastery. The circulation of this prayer is thus mapped onto a social universe in which secular composition and monastic performance are seen as mutually supportive and jointly beneficial versions of textual labor. In this vision of the circulation of the Ave Maria, the *opus dei* is brought together with the patronage of the secular household in order to create an image of writerly labor which could be see as productive and complete in itself.

Hoccleve had claimed in the *Regiment* that writing had the ability to "knit" together the subject. Similarly the knitting together imagined in "The Story of the Monk Who Clad the Virgin" must be read, I think, in the context of the ubiquitous images of psychological fragmentation that so color Hoccleve's work, as an essentially compensatory figure, as the utopic inversion of the self-division that seems so universally the outcome of writing in his works elsewhere. Only in this devotional space, made whole by the supplement of the monastic *opus dei*, is Hoccleve able to contemplate the manipulation of texts as a form of labor that both integrates the writer and assures a sure productive trajectory to his labors. It is perhaps the extremity of this situation that best shows the conceptual difficulties surrounding the representation of writerly labor in Middle English literature. The labor of the writer is never immaterial labor, but the attempt to represent the specificity of its materiality seems to drive these poets again and again into uneasy synthetic creations, in which the definition of vocation, the materiality of the labor, and the value of the commodity are all best derived from some supplement to textual labor itself. They stitch together the Virgin's sleeves and Langland's long clothes, but these costumes provide a coherent surface at the cost of hiding what lies beneath.

## Notes

I would like to thank Patricia DeMarco and Karen Winstead for their helpful comments on an earlier version of this essay.

1. Immaterial Labor is a term jointly developed, in the wake of Antonio Negri's work, by a group associated with the journal *Futur Antérieur*. The most significant treatments in English include Maurizio Lazzarato, "Immaterial Labor," in *Radical Thought in Italy: A Potential Politics*, ed. Paolo Virno and Michael Hardt (Minneapolis: University of Minnesota Press, 1996), pp. 133–46; Michael Hardt and Antonio Negri, *Empire* (Cambridge, MA: Harvard University Press, 2000), esp. pp. 290–94; and Nick Dyer-Whitford, "Empire, Immaterial Labor, the New Combinations, and the Global Worker," *Rethinking Marxism* 13.3/4 (2001): 70–80.
2. For Chaucer, see "House of Fame," ll. 652–58 and commentary in J.A. Burrow, *Medieval Writers and Their Work* (Oxford: Oxford University Press, 1982), pp. 28–29. For Usk, see *The Testament of Love* 3.4 and commentary by Paul Strohm, "Politics and Poetics: Usk and Chaucer," in *Literary Practice and Social Change in Britain, 1380–1530*, ed. Lee Patterson (Berkeley: University of California Press, 1990), p. 100. For Capgrave, see lines 47–112 of John Capgrave, *The Life of St. Katherine*, ed. Karen Winstead (Kalamazoo, MI: Medieval Institute Publication, 1999). On Hoccleve, see Ethan Knapp, *The Bureaucratic Muse: Thomas Hoccleve and the Literature of Late Medieval England* (University Park, PA: Pennsylvania State University Press, 2001).
3. The trope is Chaucerian, but for a holograph example see the final stanza of Hoccleve's *Series* in Durham University Library MS Cosin V.iii.9.
4. For another consideration of these terms, see Jacques Le Goff, "Le travail dans les systèmes de valeur de l'Occident médiéval," in *Le Travail au Moyen Âge*, ed. Jacqueline Hamesse and Colette Muraille-Samaran (Louvain-la-Neuve: Institut d'Études Médiévales de l'Université Catholique de Louvain, 1990), pp. 7–21.
5. See "Preface" to *The Problem of Labour in Fourteenth-Century England*, ed. James Bothwell, P.J.P. Goldberg, and W.M. Ormrod (Woodbridge, UK: Boydell and Brewer, 2000), pp. vii–viii.
6. On the figuration of the peasant in this period, see the masterful treatment in Paul Freedman, *Images of the Medieval Peasant* (Stanford: Stanford University Press, 1999).
7. Metaphors describing writing as agricultural labor are rooted also, of course, in the bucolic tradition. But it is an index to the seriousness of the category of labor in poets such as Hoccleve and Langland that their discussions are marked much less by this highly idealized classical tradition than they are by the conflicts marking the conditions of actual labor in their time.

8. This passage has occasioned a great deal of recent commentary, most notably perhaps in the essays contained in Steven Justice and Kathryn Kerby-Fulton, eds., *Written Work: Langland, Labor, and Authorship* (Philadelphia, PA: University of Pennsylvania Press, 1997). On the figure of Will as a poetic laborer, see also John Bowers, *The Crisis of Will in Piers Plowman* (Washington: The Catholic University of America Press, 1986), pp. 191–218; and Louise M. Bishop, "Hearing God's Voice: Kind Wit's Call to Prayer in *Piers Plowman*," in *The Work of Work: Servitude, Slavery, and Labor in Medieval England*, ed. Allen J. Frantzen and Douglas Moffat (Glasgow: Cruithne Press, 1994), pp. 191–205.
9. Citations from the C text of *Piers Plowman* are drawn from *Piers Plowman: The C Version*, ed. George Russell and George Kane (London: The Athlone Press, 1997).
10. Anne Middleton, "Acts of Vagrancy: The C Version 'Autobiography' and the Statute of 1388," in *Written Work: Langland, Labor and Authorship*, pp. 208–317.
11. Middleton, "Acts of Vagrancy," p. 249.
12. Middleton, "Acts of Vagrancy," p. 252.
13. Kathryn Kerby-Fulton, "Langland and the Bibliographical Ego," in *Written Work*, pp. 81–82. Kerby-Fulton also presents a fascinating account of the monastic background of such *apologias*.
14. In an allegorical transformation which will recur at numerous points in the poem, Will's books and prayers become embodied here as separate figures in the landscape. For a similar allegorical conceit, see the feast of texts devoured by the doctour in C 15.
15. For manuscript variations on line 44, see Russell and Kane, *Piers Plowman*, p. 289. For commentary from Skeat and Pearsall, see Walter Skeat, ed., *The Vision of Piers the Plowman in Three Parallel Texts* (London: Oxford University Press, 1924), vol. 2, p. 62 and Derek Pearsall, ed., *Piers Plowman by William Langland, an edition of the C text* (Berkeley: University of California Press, 1978), p. 99.
16. For a detailed treatment of this manuscript, see Merja Black, "A Scribal Translation of *Piers Plowman*," *Medium Aevum* 67 (1998): 257–90.
17. Pearsall responds to this syntactical difficulty, implicitly, in glossing the texts here as "the tools of L's trade." Pearsall, *Piers Plowman*, p. 99.
18. These passages have been considered jointly by Kerby-Fulton, "Langland and the Bibliographical Ego," pp. 82–97. Pearsall also points out the similarity between these passages in his commentary. See *Piers Plowman*, p. 98.
19. Cited from Charles Blyth, ed., *Thomas Hoccleve: The Regiment of Princes* (Kalamazoo, MI: Medieval Institute Publication, 1999). The physicality of labor in this scene is also discussed by Nicholas Perkins in *Hoccleve's Regiment of Princes: Counsel and Constraint* (Cambridge: D.S. Brewer, 2001), pp. 147–150. Particularly interesting is his connection between the body damaged by writing and the Roman veteran displaying his wounds before Caesar.

20. Knapp, *Bureaucratic Muse*, pp. 83–93.
21. Beverly Boyd, "Hoccleve's Miracle of the Virgin," *Texas Studies in English* 35 (1956): 116–22; Beverly Boyd, *The Middle English Miracles of the Virgin* (San Marino: The Huntington Library, 1964), pp. 50–55 and 119–22. For the spurious Ploughman's Tale, see John Bowers, ed., *The Canterbury Tales: Fifteenth-Century Continuations and Additions* (Kalamazoo, MI: Medieval Institute Publications, 1992), pp. 23–32.
22. Boyd, "Hoccleve's Miracle of the Virgin," p. 119.
23. Selections from this text will be drawn from Thomas Hoccleve, *'My Compleinte' and Other Poems*, ed. Roger Ellis (Exeter: University of Exeter Press, 2001).
24. Boyd, "Hoccleve's Miracle of the Virgin," p. 119.
25. On the *Series* and the Privy Seal, see Knapp, *Bureaucratic Muse*, pp. 174–83.
26. J.A. Burrow and A.I. Doyle, eds., *Thomas Hoccleve: A Facsimile of the Autograph Verse Manuscripts*, EETS s.s. 19 (Oxford: Oxford University Press, 2002).
27. On Marleburgh, see John Burrow, *Thomas Hoccleve* (Aldershot: Variorum, 1994), p. 25; C. Paul Christianson, "A Community of Book Artisans in Chaucer's London," *Viator* 20 (1989): 218; C. Paul Christianson, *A Directory of London Stationers and Book Artisans 1300–1500* (New York: Bibliographical Society of America, 1990), pp. 131–32; John J. Thompson, "Thomas Hoccleve and Manuscript Culture," in *Nation, Court and Culture: New Essays on Fifteenth-Century English Poetry*, ed. Helen Cooney (Dublin: Four Courts Press, 2001), p. 89; and John J. Thompson, "After Chaucer," in Derek Pearsall, ed., *New Directions in Later Medieval Manuscript Studies: Essays from the 1998 Harvard Conference* (Woodbridge: Boydell and Brewer, 2000) p. 191 n. 3.
28. John J. Thompson, "A Poet's Contact with the Great and the Good: Further Consideration of Thomas Hoccleve's Texts and Manuscripts," in Felicity Riddy, ed., *Prestige, Authority and Power in Late Medieval Manuscripts and Texts* (Woodbridge: Boydell and Brewer, 2000), pp. 94–95.
29. Anne Hudson, *The Premature Reformation: Wycliffite Texts and Lollard History* (Oxford: Oxford University Press, 1988), pp. 310–13. John Bowers, *Fifteenth-Century Continuations*, p. 24, also points out this anti-Lollard polemic in relation to the spurious *Ploughman's Tale*.

## CHAPTER 10

## THE ERASURE OF LABOR: HOCCLEVE, CAXTON, AND THE INFORMATION AGE

*William Kuskin*

> *The information age is widely understood as a technological revolution, a progressive advancement of capitalism into a post-industrial age. Kuskin argues that the transition from manuscript to print and from print to silicon chip run parallel: both demonstrate that labor is made invisible, erased, by capitalists for political reasons. This observation undermines the notion of a break from history to recall the enduring role of labor in cultural production.*

*Ideology has no history.*

—Louis Althusser[1]

In his recent monograph, *The Great Disruption*, former senior social scientist at the Rand Corporation and deputy-director of the State Department's Policy Planning Staff, Francis Fukuyama, argues for a relationship between communication technology and social production: "A society built around information tends to produce more of the two things people value most in a modern democracy—freedom and equality. Freedom of choice has exploded, whether of cable channels, low-cost shopping outlets, or friends met on the Internet."[2] For Fukuyama, individual agency is less a measure of the subject's control of his or her labor, than of freedom of choice, a benefit of participating in "a society built around information." And so Fukuyama celebrates the subject of the Information Age as largely autonomous—picking and choosing between cable channels, shopping outlets, and friends on the internet—yet nevertheless produced by the dominant ideology, capitalism, itself a progressive advancement from the past.

We can deepen such a reading of the subject of communication technology by returning to the fifteenth-century shift from manuscript to print. I offer two literary case studies: Thomas Hoccleve's work as a scribe and William Caxton's introduction of print to England. Hoccleve and Caxton both translated Jacobus de Cessolis' *De ludo scacchorum*, Hoccleve as the 1410–11 *Regement of Princes* and Caxton as his second English book, the 1474 *Game and Playe of the Chesse*.[3] In what follows, I compare these two texts in order to historicize the role of labor in the transition from one mode of production to the next. The comparison demonstrates ways in which technological transformation can be constructed to appear as an historical break from the past, and in this it illustrates Althusser's claim that the process of subject formation, what he calls ideology, erases the circumstances of its own production. Rather than abandon the category of labor in the flourish of things new, however, I argue that this observation suggests a rethinking of our approach to periodization as a whole, a renewed interrogation of capitalism and a skepticism toward historical break as a valid explanation for social change. Hoccleve and Caxton teach us that the distinction between modes of production lies less in large scale historical transitions—medieval to modern, modern to post-industrial—than in the specific historical articulation of the social relations by which capital and labor produce the individual as a subject, less of revolutionary technologies than of enduring ideological constructs for capitalizing labor.

## Thomas Hoccleve's *Trauaillous Stilnesse*

In *Chaucer's Sexual Poetics*, Carolyn Dinshaw argues that medieval "literary production takes place on bodies—on the animal skins made into pages, on cursed scribes' scalps—and the rubbing and scraping that must be done to both suggests a figurative identification here between the human body and the manuscript page, the text."[4] We can historicize Dinshaw's point through a reading of Hoccleve's *Regement of Princes*, a *fürstenspiegl* and begging poem written for Henry, Prince of Wales in 1410–11.[5] In many ways the poem is about securing paternal inheritance, from Chaucer and from Henry IV, and recent readings characterize it as consolidating poetical and political legacy in a single gesture: Hoccleve's literary authority to advise the Prince is legitimized by the poem's success as a *fürstenspiegl*; in turn, the Prince's political authority to inherit the throne is evidenced by his ability to respond to the poem as royal patron.[6] Perhaps the most pithy piece of advice in a poem of counsel—"make of necessite, reed I, vertu"[7]—is also its most succinct gloss, for the *Regement* makes necessity a virtue at every turn, and its balance of its two genres—the necessity of begging and the virtue of poetic advice to princes—is crucial to its performance of each. As a result, the *Regement* possesses a relentless logic, one that constantly threatens to collapse upon itself before it proves true. Paul Strohm phrases this observation forcefully in *England's Empty Throne* where he reads the poem as representative of the period in general: "continually at strife with its own professions, the Lancastrian text is above all a hardworking text, always striving but never succeeding in reconciling its placid surface with its external entanglements and its internal contradictions."[8] Analysis of Hoccleve's work remains incomplete, I argue, without deeper consideration of the symbolic identification between the manuscript and the subject. We see this in Hoccleve's autobiography as he describes a violence to the body and to the page that is simultaneously alienating and enabling. This is theoretically true for ideology overall: ideology cuts both ways; as much as it constrains the individual, it also places him or her as subject, however compromised. Thus, I argue that Lancastrian literary culture in the first decades of the fifteenth century seeks no real reconciliation with its contradictions at all; instead, it purposefully entangles itself in a variety of social discourses to create a symbolic structure for vernacular literary production.

The *Regement of Princes* consists of two parts. The first, the Prologue, is a dialogue between Hoccleve and the indigent Old Man he meets in the fields outside London. The dialogue alternates between the Old Man's moralizations and Hoccleve's autobiography, his twenty-four years as a scribe at the Privy Seal in Westminster, a position he held from 1387 or 1388 until just before his death in 1426.[9] Much of the conversation is preoccupied with Hoccleve's worry that "paiement is hard to gete adayes" (825), and the Old Man ultimately counsels him to seek patronage by writing an English poem to the young Prince of Wales: " 'Al-though þou seye þat þou in latyn, / Ne in frensshe nowther, canst but small endite, / In englyssh tonge canst þou wel afyn, / ffor ther-of can I eeke but a lite; / Ye straw! let be! þi penne take, and write' " (1870–74). The second half of the *Regement* is just this poem, an exemplum collection drawn, as Hoccleve announces, from the pseudo-Aristotelian *Secreta secretorum*, Giles of Rome's *De regimine principum*, and Jacobus de Cessolis's *Liber de ludo scacchorum*. The *Regement*'s Prologue therefore meditates on two axes of production: the intellectual terms of producing vernacular literature—patronage and compilation—and the material terms, the life of the scribe. Further, it argues that Hoccleve's profession gives him both the actual skills of manuscript production and the abstract knowledge of the court, of texts, and of Chaucer, to write English poetry.

During Hoccleve's tenure, Chancery was in the midst of what T.F. Tout has termed a "disintegration" of its corporate structure, an intertwined transition in its organizational and linguistic policies.[10] This process has its roots in the fourteenth century. By 1399 Henry IV shifted the clerks' daily allowance to an annuity, and after his rule few annuities were granted at all, so that the next generation of clerks had to make due with the favors, bonuses, and the open benefices they could use their position in the courtly bureaucracy to identify and their influence to secure.[11] In 1417, Henry V began a program of transforming the bureaucratic language to English in an effort to distinguish his court culture from that of the French during the Hundred Years War.[12] Tout points out that during this period the clerks reflect this overall shift in that they become increasingly secular, less a product of clerical training, and more of apprenticeship under an earlier generation of clerks who now taught out of the Inns; he tells that "the word clerk began to connote not ecclesiastic so much as writer."[13] Fittingly, the Privy Seal clerks we know much about seem to have been fairly shrewd and self-promoting, interested in courtly politics and good at keeping track of, and collecting, what they were owed.[14] As the clerks went beyond the corporate structure financially, they also went beyond its housing, so that the Chancery Inns dispersed. Hoccleve's particular situation is interesting: in the *Regement* he initially tells that he lived "at Chestre Ynne, right fast be the stronde" (5), the townhouse that the Bishop of Coventry and Lichfield rented for the clerks, but soon after that he reveals that he is married and that he expects this will move him out of the college to what he calls a "pore cote" (845).[15] Hoccleve's concerns about payment have been understood as the motivating force of his interest in patronage, but the *Regement*'s initial focus identifies vernacular writing as central to the poem's narration of its own creation at least twice over: once, in its self-reflectivity about the material and intellectual forms of literary production, and once again in its generalized anxiety about the larger social transformation such production engenders.

Hoccleve elaborates upon the work of writing in an extended contrast between scribes and artisans in the middle of the Prologue. Across a number of stanzas he complains that writing is a unique and unappreciated form of labor, which demands tremendous mental and physical concentration:

> This artificers, se I day be day,
> In þe hotteste of al hir bysynesse
> Talken and syng, and make game and play,
> And forth hir labour passith with gladnesse;
> But we labour in trauaillous stilnesse;
> We stowpe and stare vp-on þe shepes skyn,
> And keepe muste our song and wordes in. (1009–15)

Talking and singing as they work, the artisans have a harmonious relationship with their labor, which, taking place "in þe hotteste of al hir bysynesse," Hoccleve describes as a flurry of activity. In contrast, the clerks of the Privy Seal "labour in trauaillous stilnesse." Silence, *stilnesse*, should mark their subjection to institutional structure and its accompanying rewards: they should labor all day at the Westminster bureaucracy and then return to the security and comfort of the inns at night. As the terms of English writing change, this arrangement is no longer guaranteed, but they are still subjected to silence. Therefore, Hoccleve tells that though his fellow scribes are often bilked of their payment, "ne for hem speke a worde; but dombe as ston / þei standen, where hir speche hem myght awayle" (1496–97). Not only is Hoccleve silent, but he is so absorbed by thought that is he deaf as well, "he vnderstondeþ no þing what men seye, / so ben his wyttes fer gon hem to pleye" (104–105), and his sight is bleary from staring at the vellum ("Vp-on þe whyte mochel sorwe dryne," 1022). In contrast to the lusty laborers he sees in London, Hoccleve's "bysynesse" is productive only insofar as his body remains still, and in concentrating his body to this degree, his mind becomes restless.[16] This is so in the poem's first lines, which open the poem with an insomniac Hoccleve "mvsyng vpon the restles bisynesse/ Which that this troubly world hath ay on honde" (1–2), and it holds true throughout the Prologue where "bisyness" is equated with a generalized, and at times allegorized, "þoght, my crewel fo" (73). Hoccleve's labor produces material products—the letters, warrants, and dispatches his office was responsible for—but it also produces him as self-consciously alienated from the very social structure that should constitute him as a functioning individual.

"Trauaillous stilnesse" presents Hoccleve's position through contradiction. On one level, "Stilnesse" suggests his silence and his lack of movement, his literal "still-ness" at his writing desk as he stares at the sheep's skin in front of him and his stomach cramps, his back aches, and his eyes dry out (1016–22). The body occupies Hoccleve's earlier and later work as well. In the 1406 *La Male Regle* he tells us "and now my body empty is, & bare / of ioie,"[17] because, "for the more paart youthe is rebel" (65), and that poem elaborates Hoccleve's riot. In the first part of the 1421–22 *Series*,"The Dialogue with a Friend," Hoccleve reports that at fifty-three years old his "lymes sumdell now vnweldy be; / all my syght apperithe faste, and wastithe" (248–49). The terms are similar in the *Regement*, but rather than empty or wasted, here his body is actively filled up with physical pain, pain also captured in the phrase "trauaillous stilnesse": the OED records "travil" as developing from "to put to torture, torment." Still, the phrase remains contradictory, for the OED also records "travail" as becoming "differentiated from the Old French sense of work, developing in Anglo-French a

sense of 'journey', which was later differentiated into the spelling 'travel'."
At the heart of "trauaillous stilnesse," then, is 'stilnesse' as stasis and 'travail' as movement, and this too is part of Hoccleve's larger poetic, for just as the *Regement* begins with Hoccleve moving through London, his earlier and later works also focus on such London walks. *La Male Regle* tells how at a tavern "At Poules heed me maden ofte appeere, / To talke of mirthe & to disporte & pleye" (143–44), how he walked back to Westminster, where no one was "bet aqweyntid at Westmynstre yate, / Among the tauerneres namely" (177–78), and how he passed his summer days strolling along the bridge and taking ferries on the Thames (190–92). Similarly, in "The Complaint" section of the *Series* he recalls "ofte whan I in westmynster hall[e], / and eke in london amonge the presse went[e]" (72–73). *La Male Regle*, the *Series*, and the *Regement of Princes* are all begging poems that discuss Hoccleve's life in London and Westminster. Where *La Male* and the *Series* are about articulating the terms of submission at various points in one's life, the *Regement* is less resolved and as it tries to articulate Hoccleve's position, falls into contradiction. "Trauaillous stilnesse" captures this contradiction, this "restles bisynesse," and pushes it away from both closure and simple opposition to suggest a stasis that moves throughout London, a busy-ness that is productive but blocked, a labor of communication that neither speaks nor hears. As much as the *Regement* is about literary production, it is also about the unresolved violence of subjection.

Hoccleve acknowledges subjection throughout the *Regement*, in its subjection to his sources, and in his own subjection to Chancery, to Henry, and to Chaucer. These sections too are contradictory. For example, Hoccleve's discussion of Chaucer occurs in three parts, the first of which famously begins:

> O, maister deere, and fadir reuerent!
> Mi maister Chaucer, flour of eloquence,
> Mirour of fructuous entendement,
> O, vniuersel fadir in science!
> Allas! þat þou thyn excellent prudence,
> In þi bed mortel mightist naght by-qwethe;
> What eiled deth? allas! whi wolde he sle the? (1961–67)

Hoccleve figures Chaucer as a father, an identification fraught indeed. As "fadir reuerent," Chaucer is Hoccleve's master, a historical man whose excellent prudence, lost in his deathbed, might not be bequeathed. As universal father, however, Chaucer's authority is exactly the opposite: it lies beyond personal knowledge and transcends history. A number of critics have recognized that this opposition finds its precedent in *The Clerk's Tale* where Chaucer himself sets up a distinction between Petrarch's mortal body, "deed and nayled in his cheste," and his authority, the "rhetorike sweete" that "Enlymynded al Ytalille of poetrie."[18] What is unique to Hoccleve, then, is not the formula; just as he bases his discussion of Chaucer on Chaucer's prior discussion of Petrarch, he readily points out that the formula deals with the obvious and universal truth that we all die. The question, "What eiled deth? allas! whi woulde he sle the?," points to the fact that we are all subjected to death, or, as he later puts it, "like a bridel is deþes remembraunce" (2871). But the absolute truth of subjection to death only allows Hoccleve to exploit his formula, to apply it to Chaucer, and immediately reapply it once again to Gower, whose death evokes an even greater acknowledgment of universal Christian subjection: "But syn our lorde Crist was obedient / To þe, in feith I can no ferther seye; / His creatures mosten þe obeye" (1979–81). That Hoccleve's list of English writers is limited to two should not distract us from the obvious: Chaucer and Gower suggest the contours of an English canon expandable by its very application. Thus, Hoccleve's strategy is to appropriate authority by constructing it so that the figures of the canon are identifiable men, sealed away by death in history, but also transcendent, part of the ongoing process of participating in and appropriating from Chaucerian writing. The terms of subjection are also those of production; the very demands which create part one of the *Regement* as a begging poem—the disintegration of Chancery, Hoccleve's fear of death, his abject role as a disciple of Chaucer rather than a master in his own right—mobilize his authority as a counselor in part two. That the *Regement* exists in forty-three manuscripts, that Hoccleve's name is later anthologized in print with Chaucer's, Gower's, and Lydgate's argues for the success of this formulation.[19]

The contradictions within Hoccleve's symbolic creation of the vernacular canon, his rendition of English writing as simultaneously alienating and mimetic, as submissive and appropriative, also define the social relationships underpinning manuscript production. Much recent scholarship has pointed out Hoccleve's involvement in English manuscript production in Westminster and London.[20] These two communities stand in a relationship simultaneously autonomous and contingent: *autonomous* in that they independently possess instruments for literary production, Westminster in the Chancery apparatus in which Hoccleve participated, and London in Paul's churchyard, which C. Paul Christianson describes as "the apparent intellectual center of late fourteenth- and early fifteenth-century London [that] coincided with the craft neighborhood of its suppliers of books";[21] *contingent* in that high-end literary manuscripts such as the Ellesmere Chaucer and the presentation manuscript of Hoccleve's *Regement*, BL MS Arundel 38, represent the cooperation of individuals from both communities, courtiers possessing manuscripts, stationers with networks *amongst* the London trade, and artisans looking to participate in *ad hoc* work crews. A variety of guild structures lay over this fluid arrangement. For example, in 1390 the Writers of Court-Letter emerged as a corporation independent from the Textwriters and Lymners guilds, two guilds that consolidated into the fraternity of book artisans in 1403, into the Mystery of Stationers in 1440, and, again, into the Company of Stationers in 1557.[22] Still, we should not derive too rigid an organization from the existence of these early guilds. Well after 1403, the Stationers, Textwriters, Bookbinders, Writers of Court-Letter, and Limners were still recorded as separate craft organizations in at least one guild list, and individual craftsmen commonly moved between such professional designations.[23] The guild structure superimposed a coherent and hierarchical organization over a labor pool of overlapping skills. It allowed leading craftsmen to police an otherwise *ad hoc* system of production and to work with the city council in asserting social order; however, it did not present a monopoly on labor or production to the coordinated extent of the later Stationer's Company.[24] In the fifteenth century, text and craft production remained loose and fluid rather than hierarchical and defined. The medieval manuscript may project a unified relationship between poet, scribe, and patron, but in fact, it is a social object constructed by the joint participation of various agents working in temporary and entrepreneurial bonds. Hoccleve's self-presentation evokes such labor as fraught with the tensions inherent in his "troubly world," one which witnessed not only the overhaul of the Chancery system, but the Lancastrian usurpation of the throne, a war against France that seemed to have no end, and the development of an English poetic canon.

Capital underwrites this system of production in overt and implicit ways. Moving as credit, capital facilitated the temporary relationships between consumers and groups of artisans. Again, Christianson provides a useful encapsulation of this system: "Payment for labour in particular could not always wait until the book bill was settled by a patron. In the largely cashless society of fifteenth-century London, lines of credit could be extended by making a symbolic pledge of goods and chattels. Such debt transactions were entered into by various trade members...[and] represented specific instances of financing book-trade activities."[25] Capital also organized the system inherently, and in this provided its impetus for change. To capture this sense, it is worth reviewing A.I. Doyle's remarks in "English Books In and Out of Court from Edward III to Henry VII" in some detail. Doyle writes:

> If the [stationer] could procure an exemplar, whether from the author (or his heirs) or an existing owner, he could also develop further demand by

investing in handsomely decorated copies in advance of firm orders so that it would be easier, even for a would-be purchaser at court, to go straight to a stationer than to arrange for anything more than a plain copy for himself. Once a work was being fairly frequently copied and offered through the metropolitan book-trade, the courtier's advantage had gone, for members of other classes had equal access to it. Insofar as the enthusiasm for new works in English arose near the centre of the court about the turn of the fourteenth into the fifteenth century and spread through its outer circles, fringes or satellites and beyond, it must have led to the expansion or modification of the London book-trade, which was in the best position to serve it and as its records and extant books suggest did happen. Yet the court does not seem to have been dependent on the London book-trade for all its books any more than the book-trade seems to have been dependent on the court for all its business.[26]

The system Doyle describes is based in aristocratic privilege, "the courtier's advantage," a social capital of symbolic currency. At the same time, Doyle recognizes that once a book enters circulation such capital burns off as "members of other classes" gain access to it. Again, the book-trade is both autonomous and contingent; neither Westminster court nor London market are absolutely dependent upon one another; nonetheless, their activity is mutually shaping of the larger production system. The result is a twofold change in the terms of production, on the one hand a shift in the source of the literary object's capital from "the courtier's advantage" to its own authority, and on the other, the production of "handsomely decorated copies" for speculative sale that leads to an "expansion or modification of the London book-trade." Hoccleve exploits the tension within this system by structuring it as a process of exchange: he has literary capital (in his second eulogy to Chaucer he actually identifies Chaucer as capital—"Allas! my worthi maister honorable / This landes verray tresor and richesse," 2080–81); he needs financial capital. Prince Henry can grant him financial capital and, in turn, can use literary capital to his own ends. What is physical and intellectual in "trauaillous stilnesse"—the silent movement throughout London—is thus made tangible in Hoccleve's body and the literary manuscripts formed by his labor, for the body and the manuscript are subject to a system of production that is both autonomous and contingent. Hoccleve makes this parallel plain when he offers himself, like a corrupt text to a scribe, to the Old Man for correction, "and mekely yow byseche I of pardoun, / Me submittyng vn-to correccioun" (755–56).

The terms of manuscript production ultimately alter the book-trade from within. This mechanism is symbolically true for Hoccleve's production of literary authority as well. Though he may continually insist on the importance of orthodoxy for the culture at large, though he may at times appear slavishly obsequious to Prince Henry and the Lancastrian program, these statements are intertwined with an intellectual argument that often runs counter to orthodoxy. Case in point, vernacular theology is repeatedly marked as dangerous in the *Regement*, and Hoccleve aligns himself with orthodox methods of exegesis early on by having the Old Man condemn "a wrecche / Not fern agoo, whiche þat of heresye / Conuyct, and brent was vn-to ashen drye" (285–87), the Lollard, John Badby.[27] In the Badby section, vernacular exegesis, the product of too little occupation (281), is condemned as politically as well as spiritually transgressive (341), and against this Hoccleve presents the poem's most obsequious praise of Lancastrian policy (295–315). To the Old Man's rather leading inquiry into Hoccleve's own exegetical practices, " 'Sone, if god wole, þou art non of þo/ þat wrapped ben in þis dampnacioun?' " (372–73), Hoccleve quickly announces his dullness, " 'I? criste forbade it, sire!. . .ffor swiche mater, vn-to my wit to derk is' "(373–78). The bridle reappears in this context too, this time as a conceit for submitting to the clergy (365). Similarly, he later caps a sequence of Old Testament exempla by distancing himself from any sort of personal reading of the Bible, "Of swiche stories mo wolde I expresse, / But for I noght ne can, I lete hem passe; / I am as lewed and dulle as an asse" (3862–63). In such passages the poem is undeniably orthodox. After all, the Old Man's counsel is to

> Be war of þoght, for it is perillous;
> He þe streight wey to discomfort me ledeþ
> His violence is ful outrageous;
> Vnwise is he þat besy þoght ne dredeþ. (267–70)

Implying that wisdom lies in eschewing "besy þoght," the advice answers Hoccleve's social alienation with political quietism. By extension, it suggests that Hoccleve not think through the implications of vernacular literary production at all. Yet the *Regement* only endorses this view in part, for it also leads its reader "the straight way to discomfort" by indulging "þoght" at every turn. For all its protestations against vernacular exegesis by lay clerks, the *Regement* moves deliberately toward its payoff: Hoccleve's appropriation of scriptural authority for vernacular writing. We see this in the poem's last section, where he consistently uses scriptural authority to make his case: in the final passage on Chaucer, for instance, Hoccleve claims that Chaucer wrote many a line praising the virgin (4987); similarly, the Chaucer portrait leads to an argument defending iconography (5006–12), the peace section pivots on Hoccleve's reading of Jesus as an exemplum (5025), and his ambivalent argument "þat womem desiren souereynte" (5113) serves to stage his reading of Ecclesiasties 25:30 ("A woman, if she have superiority, is contrary to her husband"). In fact, even Hoccleve's recurring conceit for subjection, the bridle, is itself an appropriation from a biblical source, Ecclesiastices 7:40: "Contemplation of death is like a bridle restraining man, lest he practice vices." The result is a "violence. . .full outrageous," both a violence to Hoccleve's body and a more epistemological violence inherent in his irreconcilable conclusions, his association of orthodoxy and vernacularity, his insistence that one should not appropriate authority but nevertheless must. In this, Hoccleve's voice—his freewheeling use of vernacular exegesis to elaborate his own cause—itself appropriates its very style from Chaucer's *Wife of Bath* and *Melibee*.[28] As much as Hoccleve combines these two tales, he begs the common wisdom that the fifteenth century appreciated only a moral Chaucer; as much as he uses that voice toward vernacular exegesis, he also begs the notion that fifteenth-century literary culture was entirely repressive, absolute in any form.[29]

Autonomy is contingent upon submission. In Hoccleve this acknowledgment produces a contradiction simultaneously still and in motion, disabling and enabling, directed inward as psychological ruin and outward as propaganda, but nevertheless simultaneously and reciprocally enabling of a series of symbolic structures for literary, political, financial, and exegetical authority. Readers of Hoccleve frequently come to his work as if the categories of the debate—orthodoxy, transgression, literature, and politics—were established for him, and that in manipulating them he fell into contradiction, or worse, open hypocrisy. What must be recognized is that entanglement and incoherence are inherent in his work, not on one or two levels of the piece as unconscious error, but throughout as a fundamental quality of English literary production at the beginning of the fifteenth century. However we try to parse the poem into critical categories of genre, politics or production, Hoccleve sustains these categories long enough to enable a productive change within the existing economy. Thus, if we choose to emphasize Hoccleve's orthodox politics, we must also acknowledge that he stages this position to produce a specifically vernacular literary voice that grounds our own English canon. Similarly, if we find Hoccleve complicit with Lancastrian policy at its most draconian moments, we must also discover his silent participation in the opening outward of the book market. Hoccleve's painful silence speaks not only of the way paternity and literature construct the Lancastrian throne, but also how this construction imagines capital, identity, community, and authority in the ideological production of the vernacular subject, state, canon, and manuscript. That Hoccleve's discussion of literary production is not unified is its most profound truth.

## *Caxton Me Fieri Fecit*

Caxton printed his second translation, the *Game and Playe of the Chesse*, in 1474, directly after the *Recuyell of the Historyes of Troye*, and reprinted it in a revised form in 1483.[30] To create the *Game of Chesse*, Caxton combined (or used a composite manuscript based on) two French versions of Jacobus de Cessolis' *De ludo scacchorum*, Jean de Ferron's of 1347 and Jean de Vignay's of 1340–50, which he also compared to a Latin version and augmented with his own commentary.[31] Caxton accompanies his translation with a dedicatory prologue and epilogue to George, Duke of Clarence, and thus, like Hoccleve before him, uses the text as a vehicle for associating his literary work with royal authority. Caxton knew of Hoccleve's *Regement* but did not print it; indeed, Hoccleve is at once everywhere in Caxton—in his abiding interest in discussing literary production; in the terms of his praise of Chaucer; in the genre at the heart of all his writing, autobiography; and even his addition to *De ludo scacchorum* gravitates to a discussion of Chancery's "hell"[32]—yet nowhere to be found in his portfolio. Extant in over 200 vernacular manuscripts, *De ludo scacchorum* is obviously appropriate for Caxton's initial foray into literary culture, and I suggest that Hoccleve's previous use of the text is important as well: for the elimination of Hoccleve is part of Caxton's larger shift from the literary economy of the Lancastrian period to a Yorkist literary culture separate from the political turmoil of the Wars of the Roses.[33] With this, Caxton also erases the labor behind print production to create a story of technological effortlessness. Caxton's introduction of print involves a material and symbolic revision of English literary culture that creates the printed text as an autonomous and idealized object in its own right, less a debased version of the deluxe manuscripts of the Chaucerian tradition than a revised construction of the relationship between the book and capital that distances the subject from both history and labor.

Caxton's prologue has long been recognized as a translation of Jean de Vignay's dedication, substituting George, the Duke of Clarence's titles for Prince John of France's. Less understood is how Caxton's translation combines the pre-existing literary tradition with his immediate political context.[34] For example, in rendering Vignay's opening, "A Tres noble et excellent prince Jehan de france duc de normendie et auisne filz de philipe par la grace de dieu Roy de france" in English as "To the right noble / right excellent & vertuous prince George duc of Clarence Erle of warwyck and of salisburye / grete chamberlayn of Englond & leutenant of Irelond oldest border of kynge Edward by the grace of god kynge of England and of france," Caxton performs a strategic change as well as a linguistic one.[35] As the second son of the Yorkist house, Clarence had no secure inheritance, and though he became one of the richest—if not the richest—magnates in England by his late teens, his authority rested almost entirely on his ongoing ability to appropriate vacated Lancastrian estates and on his marriage to Isabol Neville.[36] After his return to England in 1471, Edward redistributed a number of these estates and titles though the 1473 Act of Resumption. This act was finalized by March 1474, but the process of redistribution itself was not completed until 1475, and because of it Clarence had to forfeit his estates in Nottingham, Derbyshire, Staffordshire, and Leicestershire, as well as his seat at Tutbury, worth £1,350 a year in revenues, to his younger brother, Richard of Gloucester. Caxton's recitation of Clarence's ducal title and his position as "grete chamberlayn of Englond & leutenant of Irelond" on March 31, 1474 is not merely a formulaic adaptation of Vignay's original; more exactly, it specifically itemizes Neville's old titles—the Earl of Warwick and the great chamberlain of England—and the Lieutenancy of Ireland to point out the tenuousness of Clarence's position in the face of Edward's power. By August 2, 1474, only a few months after the publication of the *Game of Chesse*, Edward had all but stripped Clarence of the lieutenancy, electing Sir Gilbert Debenham chancellor of Ireland in Clarence's name and appointing subsequent offices without involving Clarence at all. Misread as formulaic platitude, Caxton's prologue makes plain the political stakes at hand.

If Caxton underscores the weakness of Clarence's position in the prologue's opening statement, by translating "auisne filz de philipe" to "oldest broder of kynge Edward" (Caxton, 1), he offers Clarence a venue for securing his position. Caxton elaborates Vignay in what follows, proscribing Clarence's role in terms he would not want to deny:

> Right highe puyssant and redoubted prynce /. For as moche as I haue vnderstand and knowe / that ye are enclined vnto the comyn wele of the kynge our sayd saueryn lord. his nobles lordes and comyn peple of his noble royame of Englond / and that ye sawe gladly the Inhabitants of ye same enformed in good. vertuous. prouffitable and honeste maners. In whiche your noble persone wyth guydyng of your hows haboundeth / gyuyng light and ensample vnto all other. Therfore I haue put me in deuour to translate a lityll book late comen in to myn handes out of frensh into englisshe. (Caxton, 1)

Caxton's praise sets up a sequence in which Clarence can no more deny his commitment to the "comyn wele" than to Edward, can no more deny his allegiance to the Yorkist "hows" than to his own "light." Caxton finds this light imagery in Vignay and plays it out over the course of the prologue and in his original epilogue. The effect is to suggest the great circumference of

Clarence's influence, his shadow, and also to underscore that Clarence is not the source of this light, but an intermediate figure standing before the brilliance of his "hows." Of course, houses—the Neville estates and Clarence's loyalty to the Yorkist house—are exactly at issue. Caxton's prologue thus frames Clarence's power in terms of his continued allegiance to the king; in short, it makes necessity a virtue. This caution was obvious to Clarence by 1474, for he had practiced it since he abandoned Neville and returned to his brother in 1471. Ultimately, it is more useful to Caxton in securing his own persona as a Yorkist writer. For Caxton is unknown to Clarence. He tells us, "I requyre & supply your good grace not to desdaygne to resseyue this lityll sayd book in gree and thanke / as well of me your humble and unknowen seruant as of a better and gretter man than I am" (Caxton, 2). What matters to Caxton is less an actual patronage relationship—truly, patronage is not really discussed in the *Game of Chesse*—than the elaboration of a system of public legitimation through which Caxton can stage himself as counselor to kings and dukes. This should both alert us to the durability of Hoccleve's practice and convince us that Caxton sees the literary economy as embedded in a courtly milieu that operates, to a certain degree, along the same lines.

Still, if the terms of Caxton's prologue to Clarence are reminiscent of Hoccleve's to Prince Henry, by the 1470s the model of paternity for political and literary authority had changed. Thematically, the *Game of Chesse* has much to say on paternity. An exemplum collection that allegorizes estates organization through the conceit of chess, it begins with the origins of the game, reciting the story of "a kynge in babiloine that was named Evilmerodach, a Jolye man with oute Justice and so cruell that he dyde do hewe his faders body in thre honderd pieces / And gaf hit to ete and deuour to thre hondred birdes that men calle wultres" (Caxton, 10). Chess originates in patricide. Given that the *Game of Chesse* is an allegory, this suggests a more profound historical origin as well. The passage continues:

> Under this kynge than Evilmerodach was this game and playe of the chesse founden / Trewe it is that some men wene / that this playe was founden in the tyme of the bataylles & siege of troye But that is not soo For this playe cam to the playes of the caldees as dyomedes the greek sayth and reherceth That amonge the philosophrs was the most renomed playe amonge all other playes / And after that / cam this playe in the tyme of Alixandre the grete in to Egipte. (Caxton, 10)

Patricide confuses political and moral order. The syntax of the passage reflects this confusion by projecting it onto the historical record. "Trewe it is" initially implies that the Troy story contains the origins of chess, but with the announcement that "but that is no soo," the passage backtracks, demoting this truth to received opinion. Instead, the *Game of Chesse* chases the game further back into history, before Troy, to the Greeks, and before them to Babylon.[37] If the game is broadly an allegory for social organization, it is also one for social confusion, for a fundamental transgression against paternity at the origins of history that bleeds into the Trojan origins of Britain. As much as the *Game of Chesse* looks to assert order through its itemization of the chess pieces, its recitation of the estates, its characterization of these estates through its many exemplum, it cannot escape this central transgression, so if the exempla are presented to illustrate the proper behavior of each social order, they also repeatedly gravitate to bodily mutilation.

The *Game of Chesse* attempts to resolve this problem at its very end in a rearguard review in its last chapter, "for as moche as we see and knowe that the memorye of the peple is not retentyf but right forgetefull whan some here longe talis & historyes" (Caxton, 183), which inserts a long discussion of how Evilmerdoch's philosopher used the game "to amende and correcte the lyf of the kynge" (Caxton, 185), but this is truly late in the game. The fictive history the text offers is one of transgression, dismemberment, patricide, and treason at the origins of social organization, and this speaks directly to the situation at hand in England, for as rebellious as Prince Henry may have appeared to Henry IV, as usurpatious as Henry IV was himself, in the first quarter of the fifteenth century the king still stood as a figure for paternal authority that the prince had to acknowledge. In contrast, by 1473 the fathers of the Yorkist line were all dead, and the three brothers, Edward, Clarence, and Richard, were left to work out their inheritance themselves. Clarence's execution in 1478, and Richard's usurpation and the disappearance (if not assassination) of the young princes, suggests the vehemence of this process. Caxton's epilogue makes this explicit by telling Clarence that by supporting Edward, "in conquerynge his rightfull enheritaunce/ that verray peas and charite may endure in bothe his royames/ and that marchandise may haue his cours in suche wise that euery man eschewe synne/ and encrece in vertuous occupacions" (Caxton, 187). Here paternity is neither transcendent nor bequeathed; it is conquered. Caxton's point emphasizes too that such an inheritance is not simply a courtly or literary concern, but is also a mercantile issue. In this light, the prologue's earlier emphasis on "the comyn wele" of the estates, and "virtuous, prouffitable and honeste maners" broadens the stakes of conquering inheritance from courtly, political, and literary self-fashioning to economic activity in general.

The *Game of Chesse* demonstrates Caxton's translation of Hoccleve's Lancastrian poetics to a Yorkist literary culture in which the theme of paternity has changed. It also shows the adaptation of manuscript culture to print production. In contrast to Hoccleve, who stoops over the book crafting each letter, Caxton stands apart from his book. Even the placement of the table of contents occurs at some distance, for at the end of the prologue Caxton writes "And for more clerely to procede in this sayd book I haue ordeyned that the chapiters ben sette in the begynnynge to thende that ye may see more playnly the mater wherof the book treteth &c" (Caxton, 2). Caxton does not handle the book himself, rather he "ordeynes" certain changes, changes that occur, not through silent physical contortions, but in large gestures that span the entire book from "begynnynge to thende." The same language appears in Caxton's epilogue to book III of the *Recuyell*, in which he reports that he has "practysed & lerned at my grete charge and dispense to ordeyne this said book in prynte after the maner & forme as ye may here see."[38] When Caxton focuses on physical labor at all in the epilogue, he stresses the difficulty of *writing*: "And for as moche as in the wrytyng of the same my penne is worn / myn hande wery 7 not stedfast myn eyen dimmed with ouermoche lokyng on the whit paper / and my corage not so prone and redy to laboure as hit hath ben." Caxton's rhetoric here has a history stemming from Chaucer's "Adam Scriveyn," through Lydgate and John Shirley; it smacks, however, of Hoccleve's particular emphasis on literary production as hard physical labor rather than of Lydgate's and Shirley's sense of laureate illumination.[39] When print finally arrives on the scene in the *Recuyell*, it is nothing short of miraculous: Caxton tells the readers of the *Recuyell* that the book they hold in their hands "is not wreton with penne and ynke as other bokes ben / to thenede that euery man may haue attones...ffor all the bookes of this storye...thus empryntid as ye here see were begonne in oon day and also fynyshid in oon day." Factually, Caxton's claims contradict what we know to be the material demands of print production. Far from the instantaneous creation he suggests the *Recuyell* must have taken months to complete, and together with the subsequent *Game of Chesse*, the two editions represent over a year's hard work.[40] Even imagining Caxton's explanation as referring in some oblique way to the folding of folio pages, one has trouble imaging how a book the size of the *Recuyell* could be quired so that the first page and the last were printed, or even bound, on the same day. Surely there is a weak pun in here about the nature of assembling books, but the further we proceed into Caxton's prose, the greater the contradiction: for example, though fifteenth-century print runs were in the hundreds, Caxton maintains that he has simply "promysid [books] to dyuerce gentilmen and to my fiends," implying a world of personal connection to an enterprise that could only turn a profit through volume. On each level—production, dissemination, and consumption—Caxton's discussion contradicts material reality.

To a certain extent, I believe we can attribute Caxton's claims to his genuine amazement with the press. Instead of seeing contradiction entirely as a result of his naiveté, as is so often the case with Caxton criticism, we should see it as his purpose. The contradictions in Caxton's prose inherit and transpose Hoccleve's "trauaillous stilnesse" to a different register: rather than merely silencing scribal production, Caxton *erases the material labor behind his text* to blur the acts of reading and printing together in the miraculous gesture of mechanical reproduction that reads like a form of consumption. If there is any effort to Caxton's labor at all, it is financial and intellectual, the "grete charge and dispense" of its cost rather than the physical effort of stooping and staring upon the sheep's skin. Caxton describes himself less as a producer of books, than a consumer of them, like his clientele screened off from their actual making. Where idleness and "þoght" were inherently dangerous for Hoccleve, for Caxton they motivate him to read, an action which is unequivocally moral. This quality increases across Caxton's career as he begins to favor the phrase "*Caxton me fieri fecit*" ("Caxton caused me to be made") as a fitting end to his books.[41] The phrase announces a distance between Caxton and the production process that attributes the book to Caxton in such a way as to pass over the role of labor that went into it. If Hoccleve's uses *De ludo scacchorum* to form a poem about writing English, Caxton uses it to emphasize reading in two ways: generically, as an exemplum collection that continually glosses its own stories, and physically, as a symbolic object.[42]

Again, the *Game of Chesse* thematizes the issues on the surface of Caxton's writing. Chapters one and two of the third tractate, the first two pawns, allegorize the lowest ranks of the commons, laborers and artisans. The third chapter treats the pawn "whiche is sette to fore the Alphyn [the modern bishop] on the right side," which stands for "the office of notaryes aduocats skryueners and drapers or clothmakers," and, in short, "ought to be figured as a clerk" (92). The passage is worth quoting at length:

> And this pawne ought to be made and figured in this mamere / he muste be made like a man that holdeth in his right hand a pair of sheres or forcetis / and in the lifte hand a grete knyf and on his gurdell a penuer and an ynkhorn / and on his eere a penne to wryte wyth And that ben the Instrumentis & the offices that ben made and put in writynge autentyque / and ought to haue passed to fore the Iuges as libelles writtes condempnacions and sentences / And that is signified by the scriptoire and the penne and on that other part hit appertayneth to them to cutte cloth. shere. dighte. and dye/ and that is signefied by the forcettis or sheres / and the other ought to shaue berdes and kembe the heeris / And the other ben coupers. coryers. tawiers. skynners. bouchers and cordwanners / and these ben signefyed by the knyf that he holdeth in his hand and some of thise forsayd crafty men ben

> named drapers or clothmakers for so moche as they werke wyth wolle. and
> the Notyres. skynners. coryours. and cardewaners werke by skynnes and
> hydes / As parchemyn veluym. peltrye and cordewan. (Caxton, 92–93)

The passage recalls Hoccleve's discussion of writing as a craft. Still, Caxton emphasizes, not so much the Notaries's silence, but the gravity of their commission and its importance to common profit. They are knowledgeable about what they write—"therfore ought they to take good heede that they chauge not ne corrumpe in no wyse the content of the sentence" (Caxton, 94)—but their knowledge has to do with the process of transmission and the tools of the trade, not of their books' contents. As pawns they stand before the Alphyns, who "ought to be made and formed in manere of Iuges syttynge in a chayer wyth a book open to fore their eye" (Caxton, 36), and are thus portrayed as possessing the knowledge and authority contained in books. By recognizing the labor associated with manuscript production, but symbolically separating his products from that labor, Caxton reproduces the book as a symbolic form of authority. Again, for the fifteenth century, contradiction signals less a crippling incoherency, than a violence—in this case the denial of the actual production process, of the men who work in Caxton's shop—that enables subject formation.

Let me be clear about my argument here: Early printed books overlapped with manuscripts in tangible and intangible ways. Because this similarity suggests continuity with an immediate and tumultuous past, it is threatening to Caxton's overall project of installing the press in England. Caxton therefore acknowledges Hoccleve's rhetoric and his alienated self-representation, but brackets it as exclusively associated with the labor of writing. In this, he defines the printed book as representing the subject as a reader rather than a laborer, unified within himself and with other like-minded consumers across London and Westminster. The result is that Hoccleve's Chancery office seems a far cry from Caxton's leisurely study, while in fact, it is just around the corner. This has obvious allure to a nobility that identifies itself through its distance from physical work and that needs to assert its coherence after the Wars of the Roses; it also has great appeal to a non-noble class hungry for objects capable of demonstrating that they too engage in intellectual work—Westminster clerks looking for signs of their intellectual status, and London merchants desirous of announcing their economic arrival. That Caxton's logic is ultimately contradictory signals less some crippling confusion on his part, than the distance between his symbolic appeal to the various social groups at large in English culture, and the material reality.

Caxton printed his second edition of the *Game and Playe of the Chesse* during his second run of Chaucerian material. Printed back-to-back with editions of Chaucer, Gower, and Lydgate, the book stands in for the major work of the fourth English poet: Hoccleve. Caxton took this opportunity to eliminate any mention of Clarence too, rewriting the prologue and replacing the epilogue with a brief colophon. He also embellished the edition with a number of technological refinements: signatures, justified lines, and woodcuts. Unlike those of the *Canterbury Tales* of the same year, the *Game of Chesse* woodcuts are keyed to the text fairly closely.[43] This is necessitated by the text's auto-explicating nature: unlike the *Canterbury Tales*, the *Game of Chesse* insists on particular readings of its figures, and thus the details are crucial. In fact, the contrast between production and consumption I have argued for above is made graphic in the woodcuts themselves. For example, the woodcut for the Clerk presents the tools of the trade but there is not a book in sight. In turn, both chapters on the Alpyns (one decribing them, the other telling their moves) depict them sitting around a book on a reading stand. A book also appears in tract three, chapter five, the chapter on "phisicyens / and alle gramaryens. logicyens / maistres of lawe. of Geometrye, Arismetryque. musique and of astronomye" (Caxton, 118), all professions based on the possession of texts not as a process of production, but as knowledge. Further, Caxton's revised prologue underscores the importance of reading through a discussion of St. Paul.[44] The 1483 edition's woodcuts also stress its thematic interest in paternity through its very first woodcut, which shows the action of tractate one, chapter one: Evilmerdoach hacking father apart. This woodcut opens the 1483 edition, an edition printed amongst the Usurpation Crisis, far more dramatically than the 1474 edition and makes it claims for paternity and transgression more directly apparent. One printed during Edward's consolidation of magnate power speaking directly to and about political authority, the other during Richard III's usurpation, boldly depicting familial bloodshed, the two editions demonstrate the ways print technology allowed the printer-editor to aim individual editions of the same text at different political conditions.

The *Game of Chesse* demonstrates the printed book as a symbolic object on three counts. As an element of literary culture, it disseminates Caxton's revision of the legacy he inherited, his particular argument for the validity of vernacular reading, for the role of the book in generating authority, for the difficulties surrounding paternity as model for authority. In this way it speaks an ideological statement controlled, not by the author, but by the printer. The book is also symbolic as a material object. Though Caxton makes it appear unified and self-contained, it is actually remarkably fluid, a product of numerous hands. In flashes we can recognize these individual laborers: Curtis F. Bühler long ago pointed out that the *Game of Chesse*-compositors made changes to the form while they were still at press, producing variants within a specific run, and even argued that Caxton's type 2★, the type of the 1483 *Game of Chesse*, was "assigned exclusively to the second compositor; and if the view here put forward is correct, we must suppose that each compositor was responsible not only for setting up the type but also for distributing it again in his personal case."[45] We can also read across these editions for the individual compositor's silent role, so Kiyokazu Mizobata argues that the differences between the 1474 and 1483 editions show the compositor's sense of language: "the compositor presumably tried to make the text ornate by doublets, characteristic of Caxton's diction, but in the middle of his work he came, it seems, to have a different sense of style, and finding doublets wordy, he presumably began to replace them by single word-forms."[46] The compositor's intelligence can therefore be felt in minor, significant and insignificant, touches, but overall, as with the pressmen, his role and identity disappear. From our vantage point, Caxton's discussion clearly masks the material production techniques of print technology, techniques easily as grueling as those of which Hoccleve complains. From the vantage point of his readers, readers unfamiliar with the mechanics of printing, this process of erasure could not have been so transparent. Our recognition of this symbolic change, however, reveals a broader historical effect: by symbolically separating print and scribal technology, early printers facilitated the conception of the book as something new, erasing the traces of labor leading back into history.

## Rethinking Trust

Both the *Regement* and the *Game of Chesse* contain the Tale of John of Canace, a story of a father who, having given his fortune to his two married daughters, finds them aloof and neglectful. In both versions John borrows ten thousand pounds from a merchant, locks it in a chest, and promises it to his daughters if they will care for him in the present and finance his burial and bequests. And so they do. Ultimately, however, the daughters discover in John's coffers, not thousands of pounds but, in Hoccleve, a mace, and in Caxton, a club. The story revolves around the relationship between trust and capital: John trusts his daughters to take care of him in his old age, but discovering that they will not, exploits this trust to recoup some of his wealth. In turn, John's scheme can only succeed because the merchant trusts him to return the borrowed money. Ultimately, John is forced to rethink trust: he must abandon his life-long trust in his daughters and realize that they are motivated by greed. The weapon that represents their final inheritance advises them of this lesson.

The relationship between trust and capital is of increasing weight in the growing bibliography on the Information Age.[47] Fukuyama makes this case through historical contrast: "The post-Fordist factory requires, in other words, a higher degree of trust and social capital than the Taylorite workplace with its comprehensive workplace rules."[48] Fukuyama suggests a historical progression from the tangible structures of industrial production—factory, market, product—to more fluid organizational of networks based in trust that produce information. He argues that ours is a time of historical transition, hence the "great disruption" of his title, and ultimately finds in this economic model of trust and information a model for social organization as well. Thus, his description of the individual's ability to pick and choose from various options describes agency as points of contact with a larger virtual matrix of trust. In part, I am in agreement with Fukuyama. The shift in communication technology does cause concurrent changes in social formation; witness Chancery's disintegration amidst the great disruption of the fifteenth-century vernacular production. Since the market adjustments of 2001, academics, industry leaders, and the general public have become somewhat dubious of unqualified claims for the information age; nevertheless, as the United States exerts its tremendous military power abroad, America's leaders have repeatedly asked the people of the globe to trust in their view that capitalism is a progressive and benign mode of production. In the Tale of Canace the result of trust is an object of violence, and this should remind us of the coercive force within the war chest of capitalism.

In an effort toward recalling this coercive element, I suggest that John of Canace bears rereading. In Hoccleve's version, the tale is offered as a caution against "fool largesse" (4180) and his reading returns us to the laborer, to Hoccleve, when he laments, "I, Hoccleve, in swich case am gilty; þis me touchith" (4360). It is he who is the fool, and as much as the tale serves to correct him, it also reintroduces his autobiography at the end of the exemplum collection. For Hoccleve, the tale that centers on trust teaches that capital itself is not necessarily trustworthy. Thus he includes a scene in which John examines the coins: "And sigh how he amonge þe nobles sought / if defectif were any, as hem þought" (4260–61), and the mace itself bears the inscription, "Who berith charge of other men, & is / of hem despised, slayn be he with this" (4351–52). Trust—"the charge of othir men"—operates as a form of capital that alternately facilitates and obscures the movement of financial capital, but in some ultimate way returns to brute force. Caxton remains closer to the source, following Vignay in placing the tale in Tractus three, chapter eight. This chapter treats the pawn standing in front of the rook:

> And thys pawn that representeth thys peple ought to be formed in this maner / he must haue the forme of a man that hath longe heeris and black and holdeth in this ryght hand a lityll monoye And in his lyfte hande thre

> Dyse And aboute hym a corde in stede of a gyrdell / and ought to haue a boxe full o letters And by the first / whiche is money is vnderstand they that be fole large & wastours of theyr goodes / And by the seconde whiche is the dyse Ben represented the players at dyse / Rybauldes and butters / And by the thyrde whiche is the boxe full of lettres ben representid the messagers. corrours / And berars of letters. (Caxton, 146–47)

The last pawn represents an odd mix of roles: the waster, the gambler and the messenger. Clearly, the waster and the gambler are two sides of the same coin, and in that they demonstrate, by degrees, "fole large" they connect to Hoccleve's interpretation of the tale. The messenger parallels the waster and gambler through the tools of their trades: the gambler's dice, the waster's change, and the currier's epistles are all objects in transit, capable of being derailed by evil fortune. All three occupations are also attempts to circumvent labor, the wastour and the gambler in their general recklessness, and the messenger in that rather than slaving away like a scribe, he makes his money by shuttling preexiting writings from producer to consumer. In print, the messenger's "boxe full o letters" suggests an additional meaning—the case of type—and with this it develops the parallel further, for printing too is a shuttling of texts to and fro, a gamble with capital that relies in part on strategy and in part on luck, but not—according to Caxton at least—on hard physical labor. The passage imagines print production as a process capable of converting one form of capital, the codex, into another, money, through an almost magical transformation. At the same time, in introducing John of Canace, the last pawn suggests that behind the magical transformation of the press is the violence of denial.

The Tale of John of Canace underscores that trust only masks the coercive power of capital, and that it is "foole large" to believe otherwise. The lesson is still relevant today. For all the acclaim of a virtual economy, the Information Age is ultimately founded on the manufacture of hardware in the Santa Clara Valley and abroad. Chuck Carlson writes:

> Over the past two decades, business journalists, academics, and industry leaders have seized on the representations of an "information revolution" to construct a public image of semiconductors as an information technology. The result of this emphasis on what semiconductor technology does (essentially, storing, processing and routing information) has been to make the production of electronic goods, specifically, semiconductors invisible to the public eye.[49]

Carlson argues that the shift in emphasis from how the technology is made to what it does, represents a process of self-fashioning within the semiconductor industry. He locates one moment in this process at a 1985

Congressional hearing on entrepreneurship and innovation in which Robert Noyce, Charles Sprock, and Jerry Sanders spoke on trends in the industry.[50] Here, Sanders sketched a brief economic history for Congress: "The agrarian society gave way to the industrial society: the industrial society will give way to the information age," to argue, "we stand today at the beginning of a new era—the information age. It is brain-intensive, and the company that succeeds in this era believes in it." [51] Rather than framing semiconductor production as industry, Sanders tells a story in which history proceeds through a sequence of periods, naturally developing from physical to "brain-intensive" labor. As this work becomes increasingly cerebral, so do its motives; in 1991 Sanders told the *Los Angles Times*, "Noyce and his guys started companies so they could pursue what they wanted to work on, not to take a propriety technology developed at great expense and exploit it for personal gain."[52] The result is that, with the help of the academic and popular press, the semiconductor industry has fashioned for itself an identity as a clean industry without walls or hierarchies, one based on the circulation of information, rather than one based on the production of commodities.

Since the beginning of semiconductor production in California, the industry, both in the United States and abroad, has relied upon an articulated policy of using female labor for rote assembly-line tasks.[53] These workers—the industrial backbone of the Information Age—stoop and stare over their workstations in clean rooms, wearing full-body suits designed to safeguard the silicon chips from contamination rather than protect them from the hazardous chemicals with which they work. Though union organizers attempted to make inroads into semiconductor plants through the 1980s, the industry has managed to rebuff these encroachments, and the laborers in the semiconductor industry remain without the protections and earnings won by the steel and autoworkers unions throughout the century. Where the pressmen in Caxton's shop are lost to us, unrepresented in Caxton's prose, labor in the semiconductor industry remains without union representation. Ideology has no history: by pointedly redefining their industry as not industry at all, the leaders of the field—Sanders, Noyce, Sporck—claim for themselves the benefits of an historical break, one which allows them to insist that the terms of production have fundamentally changed—"begonne in oon day and also fynyshid in oon day"—and are thus free from the issues of labor, environment and fiscal responsibility that plague industry. Sander's emphasis on 'brain-intensive' work performs the same gesture as Caxton's erasure of labor: in both case labor vanishes amidst claims for a new economy.

The common logic that capitalism is an evolutionary advancement from feudalism is premised on just this process of erasure. This misrecognition plagues Althusser's understanding of history as well, and in "Ideology and Ideological State Apparatuses," he offers up the Middle Ages as a time before ideological struggle:

> In the pre-capitalist historical period which I have examined extremely broadly, it is absolutely clear that *there was one dominant Ideological State Apparatus, the Church*, which concentrated within it not only religious functions, but also educational ones, and a large proportion of the functions of communications and "culture." It is no accident that all ideological struggle, from the sixteenth to the eighteenth century, starting with the first shocks of the Reformation, was *concentrated* in an anti-clerical and anti-religious struggle; rather this is a function precisely of the dominant position of the religious ideological state apparatus.[54]

Elsewhere Althusser argues for the overdetermined nature of ideological structures—that multiple ideological relationships operate simultaneously, and often in contradiction.[55] Here, however, his view of history is totalizing: thus he argues for "the dominant position of the religious state apparatus" from which modernity is born. Hoccleve and Caxton clearly participate in a sophisticated communication system that exchanges labor for subject status through an ideological mechanism articulated, in part, through capital. Rather than the "first shocks of the Reformation" moving such ideological functions outside of the church through anti-clerical and anti-religious struggle, Caxton and Hoccleve are often theologically orthodox. What we see in the fifteenth century is a constellation of material, intellectual, and symbolic practices that often stand in contradiction. These practices produce the subject within culture, but they are hardly coherently unified as a state apparatus. In fact, the changes Hoccleve and Caxton introduce are piecemeal, at times precocious and at times backward looking. In labeling the fifteenth century "pre-capitalist," Althusser writes over this complexity in favor of a broad definition of ideology as unitary in its dominance. Althusser's misrecognition thus sustains exactly the rhetoric of historical rupture that allows Caxton, Sanders, Sprock, Noyce, and Fukuyama to make labor disappear.

If Marxist theory is to formulate a coherent rejoinder to arguments for the new economy and the broadly utopian fantasy of twenty-first century capitalism, it must single out and refute the easy assumption that historical periods are economically progressive. That is, it must recognize that historical transition is defined less by a fixed sequence of unitary changes and technological revolutions in production—a pre-capitalist feudal economy giving way to modern capitalism, which in turn develops into a post-industrial Information Age—than by continuing intellectual, material, and symbolic transformations of relations of capital, itself a social form. By theorizing such ongoing transformations and ridding itself of totalizing schemes of history, I suggest that Marxist theory can reclaim history for its argument and become critical of recent technological advances. In making this recognition, we can, hopefully, find ways to acknowledge the subject of labor during the great disruptions that lie ahead of us in the twenty-first century.

## Notes

This article has benefited greatly from discussion with Chuck Carlson, Richelle Munkhoff, Amanda Walling, and Janelle Diane Mitchell.

1. Louis Althusser, "Ideology and Ideological State Apparatuses (Notes towards an Investigation)," in *Lenin and Philosophy and Other Essays*, trans. Ben Brewster (New York: Monthly Review Press, 1971), p. 171.
2. *The Great Disruption: Human Nature and the Reconstitution of Social Order* (New York: The Free Press, 1999), p. 4.
3. In this essay I suggest that Hoccleve and Caxton represent two intertwined, yet distinct English literary cultures, Lancastrian and Yorkist. Recent scholarship has become increasingly interested in Lancastrian literary culture, and Hoccleve's *Regement* has served as a main point of exploration. Critical assessments of the *Regement* tend to be polarized. For these two views see David Lawton's "Dullness and the Fifteenth Century," *ELH* 54 (1987): 761–99, and Paul Strohm's *Usurpation and the Language of Legitimation, 1399–1422* (New Haven: Yale University Press, 1998), pp. 173–214, the argument of which is reviewed in Strohm's chapter "Hoccleve, Lydgate and the Lancastrian Court," in *The Cambridge History of Medieval English Literature*, ed. David Wallace (Cambridge: Cambridge University Press, 1999), pp. 640–61. Growing interest in Hoccleve's *Regement* is further reflected by the new TEAMS edition, *Thomas Hoccleve: The Regiment of Princes*, ed. Charles R. Blythe (Kalamazoo, MI: Western Michigan University, 1999), which contains a very useful introduction and bibliography.

   Caxton studies have been slower to develop, and as a result, Yorkist literary culture is often blurred into a generalized fifteenth-century worldview. See A.C. Spearing, *Medieval to Renaissance in English Poetry* (Cambridge: Cambridge University Press, 1985) and Richard Firth Green, *Poets and Princepleasers: Literature and the English Court in the Late Middle Ages* (Toronto: University of Toronto Press, 1980). Recent discussions of Caxton are Seth Lerer's *Chaucer and His Readers: Imagining the Author in Late-Medieval England* (Princeton University Press, 1993), pp. 147–75, and his chapter "William Caxton," in *The Cambridge History of Medieval English Literature*, pp. 720–38; and Jennifer Summit's *Lost Property: The Woman Writer and English Literary History, 1380–1589* (Chicago: University of Chicago Press, 2000), pp. 81–107. See also my article "Reading Caxton: Transformations in Capital, Print and Persona in the Late Fifteenth Century," *New Medieval Literatures* 3

(1999): 149–83, and the collection of essays on early print, *Caxton's Trace: Studies in the History of English Printing*, ed. William Kuskin (forthcoming, University of Notre Dame Press), particularly David R. Carlson's "A Theory of the Early English Printing Firm."

4. Carolyn Dinshaw, *Chaucer's Sexual Poetics* (Madison: The University of Wisconsin Press, 1989), p. 4. Dinshaw's remarks derive from her reading of Chaucer's short poem, "Adam Scryiven." In addition to Lerer's reading of "Adam Scryiven" in *Chaucer and his Readers*, pp. 117–46, see Joseph A. Dane and Seth Lerer, "Press Variants in John Stow's Chaucer (1561) and the Text of 'Adam Scriveyn,'" *Transactions of the Cambridge Bibliographical Society* 11 (1999): 468–79.

5. Blythe, *Regiment*, p. 1; Ethan Knapp, "Eulogies and Usurpations: Hoccleve and Chaucer Revisited," *Studies in the Age of Chaucer* 21 (1999): 296 [247–274], revised as chapter four of *The Bureaucratic Muse: Thomas Hoccleve and the Literature of Late Medieval England* (University Park, PA: Pennsylvania State University Press, 2001), pp. 107–28; and Derek Pearsall, "Hoccleve's *Regement of Princes*: The Poetics of Royal Self-Representation," *Speculum* 69 (1994): 387–88.

6. For discussion of this link see Larry Scanlon, "The King's Two Voices: Narrative and Power in Hoccleve's *Regement of Princes*," in *Literary Practice and Social Change in Britain*, ed. Lee Patterson (Berkeley: University of California Press, 1990), pp. 216–47, revised for *Narrative, Authority, and Power* (Cambridge: Cambridge, University Press, 1994), pp. 299–322; Anthony J. Hasler, "Hoccleve's Unregimented Body," *Paragraph* 13 (1990): 164–83; Pearsall, "Hoccleve's *Regement*," 386–410; Judith Ferster, *Fictions of Advice: the Literature and Politics of Counsel in Late Medieval England* (Philadelphia: University of Pennsylvania Press, 1996), pp. 137–59; James Simpson, "Nobody's Man: Thomas Hoccleve's *Regement of Princes*," in *London and Europe in the Later Middle Ages*, ed. Julia Boffey and Pamela King (London: Centre for Medieval and Renaissance Studies, Queen Mary and Westfield College, University of London, 1995), pp. 149–80; and Knapp, "Eulogies and Usurpations," 247–73.

7. *Hoccleve's Works: The Regement of Princes and Fourteen Minor Poems from the Egerton MS. 615*, ed. Fredrick J. Furnivall, EETS e.s. 72 (London: Kegan Paul, Trench, Trubner & Co., 1897), l. 1252. In all cases I have modernized long "s." Line numbers hereafter cited parenthetically within the text.

8. Strohm, *England's Empty Throne*, p. 195.

9. The Privy Seal began as the king's private letter-writing instrument, but by the late fourteenth century this role was filled by the Signet office, and as a result the Privy Seal became a drafting office for warrants, dispatches, and instructions from the Signet to Chancery. See Ethan Knapp, "Bureaucratic Identity and the Construction of the Self in Hoccleve's Formulary and *La Male Regle*," *Speculum* 74 (1999): 357–76 (also in *The Bureaucratic Muse*, pp. 17–44); John H. Fisher, "A Language Policy for Lancastrian England," *PMLA* 107 (1992): 1168–80; Fisher, "Chancery and the Emergence of Standard Written English in the Fifteenth Century," *Speculum* 52 (1977): 870–99;

Malcom Richardson, "Henry V, the English Chancery, and Chancery English," *Speculum* 55 (1980): 726–50; Compton A. Reeves, "Thomas Hoccleve, Bureaucrat," *Medievalia et Humanistica* 5 (1974): 201–21; A.L. Brown, "The Privy Seal Clerks in the Early Fifteenth-Century," in *The Study of Medieval Records: Essays in Honour of Kathleen Major*, ed. D.A. Bullough and R.I. Storey (Oxford: Clarendon Press, 1971), pp. 260–81; H.C. Schulz, "Thomas Hoccleve, Scribe," *Speculum* 12 (1937): 71–81; T.F. Tout, "Literature and Learning in the English Civil Service in the Fourteenth Century," *Speculum* 4 (1929): 365–89; Tout, "The Household of the Chancery and its Disintegration," in *Essays in History: Presented to Reginald Lane Poole*, ed. H.W.C. Davis (Oxford: The Clarendon Press, 1927), pp. 46–85; and Tout, "The English Civil Service in the Fourteenth Century," *The John Rylands Library* 3 (1916–1917): 185–214.
10. Tout, "Disintegration," 60.
11. Brown, "Privy Seal Clerks," 267.
12. Fisher, "Language Policy," 1171; Richardson, "Chancery English," 727.
13. Tout, "Literature and Learning," 367.
14. Brown, "The Privy Seal Clerks."
15. Ibid., 265; Reeves, "Thomas Hoccleve," 202.
16. For my discussion of the term "bysynesse" in Caxton, see "Reading Caxton," 158–71.
17. In *Hoccleve's Works: The Minor Poems*, ed. Fredrick J. Furnivall, EETS e.s. 61 (London: Kegan Paul, Trench, Trubner & Co., Limited, 1892), ll. 14–15. Line numbers from *La Male Regle* and the *Series* hereafter cited parenthetically within the text.
18. *The Riverside Chaucer*, 3rd. edition, ed. Larry D. Benson (Boston: Houghton Mifflin, 1987), fragment IV, ll. 29, 32–33.
19. *Caxton's Book of Curtesye*, ed. Frederick J. Furnivall, EETS e.s. 3 (London: Humphrey Milford, Oxford University Press, 1868), a verse courtesy manual that Caxton printed in 1477, includes mention of Hoccleve, as well as a stanza summary of "his traytye entitled of regemente" (l. 363), amongst its list of poetic "faders auncyente" (l. 400).
20. Most famously, A.I. Doyle and M.B. Parkes have demonstrated that Hoccleve participated in the production crew behind the Trinity manuscript of John Gower's *Confessio Amantis*, see "The Production of Copies of the *Canterbury Tales* and the *Confessio Amantis* in the Early Fifteenth Century," in *Medieval Scribes, Manuscripts, and Libraries: Essays Presented to N.R. Ker*, ed. M.B. Parkes and A.G. Watson (London: Scolar Press, 1978), pp. 163–210. Further, Hoccleve's third poem on the Virgin identifies Sir Thomas Marleburgh, a London stationer who at the time of the *Regement* rented two shops on Paternoster Row near St. Paul's, and who by 1423 was a Warden of the Limners and Textwriter's Guild, as his patron. See C. Paul Christianson, *A Directory of London Stationers and Book Artisans, 1300–1500* (New York: The Bibliographical Society of America, 1990), pp. 33 and 131.
21. C. Paul Christianson, "A Community of Book Artisans in Chaucer's London," *Viator* 20 (1989): 209 [207–18].

22. Graham Pollard, "The Company of Stationers Before 1557," *The Library* ser. iv. 18:1 (1937): 1–38; C. Paul Christianson, "The Rise of London's Book-Trade," in *The Cambridge History of the Book in Britain: Volume III, 1400–1557*, ed. Lotte Hellinga and J.B. Trapp (Cambridge: Cambridge University Press, 1999), pp. 128–47.
23. Pollard, "The Company," 12. Pollard points out that text producers often shift roles, 14–15.
24. See Gervase Rosser, "Craft, Guilds and the Negotiation of Work in the Medieval Town," *Past and Present* 154 (1997): 3–31; Heather Swanson, "The Illusion of Economic Structure: Craft Guilds in late Medieval English Towns," *Past and Present* 121 (1988): 29–48; esp. 42; Sylvia L. Thrupp, "Medieval Gilds Reconsidered," *Journal of Economic History* 2 (1943): 164–72.
25. Christianson, "The Rise of London's Book-Trade," in *The Cambridge History of the Book*, p. 131, repeated from his article "Evidence for the Study of London's Late Medieval Manuscript-Book Trade," in *Essays Towards a History of Book Production and Publishing in Britain, 1375–1474*, ed. Derek Pearsall and Jeremy Griffiths (Cambridge: Cambridge University Press, 1989), p. 91.
26. "English Books In and Out of Court from Edward III to Henry VII," in *English Court Culture in the Later Middle Ages*, ed. John Scattergood and J.W. Sherborne (London, 1983), p. 171 [163–181].
27. For Badby, see Peter McNiven, *Heresy and Politics in the Reign of Henry IV: The Burning of John Badby* (Suffolk: Boydell Press, 1987); Strohm, *Empty Throne*, pp. 210–11; and Pearsall, "Hoccleve's *Regiment*," 403–10; more generally on vernacular theology see Nicholas Watson, "Censorship and Cultural Change in Late-Medieval England: Vernacular Theology, the Oxford Translation Debate, and Arundel's Constitutions of 1409," *Speculum* 70 (1995): 822–64. Following Hoccleve, discussion of vernacular theology goes hand-in-hand with his writing on gender. See Ruth Nissé, " 'Oure Fadres Olde and Modres': Gender, Heresy, and Hoccleve's Literary Politics," *Studies in the Age of Chaucer* 21 (1999): 275–99; Catherine Batt, "Hoccleve and... Feminism? Negotiating Meaning in *The Regiment of Princes*," in *Essays on Thomas Hoccleve*, ed. Catherine Batt (London: Centre for Medieval and Renaissance Studies, Queen Mary and Westfield College, University of London, 1996), pp. 55–84; Diane Bornstein, "Anti-Feminism in Thomas Hoccleve's Translation of Christine de Pizan's *Epistre au dieu d'amours*," *English Language Notes* 19 (1981–82): 7–14; and Karen Winstead, " 'I am al othir to yow than yee weene': Hoccleve, Women, and the *Series*," *Philological Quarterly* 72 (1993): 143–55.
28. These echoes are well identified in Batt, "Hoccleve and...," pp. 76–81.
29. For the argument that the fifteenth century did not appreciate Chaucer's full range, see Paul Strohm, "Chaucer's Fifteenth-Century Audience and the Narrowing of the 'Chaucer Tradition,' " *Studies in the Age of Chaucer* 4 (1982): 3–32, and "Fourteenth- and Fifteenth-Century Writers and Readers of Chaucer," in *Genres, Themes, and Images in English Literature*, ed. Piero Boitani

and Anna Torti (Tubingen: Gunter Narr, 1988), pp. 90–104. There is much evidence against this view; for example, Hoccleve actually points out his use of the *Wife of Bath's Tale* in the "Dialogue" section of the *Series*, where he announces, "The wyf of Bathe, take I for auctirce" (694). This point is underscored by Blythe, who notes that "given the predominance of Chaucer's more earnest tales in the fifteenth-century editions of selected tales, it is striking that the two pilgrims whom Hoccleve makes greatest use of are the Wife of Bath and the Pardoner—pilgrims whose pronounced subjectivity and individual voice suited his own taste" (*Regiment*, p. 251).

30. Caxton printed two editions of *The Game of Chesse*. The STC lists ten extant copies of the first (STC 4920), and twelve of the second (STC 4921), but Seymour de Ricci records more: 11 existing copies and 8 untraced for the first, and thirteen existing, three untraced for the second; see *A Census of Caxtons* (1909; rpt in facsimile Mansfield Connecticut: Martino Publishing, 2000), p. 119. There is some debate surrounding the editions' dates and sources, and this has been worked out by N.F. Blake in "Dating the First Books Printed in English," in *William Caxton and English Literary Culture* (London: The Hambledon Press, 1991), pp. 75–87. The preferred date for the second edition is 1483; see Paul Needham, *The Printer and the Pardoner* (Washington, DC: Library of Congress, 1986), p. 87.

31. Robert H. Wilson identified composite manuscripts pre-existing Caxton and expanded our knowledge of Caxton's original additions in "Caxton's Chess Book," *Modern Language Notes* 42 (1947): 93–102. These sources are discussed more definitively by Christine Knowles in "Caxton and his Two French Sources," *Modern Language Review* 49 (1954): 417–23, where she clarifies Caxton's translation technique and points out that he also used a Latin text.

Caxton added three passages to the text itself. A defense of communal living based in his observations of the White Friars in tractate three, chapter two; a contrasting diatribe against "aduocats. men of lawe. And attorneyes of court," who "ete they the peple," in tractate three, chapter three; and, lastly, in tractate four, chapter one, a brief lament on "theeuis wyth in the royame or on the see"; in *Caxton's Game and Playe of the Chesse, 1474*. ed. William E. A. Axon (1883; rpt. London: B.C.M. Classics Reprints, 1968), pp. 88, 95, and 162 respectively. Further citations to the *Game of Chesse* are from this volume and are noted parenthetically within the text.

32. In his discussion of lawyers, Caxton writes "for yf they were nombrid all that lange to the courtes of the channcery kinges benche. comyn place. cheker. ressayt and helle And the bagge berars of the same / hit should amounte to a grete multitude" (Caxton, 95). Citing Caxton's *Game of Chesse*, the OED defines "Hell" as "the name of a part of the old law courts at Westminster, app. used at one time as a record office" (5).

33. See Catherine Batt, "Recreation, the Exemplary and the Body in Caxton's *Game and Playe of the Chesse*," *Ludica* 2 (1996): 27–44, esp. 28 and 37.

34. Caxton's chief biographers, N.F. Blake and George D. Painter, *Caxton and his World* (London: Andre Deutch, 1969), find the *Game of Chesse* a product

of patronage. Blake attributes the selection of the text to Margaret of York, and sees Caxton's publication as a failed attempt to obtain Clarence's patronage, concluding, "Caxton evidently wanted a patron who would recommend his work to his friends and even possibly help the printer set up his press in England. The choice was unfortunate" (p. 61). Blake goes on to suggest that in order to get rid of remainder copies, Caxton had to move to England. In contrast, Painter, *William Caxton: A Biography* (New York: G.P. Putnam & Sons, 1977), reads Caxton's prologue as a coded message to Clarence, "but the inner secret of Caxton's *Game of Chess* is only visible when we read between the lines of his dedication to George, Duke of Clarence, as no one seems to have done since Caxton's own day" (p. 65). Painter leaves unexplained why Caxton would use the tremendously public forum of the printed book to transmit secret political analysis. Neither Blake's nor Painter's reading explains Caxton's political relationship to the Yorkist house to any degree beyond a generalized patronage system, nor are they capable of suggesting why Caxton chose the *Game of Chesse* as his second text to put to press.

More recently, Catherine Batt argues that Caxton " 'solves' the implicit political question of to whom this material may be primarily directed by recasting it for a bourgeois audience in terms that do not interrogate the relation of subject to king so much as universalize the human condition and one's perspective of it" ("Recreation," 39). I have written elsewhere that the term "bourgeois audience" is insufficient to characterize the reading communities of the late Middle Ages, and is too static to delineate the dynamic relationship between Caxton and his audience ("Caxton's Worthies Series: The Production of Literary Culture," *ELH* 66 [1999]: 511–51); moreover, in what follows I question how interested Caxton is in "solving" anything, so much as in proposing new imaginative relations between the material production of books and the symbolic production of authority. Further, I disagree with Batt's conclusion that an edition opening with an illustration of the dismemberment of a king and printed in the midst of the Usurpation Crisis "might appear comforting in its enunciation of the familiar and the proverbial" (43), and that "Caxton uncritically and complacently endorses the original's portrayal of the body and its significance" (31). It is high time we stopped reading Caxton as naively conservative, placid and reactive, controlled in almost every way by an awkward combination of patronage and popular middle-brow taste, and started recognizing that he has an ongoing interest in thematic complexity, ambivalence and contradiction, and that many of the points within his writings are, in fact, in dialogue with the literary history he inherits and the texts he prints.

35. Caxton, *Game and Playe of the Chesse*, p. 1. Further citations to this text will be noted parenthetically "Caxton." Vignay's prologue is reprinted in W.J.B. Crotch, *The Prologues and Epilogues of William Caxton* (1928; rpt. New York: Burt Franklin, 1971), pp. 11–13.

36. See M.A. Hicks, *False, Fleeting, Perjur'd Clarence: George, Duke of Clarence, 1449–78* (Gloucester: Alan Sutton, 1980), pp. 124–26 and 176.

37. For the origins of the game of chess, as well as the etymology of Caxton's term for the piece now called the "bishop" see Richard Eales, "The Game of Chess: An Aspect of Medieval Knightly Culture," in *The Ideals and Practice of Medieval Knighthood: Papers from the First and Second Strawberry Hill Conferences*, ed. Christopher Harper-Bill and Ruth Harvey (Woodbridge, Suffolk; Dover, N.H: Boydell Press, 1986), pp. 12–34, and David Antin, "Caxton's *The Game and Playe of the Chesse*," *Journal of the History of Ideas* 29 (1968): 269–78.
38. Crotch, *Prologues and Epilogues*, p. 7.
39. See Lerer, *Chaucer and His Readers*, pp. 134–46.
40. See Lotte Hellinga, *Caxton in Focus* (London: The British Library, 1982), p. 48; Blake, "Dating," pp. 84–85; Painter, *William Caxton*, pp. 62–63.
41. See Painter, *William Caxton*, p. 70; Wytze Hellinga and Lotte Hellinga, *The Fifteenth-Century Printing Types of the Low Countries*, trans. D.A.S. Reid (Netherlands, 1966), Vol. I, p. 23.
42. See Lerer's discussion of Caxton's emphasis on readership in *Chaucer and His Readers*, for example, pp. 20, 143, and 168, as well as Jennifer Summit's argument for "a new model of secular learning and literary production...[as] an ideal form of intellectual labor" (*Lost Property*, p. 69).
43. See David R. Carlson, "Woodcut Illustrations of the Canterbury Tales, 1483–1602," *The Library* ser. vi 19 (1997): 25–67, and Stephen Orgel, "Textual Icons: Reading Early Modern Illustrations," in *The Renaissance Computer: Knowledge in the First Age of Print*, ed. Neil Rhodes and Jonathan Sawday (New York: Routledge, 2000), pp. 59–94.
44. See my discussion in "Caxton's Worthies Series," 519–24.
45. "Three Notes on Caxton," *The Library* ser. iv 17 (1937): 161 [155–66]. See also Bühler's "Caxton's Variants," *The Library* ser. iv 17 (1937): 62–69.
46. See "Caxton's Revisions: The 'Game of Chess', the 'Mirror of the World', and 'Reynard the Fox,' " in *Arthurian and Other Studies Presented to Shunichi Noguchi*, ed. Takashi Suzuki and Tsuyoshi Mukai (Cambridge: D.S. Brewer, 1993), p. 260 [257–62].
47. For the development of this "new form of capitalism," see Jeremy Rifkin, *The Age of Access: The New Culture of Hypercapitalism Where All of Life is a Paid-For Experience* (New York: Putnam, 2000), p. 138; Fukuyama provides a useful review of the development of social capital in sociological studies, but omits the work of Pierre Bourdieu. I have found Bourdieu's essay, "The Forms of Capital," in *Handbook of Theory and Research for the Sociology of Education*, ed. John G. Richardson (New York: Greenwood Press, 1986), pp. 15–18, and 241–58, particularly concise.
48. Fukuyama, *The Great Disruption*, p. 207.
49. Chuck Carlson, "Invisible Production in the Information Age," p. 2, unpublished paper.
50. For overviews of the development of the semiconductor industry with reference to Noyce, Sanders, and Sprock, see Paul Freiberger and Michael Swaine, *The Fire in the Valley: The Making of the Personal Computer*, 2nd ed. (New York: McGraw-Hill, 2000), and David A. Kaplan, *The Silicon Boys and their Valley of Dreams* (New York: Perennial, 2000), pp. 38–72.

51. Quoted in Carlson, "Invisible Production," pp. 32–33.
52. Carlson, "Invisible Production," p. 34.
53. Carlson, "Invisible Production," pp. 8–15; Kaplan, *Silicon Boys*, p. 56.
54. "Ideology," in *Lenin and Philosophy*, p. 151.
55. See *For Marx*, trans. Ben Brewster (New York: Verso, 1990), pp. 88–128.

# LIST OF CONTRIBUTORS

MARK ADDISON AMOS is Assistant Professor of English at Southern Illinois University. His scholarship focuses on the interanimations among late medieval cultures and their literary and documentary representations. He has published on medieval reading practices and early book production, modern theoretical approaches to medieval works, and the construction of religious, gender, and class identities in medieval texts.

CATHERINE BATT is Lecturer in Medieval Literature at the School of English, University of Leeds. She has published on Anglo-Norman, Middle English, and twentieth-century literature, and is editor of *Essays on Thomas Hoccleve* (1996) and author of *Malory's 'Morte Darthur': Remaking Arthurian Tradition* (2002).

ANDREW COLE has a Ph.D. in English from Duke University (2000) and researches and teaches Middle English literature and critical theory at the University of Georgia. He has essays in (or due in) *Speculum, ELH, SAQ, JMEMS, YLS, Rome and the North,* and *Lollards and Their Influence*. His forthcoming book is called, *Heresy et al.: Chaucer, Langland, Margery Kempe*.

KATE CRASSONS is a Ph.D. candidate in English at Duke University. She is currently completing her dissertation, *The Practice of Poverty: Litertature and Ideology, 1350–1450*.

BRIAN GASTLE is an Assistant Professor and Director of Professional Writing at Western Carolina University. His research on mercantile rhetoric has appeared in *Neuphilologische Mitteilungen* and *Studies in the Literary Imagination*, and he was a consultant for a PBS educational series on modern Fantasy's debt to Medieval Literature: *Rings, Kings, and Things*.

BRITTON HARWOOD, Professor of English at Miami University, Ohio, teaches Middle English literature and critical theory. Among his publications are *Piers Plowman and the Problem of Belief* (Toronto, 1992) and, most recently, "Psychoanalytic Politics: Chaucer and Two Peasants," *ELH* 2001.

ETHAN KNAPP is Associate Professor of English at The Ohio State University. He is the author of *The Bureaucratic Muse: Thomas Hoccleve and the Literature of Late Medieval England*, essays in *Speculum* and *Studies in the Age of Chaucer*, and is currently working on a study of Heidegger's early work on modistic grammar.

WILLIAM KUSKIN is Associate Professor of English and Honors at the University of Southern Mississippi. He has a number of articles on early printing and is currently completing two book-length projects: a monograph on William Caxton entitled *Symbolic Caxton: Fifteenth-Century Literary Culture and the Forms of Print Capitalism*, and a collection of essays on early print culture, *Caxton's Trace: Studies in the History of English Printing* (both forthcoming from Notre Dame University Press).

ANTHONY MUSSON is a Senior Lecturer in Law at the University of Exeter. He is a Barrister of the Middle Temple and Visiting Senior Research Fellow, Institute of Advanced Legal Studies, University of London, in the History of Law. His most recent book is *Medieval Law in Context: The Growth of Legal Consciousness from Magna Carta to the Peasants' Revolt* (Manchester, 2001).

KELLIE ROBERTSON teaches at the University of Pittsburgh. She has published articles on Geoffrey of Monmouth, Chaucer, Milton and postcolonial theory and is currently working on a book entitled *The Laborer's Two Bodies: Literary and Legal Productions, 1350–1500*.

MICHAEL UEBEL has taught at the University of Virginia and Georgetown University. He is the author of *Ecstatic Transformation: On the Uses of Alterity in the Middle Ages* (Palgrave). He is now affiliated with the School of Social Work at the University of Texas, Austin.

# INDEX

Abelard, Peter, 23
Adam, 19, 20, 72, 77, 145
advice, 29, 31, 33–5; *see also* gossip
Aers, David, 183
Alan of Lille, 7
Albertus Magnus, 3
Alford, B.W.E, 97, 98
allegory, 12, 138, 179–96, 214, 222
almsgiving, 4, 11, 67–85, 93–105
Althusser, Louis, 229–30, 252
*Anonimalle Chronicle*, 140, 189, 191
*apologia*, 13, 212–26
Aquinas, Thomas, 3, 4
Arendt, Hannah, 5
Aristotle, 5, 6
Ashby, George, 210
Aston, Margaret, 69, 84

Barker, T.C., 97, 98
Bataille, Georges, 168–9
Beattie, Cordelia, 22–3
begging, able-bodied, 68, 77, 81; *see also* labor laws, mendicancy, vagrancy
Bellamy, John, 136
Biscoglio, Frances M., 20
Black Death, *see* plague
Black Prince, *see* Edward, Prince of Wales
Bloch, Marc, 8
Bloomfield, Morton, 188
Blyth, Charles, 30
Boyd, Beverly, 221
branding, *see* labor laws
Braudel, Ferdinand, 8
Bühler, Curtis, 247
Butler, Judith, 22, 137

Cade's Rebellion, 3
Camille, Michael, 146
Campbell, Bruce, 8
canon law, 44–5, 49, 51; *see also* Gratian
Capgrave, John, 210
capital (and capitalism), 1, 4, 93, 236–7, 240, 248–52
Carlson, Chuck, 250–1
Carpenter, John, *see* Liber Albus
Carpenters' company, *see* guilds
Caxton, William, 13; *Game and Playe of the Chesse*, 230, 240–53; *Recuyell of the Historyes of Troye*, 240, 244
*chanson de geste*, 157–61
*Chanson de Roland*, 158–9
charity, *see* almsgiving
Chaucer, Geoffrey, 20, 42, 92–3, 169, 211, 230–1, 234–8, 240; "Adam Scriveyn," 244; *Canterbury Tales*, 9, 91, 145, 221, 247; *Clerk's Tale*, 234–5; *Knight's Tale*, 159, 180; *Man of Law's Tale*, 28; *Melibee*, 28, 34, 239; *Merchant's Tale*, 28, 34; *Miller's Tale*, 31, 104; *Monk's Tale*, 28, 34; *Nun's Priest's Tale*, 25; *Reeve's Tale*, 104; *Wife of Bath's Tale*, 21–2, 45, 57, 61, 239
Cheshire, 12, 157, 163–5
Christ as laborer, 77–8, 84, 97
Christianson, C. Paul, 235, 236
Christine de Pizan: 28; *The Book of the City of Ladies*, 21; *Epistre au dieu d'Amours*, 27
Clark, Elaine, 117
clerics, *see* labor laws
commodity, 7, 211, 251
common profit, 135, 144, 246

counsel, *see* advice
Courtenay, William (Archbishop of Canterbury), 140–7
crusades, 23

death: labor and, 4–5, 11; guild ordinances and, 102–4
Dinshaw, Carolyn, 230
disendowment, 11, 69, 73
Donaldson, E.T., 182
dowry, 44, 49; as differentiated from dower, 45; free bench and, 53
Doyle, A.I., 236–7
Duby, Georges, 8
Durkheim, Emile, 95

Edward I, 48, 163, 165
Edward III, 48, 51, 158–9, 161, 163, 170, 190
Edward IV, 240–1, 247
Edward V, 243
Edward, Prince of Wales (Black Prince), 12, 51, 163–7
Elizabeth I, 99
Elliott, Dyan, 59–60
Eve, 19, 20, 72

Febvre, Lucien, 8
*femme coverte de baron*, *see* married women
*femme sole*, *see* married women
feudalism, 3, 12, 147, 252
Fitzherbert, Anthony, 117
FitzRalph, Richard: *Defensio Curatorum*, 68–84
Flori, Jean, 169
Foucault, Michel, 9, 135, 137, 144, 148, 214
free bench, *see* dowry
Frank, Robert Worth, 182
Freedman, Paul, 6, 8, 19, 145
Freud, Sigmund, 4, 163; *Ego and the Id*, 170
friars, *see* begging, mendicancy
Fukuyama, Francis, 229, 248–9, 252
Furnivall, Frederick, 179, 181

George, Duke of Clarence, 240–3, 247
Gibson-Graham, J.K., 22
Gierke, Otto, 95
Giles of Rome: *De regimine principum*, 231
Given-Wilson, Chris, 115
Godden, Malcolm, 183
gossip, 26–7, 33; *see also* advice
Gower, John, 235, 247; *Vox clamantis*, 180, 192
Gratian: *Decretum*, 59; *see also* canon law
Groddeck, Georg, 4–5
guilds, 11, 42, 44, 91–105, 124, 189, 191, 224, 236; common good and, 94, 95, 96, 105; over-seers, 180, 192–6; returns, 184; *see also* labor laws
Gurevich, Aaron, 2, 145

Hanawalt, Barbara, 8, 34
Hardt, Michael, 2
Hasler, Antony, 30
Heloise, 23
Henry III, 165
Henry IV, 147, 230, 232, 243
Henry V, 24, 29, 230–2, 234, 237–8, 242–3
Henry VII, 93, 101
Hesiod, 5
Hewitt-Smith, Kathleen, 183
Hieatt, Constance, 157
Hoccleve, Thomas, 10, 13, 19–35, 187, 209–26, 229–53; "Address to Sir John Oldcastle," 24–9; *Dialogue*, 34; *La Male Regle*, 233–4; *Regiment of Princes*, 10, 24, 28–35, 216–21, 230–9; *Series*, 34, 223–4, 233–4; "The Story of the Monk Who Clad the Virgin," 220–6
Hodges, Laura, 20
Holinshed, Raphael, 136
Howell, Martha, 47
Hudson, Anne, 225
Humbert of Romans, 6
Hundred Years War, 164, 232

# INDEX

Huppé, Bernard, 182
Hutton, Diane, 44

immaterial labor, *see* labor
*Itinerarium Peregrinorum et Gesta Regis Ricardi*, 23

Jacobus de Cessolis: *Liber de ludo scacchorum*, 230, 231, 240, 245
Jacques de Vitry, 6
Jean de St.-Amand, 7
John of Gaunt, 51
John of Northampton, 184, 191
Judith, 27–9
Jupp, Edward Basil, 99
Jusserand, Jean, 188

Kantorowicz, Ernst, 144–8
Karras, Ruth, 6
Kempe, Margery, 58–9; *The Book of Margery Kempe*, 25–6, 61
Kerby-Fulton, Kathryn, 213–14
Kilwardby, Robert, 7
Knapp, Ethan, 26, 29, 30
Knighton, Henry, 134, 189

labor: agricultural, 13, 113–14, 121, 134, 139, 196, 212–15, 217, 220; benefits of, 68; the body and, 12, 13, 29, 98, 102, 135–8, 144–8, 185, 214–17, 230, 244; book-trade and, 229–53; clerical, 113, 121; the commons and, 85; female, 10, 19–35, 41–61, 251; gender and, 19–20, 28, 31; household, 29–30, 47, 124–5; knightly, 83–5, 166; identity and, 94; immaterial, 2–3, 10, 13, 138, 209–11, 225, 251; intellectual, 6, 10, 209–26, 229–53; literacy and, 12, 136, 138–9; manual, 3, 6, 8, 13, 22, 134, 145, 209; mercantile, 10, 13, 41–61; monastic, 6, 145, 222, 225; scribal, 13, 209–26, 229–53; *see also* guilds, labor laws, married women, scribes

labor laws, 1, 3, 11–12, 68, 113–26, 133–48, 185, 190, 212–213; branding and, 12, 121, 135–8; children and, 125; clerics and, 121, 126; corporal punishment in, 121, 134–40; enforcement, 115–24; guilds and, 100; limitations of, 120–1; local custom and, 117; private law and, 117, 120–3; master/servant relationship in, 122, 124, 139; monetary fines, 121, 135, 139–40; servants and, 113, 115, 124, 139; tax subsidies and, 164; *see also* labor, poor laws, vagrancy
Lacey, Kay, 43–4
Langland, William, 2, 9, 13, 42, 161, 166; *Piers Plowman*, 12, 61, 80, 158, 179–96, 209–26
law French, 47, 52, 165
Le Goff, Jacques, 8, 145
*Legenda Aurea*, 83
*Liber Albus*, 32, 52–4, 56, 57, 61, 188
lists, and scribal hermeneutics, 179–81
literacy, *see* labor
Lochrie, Karma, 22
Lollardy, 25, 28, 67–9, 73, 126, 141, 225, 238; *see also* Wyclif, John
London, 42, 44, 50, 93–105, 124, 180–1, 184, 187, 193, 215, 224, 231, 233–7, 246
Luttrell Psalter, 145–7
Lydgate, John, 235, 244, 247

Macherey, Pierre, 157
Maidstone, Richard, 81
Mann, Jill, 9
Marbod of Rennes, 20–1
Marleburgh, Thomas, 224–5
marriage, 31; contract, 45, 57, 59 ; and marriage debt, 10, 41–8, 58–60; property in, 59
married women: contractual capacity of, 43, 45; as *covertes de baron*, 43, 53, 55; as *femmes soles*, 10, 41–61; treated as minors, 44, 57; *see also* dowry, labor

# INDEX

Marx, Karl, 3, 5, 6
Marxist labor theory, 2, 7, 209–10, 252–3
McLaughlin, Eleanor, 59
mendicancy, 6, 67–8; anti-mendicant polemic, 71–81, 84–5; *see also* begging; Taylor, William; FitzRalph, Richard
Middleton, Anne, 9, 185, 212–13
Mizobata, Kiyokazu, 248
Mollat, Michel, 69, 84
*Morte Arthure*, 158
Muscatine, Charles, 183, 187

Negri, Antonio, 2
New Historicism, 1, 9
Nissé, Ruth, 25, 28

oath taking, 94; of laborers, 121, 134, 148
Oldcastle, John, 25; *see also* Hoccleve, Thomas
Owen, Michael, 10

Painter, Sidney, 158, 169
parliament: of 1351, 114–15, 133; of 1368, 119; of 1376 (Good), 55; of 1388 (Cambridge), 191; labor laws and, 115
Pearsall, Derek, 183–4, 193, 215
peasants, *see* labor
Peasants' Revolt of 1381, 3, 19, 55, 121, 138, 141–2, 147, 180, 189–92, 194, 196
penance, 7, 12, 105, 135, 140–4
*Perceforest*, 33
Perkins, Nicholas, 31
Perrers, Alice, 51–2, 58
Petrarch, Francis, 235
*Pierce the Ploughman's Crede*, 159
*Piers Plowman*, *see* Langland, William
plague, 1, 11, 44, 55, 113–15, 118, 123, 134–5
Pocock, W. Willmer, 99
Polyani, Karl, 7
poor laws, 99

poverty, 11, 67–85, 97–101, 183, 217; labor laws and, 126
Power, Eileen, 46
print culture, 244–8
prostitution, 6
proverbs, 19–24
Putnam, Bertha, 133, 139, 164–5

Reformation, 94, 104, 252
Richard II, 140, 147
Richard III, 243, 247
Rifkin, Jeremy, 2
Robertson, D.W., 182
Roney, Lois, 163
Rosser, Gervase, 92, 96

St. Augustine, 137, 182
St. Bonaventure, 6
St. Francis, 105
St. Paul, 41, 58–9, 83, 247
Salter, Elizabeth, 167, 181–3
Sartre, Jean-Paul, 192
Scattergood, John, 166
Schmidt, A.V.C., 182
scribes, 186–8, 209–26, 229–53; and scribal hermeneutics, 180, 187–8
*Second Shepherds' Play*, 30
*Secreta secretorum*, 231
servants, *see* labor laws
Shareshull, William, 114, 133, 157, 164–70
Shirley, John, 244
*Sir Gawain and the Green Knight*, 57, 157–8, 180
Skeat, W.W., 187, 215
slavery, 6
Smith, Adam, 105
Spacks, Patricia Meyers, 26–7
Stocker, Margarita, 28
Strohm, Paul, 231
sumptuary laws, 1, 146–7

Taylor, William, 11, 67–85
Thompson, John, 224
Tout, T.F., 231, 232
Trigg, Stephanie, 157

Unwin, George, 97, 103
Usk, Thomas, 191, 210–11
usurpation: Lancastrian of 1399, 13, 147, 236, 243; by Richard III (1483), 247

vagrancy, 6, 68, 126, 136, 138, 190, 213, 216–7; *see also* begging, labor laws
vernacularity, 231, 235, 239, 247, 249
Virgin Mary, 28, 220–6, 238; iconography of, 20

War of the Roses, 240, 246

Weber, Max, 94
*Westminster Chronicle*, 142
*Winner and Waster*, 12, 157–70, 180
women: as laborers, 83; as labor offenders, 123; *see also* labor, married women
work, as differentiated from labor, 4–5; *see also* labor
*The Wright's Chaste Wife*, 33, 61
Wyclif, John, 11; *see also* Lollardy
Wycliffite Bible, 28; *see also* Lollardy

Žižek, Slavoj, 21